NEXT STOP, VERNON!

Cordell Cross

REVISED ISBN 978-0-9696248-7-5

NEXT STOP, VERNON!
By Cordell Cross
Revised Copyright - Vanbrugh Management Ltd

Published by Vanbrugh Publishing
A Division of Vanbrugh Management Ltd.
PO Box 73038
Evergreen RO
Surrey, B.C., Canada V3R 0J2

Email: vanbrugh@telus.net

Cover art by Peter Lynde, Salt Spring Island B. C.
All rights reserved.

Cover compilation by Jana Siller - japla2003@yahoo.ca

Cordell Cross

3 – NEXT STOP, VERNON!

FOR KEN GOURLEY – MAY HE REST IN PEACE

We all miss you, Ken

Cordell Cross

OTHER BOOKS BY CORDELL CROSS

THE HIMMLER STRATAGEM
(order on net) https://www.createspace.com/3555767
Revised ISBN 978-0-9696248-8-2
 A must read if you enjoy fast moving suspense, intrigue, and mystery in a world of intense hatred and sleaze.

MANIAC (order on net) https://www.createspace.com/3604911
ISBN 978-0-9869503-0-8
When a sixteen-year-old girl disappears in the neighbourhood of Greg Britton, a Seattle police lieutenant on compassionate leave, the police officer holds nothing back and decides to find her dead or alive.

STAND BY YOUR BEDS! (order on net) https://www.createspace.com/3613071
Revised ISBN 978-0-9696248-5-1
Is the hilarious story of seven 14-year-old cadets sent to a summer military camp for six weeks training. Regular force troops returning from WW2 and Korea were also sent to the camp thinking they would be training officer cadets. When these hard-nosed battle-scarred veterans found that the boys were only 14 and 15 years old, they trained them the way they would train regular troops. The boys in turn form a very close group to survive. Both groups learn a lot about each other. Extremely funny. Get ready to roll on the floor laughing. You'll love this book.

FORM THREE RANKS ON THE ROAD!
(order on net) https://www.createspace.com/3617672
Revised ISBN 978-0-9696248-6-8
It is three years later, and the cadets continue their capers. This time they are in charge, or so they think. A refreshingly funny book.

MAP FACTS
Revised ISBN 0-9696248-3-2
The ultimate map and compass guide, is required reading for all those involved with topographical maps and magnetic compasses.

COMING SOON FROM CORDELL CROSS

WHERE THE WIND HIDES - ISBN 978-0-9869503-1-5
RUBBER GEARS NEXT YEAR! The last novel in the Vernon Army Cadet Camp series. The hilariousness continues.
RAIN ON MY TONGUE
THE STOPOVER

Cordell Cross

5 – NEXT STOP, VERNON!

INTRODUCTION

The advertisement read: *Wanted - a young person to sell Christmas trees. Compensation depends on the number of trees sold. Report to Gilford and Georgia Streets at 5:30 p.m., Monday night.*

When I turned up, I was told that I was too young, but all wasn't lost. Smartly dressed khaki-uniformed teenagers with green-feathered hackles sprouting from their headdress kept entering the giant doors of the Irish Fusiliers armouries across Gilford Street. I went in as well, found a chair on the balcony, and observed.

Thinking back, that was my introduction to army cadets. For the next two hours, I watched well over two hundred boys take their training seriously. The only time adults appeared was during the initial dress inspection and at the dismissal parade. Other than that, cadets handled their own affairs.

About an hour after I sat down, a voice behind me said, "My name's Harry Shanks. The RSM has asked me to ask you if you would like a tour?"

I stood up in a hurry and although I didn't know what RSM meant, I accepted. "Er, thanks. Did someone mind me sittin' here?"

The grinning uniformed teenager was only about fourteen and dressed immaculately. "No, that's what the chairs are for. We're having a coffee break in five minutes. C'mon, if we're first in line we'll each get a couple of doughnuts. We parade twice a week and..."

For the next hour I watched rifle shooting, lectures on instructional technique, the Bren gun, Sten gun, .303 and .22 rifles, map and compass, platoon and section tactics, signals training, motor mechanics and driving, Böfors-gun training, drill and a host of other subjects, including boxing. I even watched a busy cadet in the switchboard office seemingly talk to himself as he neatly plugged in strings of jacks and flicked switches allowing the apparatus to connect other voices located throughout the building.

On our tour, my guide saluted certain *distinct* cadets we passed.

"Why do you salute them?" I asked.

"They're officers. See the braid on their shoulders. If I didn't salute, I'd end up on defaulters after parade."

Following the dismissal, the canteen up top on the west side of the balcony came alive with normal teenage attitudes. Dispositions that weren't visible below during the evening. In the canteen, the cadets played darts, sang songs, played the piano, bought pop and told jokes. Although I was the only *civilian* amongst them and too young to join, not once did I hear a caustic remark. Instead, I was prompted to join in and sing. After I had my third pop bought for me, I had to decline offers of ten more. Also, what really surprised me was that rank didn't exist in the canteen. If it did, it wasn't evident. Cadet officers and NCOs running the show became human until they left the canteen. After putting on their headdress and web-belts, rank and protocol ruled again.

As it turned out, Harry and I went to the same school and we became good friends. He'd lost his parents in an automobile accident and was being raised by a

Cordell Cross

single aunt. They lived in two rooms of an old rooming house not far from me and many times, he mentioned that army cadets kept him on the straight and narrow.

I didn't know then that the RSM was only seventeen. Although I never got the chance to meet him that night, I did meet him many years later and thanked him.

When Chris moved on to high school, we lost track of each other for a few years. When I met him again in 1953 at the Vernon Army Cadet Trades Training Camp, he was still in the Irish, but I wore a black beret and the silver-coloured badge of the 2290 British Columbia Regiment (Duke of Connaught's Own) Cadet Corps.

Growling, he said, "You joined the Dukes? You need your head examined - they're animals! Well, near enough to it. Anyway, since it's your first year, let me explain Camp Vernon to you. It's a large camp, and…"

'Next Stop, Vernon!' is the continuing tale about cadets spending their summers at the Vernon Army Cadet Trades Training Camp in the 50s.

The majority of the boys in this story had *visited* Vernon previously but had never taken a trades' course. Two trades' courses were offered, Signals, and Driver-Mechanics, and by no means were the courses easy. If anything, cadets earned their trades badges and pay the hard way. Regular force instructors didn't understand the words, 'half effort.' They only understood and demanded 'effort-and-a-half.'

There were two ways of tackling this story. I could have stuck to the training side and bored you, or I could show some training and take you into the minds and barracks of the boys. I decided the latter would be better.

Next Stop, Vernon is the third sequel of a wonderful story. If you have read Stand By Your Beds, or Form Three Ranks On The Road, I would point out that certain *puritans* still deny that boys of the 50s swore, spat, smoked, had the odd beer, or looked at girls. They say it doesn't happen today, why would I say it happened then?

Well, I'm not going to answer that one. I don't want to burst their overly big bubble that seems to have been around for a long time. How these *people* live with themselves, I don't know.

Cordell Cross

GOD'S COUNTRY

If you want to visit an area of North America referred to as God's Country, travel to the City of Vernon in British Columbia, Canada.

Nestled against lakes, mountains and rolling hills, Vernon for some reason has maintained its early village charm probably more than Kelowna and Penticton, two other beautiful cities in the Okanagan Valley.

Named after the Vernon brothers, Forbes-George and Charles Vernon in approximately 1887, this steadily growing city can boast about having two of the world's most spectacular lakes on its doorstep – Kalamalka Lake and Okanagan Lake.

In bygone days, Vernon was the end of the line for steamers moving both freight and passengers on the lakes that caress the shores of what the Duke of Connaught referred to as, "The most magnificent setting I have ever seen. Absolutely stunning."

Kalamalka Lake is the smaller of the two lakes. At the Lookout off the highway above the lake, there used to be a sign signifying the word 'Kalamalka' meant 'Lake of many colours.' This may be correct, but officially, the lake was named after Kalamalka, an elder in the Okanagan Indian Band.

The population of Vernon in 1953 was approximately eight thousand friendly people. Today, like yesterday, they are closely tied to 'The Camp' as they refer to it.

Camp Vernon has been a part of the City of Vernon since 1912 when a Drill Hall was built on the hill south of town. That Drill Hall marked the beginning of the Mission Hill Camp the Canadian government officially established in 1915. Canadian soldiers trained there in two world wars.

In 1949, Camp Vernon was designated as a summer training establishment for Royal Canadian Army Cadets. These days, personnel from Canada's Reserve Forces use it along with cadets.

Cordell Cross

Chapter 1

When the phone rang, fifteen-year-old Douglas Brice stopped singing the hit song *Stranger In Paradise*, dropped his scrub-brush, vaulted out of the bathtub, leaped over his still-sleeping dog, and hit his right little toe on the radio sitting on the floor and blaring out the top-fifty hits played by Canada's top disc-jockey - Radio CJOR's Red Robinson.

"Damn," echoed around the bathroom and the house as Douglas bounced around on his left foot, holding up his right foot and rubbing his toe before bounding down the stairs to the hallway below.

Standing on one leg, the teen caught the phone on its fourth ring. With the telephone tucked between his chin and his shoulder, his voice hinted at his agony. "Jeez, hold on a sec ... Hello!"

Wane Banks, the *sprinter's* fifteen-year-old best friend, wasn't sympathetic. "What the hell's the matter with you? Is that any way to answer when your number one buddy phones?"

Rubbing the toe added more pain. "What the hell's the matter with *me*? Oh nothing! I'm just standing stark naked, getting the hall carpet soaked, and I think I've just broken a toe. That's what's the matter with me. Jeez, Wane, you always pick a great time to call. How come every time you phone, I'm in the bathtub?"

Laughter burst from the earpiece. "Well that's what we both do when Beverly Marcum takes a bath. I phone from the pay phone and you look through her letterbox. Don't forget it's my turn at her mail-slot next week. You'd think she'd catch on and get an extension phone put in her bathroom. What a set that dame's got. Where's your old lady?"

The swollen toe felt a little better as Douglas put some weight on it. "Don't ever tell anybody we do that. Beverly's going around with that Henry Konishi character and he'd kill us if he knew we were watching her answering her phone in the hallway in the nude. My mom's at work, and she's not that old."

A small chuckle followed. "You'd look just great if she walked in the front door right now. Anyway, do you want me to come by and we'll go to the Drill Hall together?"

Douglas glanced at the hall clock that read 5:05pm. "Yeah, sure. How long will you be?"

After a short pause, Banks said, "How's about six? We'll have to take the bus; it's pissing down out there. Say, I didn't see you on your route today, what happened?"

Brice forced some additional weight on the slightly swollen toe. "Our shack manager was late and we had two stuffings. It was a madhouse and I didn't start until three-thirty."

Wane laughed. "Like I've always told you, you should be delivering the Province, not the Sun. We only get stuffings on Saturdays. I finished my route by four."

9 – NEXT STOP, VERNON!

Colonel the dog came waddling down the stairs as if to warn Douglas the bath water was getting cold.

"Listen, Wane, do you want me to flood this old house out? I'll see ya at six ... all right?"

"All right, all right; don't get your nuts in a knot. G'bye!"

After he hung up, Douglas tackled the stairs three-at-a-time with his dog following. Just as he jumped back into the now lukewarm water, Rosemary Clooney started singing, *Hey There.*

Picking up the long-handled scrub-brush to scrub his back, he joined in with the singer. *"Hey there ... You with the stars in your eyes; love never made a fool of you; you used to be too wise..."*

Normally on rainy parade nights, at least thirty-percent of the cadets found excuses not to attend. However, on this soggy Wednesday evening in April 1954, when Douglas and Wane entered the armouries, two-hundred other eager British Columbia Regiment (Duke of Connaught's Own) cadets packed the west side of the parade square in the old Drill Hall on Beatty Street in Vancouver, British Columbia.

As the number of cadets entering increased, the smell of wet battledress uniforms blended with the main odour all armouries seem to retain - gunpowder, paint, gasoline, oil, cleaning materials and mothballs.

This night, a good number of these lads aged fourteen to seventeen would be chosen to attend the Vernon Army Cadet Trades Training Camp for the summer.

Excitement filled the air as Cadet Regimental Sergeant Major (RSM) Al Laidlaw came out of the cadet orderly room and tucked his large black drill cane under his left armpit.

"Right ... settle down! Fall in against the wall!"

Instantly all talking ceased as the 'young soldiers' marched to form a series of extended lines against the east wall of the armouries. Those who had been smoking in the jon were a few seconds behind the main throng, so the RSM nudged them along with a full frontal 'sneer.'

"Come on, you people with yellow fingers! You're in the British Columbia Regiment - not the British Columbia Dragoons! Get your asses in gear!"

As the RSM marched to the south end of the armouries, he failed to see or hear one of the smokers. A cadet by the name of Cadet Lance Corporal (LCpl) Moose Danyluk did a hustle-march talking out of the corner of his mouth to his friend, LCpl Jack East. "There ain't any yellow stains on my fingers. Here, Jack, take a look. Can youse see any yellow stains on my fingers?"

East didn't take the time to glance at his friend's outstretched arms and hands. He had his own problems trying to hide a gnawed-up chicken leg he'd just finished eating. Finally, out of desperation, he put the bone in his right pants pocket and wiped his greasy right hand on the back of Danyluk's tunic, as he said, "Christ, Moose ... you're supposed to be marching, not looking like you're sleepwalking. The only yellow stains you've got are those in your shorts."

Danyluk gave East the finger as they halted, shuffled in between two cadets, and about faced. Although Danyluk was supposed to be standing properly at ease, he

Cordell Cross

checked the fingernails on his right hand and shined them by rubbing them against his tunic.

"I use lemon juice on these gems - the girls love it. One of my *ladies* once said, 'Moose, my tender and passionate heartthrob, youse has got the fastest, softest and nicest smelling hands in the west.'"

A nearby voice whispered, "Danyluk, you've got a nerve calling those two-legged things you hang around with, *ladies*. Our kitchen table's got better lookin' legs."

"Some of his dames look like our pot-bellied stove," added another voice.

"Or the dog's breakfast," said another.

As the RSM called for markers, an incensed Moose stretched his neck forward and turned his head to find the 'mouthy' culprits.

"Youse pansies wouldn't know an exemplary body or a majestic set of legs if your lives depended on it! At least I've got dames to go around with!"

This time the RSM heard the lance corporal.

"Corporal Danyluk, get your head and eyes to your front and keep your habitual personal comments on female anatomy for your Seaforth *friends*! They can probably make better sense of them!"

The RSM then took a deep breath. "Right markers!"

Amidst snickering around Danyluk, four sharp-looking cadets marched forward, halting one behind the other in single file, in front of, and facing the RSM.

"Markers ... number!"

Each bellowed separately. "One! Two! Three! Four!"

Laidlaw took one pace back. "Stand fast the first marker! Remainder, outwards turn ... quick march!"

The three markers individually halted an equal distance from one-another, turned about, and shuffled - dressing on the first marker.

"Markers, standat ... ease! British Columbia Regiment Cadet Corps, get on ... parade!"

As the markers came to attention, all other cadets did the same and marched forward to form three ranks on their respective squadron's right marker.

Following sizing, a right dress, roll calls, an open order march, and "Fall in the officers," the commanding officer (CO) inspected his four squadrons. The RSM joined him.

Afterwards, when the officers were fallen out, the squadrons close-order marched, dressed, stood at ease, and the commanding officer called for *stickman* appointees.

Laidlaw carried out his commanding officer's wishes. "Parade, stand ... easy! Fall out the stickmen!" (Best dressed cadet in each squadron.)

As four surgically clean and adroitly dressed cadets marched forward to form an extended line in front of the commanding officer, his officers and the RSM, Jack East searched to find and wipe two breadcrumbs off the front of his tunic.

Glancing down at his chest, Jack said, "Two lousy crumbs? Two lousy crumbs stopped me from being stickman? What the hell is this army coming to? Jesus, don't they understand I've got to eat to survive? I can't see no crumbs."

Cordell Cross

Danyluk wiped visible dandruff and long blonde hairs off his shoulders. "Oh, quit bitchin' will ya? They've gone and nailed me for the inside of my belt not being shined, as well as Doris's dandruff, hairs, and grease again. If I've told that dame once, I've told her a million times. 'Keep yourself clean and youse won't have dandruff, loose hairs, or grease.'"

A nearby cadet asked, "How come she's loaded with grease? The shit's all over your back."

"I don't know. I didn't have my uniform on when we were on her couch. Nevertheless, she's like that … she's just gotta clean herself up, that's all. I even offered to give her a bath. Oh well, Confucius said, 'Upkeep of women is downfall of man!'"

"Ain't that the dame who don't brush her teeth?" East asked, still checking for crumbs. He also took off his webbelt to see the Silvo he hadn't brushed off his belt-buckle.

"Yeah that's her. I bought her a toothbrush but she uses it to brush match-red on her warts."

"Match-red?"

"Yeah … she licks the ends of matches and spreads the crap on her warts. Youse got a problem with that?"

"Hell no, Moose, she's your dame. Confucius also said, 'Man sometime discover girl of his dreams only nightmare!' How can you stand kissin' her? She's got lama breath and she sprays when she talks."

Danyluk grabbed his friend's left epaulette, then quickly let go. "How come youse got that close to her, you creep?"

Straightening his epaulette, East mouthed, "It wasn't by choice. Banks pushed me into her at the dance at the Georgia Auditorium. My nose went in her mouth, so she kissed it better. I got an affection from her tooth-marks."

Wane roared out laughing. "It's *infection*, you dummy. So you wrapped gauze around your wang, eh?"

"Up yours, Banks! My nose got contaminated and I couldn't smell anything for a week. Before I was cured, everything I ate smelled like her breath! A lama spat at me once; I know what it's like. Got me square in the face from seven feet away."

With his shoulders clean, Moose's mood improved.

"I once went around with a dame that could spit. She had a giant space between her front teeth, and she was better than a lama. The broad was good for five feet."

Danyluk's statement got the smiling squadron marker, LCpl Brice involved. "Moose, did she take you up on your offer?"

Moose's smug grin stretched from ear to ear. "Hey, Doug, how come you weren't with us for a coffee before parade? All my broads take me up on my offers! What offer are youse talking about?"

"My *batman* here, Lance Corporal Banks, was late in picking me up. I'm talking about your offer to give Doris a bath."

"Batman my ass," said Banks. "My name's not East."

East found another crumb. "Push this in your ear, Wane!"

Cordell Cross

12 – NEXT STOP, VERNON!

The expansive smile disappeared as Moose shrugged, sighed slowly, and held his hands to the ceiling. "Nah, she told me she had two weeks to go before her next bath. The dame only has two baths a month because she heats her house with sawdust. Hey, Doug, do you know what her friend Margo told her? She said… "

'C' squadron's stickman appointee, Cadet Gord Cunningham returning to the ranks, cut off the *animal*. His obvious disappointment of not winning the stick showed as he attained his original position next to Danyluk.

"Shit! That Goddamned Brooks in 'B' squadron is carrying the stick again. I think the guy's got something on the commanding officer. Any fool could see his pants weren't buttoned to his tunic. East, you owe me half-a-buck."

An expression of pure shock hit East's face! "Bull shit I do! You owe me fifty cents, you swagger!"

Cunningham continued to hold out his hand.

"Jacky, Jacky, Jacky. When are you going to learn? I said to you, 'I'll make stickman tonight, will you bet me fifty cents if I'm wrong?' Well, you creep, I was wrong!"

East thought for a moment. "You slob! I thought *I* was bettin' you wouldn't make it! Jesus, you're something else, Cunningham! Whenever I'm near you, I'm always broke!"

When Gordie accepted some pennies, nickels, and dimes, totalling East's *debt* he grimaced at the grease he got with the coins. Casually wiping his hand on Moose's back, he said, 'What's that Moose?"

"What?"

"Oh, I thought you asked me a question. Anyway, Jack, thank…kew! I've told you never to think. It's not good for you. Besides, you know what thought did, don't you? It went for a shit and the crows got it. By the way, you missed some crumbs."

Once again, the world's greatest moneymaker had silenced his chief currency-supplier. Smiling and humming *Rule Britannia*, Cunningham winked at a grinning Brice before the RSM carried on.

After giving the command, "Parade, atten … tion," the RSM turned and handed the parade over to the commanding officer.

"Thank you. Fall in please, Mr. Laidlaw!"

Laidlaw saluted and marched to a position in front of 'A' Squadron's sergeant major before turning about and facing the commanding officer, who addressed the parade.

"Parade, standat … ease! Stand, easy! My congratulations to Cadet Lance Corporal Brooks for earning the stick again. Good work, Corporal, and 'B' squadron."

Cadets in other squadrons threw a few *comments* at 'B' squadron.

"Considering the weather, I was very impressed with your turnout tonight! The majority of you look very smart, however more work is required on your boots, and I want that taken care of by next week! Also, some of you look bloody horrible without weights in your pants. I want all NCOs to explain to those people how they can make weights. Also, I will not stand for bugger-grips! Corporal Danyluk, get those sideburns cut! Do you hear me?"

Keeping his head and eyes directly to his front, Moose snapped to attention. Being in the fourth squadron, he knew the CO couldn't see him.

"Sir, I'll have fiancée problems if I do that!"

The CO moved so he *could* see Danyluk. "I beg your pardon?"

Danyluk had to think quickly. His reply had upset the CO and now SSM (Squadron Sergeant Major) Jack Battlefield appeared furious as he turned his head glaring at Moose.

Danyluk nervously cleared his throat, saying, "I said I've got a few financial problems, but I'll see what I can do, sir! How short?"

"Just so we're not stepping on them, Corporal Danyluk. Make them small!"

"Yes, sir!" Moose winked at those around him after he stood at ease. Then under his breath he added, "That'll be the foggy Friday. Nothin' I have is small."

Battlefield turned his head around again. "What did you say, Danyluk?"

The *animal* snapped to attention again. "Sergeant Major Battlefield, sir, I er, said, er, they'll be cut on Friday, sir. Even if it rains and it's soggy, I won't wait until fall."

As Battlefield re-faced his front, his puzzled-expression indicated he'd misheard the Lance Corporal. "Oh, that's all right then. Pay attention to the CO, and get that grease off your tunic."

Moose gave a quick finger to Battlefield's back, before returning his focus on the commanding officer.

"As you know, the annual inspection is coming up; therefore the regular training timetable has been changed tonight. For the first half before break, we will practise the march past! After the break, we will enter the hut at the side of the armouries and discuss the courses offered at Camp Vernon this summer.

"Setting foot in the Drill Hall this evening, I was offended by the green shamrocks painted on the main doors. Obviously, the Irish Fusiliers are up to their pranks again. Has retribution taken place, Mr. Laidlaw?"

A smiling RSM came to attention. "Yes, sir! We located our tank stencil and painted two black tanks on the main doors of the Gilford Street Armoury, sir!"

"Just two, Mr. Laidlaw? Er, surely there must be…?"

Again the RSM came to attention and stood at ease after saying, "And their other outside doors, sir!"

Satisfied, the CO confidently nodded, took some papers from inside his tunic, checked his pocket-watch, and continued to address the parade.

"We're very fortunate this year. We have allocations for 109 cadets to attend Vernon. They want our total band and we have allocations for 27 cadets to attend Eastern Canadian camps, and nine allotments for Banff. I think I can safely say that those of you wishing to go away for the summer will be taken care of! We'll go over that later."

The cadets released a few whistles and cheers of approval.

"Mr. Laidlaw, please have some people in headquarters squadron move the reviewing stand, please!"

Laidlaw shot to attention. "Yes, sir!"

14 – NEXT STOP, VERNON!

While the RSM supervised a few cadets from Headquarters Squadron (Vancouver's Saint George's School students) in moving the saluting base, Moose whispered to Banks. "Christ, I don't want to play in the band this summer."

"What are you complaining for," Wane replied. "Ya can't work up a sweat banging those damned cymbals. I'm gonna ask the bandmaster if he'll let you play the swinechord. Us drummers have to sweat our asses off."

"And buglers," said East. "If my lips get red raw, I can't eat."

"But youse can kiss the broads, can't ya?" Danyluk asked.

East thought for a moment, licked his lips, and moved his head from side to side. "Er, yeah ... I can kiss 'em, but I need nutrients in my body to get my lip-muscles to pucker."

Danyluk rubbed his crotch. "I ain't ever had that problem. My muscles act instinctively. All of 'em. Why I could be on a desert island for months without food or water, and if a broad showed up, my muscles would never let me down." He chuckled, "For that matter, they wouldn't let the dame down either."

Moose's friend, L/Cpl Lyons laughed out loud before saying, "I don't doubt it, because after you used your wang as a clam-digger, it would be nothing but muscle."

Danyluk broke up. "Hey, I can't help it if it's bi-manual. The broads would just have to put up with a little sand, that's all. Sand's sorta like resin, ain't it?" He paused for a moment recollecting Wane's words. "What the hell's a swinechord?"

"It's a hair stretched over a pig's ass. Ya hold it under your arm and pluck it with your teeth."

Moose joined those around him in laughter. Even SSM Battlefield snickered slightly, but no one saw his face. It was rumoured that Battlefield never smiled, and lance corporals warned recruits, "Don't get fooled between a gas pain and a smile. If Battlefield appears to be smiling, you're in for it."

L/Cpl named Foster said, "Ya hold it like bagpipes; that's how ya hold it. Hey, maybe those Seaforths play swinechords, not bagpipes. They probably blow air into pigs' asses. It's a shitty job, but somebody's gotta do it, and I get the impression the Scots love it."

Banks quipped, "They probably do if it's shitty."

Foster was on Moose's 'shitlist.' "Hey, Foster, that *supposed* Spanish Fly youse sold me, smells and tastes like horse shit. Ethel got sick the other night when I slipped it in her coke."

"I didn't say it was *real* Spanish Fly," Foster shot back, grinning. "Cunningham suckered me into it for three bucks. I couldn't stand the smell either, that's why I dumped it on you."

Moose couldn't believe what he just heard. "Just what the hell does that mean? I pay youse five bucks for..."

The RSM's voice stopped Moose.

"Right, pay attention here! On the march past, I want to see all arms up, chins up, and chests out! Watch your dressing and dig in your heels! Push down on your thumbs. Drive the arms straight back and don't wipe your asses. On the eyes right, look at the commanding officer's eyes! Parade, atten ... tion! Move to the right in column of route, right ... turn!"

Cordell Cross

15 – NEXT STOP, VERNON!

All squadrons turned to the right and the supernumeraries went to their new positions.

"The British Columbia Regiment Cadet Corps will march past in column of route, headquarters squadron leading! By the right, quick ... march!"

For the next hour, cadets of the 2290 British Columbia Regiment (DCO) practised the march past without members of various squadrons forming the band.

During the ceremony, several cadets were asked to leave the ranks for individual instruction. Lance Corporals worked with them until they improved.

At 2015 when they were fallen out for a fifteen-minute pop break, Danyluk glowered at Foster like a bee ready to sting. "Here's the bag; gimmee back my fiver!"

Like the others, Foster received a free KiK Kola and two doughnuts, but these didn't improve his ungenerous mood "Not on your life, Moose; you used some of it. Listen, a business deal is a business deal. I had to sell it to you, so go sell it to someone else."

Frustrated, Moose didn't know what to do. Then after a second or two, a smile appeared.

"Okay, ya pongo, but I'll getcha for that one. Where's Doug? Ah there you are. Doug, ol' pard, ol' pal, ol' buddy, let me buy youse another KiK-Kola."

Douglas backed off quickly. He knew Moose needed help when the *animal's* nose hit his.

"I've already got one. All right, tell me what's going on?"

"I need the assistance of *Musketeer Sales Plan Three*. Just follow me and plead, offering me five bucks. Okay?"

Douglas agreed. 'Musketeer Sales Plan Three' had been designed and developed by their buddy, Bergie, a Royal Canadian Electrical and Mechanical Engineers (RCEME) cadet they'd met at Vernon the previous summer. The system came in handy when one of them was broke and wanted a *flounder* to spring for a cold pop.

Moose wound himself through the crowd looking for a certain individual and paying no attention whatsoever to Douglas who had hold of Moose's uniform's left sleeve.

"Come on, Moose! I'll give ya five bucks for it. Listen, five bucks is a good deal ... I started bidding at three bucks. C'mon, Moose, sell it to me, *please!*"

Danyluk's face remained adamant. "It's six bucks, or nothing! I've told youse that, Doug. Fork up six bucks and it's yours! Jesus, youse has got a nerve. Commerce is commerce, and I want six bucks for it!"

"Aw, c'mon, Moose? I... "

Brice didn't have to continue because a fish bit the line. Tommy Johnston, a curious baby-faced cadet joined them. "What ya sellin' Moose?"

"Youse is too young, Tommy, and cheapskate here is only offering me five bucks. Listen, Doug, where can youse buy a bag of genuine Spanish Fly for five bucks? Answer that one. I'm keepin' the stuff for my broads."

A worn out LCpl Brice still persisted a little and searched one pocket for the money.

"All right then, five dollars and ten cents."

Cordell Cross

With the sneakiest gleam on his face, Johnston grabbed Moose's other sleeve.

"What? Genuine Spanish Fly? Jeez, er, Moose ... I'll..."

Tommy's hands reached for his pockets. "Yeah, I'll buy it from ya! Here, Moose, here's the dough."

Moose scooped up the small wad of six one-dollar bills and handed the bag to Johnston. "Okay, Tommy, but watch what ya does with that stuff. It's powerful and used on the farms, ya know. I'm sorry, Doug, but money speaks."

Feigning betrayal, Brice slowly sauntered away, muttering, "You mean *talks*. Some friend you are, Moose."

In seconds, five guys gathered around Johnston expressing their views as the *buyer* sniffed, displayed, and explained his *excellent* knowledge of the *exceptional* purchase.

"Jeez, really? Are you serious? Wow," said a nearby cadet eyeing the bag. "I heard about a dame that took some and satisfied herself by sittin' on a gear shift."

"Can I buy a bit off ya?" another asked.

"The genuine stuff? Tom, you'll be skin and bones."

"Skin and all bone," a confident Johnston replied.

"Christ, you lucky stiff! I'll give ya seven for it!"

A hand grabbed Johnston's arm, forcing it over so a nose could enter the bag.

"Phew, Spanish Fly smells like horse shit."

The proud new owner pushed the 'sniffer' away, gulped down his pop, and pocketed the pouch. He knew the RSM was about to fall in the parade.

"Lookout dames," Johnston said, feeling and acting like the sex-king of the world. "Tom the bomb ... the walking, talking, lust-machine is on the loose. What a good buddy Moose is."

"Form up in your squadrons!"

A minute later, the RSM carried on. "Parade atten ... tion! Move to the right in threes ... right ... turn! Peeling off from the rear rank of 'C' squadron, into the hut ... Quick ... march!"

Two wings of a normal 'H' hut without the centre section stood outside the armouries. One wing housed the Regiment's Men's Canteen, the other, a lecture hut. Laidlaw called the jammed-to-the-brink lecture hut to attention when the commanding officer and his officers entered. Cadets seated on benches behind wooden folding tables sat to attention as the CO made his way to the front with his officers following. Those who were standing stood to attention.

"Thank you. Just relax and take off your berets!"

Two duty lance corporals took out their 'little black books' to note the names of those who weren't paying attention or didn't have proper haircuts.

"We've reviewed your applications and we've done the best we can to send you away this summer. Unfortunately, most junior non-coms (non-commissioned officers) have applied for the driver mechanics course. Sorry lads, we've only got twenty-one vacancies for that course and we've allocated them to the senior guys."

Grumbling filtered through the assemblage. Every cadet had his heart set on receiving a military driver's licence.

"So, the following cadets have the option of not going, or taking the Signals RT (radio telephone) course. The choice is yours."

The commanding officer read a long list of names he had chosen to attend the sigs course at Vernon. His list included, Brice, Banks, Danyluk, East, Lyons, and Cunningham.

Wane appeared upset and it showed as he stood up.

"Yes, Banks! What's the problem?"

"Er, sir ... last year you allowed some of the younger cadets, like Lance Corporal Lyons here, to take the Driver Mechanics Course. Why not this year?"

"Last year they allotted us more positions. Also, because Lance Corporal Foster applied for Driver Mechanics Course last year, but had to take signals, we've put him on Driver Mechanics Course this year! In 1953, most of you people wanted to take Instructors' Basic Training ... remember?"

Someone whispered, "Foster, you lucky stiff."

Foster didn't say anything as the commanding officer continued speaking. He just stuck out his chest and stroked a non-existent beard.

"I think I can confidently say that those of you taking signals this year will have the opportunity of taking driver mechanics next year. Sorry chaps, but listen, I don't know why you're complaining ... the signals course at VACC is an excellent trade qualification course. You'll receive the same trades' stipend as those taking D&M. Anyway, please let me get on with this list!"

At 2130 hours, the corps left the hut and formed up in squadron formation for the nightly dismissal. Further advice was given to everyone before the final salute.

"A week this Friday, the regiment is going to Nanaimo. (The British Columbia Regiment had six tanks at its Nanaimo training base on Vancouver Island. Members of 'C' squadron of the Regiment lived in the Nanaimo area.) Those who wish to attend, give your names to your squadron sergeant major! I also want you to keep in mind that this whole cadet corps will be going to Nanaimo again next month. We'll be on the ranges for the weekend. In May, we'll be at Blair Range for a weekend and in June, one week prior to the annual inspection, we'll be joining the regiment at the same range for the Blair Shoot! Some of you will be in the Butts ... the remainder doing other odd jobs! Are there any questions?"

Lance Corporal Danyluk came to attention and spoke.

"Sir, why is the Nanaimo Indian Hospital out of bounds?"

(The Nanaimo Indian TB Hospital was housed within the confines of the camp.)

Cringing, a grin came to the commanding officer's lips. He recognized the voice. "Because, Corporal Danyluk, the female patients in there have got tuberculosis and they need rest. Do I make myself clear? They need rest! It wouldn't be impossible for them to get any rest with you walking the halls with your usual bag of candy and monumental erection!"

As Moose stood at ease and put on his hurt look, howls of laughter filled the armouries. Suddenly he came quickly to attention again.

"But, sir, I'm just trying to make them feel cheery! You know, cheer them up? I just want to give them a laugh."

"No, Corporal Danyluk, you want to feel them up, not cheer them up! As far as giving them a laugh is concerned, that thing will frighten them to death! I don't care whether you're just trying to make them feel or be felt, or if you've named that thing of yours 'cheery' or not - the Nanaimo Indian Hospital is out of bounds, is that clear?"

Laughs reached the rafters and dulled the sound of the pounding rain.

"Yes, sir."

"I can't hear you!"

"Yes, sir," a forlorn Danyluk replied, standing at ease again.

After about ten other questions and as the squadron sergeant majors wrapped up taking names, the commanding officer called the parade to attention. His officers stood at attention behind him.

"Mr. Laidlaw!"

"Sir!" The RSM marched and halted in front of the commanding officer and saluted.

Upon returning the salute, the commanding officer said, "Dismiss the parade please, Mr. Laidlaw."

The RSM saluted and the commanding officer returned his salute before Laidlaw turned and faced the parade.

"Officer on parade! British Columbia Regiment Cadet Corps, dis ... missed!"

Laidlaw turned and saluted the commanding officer while the rest turned to their right and saluted. The officer returned the salute.

While two hundred cadets dispersed quickly, Lance Corporals' Brooks and Doucette both called for 'defaulters.' (Those whose names had appeared in 'little black books' throughout the evening.) Defaulters received fifteen minutes of extra drill by the two lance corporals. Also, the defaulters had their names placed on the 'Defaulters-Board in the orderly room. Lance Corporals were gods because they controlled the 'little black books.' If a sergeant or a higher rank saw something wrong, lance corporals would sort out the problem.

After gathering their raincoats or greatcoats from various hiding places, the cadets of the British Columbia Regiment left the armouries and headed across the street to the restaurant in the bus depot, or headed home.

(Author's note: Unlike the Irish Fusiliers, the BCR cadets didn't have a cadet mess to enter after parade. The Irish had a mess and a piano that inaugurated many 'songs' one of which always stood out. Fierce competition existed between the Irish, Dukes, and Seaforths. *Shamrocks of green, standing stately with pride. Irish we are, the rest move aside.*

Bring on the women, the enemy too. And we'll get the job done, better than you."

A chorus sang: *"That means you, Dukes and Seaforths!"*)

After leaving the Drill Hall, Moose Danyluk crossed the road with Banks, Brice, East, Lyons, and Cunningham. The wind and driving rain forced them to pull up their collars.

"All I want to do is cheer them up, and he says I want to feel them up. Jesus, my reputation is really going downhill. Can youse guys believe that?"

19 – NEXT STOP, VERNON!

East counted what small change he had left. Cunningham had nearly cleaned him out. "Can we believe what? That you really want to feel them up?"

Moose pushed East forward out of the way of a passing car. "Well, I gotta do what comes naturally, but I can make 'em cheery while I'm doin' it to 'em. I do it with style ya know. I don't use Cunningham's method. Every dame in the world wants to be felt with these smooth, lemon-fresh hands."

Searching his pockets for more change, East said, "Casanova didn't even have to feel his broads. He could lay 'em without foreplay."

As they entered the bus depot, Cunningham took off his beret and shook it. "What the hell's that supposed to mean - that you don't use my method? Just because I train my dames how to gamble, doesn't mean we don't get it on occasionally. Unlike you, I use a little savoir-faire. I don't go up to a broad and say, 'Hey, I like your big tits, can I see if they're real or rubber, my dear?' Moose, you are one crass individual. And Casanova didn't have yellow stains on his fingers, either."

Danyluk checked his fingers again and ordered his usual cheeseburger and orange drink.

"When have youse ever seem me do that? Doug, Wane, have you ever seen me do that? I take 'em gently by the hand ... looks into their eyes, and then I ask 'em. I use diplocaxy, er, diplimatty."

Lyons winced. "The word's, diplomacy, you ayrab!"

Cunningham also ordered a cheeseburger from a waitress oblivious to the conversation.

"You call that diplomacy? It's where you put their hands, you creep. The dames don't even know you and the next minute you've forced their hands onto your crotch."

"Well, what's wrong with that?" Danyluk, yelled, before realizing he was too loud and lowering his voice. "Let's get off the subject. My methods work better than the techniques youse virgins use. I get 'em in seconds, not months. And these surgical fingers of mine don't have nicotine stains. Christ, I'm gonna be a ginnyologust. Ya can't have yellow finger-stains doin' that stuff."

Lyons recoiled again. "The word's *gynaecologist*, you moron."

Moose checked his fingers. "Whatever. I ain't started yet. After I take the course I'll know how to pronounce it, won't I, smart ass?"

"Jack, why haven't you ordered?" Wane asked.

A grim and always famished East responded, "How can I eat when Cunnilingus has got all of my dough?"

Cunningham bit into his burger. "That's right, he ain't eatin'. Jacky, my boy, if you continue to bet with me, you'll be as skinny as Moose here."

Wane produced a one-dollar bill. "Here, you can pay me back at shooting practise on Saturday."

East's face lit up. "Thanks! How about at band practice on Sunday? I don't get my allowance until Saturday night."

Gordie swallowed quickly. "Allowance? Jeez, why don't you get a job like the rest of us?"

Cordell Cross

Humbly, East took the dollar. After he thanked Wane again, he glared at Gordie. "I do have a job, you creep. It takes my job and allowance just to support you."

Chuckling filtered around the table. Even other BCRs close by, joined in.

A very proud cadet sitting in the next booth and protecting a small paper bag turned around and tapped Moose on the shoulder.

"Hey, Moose, I'm gonna slip some of this stuff in Hilda's drink tomorrow at school. Do ya think she'll rape the teacher right there and then?"

Moose turned his head. "Who's sittin' the closest to her?"

"I am," replied the soon to be sex maniac.

"Then youse better loosen your belt and pants, because if ya don't, she'll rip 'em off youse right there and then."

A serious look took over Johnston's smile. "Jeez, in school? I'd better wait until we're in her house."

"I would, Tom, and don't give her too much. We don't wanna lose ya."

"If he gives her too much, she'll be *neighing*," Gordie whispered out of the side of his mouth.

"She'll also be *hoarse*," Douglas added as the group muffled their howls.

At Johnston's table, his 'friends' decided they would all be taking their girls over to Hilda's house after school. Funds changed hands quickly as small amounts of the *sexy stuff* were dished out of the bag and wrapped up in individual serviettes. After the sales, a self-satisfied look returned to the *supplier's* face. He'd made his money back, and still had half-a-bag left.

Thirty minutes later all boys said their goodbyes, departed, and Douglas and Wane headed for the bus stop together.

The night-wind whipped up sheets of rain, and those without coats were quickly drenched.

Chapter 2

Time slows down when leaving for Vernon is getting close. Over the next few months, the cadets of the British Columbia Regiment (DCO) attended the Nanaimo Military Camp twice, and Danyluk was true to his word. Although it was tough for him, he stayed away from the Indian Hospital. Some female patients did lean out their windows calling for him, but the Moose just rubbed his crotch, sighed, and ignored them *in the line of duty*.

When Blair shoot time rolled around, the BCR cadets did odd jobs for the various regiments attending the Blair Trophy shooting competition at Blair Range in North Vancouver, B.C. All attending regiments took their cadet corps with them and this particular year the weather was wonderful. At the presentation parade following the two-day shoot, the British Columbia Regiment (DCO) had won the Blair Trophy.

"The reason the Seaforths lost is because their asses were cold," Wane said to Douglas. "Why they wear those goddamned kilts at a shoot like this, I'll never know. Every time one of 'em hit the ground, his kilt was up around his neck. They didn't have the time to pull their rags down."

Lighting up a smoke, Moose laughed at Wane's usage of the word *rags*. "It's because they want them up. They wanna show their asses … that's how those *kilties* get the dames."

"I think you're right Moose," Douglas said. "But the Canadian Scottish don't wear kilts when they're here."

East strolled by eating a chicken breast. The *beast* had managed to get his favourite job of assisting the cook for the entirety of the event. "That's because they're not exhibitionists like the Seaforths," he said. "Anyway, those Seaforths eat smaller portions because their asses are always cold. That means more for us."

Wane smacked his chewing buddy's back. "You mean more for you,"

"No, you creep, I mean it's more for all of us," East reiterated, dropping the chicken bone in a Westie beret lying on the ground. "Those antler-lovers with the kilts eat like sparrows because they've always got colds or something wrong with themselves. They should be wearin' shorts of some kind under those rags. Even hot-water bottles."

Douglas chuckled at East now using the word *rags*. He knew Jack wouldn't say it if a 'kilter' was near. "C'mon, you two doctors, let's go to the back of the Butts, and see if we can find some slugs to make proper weights."

After the presentations, Cunningham roamed the swarm searching for cadets that had placed bets that the BC Regiment wouldn't win the shoot.

When Cunningham had his antennae out, no one, young or old escaped paying. Once again, the world's richest young gambler was wealthier - this time by $67.00 of which $33.00 had been won playing stuke and poker in the Butts and huts during the two-day event. In the Butts, he even bet the cadets next to him where the next shot would hit their targets. If the Heavens had opened up as they did the year before, it wouldn't have mattered. Absolutely nothing took the gambler's mind off his goal. Gordie Cunningham's incessant smile indicated his eagerness to initiate or fully participate when his ears picked up the words, "game," or "all money in the pot."

Johnston's face, however, wasn't beaming. For the past few months, he'd been glued to Danyluk, trying to get his *Spanish Fly* money back.

"Listen, Moose, our school's got sick dames all over the place. Hilda's breath even smells like horseshit. She dumped me because I ain't kissed her for two months. I've got half a bag left and I've sprayed it with perfume; gimmee three bucks for it, will ya?"

The Moose wasn't gentle. "It's Corporal Danyluk to youse, Johnston. I thought it was the real stuff and if I had sold it to Doug, he wouldn't bitch nor have the nerve to ask for his money back. You got most of your dough back by proportioning it out. Sell the balance to someone else, you pongo. You're surrounded by Irish and Seaforths ... get with it."

Johnston's pout changed to a devious smirk and before long, the half-bag went for ten dollars. A 'cold ass' cadet, surrounded by other 'cold asses,' became subjected to the same treatment Johnston went through earlier in the year.

"Ya lucky shit," one Seaforth said. "I would have paid him eleven bucks."

"Phew, it smells like a combination of that *Evening In Paris* perfume stuff, and..."

Another said, "Hey maybe my mom must wear Spanish Fly?" "No it don't! That's horseshit! It smells like *Evening at the Stables*. No wonder they use it on animals."

A tall Irish cadet moved in. "I'll buy some off ya, okay? I'm takin' out a new dame who used to go around with some BCR cadet by the name of Johnston. She's been sick lately; maybe the stuff will get her in the mood. How are ya supposed to use it?"

The current owner now became the teacher. "Ya slip it in her KiK-Kola, ya dummy. What's the dame's name?"

A stately smile followed the name, "Hilda."

As the Canadian Pacific Railway's *troop* train coiled its way through the dark in British Columbia's Fraser Canyon, weariness showed on its occupants faces. Friday had been a very long day for them, what with packing and making last minute arrangements with friends so that chores and jobs would be done while they were away.

Prior to boarding the train, the station boiled, and for some reason this year, every railcar had a regular force non-commissioned-officer aboard. These *gentlemen* perused and *listened* to certain suitcases and duffel bags to detect the smuggling of beer. They even joined the occupants of their cars for meals, which kept down the usual tomfoolery.

Earlier, upon arrival at the depot, the BCR musketeers, Brice, Banks, Lyons, Cunningham, East, and Danyluk, met their previous-summer's friends, Bergie, Earl Jackson and Harvey Rothstein, who were about the same age but served in other regiments. As luck would have it, they each mentioned that they were also taking Signals. This meant that the original seven musketeers were back together again; Lyons became the eighth, and Cunningham, the ninth. They called themselves musketeers because they worked as a team to survive the rigors of Vernon the year before. It was, all for one, and one for all.

Although the non-BCR Musketeers occupied different cars, the boys' managed to visit back and forth a few times as the group of them brought themselves up-to-date on what was happening in their *world* of cadets.

After Douglas Brice changed into civvy PT shorts, a T-shirt, heavy socks, and running shoes, he decided to explore the long train. The train-ride to Vernon the previous year had been a riot even though the travellers had been warned what lay ahead of them in the sunburnt hills of Vernon.

Walking through each car, Douglas found the atmosphere the same. With NCOs present, all cars were quieter than usual. Cadets who had never been away from home stared blankly out the windows observing more of a reflection of themselves than the sparse lights that sped by shattering the darkness of the night for a fraction of a second. Other boys read comics, last-minute letters from girlfriends, or shined their brass and boots while lonely songs originating from large portable-radios contributed to the scene. A few had even brought guitars, and slow-moving fingers subliminally picked at strings playing melodies that reminded cadets of home.

Some of the newcomers had taken off their shirts and just sat around in battledress pants. The pants were crumpled at the bottom of each leg, exposing seams that had been opened to thread a piece of string or a shoelace through so the bottom of the leg could be drawn in before being submerged in puttees or gaiters. Other cadets just rested in their undershorts, or undershorts and khaki shirts. They had been warned not to bring civvy clothes and already this world of khaki felt strange and uncomfortable.

Walking through cars, Douglas observed the homesick looks of new cadets that hadn't yet made friends. Hours earlier, they had excitedly grinned and waved goodbye to family members with welled-up watchful eyes standing on the railway platform. Forever dreading this day, mothers, fathers, sisters, brothers, grandparents, aunts, and uncles knew the time had come to loosen the cord of attachment so their young loved-ones could explore the reality of the world far away from a caring home.

Although the departing youngsters didn't know it then, before long, they would make new friends and the thread of loyalty would forge a bonding relationship that would last a lifetime. As such, new families would be brought together - not blood-kinship, but near enough to it.

Close to the *abandoned* cadets waiting for someone to say hello, sat the boisterous, the egotistical, the unconcerned and the smart-alecky boys. Even a good portion of these young fellows just put on a front to hide their real feelings. That's the way they had been brought up. Indeed, very soon, they too would be made to see that the light. Close camaraderie made it easier to drop false fronts that weren't necessary in the first place, nor tolerated at Vernon.

Like millions of youngsters before him, on his way back to his own car, Douglas stopped and stood on the middle of a moving partition between cars. The consistent action of the concertina-like material covering the cars' steel joining-platforms and clickety-clack sounds the wheels made on the tracks never failed to intrigue him. The rush of country-fresh night air mixed with the smell of the train, and the echo of its lonely whistle triggered memories of his first train trip to Camp Vernon. The upcoming excitement of seeing Diane, the girl he had met the summer before was on his mind. His memory of her was constant, as was his longing to revisit the camp and the Village of Vernon in 'God's Country.'

Sticking his head out and allowing the blast of night-air to ruffle his short hair, his yell, "It's great to be back!" was absorbed and hidden in the majestic canyon's walls.

As Douglas wiped his wind-strained eyes and pushed open the heavy door to his car, Moose Danyluk's voice boomed. The *animal* was bugging Bergie again and the combination of Moose's voice, the train trip and being able to share six weeks with his best friends thrilled Douglas Brice. He loved this exhilarating portion of his life the army provided.

"Where the hell have you been?" Banks asked, joining Douglas in his berth. "And why are you crying?"

"I just took a walk through the train and stuck my head out. Was I missed?"

Wane grinned. "No, we didn't miss ya, but East thought you'd flushed yourself down the jon."

As usual, East spoke with his mouth full. "Yeah, I did. While you were gone, Cunningham was on his hands and knees trying to sucker us into a game."

"Then I'm glad I wasn't here," Douglas said, still wiping is eyes.

Elated to be back with Bergie, his *guru*, Danyluk stuck his chest out a mile as he sat on the edge of his upper berth. The year prior, Bergie had taken these BCRs under his wing, along with Earl Jackson and Harvey Rothstein.

"Bergie, youse old pal 'o mine. So ya made sergeant, eh? Get up here and tell old Moose about it. Hey youse guys, I've always told ya Bergie's got the smarts."

Bergie's smile widened. "Moose, don't talk about me making sergeant. The fact that you've actually made it to lance corporal amazes me."

Leaning down and giving Bergie a mock punch, Moose said, "Yeah, I know - thanks, Bergie. It's been tough though. This past year I've been a lance corporal more times than you've been to the jon. My dames are gettin' fed up sewin' my stripes back on. One of 'em even said, 'Darlin' I've sewn your stripe back on three times ... don't that make you a sergeant?' I said, 'No, baby, it makes me a general.' So she now calls me General Moose. Olive's not too bright, but what a set of melons she's got. She's the one that won't wear a bra."

"Why's that," asked Jackson.

A grinning Moose replied, "Cause I told her wearin' a bra causes ringworm. Youse all knows that ringworm is contagious. I sure as hell don't want it."

East swallowed. "Ya can't get ringworm from wearin' a bra. Jeez, Moose, get with it."

"Maybe youse can't with your bra, but she might with hers. Anyway, it always works. I've got three more dames ditchin' their bras because they think they might catch ringworm."

25 – NEXT STOP, VERNON!

East stopped chomping for a second. "Er, what did you say? My bra? Did you guys hear that? Up yours, Moose!"

Wane threw his comic at Bergie. "I thought you weren't coming back?"

The *sergeant* caught it and jumped up next to Moose. "So did I, but if I wasn't around, who would look after the living, walking-talking wang, here?"

"Hey, youse didn't look after me! It was me who kept ya in clean gaunch! Not this year, though, 'cause Heavenly Helga's bought me some new-style Norwegian cotton briefs. There's only one problem. I..."

Bergie already knew. Living with Moose for six weeks the previous summer had really clued him in. "Don't tell me. There's no room for the family jewels or the unemployed."

"Ya got that right; a flea couldn't fit in 'em. Hey, who sez they're unemployed? If anything, they're overworked and undernourished. Jesus, these things are tight, I can't even cross my legs."

Bergie slapped his friend's back. "Moose, I keep tellin' ya, I wouldn't wear a pair of your gaunch if my life depended on it. And don't borrow mine this year."

East eagerly rooted through his duffel bag. He had already changed into comfortable civvy PT shorts - now he craved food. "You're welcome to look after him, Bergie. We've gotta take care of him for the other ten months of the year and…"

East's expression suddenly changed as his hands waded through his bag.

"All right, who's the wise asshole that's gone south my bag o' fried chicken?"

When Lyons popped his head out his curtain, he didn't try to hide the chicken leg he raised to his mouth. "Mighty good, too, old chum."

Faster than a bolt of lightning, East leaped up into Lyons' berth. "Two pieces! You've eaten two pieces of my delicious chicken? Why you...!"

It wasn't difficult for the others to hear the choking sounds accompanied by Lyons' pleas coming from behind the swaying curtain. In thirty seconds a smiling East appeared with four pieces of chicken, a paper cup, and a bottle of warm beer. He used his *church key* (bottle opener) attached to the end of his lanyard to open the bottle. (All BCR cadets carried *church keys*.)

Lyons hadn't brought his LPB (Lyons' personal bar) with him this year. He'd only managed to bring five warm bottles of beer, which he'd hidden in his bass drum. Jack now had one of those beers.

The cadets of the British Columbia Regiment (DCO) were forming the band at Vernon this year, so many drummers used their instruments to conceal illicit *liquids*. Danyluk of course always complained that he was constantly on the losing end because he couldn't store anything in his cymbals, except "sweet smelling" garterbelts which he used for straps. The items apparently helped him too, because he always boasted, "When I clash my cymbals, the compressed air forces the perfumed aroma to my nose. It keeps my spirits up, amongst other things."

Lyons interrupted the quiet of the car as the Musketeers talked about their past exploits. The regular force corporal didn't appear very often after supper, so it was impossible for him to monitor the *chubby one's* burping and singing.

Cordell Cross

"She went into the water and she got her toes all wet. She went into the water and she got her toes all wet.

"She went into the water and she got her toes all wet. But she ain't got her..." Although the other guys were involved in deep conversation, they all subconsciously clapped twice.

"...wet yet!"

As Lyons belched and sang behind his curtains, Douglas asked where Cunningham was.

"The last time I saw Gordie," Harvey Rothstein said, "He was heading to the dining car with a deck of cards. I'll go find out. Maybe he's peeved 'cause he couldn't take our dough?"

Moose felt for his wallet. "He ain't gettin' any of mine. I gets it from my rich dames and it goes to my poor dames."

"Sorta like Robin Hood, eh, Moose?" East asked.

"Yeah, youse could say that, Jacky, my son. Moose Hood's the name, and Cunniligus ain't no Cop of Snottingham."

"It's Sheriff of Nottingham, you dummy."

"Whatever. Come on now, Bergie my boy, tell us the truth on how youse made sergeant. I know it's easy to get rank in the RCEME, but I didn't think it was that easy?"

His tiredness showing, Bergie yawned and jumped down saying, "It's called brains, Moose. While you're out at night spoonin' with the moon, I'm studying. When I think..."

A *soaring* Lyons suddenly cut off Bergie.

After mouthing the words, "I've gotta piss like a rhinoceros," Lyons had flung his legs over the side of his upper bunk to jump down, but couldn't stop his momentum. The chubby boozer's body came flying out of his unbuttoned-curtained upper berth and landed full-force on Bergie. The swift action took both of them into East's darkened unbuttoned lower berth. Obviously, Lyons had been partially sitting up swaying his beer to the sound of his singing. A pillow in his other hand indicated he'd tried to grab something prior to his *flight,* but unfortunately, the pillow wasn't strapped down.

Furious, Jack East didn't know his distress would worsen. Not only did Lyon's action cause East to spill his own warm beer all over himself, but he got a chicken leg pushed down his throat. The bottle of 'suds' in Lyons' other hand spewed out all over East's sheets, blankets and Bergie. Anyone passing at the time would have wondered why a wiggling wet cadet was being smothered by another wet cadet, who was in turn being suppressed by a chubby wet cadet holding onto a pillow with one hand, and an empty bottle of beer with the other.

Occupants of the car erupted in laughter just listening to the banter as Bergie yelled, "Jeez, Lyons, you've broken my neck! Get off me, you creep! I smell like a brewery and I ain't even had one yet."

Lyons couldn't move because he'd got his feet ensnared in East's curtains. He didn't seem to care anyway.

"Where am I? Hey, let's all sing Queen Farina. *Queen Farina, Queen of all the...*"

Cordell Cross

As Bergie pushed Lyons onto the aisle floor, he didn't feel his other elbow shoving the chicken-leg further down East's throat. Now a blue and wet wiggling East had even more to worry about.

Realizing Jack's predicament, Bergie yanked the bone out quickly - the sound imitating a plunger exiting a toilet bowl.

Coughing and spitting out pieces of chicken, East became maniacal. "I can't breathe and I think I've lost a tooth! I can't breathe! Let me up! Let me up, God damn it!"

The *beast's* teeth were still intact other than being covered in chicken-skin.

"Ah, that's better! Jesus, I'm soaked! What happened, you idiot? I can't sleep in these sheets."

Bergie wasn't apologetic. "It wasn't me, you 'ayrab' ... Lyons fell on me!"

Wane didn't help matters when he said, "Jack, that's the first time I've ever seen you want to get rid of food."

"Up your nose, Banks! God, I nearly swallowed that chicken-bone! Thanks for helping me, Bergie."

Now Lyons lay on his back in the middle of the aisle.

"Hey, palsies, let's sing the sheep's song. *We are poor little sheeps, who have lost our way. Blah, blah ... blah!*"

Rothstein rushed back into the car, yelling, "You guys, Cunningham's cleaning out all the NCOs and the dining car staff. You should see the dough he's got! What are you doin' on the floor, Lyons?"

"We are little black sheeps who have gone astray, bla, bla, bla...!"

It took two minutes for a chanting Lyons after he returned from the washroom to have his pillow and an empty beer bottle wrenched from his hands before being thrown between two soaked sheets in East's berth. Shortly, clothes and other personal objects were exchanged and Jack had a dry upper berth. When Lyons' curtains were being buttoned, the *vocalist* still remained in good spirits. "*Over there, over there, send a word, send a word, over there. ' Cause the Dukes are comin' - the Dukes are comin'* ... Hey, who pissed in my bed!"

The car was quiet after that except for the snoring of the one-man-choir and the laughter after Jackson asked, "*He* sure as hell hasn't changed, has he? Thank God last year's sergeant with the sore hand isn't here; he'd throw the drunk off the train."

A few moments later, they all said goodnight and went their separate ways. Friday had been a tiring day and the swaying of the train was putting them to sleep.

At two o'clock in the morning though, no one heard East and Lyons' conversation after Lyons had somehow managed to unbutton his curtains to get up and visit the jon. East was awakened from a deep sleep by getting a knee and a nose in his face as Lyons tried to climb into the same berth.

"What the...? Lyons, what the hell do you think you're doing here? My God, you reek of beer and onions!"

A little more sober, Lyons' face looked puzzled. "What am *I* doing here? What the hell does it look like I'm doing? What are you doing here? I'm going to bed, you asshole!"

"Not in this bed you're not! You moved to a lower berth!"

Cordell Cross

"I did? When did I do that? Hey, where's my celery, sugar and onion sandwiches?"

East pointed. "In your new berth, right there, you creep! Now bugger off!"

"Ya got any chicken left, Jack?"

East pushed Lyons and the thump was loud as the *boozer* hit the deck. Not worrying about his curtains, Lyons crawled between his sheets.

"Jack, I musta wet the bed! Did ya hear me, Jack? Damn it, I've pissed the bed! Hey, Moose ... can I move in with ya?"

Danyluk's snoring now rocked the car, so Lyons never asked again. Shortly, his snores were louder than Moose's.

"Next stop, Vernon! Next stop, Vernon! Vernon's the next stop! Fifteen minutes to Vernon!"

Briskly moving through the only car with curtains still up, the conductor made it quite clear which town lay ahead.

One and a half hours earlier, the 'warm beer hoarder' had slept through the racket of everyone getting up to attend breakfast, but he wasn't about to sleep through the regular force corporal's *awakening*.

"You, you horrible little man ... What the hell do you think you're doing?"

Still partially asleep, Lyons replied, "I'm in my girlfriend's house and she's pouring me a glass of sherry. Fill it to the brim please, Louise. Your parents won't know it's missing."

The massive arms of the NCO *gently* moved Lyons into the aisle, bedding and all. "Really now, is that right? Well Lovernuts, you've got exactly five minutes to get your nose out of the sherry, get washed, dressed, and packed up! Five minutes ... do you hear me? If it takes longer, you'll wish you hadn't been born! Is that clear?"

Although his head pounded, Lyons recognized the expression. He'd heard and heeded it the previous year. With great difficulty and as best he could, he stood to attention.

"Yes, er ... Corporal!"

"I can't hear you!"

"Yes, Corporal!"

Helped by his friends, Lyons made the five-minute deadline. With red eyes, uncombed hair, unbrushed teeth, no spiffy, unrolled puttees and sleeves, loose bootlaces, a noose for a tie and a dishrag for a shirt - Lyons stood to attention.

The corporal's lips formed the semblance of a gas pain. "My God, man, you look like you've spent the night under the train. Would you like that glass of cheap sherry now?"

Finding it difficult to stand, Lyons winced and nearly threw up. Just the thought of a glass of sherry made him nauseous.

"No thank you! Actually, her parents buy only the best! I can remember the time…"

"Get out of here and get yourself straightened up!"

"Yes, Corporal!"

"What regiment are you with?"

With difficulty, Lyons thought for a moment. He knew the procedure.

"The Irish Fusiliers, Corporal!"

"It figures!"

For the next ten minutes, those who berthed around him received the wrath of the *hobo* who supposedly had slept under the train.

"My friends? You guys are supposed to be my friends? Jeez, you let me sleep in ... I feel like a ton of shit ... I smell like a brewery, and I've only got ten minutes to make this perfect-looking body presentable to the girls of Vernon. What's with you pongoes?"

"Every one of us tried to get you up," said a smiling *gambler*, shuffling a deck of cards. "Moose even dumped two paper cups of water on you."

"What? No wonder I was soaked! Moose, you creep!"

Moose wasn't around. He was between cars with Douglas and Wane. They'd opened up the upper half of the door.

"Smell that fresh air! It reminds me of all my evenings alone with Alma in Polson Park. Do youse guys wanna know something? There's nothin' like Vernon air to get your wang up! I never wake up with a hard-on at home, because the atmosphere ain't the same. When I'm here in God's country, the air won't let it go down."

Wane squeezed in between the two. "That's bullshit, Moose, and you know it. I suppose Nanaimo's air don't help you out?"

All three of them now had their heads out the door, allowing the hot morning's Okanagan air to explore their necks and faces.

Moose pulled his head back in. "Well, er ... it's the pulp-mill smell that keeps it up. Wane, are youse tellin' me this scent don't help youse get it up?"

Banks didn't answer. It was great to be back in the Okanagan Valley. The look on his face mirrored Douglas'. The beauty of the surrounding countryside combined with the fragrance of the fresh forenoon air brought back all the memories of the summer of 1953. As far as Wane was concerned, nothing in the world could match the splendour speeding by. This wasn't the big city, where one could get lost in the crowd. This was the Okanagan Valley and the unique and lovely Village of Vernon. The astonishing quietness and bouquet of peacefulness of the area allowed one to disregard all big city clamour. The cadets were about to re-enter a special place where time slowed down, *and* Banks could hardly wait to get his hands on another pair of Debbie's panties.

Wane's feeling didn't last for long though, because Cunningham and Foster appeared.

"Jeez, there you are," the *gambler* said, still shuffling his cards. "C'mon you pongoes, the corporal's doin' a head count! Are you guys all packed up?"

When Douglas brought his head back in, the serene expression on his face indicated he'd painted a canvass of enchanted reminiscences and uncorked a bottle of the sweetest elixir ever created by the Master of the universe.

"Hey, youse guys don't hafta worry about me," said Moose. "Who got us up this mornin' to be first in line for breakfast? I did!"

Wane ran his comb through his short hair. "How's Lyons?"

"You mean the *dragon* of railcar 2044?" Gordie asked, grinning. "Oh he's up. Right now he's accusing East of eating his ... er, I think he said, 'celery, sugar and onion sandwiches.'"

Cunningham was right, because after they entered their car and the corporal ticked off their names, the accusations came hot and heavy.

"Oh really? I smell fish and onion on your breath and you never touched 'em! Whatsamatter with you, East? You eat breakfast and then help yourself to my sandwiches? I get hungry too, ya know?"

East exhaled in Wane's face. "There ain't no onion on my breath, is there? Wane, can you smell onion my breath? Lyons, I wouldn't eat your goddamned beet root, sugar and cabbage sandwiches."

Wane quickly backed away. "Jesus, Jack, just what *did* you have for breakfast ... kippers?"

East folded his tunic and placed it in his duffel bag. "Yeah, I like kippers. I had an extra helping because no one else ordered them. The cook was nice to me."

Still searching, Lyons yelled, "Well, if you didn't eat 'em, who did?"

"Lyons you idiot, you did! I keep tellin' ya that! I heard ya crunchin' about half-an-hour after you tried to crawl into bed with me. You were belchin' and singing some Seaforth song! Even though your bed was soaked, you were happier than a pig in shit!"

Lyons grinned and calmed down for a moment, but only a moment, as he took out his wallet to count his cash." All right, Jack, I apologize old chum. I thought..."

Lyons eyes bulged as he opened up his wallet. "What the...? I've been robbed! Where's my money gone? Okay, you creeps, where's my dough?"

Although slightly embarrassed, the *gambler* forced a smile and held his chin in the air. "Ya lost it to me at three o'clock this morning. Jack's right, you did eat your sandwiches. It's a wonder I could play cards with that breath of yours suffocating me."

Lyons was about to lay a barrage that would stop a herd of elephants, but the train had nearly come to a halt, allowing two impeccably dressed regular force artillery sergeants to enter the car from separate ends. Their finely pressed bush uniforms looked immaculate and their boots shone like mirrors.

The sergeant nearest the musketeers didn't waste any time after a serious partial gas-pain hit his face. "This car smells like fish! Stand in the aisle by your berths and place your duffel bags on your right! Quickly now, quickly! You, where's your headdress?"

Lyons didn't have a clue where his headdress was. "I, er ... I seem to have misplaced it, Sergeant. This doesn't happen very often. As a matter of fact..."

"Don't give me your life story! I'm not your mother! Do I look like your mother?"

Lyons' bloodshot eyes weren't the greatest. He scratched his head. "Well, ... er ... not really. Now where did I put my beret?"

"What did you say?"

"No, you don't look like my corporal, Mother!"

"What did you call me?"

"Er, Sergeant, you don't look like my sergeant, Mother!"

"What?"

"My mother, Sergeant!"

The Sergeant glanced at his counterpart at the other end. "My God, Charlie, will you take a look at this! The train hasn't even stopped and I end up with this bliffy shower of shit! What regiment are you in?"

All BCR eyes stared at Lyons. Once again he knew the script when a question was asked that could embarrass *the* Regiment.

"Er, the Irish Fusiliers, Sergeant."

"I can't hear you!"

"I'm with the Irish Fusiliers, Sergeant!"

"Oh, really? God give me strength! The Vancouver Regiment, eh? What the hell is the matter with you Irish? Right! Pick up your duffel bags and start heading out the forward door! Those of you who brought band instruments, you may keep your bugles with you, but drums and other large items must be placed on the platform cart."

It was fortunate that the sergeant didn't catch on to the fact that Lyons wore a black webbelt and black puttees. The Irish wore khaki items.

"Now, all of you - take one last look to be certain you've left nothing behind! You! What's that in your left hand?"

Cunningham swallowed heavily. "Playing cards, Sergeant! Would you like to...?"

The sergeant hadn't yet heard of the *gambler's* steadily growing card-playing reputation.

"Cards? You'll have no time for them here! Put them in your pocket! Playing cards? What do you people think this is ... a goddamned boy scout holiday camp?"

Cunningham glanced at a nearby red-faced corporal he'd *cleaned out* during the night. The NCO didn't say anything; he knew Cunningham's knowledge of cards was far more advanced than that of a boy scout.

As the trainload of cadets formed up in three ranks on the platform in front of the tiny Vernon railway station, the scorching sun's rays hit them with the ferocity of a blast furnace. Each cadet had packed his tunic, suspenders and tie, and was dressed in half-serge with webbelts. In addition, they had rolled up and buttoned their sleeves approximately three inches above their elbows. Each, that is, except Lyons. Although he'd combed his black hair, the rest of his uniform looked like he'd slept in it.

After Danyluk placed his cymbals on the cart, he stretched his neck searching for *friends*. Other than NCOs, drivers and railroad employees, hardly anyone was at the station.

"Where's the dames?" Moose whispered to Douglas.

"We've arrived an hour earlier than planned. Boy, they're gonna be upset," Douglas said out the corner of his mouth.

"Keep your mouths shut! Welcome to God's Country! You're going to love it here! By the time we're finished with you, you'll be qualified to sit on the right side of the omnipotent being, Himself! Is that clear?"

"Yes, Sergeant!"

"I can't hear you!"

"Yes, Sergeant!"

A small cadet in the 43rd Field came to attention and *proved*.

The Sergeant glared. "What is it lad?"

A timid voice said, "Ain't all sergeants, Gods, Sergeant?"

"Speak up, man! You're not in your girlfriend's bedroom! Now, what was your question?"

"I said, ain't all sergeants, Gods, Sergeant?"

A gas pain appeared on the NCOs lips. This young fellow spoke the senior non-com's language.

"What's your name, my boy?"

"Cadet Glendenning, Sergeant!"

The NCO's nose and gas pain smothered Glendenning's face.

"You are absolutely right, Glendenning! Undoubtedly you're going to top your course here at Vernon. Did every one of you hear him?"

"Yes, Sergeant!"

"Good, and don't you ever forget what he said! Are all artillery cadets sharp like you, Glendenning?"

"Yes, Sergeant," Glendenning announced, ignoring the word, "suck" uttered from most people around him. The NCO, however, now respected the boy.

"We will now march toward the trucks. This mob, atten ... tion! Pick up your gear! Move to the left in threes, left ... turn! By the right, quick, march! Left ... right ... left ... right ... left ... right!"

As approximately seven hundred cadets stomped in the direction of the waiting three-ton trucks, the minds of those who had *visited* before, released memories of previous summers. The rest remained wild-eyed. Their cadet sergeants had told them about this place. They were about to participate in six weeks of training that would seem like eternity, with benefits lasting a lifetime.

After the cadets loaded up, the trucks rolled through Vernon's main drag and headed up the hill. Along the route, newcomers were subjected to many excellent tour-guide commentaries offered by *professional old-timers*.

"There's the theatre! Obtain a midnight pass and try and get the back-row seats!"

"See that jewellery store? They have old capbadges in there! And they're cheap, too."

"There's the fruit union exchange. If ya ask nicely, they'll give you some free fruit!"

A voice said, "I don't need any, Danyluk's here!"

Moose shot back, "Up yours! And I ain't free!"

"Er, sorry ... little joke, there, Elephant!"

"It's Moose to youse."

"That's Polson Park! Hey, Brad, do ya remember the time we met those dames and..."

"It's easier drivin' than walkin' this hill!"

"That's the Vernon Hospital! Ya can neck in the bushes in the back!"

"Say, Wane," Jackson said. "Do ya remember when you put that silver cigarette paper on your epaulettes and became an *occifer*?"

"Sure do, Earl. There's where we got chewed out by those Irish creeps!"

East joined in after he'd eaten an apple and slipped the core into an artillery cadet's pocket. The recipient didn't feel anything because a nearby friend kept explaining the many benefits of visiting Polson Park.

East yelled, "There's Hop Sing's Laundry. Hey, Moose, do ya think you'll make it in there this year?"

Automatically, Danyluk came to attention, rubbed his crotch, and saluted the old building.

"Beastie, youse can bet your life on it! I've given it a lotta thought and I'm applyin' for a job there on Saturday afternoons. Move over, Hop Sing ... The Moose is back!"

Some Canadian Scottish Regiment (CScotR) rookie said, "Jeez you BCRs are weird if ya like workin' in laundries."

Moose glowered at him. "I'm not goin' in there to work, you virgin; I likes gettin' into dames' laundry!"

The *greenhorn* didn't care for the label Moose gave him.

"Who the hell are you callin' a virgin? You referrin' to me?"

Moose became a hornet. "Yeah, you!"

The lad thought for a moment before perspiration appeared on his forehead. "Oh, well that's all right, then. I'm sure there's a few of us here. All virgins hold up your right hand."

For some reason, *miscellaneous conversations* started. No one needed that question and each pretended he didn't hear it.

Danyluk didn't let the matter rest. "So that makes you the only virgin, eh?"

"Er, well, we all gotta learn sometimes, don't we? When did you start, Water Buffalo?"

"It's Moose, and youse is askin' a personal question. Lemmee see now ... it was just before I started to walk. Yeah, that's it! When I was six months old, the neighbour's dame and me was sharin' a crib. She was only five months old and asked me if I had a rubber and..."

Moose gave a small bow and shrugged aside the many comments thrown at him when the whole truckload of cadets burst into laughter.

"Well a stupid question deserves a stupid answer, don't it? How the hell do I know when I started? It's too far back to remember!"

As the three-tons turned left off the highway leading to the parade square overlooking the golf course, the young CScotR gawked in awe at Moose.

"Jeez, then you're a pro?"

Danyluk smiled and smacked the kid's back. "Youse has got that right, and at least you're honest. I'll betcha there's a hell-of-a-lot more virgins in this truck. I'll try and get youse into Hop Sing's with me."

"Er, thanks anyway, but I don't wanna work in laundries."

"That joint ain't just any laundry," Moose said, grabbing the front of the Scot's shirt, before letting go and firming up his own non-existent breasts. "It's more than a laundry! Now do youse knows what I means!"

"Oh, er, really? Yeah, shit, count me in; I'm willin' to learn. How much is it?"

"Does price matter to youse Scottish gentlemen of the world?"

"Er, I've only got ten bucks ... will that do?"

Although Cunningham sat at the other end of the truck, his famous dazzling white smile instantly appeared, along with, "Ten bucks? Say, soldier, do you play cards?"

Moose pushed the *gambler* aside. "The dames are really nice. What size do youse likes 'em?"

"Big!"

"How big?"

"Really big! I've heard if they're big, ya got something to hold onto!"

The *animal* smiled, shook the kid's hand and replied, "Hop Sing is going to think you're a master of the *art*. What's your name?"

"Patterson."

"And your first name?"

The cadet paused for a second. "Gunther."

The grin widened on the *animal's* kisser. "Gunther?"

"Yeah, Gunther."

"Youse can't be Scottish with a German name. As of now, you're Haggis Patterson. Right?"

Danyluk's smile transferred to the Scots face. "Right! Haggis it is! Yeah, I kinda like that!"

A good-hearted broad grin also appeared on Doug Brice's face as he listened to Moose's conversation with the *would-be client* of Hop Sing. As far as Douglas and all other BCR cadets were concerned, Moose Danyluk was really one of a kind. Life in cadets would not have been the same without the *animal*. When things got tough in Vancouver, Nanaimo, or even in Vernon like the previous year, Moose's jovial presence made real-world problems disappear almost instantly. Danyluk's hilarious contrived flippancy allowed those who were close to him to step one-pace back to observe life's everyday obstacles from another angle. It was always hard to tell if the Moose was earnest or not. As far as the ulcer department was concerned, Danyluk could never get an ulcer because very rarely did he allow anything to get him down. Also, insofar as Moose's female-exploit-bragging was concerned, when he expounded on his lustful conquests and had everyone's solid attention, a smile would appear on his lips indicating he'd suckered them once again. His joyful facial expressions were always accompanied with a wink, leaving his audience wondering.

The small talk stopped as each truck left the highway and entered the camp proper. Camp Vernon is grid with two H-huts to a square. The huts and the roads were empty and the only activity of any kind were water-sprinklers trying to entice individual blades of grass to raise their tips from two inches of dust that had been turned into mud moments before reverting to dust again. The horrendous heat didn't allow mire to form for long and most of the water evaporated before it hit the ground.

Eyes and ears of cadets who had attended Vernon in years past could see and hear the seemingly eerie sights and sounds of yesteryear hauntingly emanating from the parade square, open doors, and windows of empty buildings. Although this was a new year, the *old timers* knew that within moments the exact same screeching and hollering of former years would be regenerated. Although cadets and courses changed, barrack-room life didn't. Life in the barracks remained constant because the spectrum of personalities didn't alter. Kids are kids, and eagerness and innocence hadn't yet been turned into adult caginess and one-upmanship.

Newcomers expressed astonishment at the size of the camp, remembering what their *old pro* friends had said referring to survival in the barracks and on courses. *"Pay attention. Keep your nose and body clean, and your mouth shut. Use the eyes in the back of your head and you'll make it. If you don't, God help you."*

As the vehicles passed the cannon in front of the headquarters building, Douglas remembered trying to save some baby birds, and his *introduction* to Colonel St. Laurent, the camp's commanding officer the year before. He could also see B-21 and the tree where Sergeant Beckford had given him some fatherly advice.

As he perused the camp, a lost smile came to Brice's lips. Slightly shaking his head, he thought to himself, wow, wouldn't it be great if these old huts could talk.

When the convoy finally came to a halt on the parade square, regular force and militia non-coms turned up out of nowhere.

Tailgates swung swiftly and once again the sounds of the 'good old days' became standard. When the trucks drove away, the Vernon Army Cadet Trades Training Camp had opened for business.

"Form up in three ranks! Quickly now, quickly! Bring your duffel bags with you, and get a move on! You, you horrible excuse for a human being. What's that in your hand and what's that all over the front of your pants?"

The artillery cadet cringed. He had an apple core stuck in his hand and the juice and pulp from the item had oozed through his pocket onto the front of his pants.

"It's the remains of an apple, Sergeant, and I…"

"Speak up, man, and stand to attention when I'm addressing you! Have you been playing with yourself in the back of the truck?"

To the laughs and applause of hundreds of cadets, the extremely embarrassed *standard-bearer of the apple-brigade* snapped to attention.

"No, Sergeant! It's an apple core, Sergeant, and I'm not too certain where it…"

"Do you always walk around with an apple core or *other* things stuck to your hand? Well, do you?"

"No, Sergeant! I don't know where…"

"You say that's what caused the mess all over the front of your trousers?"

"Yes, Sergeant!"

"What's your name?"

"Gourley, Sergeant!"

"Well, Gourley, put that decaying thing back in your pocket! What are you going to bring out next … half a banana, or a baby's half-full bottle of sour milk?"

"Sergeant, I don't know *where* it came from!"

The sergeant's breath drenched Gourley's face. "It came from a tree. That's where apples come from, and as far as you're concerned, they should stay on the frigging trees."

Again, chuckling filtered throughout the ranks, but one BCR cadet laughed the loudest and the sergeant wanted him instantly.

"You! Yes you! Get out here!"

East *sobered* up quickly; marched out and stood at attention in front of the Sergeant.

"What's your name, laughing boy?"

"East, Sergeant!"

The Sergeant backed away fast, flapping his hand in front of his face. "My god, son ... what did you do, brush your teeth with fish-paste?"

"No, Sergeant! I had kippers for breakfast!"

"East, by the smell of your breath, you've had them for breakfast, lunch and supper all week."

Laughter rang throughout the ranks as the sergeant continued saying, "Gourley, come here! I'm giving you permission to wipe your hand on the front of this man's shirt ... Do you understand?"

Gourley smiled and hesitated. "Yes, Sergeant. Uh, on his shirt, Sergeant?"

"Yes on his shirt! Well, get on with it, man!"

Amidst howls from all but East, a bewildered Gourley thoroughly wiped his right hand finger by finger over the front of the instigator's shirt.

"Now, both of you fall back in!"

As a red-faced East marched back to his position, the still-puzzled Gourley stood at ease while the sergeant backed up and faced the four three-rank-long columns of *troops*. Neither Gourley, nor East knew this particular sergeant had been riding in the cab of the truck behind them. He had seen East's *dirty work* with the apple core and had remembered their faces. Sergeants have a habit of not missing too much. While East thought he was picked on for laughing out loud, and a baffled Gourley wondered how the core had gotten into his pocket, justice was served.

"Right! Atten ... tion! Standat ... ease! Stand ... easy! Pay attention here. You will notice there are seven tables on the side of this parade square. Each table has a course-sign displayed! Table 1 is Signals, table 2 is Driver Mechanics, tables 3, 4, 5, 6, and 7, are marked Instructors' Basic Training! When I fall you out, you will form up in single file in front of one of those tables, making certain you have your joining instructions ready. Keep the lines even at the IBT tables! Is that clear?"

"Yes, Sergeant," echoed around the nearby huts.

"Right! Vernon army cadets, atten ... tion! Fall ... out!"

Mayhem pursued after the cadets turned to their right for the standard count of two-three. Instantly, the commotion on the parade square resembled the main deck of an aircraft carrier when the order "Man all stations," is announced. Eventually, long lines persisted in front of each table.

For the next hour in unbearable heat, the sounds of shouted names and instructions reverberated throughout the camp.

37 – NEXT STOP, VERNON!

Banks became the first to approach the captain owning bushy eyebrows and a large chin. When Wane saluted, the officer didn't look up or smile. Instead, a sergeant next to the officer bellowed, "Last name first, and first name last!"

Wane placed his instructions in the officer's outstretched waiting hand. "Banks, Wane, sir!"

Both the officer and sergeant ticked Wane's name on their lists before the officer finally glanced up and handed him a blue ribbon and a medical card.

"You will wear this on your left epaulette for the remainder of camp. Take this card and report to that corporal, right ... there! Next!"

As Douglas Brice approached the officer and saluted, Wane became the right marker of Signals Company

Approximately a-half-hour later, 'F' Company, or Signals Company as it was later referred to, came to a halt at the side of the camp hospital located at the extreme southern end of the lower camp's main road. A red-haired sergeant with a nametag that said Pennington called the step and he halted and retired the company making certain cadets had their backs to the sun.

"F company, Halt! The company will retire, right ... turn! Standat ...ease! Stand ... easy! Pay attention here! My name is Sergeant P. G. Pennington! The 'P' stands for Prichard, but my friends call me, Red. My middle name is Grand, and I've never forgiven my mother for choosing that name! That should indicate to all of you that I'm not a very forgiving person. You are not my friends! You never will be my friends! I don't have many friends, and the ones I do have don't particularly think I'm very nice! However, that's all right, I don't really care for them, either! Now that I've made that clear and you know my name, you will you refer to me as what?"

While the main group bellowed out "Sergeant," Danyluk cupped his hands around Bergie's ear. "With a name like that, we should refer to him as the Big Red Prick!"

Like all sergeants, Sergeant Pennington used his God-like qualities. He had eyes in the back of his head and if he wanted to, he could hear a pin drop at the horse races. Marching over to Moose, but scanning the company, he said, "Perfectly correct! You will refer to me as, Sergeant, or Sergeant Pennington!"

The *unlikeable* fellow sporting a very casual look on his face halted in front of Danyluk, and quietly asked, "What's your name, son?"

Moose nervously came to attention. "Danyluk, Sergeant!"

"Did you know I can read lips, Danyluk? Even if they're shut, I can actually read them." Pointing at Bergie, the sergeant asked, "What did you say to him?"

Moose swallowed hard. "I ... er..."

"Speak up, man!"

"If you can read lips, you should know, Sergeant!"

Nearby chuckles grew into roaring laughs, but the sergeant didn't join in. He just changed his voice to a whisper. "Oh, we're a smart one, are we? Please don't get smart, Danyluk. I don't like people who get smart with me."

"I ... er ... simply answered his question, Sergeant!"

While the quizzed expression on Pennington's face indicated he hadn't seen Bergie's lips move, Bergie's facial cast became one of pure fright. After rolling his eyes to the sky, Bergie's utterance of the words, "Christ, not again," went unheard.

The Sergeant directed his attention to Bergie. "What did you ask him?"

Perspiring slightly, Bergie came to attention saying, "Sergeant, I asked him if he ... er ... knew what trades qualifications you would have. He said, if you're instructing on this course, you must be a group four signalman,' Sergeant! He also said, 'a group four signalman is one of the most qualified trades in the army. That your credentials, 'are, er ... as big and as solid as a' gold, er, 'lead brick,' Sergeant!"

Cocking his head and clearing his throat, the usual gas pain came to the sergeant's lips. The NCO felt angry at the thought of being so paranoid. These two *nice* innocent boys were actually giving him compliments.

"Not bad, I like that comparison. Big, and solid as a lead brick, eh?"

"Definitely, Sergeant!"

The eyes of 'God' stopped burning through the lads.

"Big, and solid as a lead brick. Yes, I like that. I like it so much the two of you can get down and give me thirty, right here and now."

Upon completion of the punishment, Sergeant Pennington faced his troops. "Big, and solid as a lead brick. Yes I really like that. You boys make me feel really proud.

"Right! Pay attention here! I'm not going to fall you out formally! Taking your kit bags with you, I want you sort yourselves out alphabetically and form up in a single file in the shade of these two buildings. Once that's done, I want you to take off your headdress and put it in one of your pants pockets! Then, take off your puttees and weights and loosen your bootlaces. Also, take off your shirts and place them on top of your duffel bags. Do not take your kit into the building. Just leave it outside and return to it when you're finished. As you enter, have your medical cards ready! Any questions?"

There were no questions, but an eager Moose's voice disturbed Sergeant Pennington's thoughts.

"Er, Sergeant Pennington ... er...?"

This time, the sergeant's attitude towards Danyluk was quite different – a little warmer. "Oh, it's you, you brilliant deep thinker. Solid as a brick! Yes, I like that, Danyluk! What's your problem, son?"

Holding the medical card in his teeth, and wringing his entwined hands, a grinning Danyluk replied, "Thank youse! I don't have any problems, Sergeant, but my friend doesn't seem to know if the same nursing sisters are here this year. Would youse happen know if last year's crew returned?"

"Get that card out of your mouth! Would I happen to know what?"

"Er, if the same broads, er, nursing sisters are here, Sergeant?"

Why, do you know them?"

Rubbing his crotch, Danyluk answered, "No, but I sure wish I did, Sergeant. Do youse knows if they're doin' the weighin' and the feelin'?"

Some Seaforth cadet said, "Christ, look Glen, it's him again. Six weeks with him last year was enough." Then he tapped another of his friends on the shoulder. "Hey Glasgow, that peculiar BCR bastard's back."

Glasgow pushed his glasses up his nose and stared at Danyluk. "Is he the one who farts in the showers?"

Moose heard the comments and gave both Seaforths the finger before continuing. "The sisters have got the touch of a delicate spring rain exploring a newly-sprouted tree, Sergeant!"

"Leaf." Bergie whispered. "You mean 'leaf' Moose."

Danyluk caught on fast. "Er, a newly-sprouted leaf, Sergeant!"

Another gas pain hit Pennington's face. "What are you ... some sort of a depraved sex fiend? How old are you?"

Moose winked. "Fifteen, goin' on thirty, Sergeant. If youse knows what I means?"

Pennington moved to the head of the line. "Yeah, I know what you mean! It means you'll have it worn out by the time you're sixteen!"

"They said when I tried on my first rubber at age two, but it ain't happened yet, Sergeant!"

As Sergeant Pennington stood by the door shaking his head, a wide smiling, eager-to-please Moose Danyluk couldn't get inside quick enough. Still wringing his hands, the *animal's* head and neck resembled a submarine's periscope searching for prey.

When Moose finally entered and progressed through the MIR (Medical Inspection Room), his card stayed with him. After a medical orderly checked his feet, another NCO inspected his scalp, eyes, ears, teeth and throat. When the corporal told him to remove his pants before entering the next room, an anxious and grinning Moose accommodated him quickly.

"I said, your pants ... not your pants and undershorts! Jesus, put that flimsy garment you call shorts, back on. Do you want the nursing sisters to have heart attacks? Christ, get your thing down man. This is a hospital, not a bordello!"

"I can't, Corporal ... it's trained," Moose replied.

Like the episode with the nursing sister in 1953, after a slight tap with a rubber mallet, followed by "Ow," Moose's *clam-digger* was back to normal, but only for a moment. When he entered the next room, six nursing sisters standing next to weighing-scales had to *bear* witness to a *healthy* giant-sized robust erection sticking up and out of the elastic of his miniature white-cloth *leaf*. The throbbing action resembled that of a divining rod searching for water in the middle of a lake.

The sight did seem to collect some snickering from five of the sisters, however the one to which Moose was assigned appeared quite serious when she asked him to step on the scales. After she noted his height and weight, she examined his back and chest with a stethoscope and told him to step down.

With their faces only inches apart and his eyes never leaving hers, Moose stayed where he was, smiled, puckered and gave her ten energetic kissing sounds.

"Have you got something wrong with your lips, young man?"

Cordell Cross

The sister's voice sounded angelic and Moose was now in love with blue eyes that could match the glittering water in a calm deep wishing well. Her skin appeared smooth and he thought the Okanagan sun at Kalamalka Beach must have nurtured its olive colour. He could also smell her perfume and it took him one-step closer to Heaven.

"Nothing that you can't cure, Sister. Can I make an appointment for later?"

The officer took out her pen. "You certainly can. What's your name?"

"Danyluk, but youse can call me, Moose."

The sister wrote down his name. "I'd like you here at six o'clock. How does that sound, *Moose?*"

Totally in *lust,* Moose hopped off the scales and put on his best Adonis pose.

"Great! Youse will notice I'm lean, mean and all protein," he said, heading for the medical officer's office. "Finally, my prayers have been answered. Would youse like me to wear these here shorts, or are they necessary?"

With a beautiful smile, the sister replied, "You just dress appropriately, *Moose.*"

Completely lovesick and in a daze, Danyluk was lost in a world of enchantment as he faced the medical officer who twice asked him to "lower his undershorts."

"Did you hear me, young man? Please take down your shorts!"

A glazed-eyed Moose still didn't pay any attention before his briefs were ripped down and he was asked to cough. Afterwards, he picked up his battledress pants and straddled to the door leading to the road.

The doctor yelled, "Where the hell are you going? Your shorts are around your ankles."

Danyluk slowly turned around and remained otherworldly as he answered, "Out in the beautiful Okanagan sun, sir. Ain't life wonderful?"

"It isn't sunny in the guardroom, mister! Pull up your shorts and put your pants back on!"

The word *guardroom* straightened Danyluk out quickly, but outside when the blinding sun hit his face he remained in his dream world.

After mumbling, "Bloody hell, that last cadet should be at Sunny Farms," the frustrated doctor shouted, "Next!"

Kipper-breath was next because he'd been rushed through the MIR at great speed. When he breathed on the captain after being asked to cough, the medical officer with his arm fully extended had to turn his head away.

Trying to hold his breath, the doctor asked, "What regiment are *you* with?"

East pulled up his shorts. "Er, I'm in the Irish Fusiliers like that buddy of mine who just went out."

"Oh yes, him! Is your breath always this bad?"

"No, sir - I had kippers for breakfast."

The doctor opened the window. "How many, fifty?"

East laughed, so the window was opened wider. "No, sir; four, and they were really good. You like 'em too, eh?"

The Medical Officer couldn't get rid of this cadet fast enough. "Yes, yes, fine! Quickly now, put your pants on. That's good now out you go! Sister, hold the next patient for a few moments, please!"

Cordell Cross

41 – NEXT STOP, VERNON!

When East walked down the stairs, he actually passed under the doctor's head sticking out the open window as the doctor attempted to get some fresh air.

"And I eat the skin too, Doc. My mom says it's the best part of the fish, and..."

Talking to himself, the doctor slammed the window shut.

"Irish Fusiliers? What the hell's happening to that once fine regiment?"

Sergeant Pennington allowed cadets who had already gone through the MIR to sit against the outside hospital wall and the wall of the H-hut across the road. As if by magic, when the last sigs cadet came out, trucks appeared carrying the Driver Mechanics Company. The D&M cadets had already been through the camp clothing stores; they were wearing blue PT shorts, white T-shirts, heavy socks and running shoes.

"Keep your hands and eyes off my nursing sister," Danyluk yelled.

Immediately after signals formed up and boarded the three-tons, the dusty ride to the upper camp only took two minutes.

Bergie jumped on Moose instantly. "Moose, I'll get you for that big red prick *sting*. Jesus, why is it always me?"

Danyluk put his arm around his friend's shoulders. "You would have done the same thing. I'm just keepin' youse on your toes, that's all. We are now Pennington's number-one chums."

"On my toes? I was nearly on my ass. Shit, if that's what he's like with his friends, I'd hate to be his enemy. I'll getcha for that one. Jeez will I ever. That son of a bitch had already told you he doesn't have any friends."

"When the hell are they going to pave this thing?" a brown-faced Cunningham said to Banks. "We slave and wash and shine only to have our efforts completely ruined by spending one second on this *road*."

"I think it's part of the training," Wane replied. "If we're always clean, we ain't been active enough."

The truck the BCR cadets rode in didn't have a tarpaulin, but it wouldn't have mattered anyway; dust, swirled upwards by the tires of leading trucks found every part of their exposed skin inviting. By the time the vehicles came to a halt in front of a large hanger, all occupants appeared like French Foreign Legionnaires who had taken on the Sahara and lost.

Sergeant Pennington and the driver unfastened the tailgates.

"Leave your bags on the vehicle and jump down quickly! Make sure you remember your truck! Form up in three ranks! Quickly now, quickly! You, yes you! Quit scratching your balls. Get your hands out of the front of your pants and fall in!"

No one had his hands in his pants, but those cadets close to the sergeant scrutinized each other with contempt. While falling in, Danyluk, who was used to this *treatment* thought he'd have some fun.

"How come youse Westie pansies always have your hands in your pants?" he said to a group of Westminster Regiment cadets. (Now, the Royal Westminster Regiment.)

The reply was quick. "Jesus, it's you again. I never thought you'd survive the winter. It's better than having them stuck up our asses like you guys in the BCRs."

Cordell Cross

"Or someone else's ass." another said.

"Picky, picky," replied Moose. "Jealousy won't get you anywhere."

"How many dames have ya raped over the winter?" a *Westie* asked.

Obviously two of the Westies had bunked in hut B-21 the year before. They recognized Danyluk immediately and one commented, "Hey guys, this sex maniac would violate a hibernating female bear if he thought he could get away with it."

"Who says it has to be female?" added his friend.

Another said, "I saw that pongo reaching for a cigarette once and someone stepped on his hand."

Danyluk hadn't counted on such a response but he couldn't back-down now.

"Hey, ain't youse the two Westie homos who used to wash each other's hair in the showers at five o'clock every morning? You know, before anyone else got up? Hey fellas, look who's with us again. It's the Palmolive duo that stunk out the hut with their perfume."

"Do you pongoes still paint your toenails?" East asked, adding, "Gordie, take a good look at those two and don't forget their faces. Not that it would be difficult because you'd notice their lipstick. When ya can't see 'em, they're walkin' behind ya, and they even whistle."

"I never let them walk behind me," said Wane. "Those two should be in a circus. Ten shows a day wouldn't even slow 'em down."

Two red-faced Westies tried hard to make a comeback with the help of some Provost cadets, but when the CScotRs joined in with the BCRs it wasn't a contest. For some untold reason, Canadian Scottish cadets always teamed up with the BCRs. That is until kilt jokes started and Scottish pride was on the line. When the 'Canned Scots' united with the Seaforths, Calgary Highlanders and other Scottish regiment cadets, frays were never extended because the highlanders always won.

Chapter 3

It took an hour for summer clothing to be issued. Cadets followed their clothing and bedding cards down counters where civilian storesmen *threw* individual items of clothing at them. Past experience had made the storesmen very proficient because after one glance at the person on the other side of the counter, the clothing they tossed usually fit.

Before emerging into the open inferno again, each cadet signed his clothing and bedding card and was informed lost items would have to be paid for at the end of camp.

Moose checked his khaki shorts. "Hey, I think these will actually fit. Last year they thought I was a midget."

Rothstein laughed. "No, you'll just have to remember that there are only two sizes - too large, and too small. Last year they never took into account that your nuts are like soccer balls."

With the trucks loaded and running, clouds of dust rolled across the field to the lower camp. The vehicles stopped at the south side of B-25 the first cadet hut facing Highway 97, a two-lane highway running through Camp Vernon. Only two cadet H-huts face the highway and an H-hut kitchen sitting further back separates them.

After forming Signals Company up in three ranks, Sergeant Pennington bellowed out further instructions. "This is going to be your home for the next six weeks! Did you hear me? I said it's going to be your home! As such, it will be kept spotless at all times!"

The sergeant glanced at his watch. "Now pay attention here; there are four platoons in this company and they are numbered from 21 to 24. Twenty-One Platoon is in the south end and Twenty Two Platoon is in the north end of the west wing. Twenty-Three Platoon is in the south end and Twenty Four Platoon is in the north end of the east wing! When you enter the hut, go to the respective bulletin boards in both wings, and find your platoon! Then go to your specific platoon area and find a bunk! When you've chosen your bunks, your platoon corporal will mark your name on the end of them!"

The Sergeant glimpsed at his watch again. "Right, lads ... pay attention here! The Prairie cadets will arrive tomorrow and make up the balance of our company! Right now, you have an hour before lunch! Hang up your battledress and unpack your clothing! Grab a shower and get dressed in your PT shorts, T-shirts running shoes, and heavy socks! I want you formed up in three ranks on this road (the south road running east/west by both wings) at 1200 hours! You will not wear your headdress! Is that clear?"

The noisy reply of "Yes, Sergeant!" bounds off the huts.

"Right! Signals Company ... atten ... tion! Fall ... out!"

The rush was on. In seconds, approximately seventy cadets hurried into both wings and headed straight for the bulletin boards. Those who couldn't find their name in one wing, quickly headed through the sink area to the other wing.

The Musketeers were already organized. They knew they would all be together because the joining instructions had asked them which friends they wanted to be

Cordell Cross

near in the hut. As such, seven waited on the road while Jackson checked out the east side and Rothstein checked out the west side.

Harvey Rothstein appeared first. "Hey, guys, we're in Twenty One Platoon! I'll get Earl!"

Although some bunk exchanges had to be made, in the next five minutes nine 'old soldiers' of the Vernon Army Cadet Camp claimed four sets of bunks in the extreme south-west corner of B-25, right next to the wing's southern door. This way the corporal whose cubicle was located at the northeast end of the wing wouldn't bother them. Lyons, being the *autonomous-intellectual* he was, decided to bunk with a Seaforth cadet across the aisle. The lad introduced himself as McLeod. His thick coke-bottle eyeglasses matched Lyons', and within minutes the *brainy* duo were playing chess.

Danyluk and Bergie took the first bunks, with Moose up top. East and Jackson took the next set, with Jackson in the upper bunk. Wane insisted on *his* usual top bunk above Douglas in the third set, and Cunningham and Rothstein shared the last set of bunks, with 'Rothie' in the *loft*. Actually, Harvey wanted the lower bunk but bowed to Gordie's *pressure* that it was hard to play cards when "a person's feet ain't touchin' the floor."

"OK, you can have it Rothie, but my suckers ... er, my playing partners will always be sitting on your bunk."

"Oh, er, that's all right then, Gord. I'll, er, take the upper bunk."

The position of the *gambler's* bunk allowed for undetected card or dice games. Far enough from the end doors and the centre area, *games* in progress could be stopped instantly when officers or non-coms entered.

Upon opening the window next to his bunk, Moose said, "This is gonna be neat. I can lean out the window and invite in all the dames drivin' by. Bergie my boy, we're going to have the summer of a lifetime. With my brawn and your brains, we'll meet the best dames in the whole Okanagan. Not today though, 'cause I've got that nursing sister at 1800 hours." Wringing his hands, he added, "She actually invited me back, can youse believes it?"

Bergie did believe it, but had reservations. "Moose, she's got to be twenty five or twenty six. She's too old for you. Besides that, she's an officer. Ya can't go around dating the officers."

"Hey, who says I can't? Bergie, you're always the one that says many a new tune can be played on an old fiddle. Well, I got some new tunes. You're just jealous because I've finally found someone with ... er, er, sleuth and sculpture."

Bergie stopped making his bed. "What?"

Rothstein interjected. "He means couth and culture."

Moose went over and jumped up on Rothstein's bunk and placed an arm around Harvey's shoulders.

"Right, Rothie! Couth and culture is what she's got. Rothie, youse spotted it too, right? Who knows, this could lead to sumpin' big. She could be the first dame to ride in my hearse when it's completely finished. A flashy broad like this appreciates the importance of a limousine and its owner."

Cordell Cross

45 – NEXT STOP, VERNON!

Bergie hadn't heard of the *vehicle* Moose had been working on for two months. Cringing, he asked, "Jeez, you bought a hearse? Next you'll be telling us you also bought a coffin."

Danyluk appeared insulted. "Hey, the word's *casket*. Yeah, the casket came with it. I bought a 1936 Packard with a straight eight, and two spare tires in continental kits. It cost me two-hundred bucks and youse should see how the casket rolls in and out. It's even got pins to lock it to the floor."

Bergie laughed. "Classy broads wouldn't ride around in a 1936 Packard hearse with a coffin in the back."

Moose jumped down, strolled over and sat on his own bunk. "Youse talks about me bein' ignorant. Get your facts straight, Bergie. It's not called *the back*; it's called the *trailing pagoda*. Well, my trailing pagoda's got padded red plush velvet and I've had the casket cleaned. I paid East to clean it. Ain't that right, Jack?"

East quickly finished off his banana. "I cleaned it, but I couldn't get rid of the smell. How man dames have you had in that coffin, Moose?"

Banks got his two-cents worth in. "None, because they've probably all seen those vampire movies. One look at the size of Moose's *lower tooth* and they faint."

Danyluk briskly stood up and stuck out his chest. "That's bull! Every dame in town wants to get into my casket! The feature lights make the mahogany shine like my body! Also, the organ music makes the broads feel like they're lookin' up at the face of God!" A Charles Atlas pose followed. "Which of course, they are!"

Jackson couldn't take it. "If that's the face of God, I'm becoming an atheist."

"Up yours, Earl! Even I know a jewel ain't like God!"

"I said atheist, not amethyst, you pongo!"

"Oh! Well, youse guys are just envious. When I turn on the organ music, the low lights automatically come on and the casket locks in place. Even my pagoda door locks itself. I just pull the tassels and the curtains close leavin me with the dame, the casket, the music, and the beer cooler."

"Didn't some dame once get stuck in that coffin?" Douglas asked.

"Casket! Er, yeah ... Hilda did, but nobody could hear her screamin' because my hearse's soundproof. I got her out when I found the secret latch."

Wincing, Douglas asked, "How long did that take?"

Moose lowered his voice to a whisper. "Only an hour. Jeez she was pissed off. She hadn't yet recovered from the Spanish Fly *incident*. Anyway, it's runnin' now. Might be a bit slow on the pickup because it weighs about six thousand pounds, but I can go anywhere because I've installed a long distance tank. My baby cruises at seventy with no trouble at all."

Cunningham appeared with ten one-dollar bills in his hands. He'd been gambling in the other side of the hut. "The shower room's clear. Let's get in there."

Quizzed looks appeared on their faces. The seven had been so busy talking, they'd forgotten about getting the hot water first. The excitement of arriving in Vernon had slowed down their organization.

Banks glanced at his watch. "Hey, we've got to fall in for lunch parade in twenty minutes; let's get our brains in gear."

Cordell Cross

In no time, clothes were unpacked and locked away in single barrack boxes that had to be shared by both bunk occupants. Later, each pair would obtain a piece of cardboard to place in the middle of their box, thus creating two compartments.

In a few moments, the nine had the shower room to themselves. For some reason, probably the fact that the Prairie cadets hadn't yet arrived, there was still plenty of hot water.

Danyluk entered last. "All right, Bergie, where is it?"

"Where's what?" Bergie asked.

"My soap, you creep. I can't find my soap."

"Don't look at me, Moose. I wouldn't touch your soap. I don't think anyone in his right mind would."

A frustrated Danyluk believed him. "Son of a bitch," he yelled, grabbing a large bar of brownish-grey sergeants' soap out of a bucket. "I swore after last year I'd never use this stuff again. It rips the skin of one's nuts."

East put half of his apple on the window ledge. "So that's what the two-inches of crud was covering the floor ... the skin off your balls. I always thought it was soap flakes.

"Stick it in your ear, East! Oh, well, sorry fellas!"

"You don't have to apologize to us," Rothstein said, closing the window.

A serious Moose grimaced as he glanced downward. "I ain't apologizin' to youse; I'm apologizin' to *them*. The jewels o' my life."

Signals cadets relaxed the rest of the day. Only Sergeant Pennington and four regular force corporals walked the aisles of B-25. Officers weren't seen, nor for that matter other sergeants or the balance of the hut's corporals.

Each cadet received a 'responsibilities' envelope' containing a timetable and schedule of events. These instructions informed them of the usual routine as well as what was expected of them. They were to prepare their kit and their bed spaces in accordance with the example and explanation on the bulletin boards, and they were to familiarize themselves with the lower and upper camp. Although they were confined to camp that day, the commanding officer had allowed them Sunday off, and they could visit downtown Vernon. If they decided to go into town, their dress had to be approved by the Provost (Military Police) at the Provost shack. In B-3, Saturday night's movie was *Wolf Pack,* and on Sunday night *All Quiet on the Western Front* would be shown. A brunch would be served from 0700 until 1300 on Sunday and there wouldn't be a church parade. Also on Sunday, the cadets from the Prairies would arrive by 0900 hours and if cadets went downtown, they were expected to be back in camp by 1630 hours.

After lunch, quietness filled B-25 as the nine lay on their bunks just shooting the breeze. It was great to be back. They had tried to call the girls they had met the year before, but the mile-long line-up at the lone phone in the cadet canteen made it difficult. Some cadets were homesick already and needed to hear the sounds of loving voices from home. Not Jack East, though. Just his noise from chomping on an apple drowned out sounds of loneliness.

Cordell Cross

"Ya know, I really love the grub they serve here. I don't know what it is, but if I could, I'd live in this camp year 'round. Today's three choices were out of this world. Did you guys taste the...?"

Wane interrupted the *beast*. "Did you actually go back and get the three selections?"

"You bet! I even made friends with the serving ladies. One of 'em said she has a son who eats like me. She says she only sees him when the circus comes to town."

"What does he do in the circus?" Banks asked.

"She said he's the star ... *The Fatman*. I think she said he weighs 780 pounds."

Jackson put down his comic and leaned over, saying, "That's what you're gonna look like if you don't slow down."

East gave Jackson's springs a *kick*. "It wouldn't bother me. Just think of the scoff the guy must get. His mother said her son doesn't even have to stand up to get his food; they just shovel it to him in his bed. He ain't been up in six years, and he makes a thousand a month."

Putting his dice and cards away for a few minutes, the *gambler* asked, "How does he take a piss or a dump?"

"How the hell do I know? Do you think I'd ask her that? Jeez, Cunningham, you come up with the weirdest questions. I wouldn't ask her that, would I Moose?"

Moose stopped reading a love-letter handed to him before he got on the train. He'd forgotten about it. "Would youse what?"

"Would I ask the mother of *The Fatman* how he takes a dump or takes a leak?"

Danyluk really wasn't paying attention. "Why not? Sure youse would."

Jack threw his pillow at Moose. "Bull shit I would! The guy probably gets his bed emptied out by the elephant cleaner, and I'm gonna ask her that?"

Moose threw back the pillow. "Elephants? What are youse talkin' about, East? Are youse makin' wisecracks and speakin' about my Doreen again?"

"No, I was taking about..."

Danyluk didn't let Jack finish. "Hey, guys, listen to this: My *Darling Moose: I can't forget the night you sneaked me into your garage and let me lie in your limousine's bed. It was so dark I couldn't see a thing. The feel of the satin sheet beneath me was just wonderful, but what I can't understand, my darling, is why you didn't make the bed wider. It was so cramped I could hardly breathe, and when I did breathe there was such a pungent odour. When you got up to get a beer from the cooler, I tried to cover myself with the upper sheet but there wasn't one and your upper bed door slammed shut on me. Moose, my baby, when you get home I want to share your bed in the daylight and I'll buy you an upper sheet. Also, darling, you need a new mattress. I'll miss you, you great big hunk. Always ... Claire with the hair you love.'"*

Rothstein howled laughing. "You got some dame in your coffin and she didn't know it...?"

Now eight gathered around Moose's bunk as Rothstein asked, "You told her it was a bed, not a coffin?"

Danyluk's eyes lit up and a sneaky-grin came over his face.

"Hey, what would youse do? This dame's afraid of her own shadow. What she don't know, don't hurt her."

"What about the feature lights and the organ music?" asked Bergie.

Cordell Cross

"I didn't have 'em fixed yet," replied Moose. "It was just as well. I gotta get rid of that smell though. Jack, you owe me another cleaning."

"Bull shit I do! I wouldn't have taken the job in the first place if you hadda told me it was a coffin!"

"Casket, *please*."

"Casket, gasket, whatever! Go screw yourself, Moose!"

"If ya give it a second cleaning, I'll let youse and your dames use the casket."

"Take a hike, Moose!"

"Hey, where are you two going?" Cunningham asked Douglas and Wane. Both cadets' arms were loaded down with the clothing they had just been issued.

Brice turned his head, "Have you guys taken the time to smell these things. They reek of mothballs."

It didn't take long for three other barrack boxes to be opened. Douglas was right because their area of the hut instantly took on the smell of the little white round chemical spheres. Now six other cadets headed to the sinks in the middle portion of the building. For the two hours, the boys used scrub-brushes and sergeants' soap to get the garments clean smelling and spotless. Brice and Banks volunteered to take ten minutes watching the clothing while it dried spread out on the centre stairs facing the highway. After drying, the garments were ironed and put away.

With their clothing prepared and their belts, pith helmets and boots cleaned, the nine cadets separated in groups to rediscover the camp they had known so well one year earlier. Douglas and Wane headed for their favourite place, the ground overlooking Vernon's golf course. A hole in the fence allowed them to head down fifteen feet to a flat spot where they could sit and take off their berets and not be noticed by officers, NCOs or the ever-prowling military police.

The breathtaking serenity of the countryside allowed them to relax even on the hill's furnace. In the valley below, the beautiful green golf course resembled the image of an oasis in the middle of a rugged desert that time had forgotten. Two giant fluffy clouds peered down on the distant hills, their shadows casting welcome relief from the sun for the few head of cattle searching for grass.

Shading his eyes, Douglas counted the small number trees on the far-side hill. He thought their roots must have fought for every drop of water that had gushed over the aeons and formed long-downward depressions in the hills.

"Remember the time we walked over that hill?" Wane asked.

Douglas nodded. "I sure do. We thought it would only take us an hour or so, but we didn't account for the 'dead' ground. It was worth it though; the view of Kalamalka Lake from up top was something else. Should we do it again?"

Wane chuckled. "Are you out of your mind? We had emptied our water bottles and our lips were swollen by the time we got back. Doug, that took us all day. What I'd really like to do is climb up Silver Star Mountain and take in that view. At least we'd be climbing in shade."

Turning his head to his left, Brice glanced at the green Silver Star to the north. "Silver Star? Just look at it; it's ten times the height of these hills. It would take us a weekend to climb that baby."

49 – NEXT STOP, VERNON!

Small talk ensued for the next hour. Both boys thought it was great to be back. While the camp and the countryside hadn't changed over the year, they were a little intimidated by the strange course they were about to take. They had seen and heard the hustle and bustle taking place in the instructors' basic training huts, but signals seemed more relaxed. Sergeants and corporals weren't appearing out of the woodwork. Their welcome had been very reserved and no one was bothering them. They enjoyed this, but in their minds wondered if this was the lull before the storm.

Finally, Wane broke the silence. "Ever heard of SOD - Signal Office Duties before?"

Douglas took out the timetable stuck in the elastic waistband of his shorts. "Nope. I've also never heard of the UCL Ten-line switchboard, Tele-L sets, line laying, ground returns or the like. We've heard of Nineteen sets and Thirty-eight sets 'cause we saw them in Glenemma last summer. I also think Morse code is gonna be a blast."

Wane took hold of the paper for a moment, then handed it back. "Yeah, I spoke to Foster about that, but I forgot what he said about how many words per minute we're supposed to transmit. It ain't easy. Did you know that last year Foster and a group spliced up a line to the RSM's phone? They knew his every move."

Both boys laughed when Banks added, "And they heard him call the MIR about some Danyluk *character*."

Douglas stood up and put on his beret. "You've gotta be joking? Our Moose?"

Walking back up the hill and through the hole in the fence, Wane said, "Yeah, Foster told me on the train and he was talking about our *one-and-only*. Apparently, the RSM asked the medical officer if he would review Danyluk's file. When the MO said there wasn't any file, the RSM said, 'But there's gotta be one. We have a walking-talking sex-machine on our hands. This kid's almost a hazard'"

Douglas shook his head, asking, "What happened then?"

"The MO told him to calm down - that boys will be boys and Danyluk's just going through his growing-up stage. Haaa, little did he know Moose went through that level at the age of six months."

Their laughter caught them off guard for a moment because the *man* himself, RSM Gardiner, appeared out of nowhere. "You two! Yes, you two! Get in step and get your arms up! Where the hell do you think you are, in cub camp?"

Both cadets halted with their arms stiffly by their sides, head and eyes to their front.

"No, sir!" they said in unison.

"Right! Carry on! I'll be watching for you two!"

In perfect step with their arms up, Wane whispered out the corner of his mouth. "Jeez, RSM Gardiner's back."

A grin appeared on Brice's face. "Yeah, I can't wait to tell Moose."

Douglas didn't have to wait long because the supposed 'living-walking-talking' human *abnormality* stood waiting with the others when the duo walked into the barracks.

"Hey, youse two, we've been waitin' for ya! Jack East's over at the mess hall savin' our seats. Where the hell have youse been?"

After a quick explanation that included laughs and a wash, eight of the nine headed over to eat where Moose fumed tearing into his steak. "A walkin'-talkin' sex machine? A hazard? I'm really ticked off. This guy is gonna ruin my reputation. I ain't that bad."

Not receiving any attention, Danyluk followed through. "Hey, I said, I ain't that bad ... am I Bergie?"

"Well, er, Moose. You, uh, do admit to the fact that you're a living legend, don't you?"

Danyluk stopped eating. "Yeah, er, well I guess I am, Bergie. The ladies tell me I am."

"I'll bet they do. And with such great status you do admit that living the life of a man of such admirable exploits must subject you to scandal, chatter, gossip, lies, innuendoes, insinuations, sly put-downs, and the like?"

Moose's serious expression nearly had those at the table howling.

"Yeah, well, er, if youse sez so, Bergie."

"Then my answer to you is ... undoubtedly; you are that bad. Good for you, Moose."

Deep in thought, Moose sat back scratching his head. "Hey, youse is right! An idol is cherished, and respected! Admiration comes in strange ways don't it, Bergie?"

Danyluk went back eating not noticing Bergie's wink to the others when he said, "You're one of a kind, Moose, and as such you will always receive bizarre reverence. It doesn't matter how it arrives, the fact that it's offered, you have to accept it with grace!"

Nodding his approval, Moose picked up his glass of milk. "Youse is right! The RSM really respects and appreciates me! He just has difficulty expressing himself! Right?"

"You've figured it out, Moose."

"The more shit he heaps, the more he likes me! Right, Bergie?"

"Exactly, Moose."

"Deep down inside, he thinks of me as the son he never had! Ain't that right Bergie?"

"Er, don't push it, Moose. Now you've got it."

Danyluk slid back his chair and stood up with his glass of milk. "Rise with me in a toast to a man that admires me more than life itself! To RSM Gardiner!"

The rest stood up. "To RSM Gardiner!"

"And God bless him," Said moose.

"And God bless him!"

Two tables away, a Seaforth cadet said, "Did you guys hear that? Next, he'll be saying the commanding officer wants to be his mother."

Three other Seaforths turned around, and one mouthed, "Jeez, it's that weird BCR again. The guy with the body attached to his prick. Avoid him at all costs. I think his name is Hippo or somethin' like that. He's the only one that can stay in the shower room when that abhorred Canadian Scottish pongo, East, starts farting."

Moose stood up with his plate. "Fellas, the next time I see RSM Gardiner, I'm gonna make it easier for him to respect me! Right, Bergie?"

Cordell Cross

"I would Moose. Where are ya going now?"

Danyluk stuck out his chest. "I'm off to see my Nursing Sister friend. Eat your hearts out, you jealous pongoes."

As he passed the *Seaforth* table, a Scottish *spokesman* by the name of MacKay said, "Hey ain't you the cadet the RSM admires?"

Always leery of Scots who speak without being spoken to, Moose stopped for a moment – his face suspicious. "News travels fast, eh? Yeah, I'm the one he respects. What's it to youse haggis stuffers?"

The serious Scot asked, "We've heard the RSM likes workin' on Austin cars. Is that right? Is he really a British car enthusiast?"

Another said, "Yeah, and does he eat prunes by the truckload after his sister joined the American Navy."

The first one added, "Also, does he really hate playing bridge?"

Danyluk was lost for words as he thought to himself, *God, I'm the man's idol and these sheep shit and heather types know more than I do.*

"D'ya think I'd tell youse creeps what the RSM likes and what he don't like? Cold asses askin' me? Find out on your own. What the hell does youse thinks I am, a walkin' er, enclopedia?"

"Don't you mean encyclopaedia?"

"Yeah, whatever. Go earn yourselves the status I've got."

Cocking his head and strolling away, Moose mumbled to himself, "Jeez, I'd better start findin' out what the RSM likes and don't like. I should know these things."

After the *animal* was out of sight, six Seaforth heads met at the centre of their table. One asked. "I didn't know the RSM likes workin' on Austin cars and his sister joined the American Navy?"

"Or that he hates bridge and eats prunes," said another.

One of the *highlanders* grinned. "My old man knows Gardiner. He says there are two things the man hates - Austins and prunes. He never had a sister and his favourite card game is bridge."

Laughter erupted as a Seaforth by the name of Neish said, "Glen MacKay you're a genius. Knowledge like that can be dangerous in the wrong hands."

MacKay slapped Neish's back. "You're right, Andy. And now it really is in the wrong hands."

Seaforth grins disappeared as the boys passed the musketeers table on their way out. After the screen door slammed shut, the grins turned into bursts of laughter.

In deep conversation with the other musketeers, Bergie casually watched the Seaforths leave. One of his *tasks* was to check what was going on around the *protective-group.*

"That particular group of Seaforths are a snobbish bunch. I don't want to sound paranoid, but they were laughin' until they passed our table. We'll have to keep our eyes on them. Something's up."

Earl asked, "Is your sixth sense acting up again?"

"Seventh and eighth senses as well," Bergie said, standing up and grabbing his plate, cup and utensils.

Cunningham felt for his small money-belt pouch he wore with his PT shorts. "The movie starts in one hour. Who wants a pop in the canteen? I never thought I'd say this, but since this is our first day, I'll buy."

The *gambler* didn't have to ask a second time. In a fraction of a second, Bergie, East, Rothstein, Jackson, Banks, and Brice trampled him. East led the parade. "And potato chips, eh, Gordie?"

"Screw you, Jack. Don't forget you still owe me a buck-ninety-eight. Lyons, are you coming?"

Too busy playing chess with his new bunkmate, Lyons simply waved the 'gambler' away.

As the eight headed to the cadet canteen, Jack East's voice echoed between the huts - the same normal voice that always reverberated between the Drill Hall and the bus depot in Vancouver. East had nearly choked on his apple after Cunningham asked him for money. "Bull shit I owe you one-ninety-eight. I sold ya my good weights for that one-ninety-eight! Wane, you saw me sell them to him, didn'tcha?"

"Yeah, I saw it."

"Bloody true ya did! So up your nose, Lingus!"

"I'll remember that, Jack. Better take it back."

"So what if you remember? I ain't borrowing or gambling with you in Vernon."

"Yeah, but what about when we get back home?"

"Er, okay, I'll take it back. On second thought, stick it in your ear, Cunningham."

The night air boiled as the main doors of B-3 opened and its occupants emerged through clouds of cigarette smoke. Although the projector had broken down three times, the musketeers indicated they had enjoyed the movie and it became the main point of discussion as they marched back to their barracks.

"You wouldn't get me in one of those U boats," East said, reaching into the front of his PT shorts.

Earl nudged him. "Jesus, will you quit playin' with yourself. You've done nothing but fidget throughout the whole movie."

"I ain't playin' with myself; I'm trying to find the chocolate bar I hid in my gaunch."

"You ate that fifteen minutes ago when the last freighter got sunk. Remember, the chocolate was so soft it was all over your hands? By the way, I saw you lean forward and wipe 'em on that big guy's shirt when you asked him if he was the parade commander last year?"

A smile came to East's lips. "Yeah, good thinkin' eh?"

"Good thinking? You're lucky it was dark in there. That poor bastard would be up all night trying to find you if he knew what you looked like. Someone's gonna tell him he's got shit all over his shirt. Why'd you pick him?"

East chuckled to himself. "He's in the Irish."

Rothstein's thoughts were still on the movie. "I like the way that destroyer cut the U boat in half. Then it rescued the bastards. Why'd they do that? Those Nazi bastards never saved anyone."

Cordell Cross

Bergie entered the conversation. "It was only a movie, Rothie. They gotta make it look like we're the good guys all the time. I don't think either side helped the enemy."

East was going to put his hand on Bergie's shoulder but thought better of it. "Oh, yeah! What about the Genova Convention? There are rules ya know."

Bergie cringed. "It's the Geneva Convention you ayrab! If it were the Genova Convention, all those Nazis would be gettin' rubdowns. Also, do you think Hitler and his creeps paid any attention to the Geneva Convention? If you do, you're nuts."

With a determined look on his face and his teeth gritted, Harvey slapped Bergie on the back. "Use the word filth for them. Okay, Bergie?"

Bergie's face turned sombre as he paused for a moment looking into Harvey's eyes. Then in a low voice, he said, "Yeah, you're right, Rothie, and even the word *filth* is too good for the bastards."

Moments later they were back in B-25 and although the Prairie cadets hadn't arrived, the place had already taken on the look of B-21 a year before. Inhabitants in their undershorts leg-wrestled, arm-wrestled, ran up and down the aisles sloping arms with broom sticks, squirting the fire extinguishers, picking their mattresses and bedding off the floor, re-making their beds and hopping from one upper bunk to the next. In addition, some were ironing, shining, writing letters, gambling, trying to get into their barrack boxes because the combination was inside, and nearly everything else cadets do when they're left on their own. In addition, it didn't matter if the hut faced the highway, all windows remained open.

One event stood out amongst the others. Moose Danyluk was already in bed, reading a comic. His combed hair and spotless face indicated he'd had a shower. With a smirk, he said, "Don't ask."

Bergie wasn't listening. "Moose, my boy! Was she so good she wore you out?"

Danyluk threw his comic aside and sat up displaying the blisters on his hands.

"She wore me out all right! From the minute I entered the hospital until thirty minutes ago, I've been on my hands and knees scrubbin' the floor. She wasn't even there. Some orderly read the note she'd left! Jeez, I'm sure all over!"

Now the eight howled with laughter as they gathered around Moose. Both his hands *were* full of blisters.

After a corporal turned out the lights and told everyone to hit the sack, Bergie nearly had the last word. "I've seen ya leave the jon with more blisters than those, Moose!"

It had been a long day. Moose didn't verbally retaliate. Instead, he made a cardboard cup appear out of nowhere. A moment later, its contents of cold water found its mark.

Bergie couldn't move out of the way fast enough. "Bloody hell, my crotch is soaked!"

Moose had the last word. "And I've seen youse leavin' the jon with your crotch lookin' like that, Bergie!"

Wane leaned over. "It's like we haven't been away. Good night, Doug."

Cordell Cross

Douglas' springs squeaked as he rolled on his side. "I actually thought I missed this place, but now I'm not too sure. G'night buddy."

As B-25 cooled down, the only sounds splitting the silence were those of passing cars or trucks, some nearby crickets, flying bugs circling the outside lights, and bedsprings squeaking when cadets rolled on their sides. Above, a smiling wise old moon knew another summer had begun.

Chapter 4

Action took place all around Douglas Brice but he couldn't quite gather his senses together to figure out the noise. He'd had a fantastic sleep - a rest he didn't wish to wake from but had no other choice.

Pulling a blanket over his head, Brice's mind sorted out just one fact - Danyluk's radio was loud as the Moose changed radio stations.

"So, Elsie, we know you bake the best pies in Vernon ... just what is your secret? Is it because you use Vernon blueberries, or are you...?"

Douglas popped his head out of his blanket just in time to hear Danyluk's raving. "Oh my God, that's the same pie-baking dame that was on the air every Sunday morning last year. She probably slips the announcer a pie, before he slips her ... Ah, this is more like it. It's Bill Haley and the Comets."

"...kitchen, and rattle those pots and pans..."

"Hey youse guys," bellowed Danyluk, "It's Bill Haley and the Comets singin' *Shake Rattle and Roll!*"

Douglas sat up wiping his eyes and glancing around. His watch read 0930 and the hut hummed with activity. In the aisle, the lower part of a naked Moose gyrated to *Shake Rattle and Roll*, and the *animal's* dancing partner was a mop that didn't talk back.

"Youse may have grey hair, my love, but to me it shines golden blonde. Have we met before? Have I showed youse my limousine?"

It didn't take long for Douglas to figure out what was going on. Cadets from the Prairies had arrived, and were unpacking. Adding to the confusion, Rothstein ironed, Cunningham threw dice with new *suckers*, but with no cash in sight, Scottish types demonstrated how they wore their kilts, East sat eating an orange while shining his boots, a couple of Rocky Mountain Rangers squirted the fire extinguishers, cadets straightened out their barrack boxes, boys appeared from the showers flicking their towels, others made their beds, corporals walked the aisle checking names, Sergeant Pennington sat on a Prairie cadet's bunk and wrote on his clipboard, Lyons persisted at chess, and Jackson lay on his bed howling at a Bugs Bunny comic. Throughout, the sounds resembled those of a carnival on a busy day.

After throwing his bedclothes aside, Brice kicked the springs of the upper bunk. "You up, yet?"

Before he saw Wane's smiling face, a hand appeared holding a Captain Marvel comic. "Nope. I thought I'd wait until you got up. Wanna grab a shower before the hot water's gone?"

"When did *these* guys arrive?" Douglas asked, referring to the Prairie cadets.

"About eight-thirty. How you slept through an hour of this clatter I'll never know. Jeez, you must have been tired."

Danyluk waltzed over - his chin nestled into the *locks* of his 'blonde-haired sweetheart.'

"Nice, ain't she? A little thin but accommodating as hell. Take off, Bergie, she only dances with me!"

Cordell Cross

56 – NEXT STOP, VERNON!

Bergie didn't want to dance with the *wooden wench*; he was on his way to the showers when he tapped Moose's back.

"She's all yours, Moose! That was probably the mop we used to clean out the jon last year! Who's for a shower?"

Rushing to grab his towel, an embittered Danyluk threw his *sweetie* aside.

"You jezebel! Here you've been dancing with me, but all along youse has been used by others. I take it back … you'll never see my limousine."

Douglas laughed watching the *animal*. "I don't know why, Moose? That thing would probably want to get in your coffin."

"Casket, please."

"Er, sorry. Casket, of course."

Brice, Banks, Bergie, Rothstein, and Danyluk decided to have showers. East had showered before the mess hall opened for breakfast. Jackson was too immersed in Bugs Bunny, and Cunningham had *suckers* two-deep gathered around his dice area. Scrutinizing the chessboard, Lyons declined the offer of a shower as he cleaned his glasses on his upper sheet.

Danyluk covered the nozzle of the showerhead and released the water in spurts. "I had the weirdest dream last night. I was drivin' by the camp on Highway 97 here and my casket opened in the trailing pagoda. Some Goddamned skeleton got out and sat beside me in the front seat."

As usual, Banks covered his body with shampoo. "Was it that scarecrow Clara? You know! The broad you took to the last dance? The dame with the neck that looked like a carrot?"

Moose smeared his bar of sergeants' soap. "Nah … I know Clara's thin but this was an actual skeleton. The bones clanked as she climbed into the seat next to me. Jeez, I was scared. Then she rested her bony fingers on my right leg. When I threw her hand aside, it separated at the wrist and fell on the floor."

Rothstein asked, "How did you know it was a dame?" "Maybe it was a weird."

"Hey, we're talkin' about the Moose, here! Only dames get into my casket! Besides, this skeleton was wearin' a bra and panties."

Bergie belly laughed. "That's the first dream you've had where the dame wore clothes. Also, the fact that you took her hand off your crotch means you're startin' to get civilized."

"It was my leg. Bergie, even youse would throw off a hand like that," retorted a grinning Moose. "When she reattached the thing she put her arm around me and started nibbling on my ear. Jeez, I didn't know what to do. Her bones kept clinking."

Rothstein finished showering and started drying himself off. "Well in your case, your *bone* would be clinking. Why didn't you do your usual and slip her the tongue?"

Harvey's question had Wane in stitches. He had to open the window for air. The rest roared out laughing as well.

"Hey, I couldn't give this broad the tongue … she had no lips. Nothin' else either, for that matter. Anyway, when she took off her bra and threw it in my face, I nearly drove off the road."

"Why, what happened then?" Douglas asked.

Cordell Cross

Moose turned off his shower. "Nothin' happened. I remember I couldn't get the thing off my face, and it reeked of decayed flesh and mothballs. I woke up in a cold sweat and looked at my watch. It was 0300 hours. Jeez, that dream was real. I got out of bed and nearly drank the water-fountain dry. I think it was a warning dream. No more thin broads for me. From now on, it's dames with lotsa meat on 'em."

Bergie flicked his towel at Danyluk, making certain he missed. "Until a thin broad comes along, eh Moose?"

Moose pumped out his chest. "I don't know, Bergie. Oh, what the hell ... yeah, probably. If thin dames want the body-beautiful, I'll just have to give in."

After eating brunch, making their beds and mopping out their bunk spaces, nine 'old pros' passed the dress-inspection of the 'eagle-eyed' Provost Sergeant grunting his approval for them to leave camp. Although the temperature hovered in the middle 90s, marching down the hill was no problem. Their finely pressed khaki shorts and shirts kept the immense heat to a minimum. Over the next six weeks, however, their bodies would become *attuned* to these items of summer clothing. Even if the boys were nude, the sun's rays would become unbearable as the Musketeers and other cadets learned and practised their trades on the windless *fireball's anvil* - the military compound on top of 'the hill.'

"It looks like everyone in camp is visiting town today," said Cunningham, marching, but still managing to take a fifty-cent piece out of Jackson's ear.

Danyluk wrung his hands before placing them to his sides and giving the "Eyes, Left."

Instantly, without hesitation, eight others cut their arms to their sides and shot their heads and eyes in the direction of Hop Sing's Laundry on the other side of Highway 97.

Smiles remained steady after the "Eyes, Front!" Then nine pairs of eyes continued staring at the small run-down building with little or no activity taking place inside.

"I'll betcha all the *action* takes place in the back," Rothstein said, referring to the well-known scuttlebutt that the laundry was a front for a house of ill repute. "We should do a recce (reconnaissance) some night and watch the action. I'll betcha half the officers and NCOs are there. They've gotta be because they're always smilin' while they're givin' us hell."

Banks nodded. "Yeah, no wonder. When they take their shirts in, they probably give ol' Hoppy a wink and say, 'Er, Hoppy, old sod, these here shirts ain't that dirty, but er, well, er, you know?'"

Amidst chuckles, Wane continued his story. "'You come back rater, or you want tleatment now?' asks Hop Sing."

"'Er, well, I'll have the *treatment* now, er, if it's all right with you, Hoppy?'"

"'Here's your tickee; you go to back door. You knockee twice and say password.'"

"'Er, I've forgotten. What's that password again, Hoppy, old friend?'"

"'You say, 'Roretta my rovery, I not here for the raundry. I here for the rub.' She then ret you in.'"

Cordell Cross

Other cadets marching in front and behind the Musketeers couldn't understand what was so funny as Banks intimated what Hop Sing would say. They also failed to comprehend why Danyluk pumped his crotch in and out and lost his step from laughing so hard, mouthing the words, "Roretta my rovery. Haaa, that's mint."

Then a serious look came over Moose. "Hey, Banks, youse ain't talkin' about my lovely Loretta are ya?"

"No, Moose. *His* rovery Roretta. There's more than one Roretta, ya know."

Bergie checked his watch that read 1400 hours. "We're late. Earl, what time did you ask the girls to meet us at Polson Park?"

"Thirteen-thirty, but they'll understand."

Douglas took a deep breath. "It's great to be back, eh, guys? Nothing has changed. Jeez, I'd love to live here. Smell that air."

"You won't be saying smell the air when we have to hike up this monstrosity," East quipped, dying to take a chocolate bar out of his pocket, but knowing full well the military police would spot him if he didn't march with his arms waist high.

A concerned Danyluk moved next to Bergie. "Hey, Bergie, what's a neckrepile? East says it's like a crocodile ... is it?"

East didn't like being quoted. "I didn't say a neckrepile was like a crocodile; I said a necktareptile was a part of the alligator family. Get with it, Moose!"

"Whatever."

The others had heard Moose's *serious* question, but not one of them knew the answer except Bergie.

Giving Danyluk a weird look, Bergie asked, "You mean what's a necrophile? Is that what you mean? Jeez, Moose, don't tell me you're into *that* stuff now? Is that why you bought the hearse?"

"*What* stuff? Keep my hearse outa this, Bergie. Youse also knows there's nothin' wrong with my neck. I ain't got piles, especially on my neck. Sergeant Pennington called me a necro ... er ... somethin' when I was marchin' too close to some guy he called, an 'expired shower of shit.' He also said the guy was, 'dead from the ass up.'"

The rest of the group still didn't know the answer so they kept their mouths shut and watched an ear to ear grin hit Bergie's face.

"Well, I'm not too sure, Moose, but I think it means someone who likes screwin' dead bodies."

East yanked out his chocolate bar. "Bull shit, Bergie! Dead bodies don't screw! Did you guys hear that? Dead bodies gettin' it on? It ain't possible, and besides, it's Latin for alligator!"

Danyluk's face indicated his bewilderment as he stopped instantly, forcing others marching down the hill to go around the now newly formed circle of Musketeers.

"So that's what Pennington meant? Why that louse! I..."

East quickly pocketed his chocolate bar before a passing military police jeep *gently* moved them on. "You people! What do you think you're doing? Continue marching and get your arms up!"

Now back in pairs and marching, Danyluk was mad as hell.

"That son of a bitch! Just because he called the guy in front of me, 'a dead shower of shit,' doesn't make me a necro ... Er ... How do you pronounce it?"

Bergie assisted. "Necrophile."

"Yeah, necrophile! That's bloody disgusting! If it ain't live, I wouldn't touch it! And even if I did, it has got to be female! Annabelle is the closest thing to necrophile bait I've ever been out with. She's stiff as a board and don't even talk when we're doin' it!"

A still-upset East wouldn't let up. "How the hell could ya screw a dead body? What about the smell?"

Moose's expression changed from earnestness to amusement. Offering a camp cliché, he said, "Jack, once youse gets past the smell, youse has got it licked."

East feigned throwing up. "Danyluk, you are one sick necrophile!"

"Up yours, Jack. Everyone at the Drill Hall knows youse has a corpse in your basement. You've told everyone that."

The chocolate bar was now out again and although East's mouth was full, it opened wider than ever.

"Bull shit I did. Wane, Doug, did you hear that? The family that lives in our basement is named *Copps*. Their daughter's name is Clara and she's built like a brick shithouse, so there! It's Copps, not corpse you ayrab!"

Moose winked at Bergie. "Well, from what I've seen, she looks like a corpse. Ain't you the one that said you slipped her the tongue and injured yourself?"

East's face turned red as he mumbled something.

"We can't hear ya, Jack. What did you say?"

"I said yeah, but she kept her teeth shut and I cut it on her braces! Shut your face Moose, these things are personal!"

Two Irish cadets marching in front had heard Danyluk's *scuttlebutt*. The taller of the two said, "Don't look back, Paddy. It's that weird BCR cadet they call Bison or somethin' like that. Now he's into necrophilia."

"What's necrophilia?" his friend asked.

"He likes makin' love to the dead. We bunked close to him last year. If anything walked, he'd screw it. Now it appears it don't even have to walk or even move for that matter."

Paddy couldn't help glancing back and muttering out the corner of his mouth. "Jeez, he looks normal. How sick can a guy get?"

"What are youse lookin' at?" bellowed Moose.

Paddy quickly turned his head to his front. "I see what ya mean. Are all BCR cadets like him?"

"Near enough," replied his buddy. "They're almost as bad as Seaforths."

The Musketeers turned right at the bottom of the hill and entered Polson Park. The last time they were here was August 1953 and the lush-green oasis was still as beautiful as they each remembered it. The flowers, giant trees, and manicured lawns allowed relief to all cadets who entered. Instantly, weary *soldiers* forgot about the intense heat and dust of the camp above.

"Where are the girls?" Rothstein asked.

"They're gonna meet us in the bleachers," Earl said. No sooner had the words left his mouth, the girls walked out of the stands and shyly waved.

"Alma, my one and only," screamed Moose, rushing to pick up his long lost *sweetheart* and swirl her around.

Alma didn't reply. Like the others, her bashful expression said it all. She was in love and her knight in shining *skin*, er, armour had returned.

Beaming demure facial expressions replaced words of devotion as the teenagers paired off heading in different directions, holding hands and staring into each other's eyes. They had been away from each other for a long time, and all their intimate personal confessions spoken via the telephone or written on page-after-page of near-daily letters came to the forefront of their innermost thoughts.

Subliminally guided after they had delicately said, "Hi" to each other, Douglas and Diane found themselves in their usual spot under the weeping-willow tree by the babbling stream. As usual, he took off his beret before he lay on his stomach next to her with an arm around her waist.

With her eyes excited and starry, Diane softly asked, "Did you get my last letter?"

After their lips met, Douglas explored every inch of her face. Grinning impishly, he answered "Yes, and did you mean every word of it? Even the part about us...?"

Diane's cheeks turned rosy, and she turned her head away while placing a finger over his mouth.

"I, I think so. Well, I know that..."

She couldn't finish, and her eyes remained down until he lifted her chin, stretched out his left arm and nestled her next to him. Her head rested on his upper arm and their faces almost touched as he gently caressed her hair.

"I'm sorry, Di. I didn't mean to bug you. I've thought about you day and night for a year. My mom, Wane, teachers, RSM Laidlaw, Sergeant Major Battlefield, and my shack manager have given me blasts for not paying attention. How the hell can I pay attention when I'm always thinking of you?"

When their eyes met again, both teens chuckled before Diane said, "It's been the same here. The other day I bumped into a lamppost and I still have a swollen nose to prove it. Yesterday when my mom phoned from the hairdressers and asked me to put the pork chops on she'd left out for supper, I put 'em back in the ice-box and started boiling four eggs."

Douglas kissed the tip of her nose. "Does that make us a couple of gormphs?"

"Yes, but nice gormphs. I wouldn't want it any other way."

For the next hour, each couple remained lost in their own enchanted world and as usual, it was Jack East's yell that put their magic spells on hold.

"Hey everyone ... let's go grab some banana splits!"

Shortly, eight couples headed towards the Capitol Cafe. Lyons and his girl, Zelda, remained immersed in a game of chess, so they stayed behind.

Zelda's face remained down but her eyes had observed the others as they left.

"Don't those other cadets bore you, my dear? I mean, they're so terribly uninteresting."

"Check! Oh I put up with their little minds," Lyons replied. "What more can I do, my pet? Not everyone in this world is as bright and rational as you and I, you know. We just have to make do with those around us, don't we?"

Zelda nodded. "Yes, I guess you're right. Check! Do those boys drink alcoholic spirits?"

"Yes, my dear, they do. I keep trying to reach out to them with my wisdom on the advantages of abstaining and consistency in keeping the body pure, but I'm only one man. It would take thousands of people to elucidate to them why they should alter and improve their immoral ways. Checkmate! Another game, my little heartthrob?"

"Oh, Don. You're so wise and understanding."

"Yes, I know, my sweet. Sometimes it seems I'm fighting the world all alone. Uh, are your parents at home today?"

"No, they've gone to Penticton."

"Excellent! Er, I mean how unfortunate. Shall we go to your house for another game of chess?"

Zelda giggled. "Absolutely, my pumpkin. Are you certain that is all you wish to play?"

"Ha, ha, ha. What other enjoyment is there, my turtledove? I mean other than...?

"Oh Don, you're so romantic when your upper lip perspires and twitches."

"Yes, my little cupcake, I know. Say, er, does your father still have his favourite liquor cabinet? You know the one with all of that nasty, frightfully appalling sherry, port and other insipid liquids?"

"Daddy? Yes, but he locks it now."

"Damn! Er, I mean, how unfortunate it is that he can't trust people. When did he start locking it, my buttercup?"

"Last year, just after you left for home."

"Oh good for him. Er, shall we join the others at the Capitol Cafe? Time is moving on rather rapidly my sweet and my throat is getting dry."

That afternoon, time stood still for eight of the nine couples reminiscing as they toured the town, bowled, danced, and just had fun. Being together again felt absolutely wonderful. The ninth couple, Lyons and Zelda discussed the *intelligent one's* theory that the number 'zero' didn't exist. Lyons believed the world's numbering system should go from one to nine, and he kept saying, "After all, zero does count as one, you know?"

At 1630 it was time for the boys to tackle the hill. All cadets had to be in camp for supper. Although a movie was scheduled for B-3 that night, tomorrow was a training day and their kit had to be prepared.

Sweating while heading up the hill, the group was joined by a small CScotR cadet with a kilt nearly bigger than the boy.

"Hey, Mr. Moose, remember me? I'm Haggis Patterson, the virgin you met in the truck. I don't think I'm gonna go without it for long 'cause I met a dame in town. Her name's Audrey and this is her picture. Big ones, eh?"

Cordell Cross

A heavily breathing Moose lost his step perusing the photograph. "Just Moose will do. Not bad, but if youse thinks those are big ones, Haggis, ya gotta have your head examined. My cat could match those."

The Scot snatched his picture back. "Yah, sure, sure ... and I suppose your cat works in Hop Sing's like Audrey does, eh?"

At once, the world stopped turning and all ears perked as the musketeers encircled the young *kilter*. Moose even placed an arm around the shoulders of his newfound friend. "What? Your dame works for Hop Sing? Er, what does she do?"

Sticking his chest out, the young fellow replied, "She sorts laundry on Sunday mornings. I asked her if Hop Sing's was a whorehouse and she slapped my face. Look, it's still swollen. She says it ain't a whorehouse. All they do is laundry."

The military police jeep didn't stop. "You people get yourselves in pairs and start marching!"

Danyluk wasn't lost for words as he started taking on the hill again.

"Laundry? That's bullshit! Everyone knows they do more than laundry! Maybe she was too embarrassed, or the *girls* take Sunday off?"

"Yeah, like, er ... never on Sunday," East said, adding, "Ya can't go to church and then start screwing the customers. It wouldn't be right!"

The Scot nodded. "Well, that's what she told me. I asked if I could look inside next Sunday and she said sure. She thinks I'm a real weirdo wantin' to watch her sort people's dirty laundry. I'm gonna take my camera and she said she'll pose next to the bed-sheets. Her and her mom will be the only ones there."

Moose couldn't control his excitement. "Jeez, what a break! Then she'll let us in?"

"No, I asked her, but it's against Hop Sing's rules."

"I'll bet it is," Rothstein said. "Hop Sing's probably in the other rooms getting rid of the evidence. Take pictures of the separate rooms as well. Moose could sell 'em to the Seaforths and the Irish."

"Screw those jerks! Youse knows I could sell 'em to anyone! This is too good to be true. Finally, we get to see inside that consygerated establishment! What a summer this is gonna be!"

"That's *consecrated*, Moose," Rothstein offered.

"Whatever, Rothie, my boy. Mere words won't never explain the real tender and refined feelings I have for that joint. Son of a bitch, I'm gettin' a boner just thinkin' about the place."

East opened a small bag of peanuts. "Do ya think Hoppy gives credit?"

Jackson laughed. "Not to us he wouldn't. But he probably gives it to the commanding officer and the medical officer, I'll betcha."

"And the padres," Cunningham uttered. "Especially the padres. They all walk around with persistent silly smiles on their faces. I know they ain't gamblin' so they must be droppin' their *load* off at Hop Sing's."

Shortly they gave an 'eyes right' to the launderer's *revered establishment*, and as the group marched past the Provost shack, Danyluk had the last word. "Jesus, I wonder if I could borrow one of those priest's collars. Father Danyluk has a nice ring to it."

Bergie winced. "You wouldn't, would you? Jeez, here we go again. Just keep me out of it."

"No way, Bergie - you're in. I'll find you a collar also. Brother Bergie sounds apprapa ... er, appripate."

Cringing again, Bergie said, "Appropriate?"

"Yeah, that'll do."

Although they had seen it many times, after the movie *All Quiet on the Western Front,* and mug-up, B-25 became alive with activity. Cadets who had taken the day off instead of preparing their kit had a lot of catching up to do.

In addition to the incessant whining of an overloaded washing machine, loaded sink-ledges overflowed with wet garments being scrubbed and smeared with Sergeants' soap. At least fifty cadets gathered in the sink, toilet, shower, and drying-area of the H-hut, and none were gladdened with the stench originating from the jon.

"Who saved up for a month before taking a crap?" gagged Rod McKee, a Calgary Highlander cadet, placing a clothespin on his nose as he scrubbed his khaki shorts. "If someone lit a match in here, this whole building would go up. Nobody's dump should smell that bad. Hey, fella, whoever the hell you are, you'd better have your stomach examined and pumped, and after that, have your asshole sewn up. Your smell could gag a maggot!"

All cadets in the immediate vicinity pinched their noses as the unseen *haze* explored the entire centre section.

"Jeez, they should issue gas masks in this hut," said another, pinching his nose with one hand while wiping the tears from his eyes with the other. "Whoever the hell's in there, you must have an asshole the size of a cannon. If ya flush that thing, you'll probably flood the joint!"

"It would have been worse last year with no doors on the shitters," a teary-eyed cadet said at the washing machine and in effect, ground zero. "There's no one in here! I looked under the cubicles. Whoever it was must have had a quick dump and took off! Probably a Westie! They don't waste any time doin' those things! To them it's the same as screwing! Wham, bam, thank you, ma'am."

Still holding his snout while trying to get his washing out of the machine, the *crying* cadet's laundry appeared dirtier now than before it went in.

Another yelled, "Or probably a sally's light horse type! (South Alberta Light Horse) Jeez, man, how can you stand it in there?"

The 'laundry' cadet wiped both eyes before cupping his hands over his mouth and taking a deep breath. "Last year I bunked close to an Irish cadet named East. I think he said he was in the Irish ... or was it the Seaforths? Anyway, hell, this is mild! When he farted, we had to take off fast, otherwise it was game over! The paint on our bunks blistered."

Even in such difficulty, McKee managed a smile, saying, "Silent but deadly, eh?"

The 'breath-holder' emerged with his wet clothes. "You can say that again. Even the local flies died quickly. He never had any fly-catchin' paper over *his* bunk - they just croaked from unnatural causes!"

Cordell Cross

Chapter 5

Although Vernon days are extremely hot, early mornings can be quite cool. Throughout the night, some cadets had kicked off their blankets and were just wrapped in their upper sheet. Others had cast off all their bedclothes and had assumed the foetal position, subconsciously wondering why they were cold.

On Monday morning when reveille sounded and a strange fully moustached regular force sergeant stormed into the hut, getting warm *his way* was the last thing on their minds. The walls, ceilings and floors of the barracks and its occupants, including their bunks and barrack-boxes, shuddered from the sound of his voice when he *introduced* himself.

Due to the ferociousness of this one-man hurricane, even the new day's sun appeared to falter at the start of its long westward journey.

Blankets, mattresses, sheets, towels, bunks, barrack-boxes, buckets, mops, brooms and yes, even bodies were tossed to the sound of: "You people in Signals Company have exactly one minute to form three ranks on the road! Do you hear me, you miserable excuses for living, breathing, walking-talking Homo sapiens? My God, two-thirds of the world's peoples have already started their day, and you lazy lot sleep your lives away! Get out of it! You, and you, and you, get your asses in gear! What am I dealing with here? Did your mothers throw away the baby and keep the after-birth? Never in my life have I seen such slothful people! You, get your finger out of your nose and quit scratching your ass! And you, you with the money-belt on, you've got enough lint in your belly button to build a bedstead! I'll be back and..."

Cunningham checked out his belly button and quickly hid his money-belt as the sergeant's voice trailed off through the centre portion of the H-hut.

After *gently* awakening the other side, the living tornado arrived back and the whole building shook again.

In what seemed like millionths of a second, approximately one-hundred-and-fifty cold, confused, bewildered, dazed, and thunderstruck fragments of *after-birth* bumped and stomped into each other attempting to put on PT strip.

Amidst yawns, bickering and scratching, barrack-box lids slammed as arms, legs and torsos flapped out the southern-end doors of the building. Those who were stuck in the middle of the doorways quickly got over the bruises and cuts. For some untold reason even gashes stop bleeding when they receive the scrutiny of angry sergeants.

Though sweet smelling, the cold air took its toll as a hundred-and-fifty sets of bleary eyes attempted to focus on the grinning *sadist* in front of them. Throughout the camp, other Cheshire-cat sergeants received the same observance. These *loyal non-commissioned officers* of the Queen weren't smiling at all. Having to arise at such an ungodly hour after staying late the previous eve in the sergeants' mess, brought on the release of stomach vapours - the result of which created uncontrolled gas pains that contorted their faces.

"My name is Sergeant Bentley! I am a member of Her Majesty's Black Watch regiment!"

Cordell Cross

"It figures," Danyluk whispered to a shivering Bergie. "Another 'cold ass' who couldn't sleep so he takes it out on us. Jeez, put some underwear on those sheep-shit and heather types and they could become almost human."

This 'cold ass' sergeant was the same as the others. His ears appeared normal, but he was a three-striper, and three stripers have ears that work above human normalcy.

"I will do the talking! What did you say?" Sergeant Bentley asked breathing in Moose's face.

When Moose came to attention, his untied right running-shoe lace whipping both his legs. "Me, Sergeant?"

When the sergeant bellowed, "Yes, you," Bergie flinched. He knew what was coming because Moose always included him.

"I, er, simply stated to my friend here..."

Danyluk pointed at Bergie, who rolled his eyes up to the sky.

"That the Black Watch is a fine regiment, Sergeant."

Bergie's face received a full-frontal assault of the fumes from the gaseous mixture in the sergeant's stomach.

"Did he say that?"

Moose's *friend* assumed the position of attention.

"Yes, sergeant! He wants to join your regiment when he *grows* up!"

A real grin hit the sergeant's face. "Wonderful, just bloody wonderful! Well, let's start with my regiment's indoctrination process right now, shall we? Both of you get down and give me fifteen! I'll do the counting!"

After each cadet completed thirty push-ups, Sergeant Bentley continued.

"Don't ask me why I'm here! I don't know why I'm in Vernon! I didn't ask to get posted here and I certainly didn't put the make on the Regimental Sergeant Major's (RSM) wife to receive it. I just do my job well! Maybe that's why I'm here? I do my tasks so effectively and efficiently, they want me to impart my exceptional knowledge, together with my sweet-tempered good-natured and kind-hearted disposition on you people!"

Moose attempted to whisper again, but Bergie beat him to the punch. "Moose, for Christ's sake, keep your mouth shut!"

"Yes, I think that's why I'm here," Bentley continued. "So that is exactly what I intend to do!"

"Right now, I'm not going to talk about this signals course! Instead, we're going to run two miles and get our bodies limbered up! Are there any questions? No? Then there must be some complaints? No? Phenomenal ... just bloody phenomenal!

"Signals Company, atten ... tion! Move to the right in threes, right turn! By the left, double quick, march!"

After the company had crossed the highway, heading on the dust covered road to the upper camp, the sergeant bellowed, "We're all going to sing this morning! I'll sing the verse and you'll repeat it! Is that clear?"

The words, "Yes, Sergeant," were released by half the members of the company who weren't breathing hard.

Danyluk muttered to Bergie, "What does he think we are ... Goddamned birds? Even they ain't up at this ungodly hour. Jeez, I don't sing this early unless the dame of the day joins me in the shower."

Bergie puffed, "What if the dame of the day is Doris?"

"Like I've already told youse, Bergie, my Doris don't like soap and water. I ain't never sung with her because it would take me a week to get her hairs and dandruff outta my bathtub. There're limits to who I shower with Bergie."

Bergie stumbled but quickly regained his balance. "Don't bullshit me, Moose. I know you've showered with Hairy Helga the dame with..."

The Sergeant's voice cut Bergie off. "I can't hear you! You all want to sing, don't you?"

Before Moose and every other cadet reluctantly replied, "Yes, Sergeant," the *animal* got the last word in. "Hairy Helga don't shed. She shaves, but she don't shed. Nice broad, Helga. She looks great after she combs her face."

The company's *willing* reaction pleased the sergeant. "Good, that's what I thought! Right, here we go! You repeat the words that I sing! *D&M types work with nuts and bolts, 'cause D&M types are mostly dolts!*"

Repeating the words got the whole company laughing.

"D&M types don't have class; 'cause all their brains are in their ass!

"If ya try to go to heaven in a D&M jeep; you'll go the other way, 'cause it's driven by a creep!

"The devil will welcome them by name; because they've done everything wrong to bring on the shame!

"IBT bodies ain't kept fit, 'because they're skins are stretched over bags of shit!

IBT creeps don't have a name - and they sure as hell don't share signals fame!

"We're in signals sharp and true; because we're the ones that have got a clue!

If ya wanna be great right from the start; to work in signals, ya gotta be smart!"

The sergeant and cadets introduced other verse and song of company brotherhood as signals made its way around the upper camp and back to its own lines. Spirits were high during the whole jog as loud and proud company laughter greeted *other* assemblages jogging nearby. Needless to say, all sides exposed middle fingers throughout.

After halting and standing the cadets at ease, Sergeant Bentley's gas pain turned into a smile of reverence, and he winked at the company, saying, "Very good, my lads, very good! Not too bad at all for our first day! You have my permission to sing those songs whenever you want, except in the mess halls, downtown, church parade, or at home!

"Now, when you get inside, I want each of you to shower, brush your teeth, comb your hair, and get this barracks in signals shape! You will notice I said signals shape, not IBT or driver-mech shape! Is that clear?"

"Yes, Sergeant!"

"I can't hear you!"

"Yes, Sergeant!"

"That's more like it! After that, I want to see the sharpest company in camp on parade! Signals Company, atten ... tion! fall ... out!"

Cordell Cross

After the customary turn to their right, all cadets marched forward five paces and enthusiastically dispersed.

Wane put his right arm around Douglas' shoulders. "You know, Doug, I thought he was going to be a real bastard, but he's like the rest of 'em, he's all right. He reminds of Sergeant Beckford from last year."

Douglas didn't have time to answer because the other musketeers moved in.

"They all come from the same old mould," Danyluk said, stretching. "It must be the way they're taught. It's personraly persified. That's the way I'm gonna be with my victims, uh, customers when they come to my doctor's place."

Rothstein cringed. "You mean personality *personified*, and don't you mean *patients* that come to your *office* or *clinic*?"

Moose pushed Rothstein through the wing door into the entranceway and whined, *No I don't mean patients, office or clinic*. My shingle will read: 'Doctor Danyluk's Place For Dames Only.' I've even thought of my slogans. How do these sound? 'If youse's gonna let him rub it ... allow me scrub it!' Also, 'After he slips youse the root ... I'll keep it a beaut!'"

The musketeers howled their heads off entering B-25. Only one person wasn't laughing and that was Moose. Although he wore a small smile, he remained a little upset that his friends didn't appreciate his dedication to the medical profession. Moose also couldn't understand why they failed to recognize what he considered his *exceptional* grasp of the English language.

"Youse won't laugh when ya send your wives to my doctor's place! No siree."

After breakfast and last minute alterations to the alignment of barrack boxes, bunks, dust covers, hung battledress, washbasins, and items on shelves, the company formed up in three ranks on the east/west road at the southern end of the Hut B-25.

In accordance with the timetable and instructions, only 21 and 22 Platoons wore khaki shorts, hosetops, boots and puttees. Platoons 23 and 24 wore KD longs with puttees and weights.

In front of them stood their company commander, his second-in-command, four platoon commanders, the company sergeant major, four platoon sergeants, and eight platoon corporals. Gas pains were evident everywhere - even on cadets' faces.

"Son of a bitch," muttered Danyluk. "Bergie take a look, it's..."

This time Bergie responded appropriately, not turning up his eyes to the sky as he normally did when Moose mumbled in the ranks. "I see him. Jeez, it's Sergeant Major Genova."

Whispers indicated quite a few cadets spotted the man with the devious smirk hid under his giant nose and beady-eyes, standing there observing the group while rubbing his hands together.

In Vernon the previous year, and at their home corps, a good number of the BCR cadets had come to dislike this ex member of the British Columbia Regiment (DCO) who showed favouritism and had *peculiar* ways. Some cadets though, thought he was all right, and were quickly promoted for their *vision*.

"He ain't smearin' Vicks on me if I get a cold," East quipped. "I don't want that creep within fifty feet of me."

Moose grinned and nudged the *beast*. "You'll never make sergeant that way, *darling*."

"Screw you, Moose. You go and get a cold."

"Not me! It's always Lyons who gets the colds. Maybe he'll even get newsmonia."

The chubby intelligent one in the centre rank turned his head. "It's *pneumonia*, you idiot. Not this year I won't. Go and violate yourself, Moose."

"Such diction. Why Don, my old friend, I didn't mean to insult youse. Bullshit, on second thought, I did. That body of yours needs some Vicks. It'll limber youse up for that Zelda broad."

"Go trip on your wang, Moose."

"Picky, picky," Danyluk replied.

Over the next half-hour, the cadets of Signals Company went through the process of being introduced to their company staff before being inspected by their individual platoon commander and their company commander, Major Hansford.

The musketeers' platoon commander introduced himself as Lieutenant Preston, and to their surprise, the cadets found out that they had already met their *singing* platoon sergeant earlier that morning.

Corporals attached to 21 Platoon were Corporal Sherdahl from the Princess Patricia's Canadian Light Infantry, and Corporal Francois from the Royal Canadian Corps of Signals.

During the morning inspection, a few names were taken because uniforms weren't pressed properly, or cadets forgot to wear their coloured ribbons. Overall, though, Major Hansford, a short man of few words, was pleased. He advised them that the company staff would inspect them each morning, and that a cadet rank system would be arranged within the next few days. He also advised them that he was extremely happy with their barracks.

At 0830 hours, the officers and Sergeant Major Genova disbursed notebooks, pencils, pens and various CAMTs (Canadian Army Manual of Training). Afterward, as 21 and 22 Platoons marched over to nearby lecture rooms, 23 and 24 Platoons boarded trucks to take them to Area 10 in the upper camp.

Although all windows were open, the heat jolted members of 21 Platoon entering their lecture hut. Inside, enough folding military tables had been assembled to seat everyone. Each table held a Nineteen radio set, two sets of earphones (headsets), a microphone and two Morse-code keys. Cadets sat in pairs at each table, facing their set and the blackboards and lectern at the front of the room. Their platoon officer, Lieutenant Preston stood at the lectern. Through the hut windows, the cadets could see Sergeant Pennington and 22 Platoon's officer in the adjacent hut.

Cadets engineered their own seating plan, therefore, Wane sat with Douglas, Danyluk with Bergie, Rothstein with Cunningham, Jackson with East, and Lyons sat with his Seaforth chess playing bunk partner Cadet McLeod,

As it turned out, most cadets sat with their bunk partners. The platoon corporals noted individual names on a seating plan and passed it to the front.

Forthwith, all hands were on the dials, knobs and switches of the Nineteen sets.

Cordell Cross

"Please refrain from touching the sets until you start receiving instruction on them," Lieutenant Preston stated.

"During the next three periods, we're going to discuss Signals Office Duties. As your timetable points out, there will be a break after the first period and following the third period, you'll have half-an-hour to clean up for lunch. Right, please remove your headdress. I realize it's unbearably hot in here, but try to make yourselves as comfortable as possible."

Lieutenant Preston didn't waste any time getting to the *meat* of the first lesson as the two platoon corporals passed out pads of message forms.

"Now, everything we do in signals has to be exact. There can be no excuses for passing out improper information such as misspelled names, places, or orders. That also means there can be no errors in reporting dates, timings and co-ordinates, etc. Your job as signallers is to make certain everything you do is perfect. The lives of men depend on your precision, and while taking this course I want those facts to be constantly on your mind. Now, let's look at the top of this form. In the upper left corner you will see..."

Fifty-five minutes later, the eager and willing cadets of 21 and 22 Platoons left their berets in their huts and gathered under the shade of some nearby trees. A pop truck had already dropped off cases of ice-cold KiK-Kola and now the rush was on to buy tickets from one NCO to pass them on to another NCO for a bottle of pop.

Of course, some cadets, such as East, forgot to bring money, but Cunningham looked after them. His bank was now open and his interest rate was fair considering the *qualifying* factors.

"Do you want a loan, or don'tcha?" Cunningham asked a fuming East.

"Twenty-five percent is highway robbery. Who the hell do you think I am, Henry Ford? Jeez, give a buddy a break will ya?"

The banker had no time to listen to East's pleas; other *pigeons* were pushing forward.

"No? You don't wish to negotiate a loan? Fine! Next!"

East wiped his brow. He needed a pop now more than ever before in his life. He figured the temperature had to be in the high nineties.

"Er, alright, alright! Christ ... twenty-five percent? I think I'll change my name to Lance Corporal Moneybags."

The young entrepreneur passed a one-dollar bill into the anxious outstretched hands of 'Lance Corporal Moneybags.'

"Wonderful," Cunningham said. "Just sign here."

Still mumbling to himself, East signed next to the amount of the debt, then bewilderedly strolled over to the corporal with the tickets. The price of a KiK-Kola was now ten cents.

"Ten tickets, please, Corporal."

After East got his pop, he joined the others as Rothstein took a long swig from his bottle, swallowed, and said, "I think I'm really gonna like this course. Did you guys see the Russian writing on those Nineteen sets?"

"Rothie, we supplied them to the Russian army," Bergie replied. "I don't think we do now."

While Rothstein nodded, a puzzled look came over Jackson's face. "The Russians? Hey, ain't they our enemy. Look what those bastards did in Korea."

Bergie knew the answer. "Yeah, but they weren't our enemy during World War Two."

"Did we get 'em all back?" Moose asked his chum.

Bergie gave Moose a frustrated look. "How the hell do I know? Do you think I went out and counted them all?"

"Hey, I only asked, Bergie! What's bothering youse?"

Bergie stood up and slapped the dust of the back of his shorts. "I sit next to you, right?"

"Yes, youse is my partner," Danyluk answered. "So what?"

"Well on the top of the message form where it says, *date*, you don't write, '*Natch, they're guaranteed.*' How can the words, '*Natch they're guaranteed,*' be a date? The officer's going to think we're a couple of idiots. Also, why did you write the words 'eight hours' where it said *time*? Did you mean 0800 hours?"

Moose glanced egotistically at his friend. "Hey, the form asks personal questions! I've never gone short of a date in my life, and when I do take a dame out, it's usually for about eight hours. So there, smart ass!"

While Moose's *rational* started the others laughing, Bergie stood there with his mouth open shaking his head. He couldn't believe what he had just heard. It wasn't until they were walking up the steps to the lecture hut that Moose put his arm around Bergie's shoulders and told him he'd handed in a duplicate form with the proper information on it.

"Gotcha, didn't I? What the hell do youse thinks I am, Bergie ... a Westie?"

As Moose was pushed through the door, Bergie replied, "Worse! For a moment I thought you were in the Irish."

Following the pop break, their platoon sergeant, Sergeant Bentley stood behind the lectern. He had his headdress off and except for a few grey hairs above his ears, his scalp of short jet-black hair matched the colour of his moustache.

As the corporals passed out booklets entitled, *Morse Code -the essential language*, the senior non-com said, "Right fellas - don't touch the Nineteen sets! We won't be getting to them until after lunch!

I have decided it is too hot in here, therefore I've had a portable blackboard set up outside in the shade. You people in the front row, I want you to do me a favour and move this lectern out! Thank you!"

Banks whispered to Douglas. "Did you hear what he said? He said, 'Do me a favour,' and he used the words, 'thank you.'"

Douglas nodded. His mind recalled Sergeant Beckford, their sergeant in 1953. "They come from the same school. They're decent guys," he replied.

It *was* cooler outside and the cadets appreciated Sergeant Bentley's consideration. Sitting under a tree on dusty burnt grass was much better than roasting and falling asleep on a wooden bench.

Sergeant Bentley took a deep breath and allowed his blue eyes to scan his class. "Communication! A word containing thirteen letters. Communication is the reason the human race is superior on this planet. We communicate!

Cordell Cross

"We use various methods to communicate with our fellow man, and animals ... What are they?"

The sergeant had *thrown out* an overhead question. He now faced raised hands as he reviewed the names on his seating plan.

"Banks?"

"Speech, Sergeant!"

"Good!" He wrote the word on the blackboard. "Yes, speech! In addition, are there other methods? Er … McLeod?"

"Writing. The written word, Sergeant!"

"Excellent!" Bentley said, writing the word out and facing the class. "Are there more? ... Danyluk?"

Bergie also had his hand up, but slowly lowered it and let loose with a constrained gas pain.

"ESP ... er, er, excellent sensory perspiration, Sergeant?"

The Sergeant tried not to laugh with the class. "That's close, Danyluk. Not bad, but don't you mean, extrasensory perception?"

Bergie glanced at Danyluk and he could tell from the look on the *animal's* face, those words were *not* what he meant. Whispering he pleaded, "Say yes, Moose. For God's sake, say yes."

Moose shrugged off the advice. "Er, not really, Sergeant! When I'm with my broads ... er, dames ... er, they sense something excellent is going to happen to them, so they sweat, er, perspire! Nothin' is said between us, but they knows what I'm thinkin' ... and I'm sure they knows what's comin'."

Howls from the platoon echoed against the nearby huts.

An Irish cadet laughed and leaned over to his friend. "Shit, it's him again. Any broad would know what's comin' if they're out with him. It's like the sun rising and setting. They're gonna get sixty-pounds of raw sausage meat whether they want it or not."

His friend replied, "Doesn't he asked them first?"

"Not him. Hell, he takes them for granted the second he introduces himself and grabs their rear ends."

Sergeant Bentley regained his composure and turned half his body towards the blackboard. "Well, I think you mean extrasensory perception, Danyluk! Yes, that's one. Give me another … Brice?"

"Sign language, Sergeant!"

"Good, very good! Moreover, there are various kinds of sign languages. We've seen the deaf communicate. Also in 1792 a Frenchman named *Claude Chappe* developed a mechanical contrivance consisting of moveable arms attached to a post. The position of the arms indicated various letters and numerals. That was the start of semaphore and it is still used today.

"Fellas, the Romans used signal fires, the Greek army used polished shields to reflect the sun, and American Indians used smoke, drums and torches. So you see, communication by sign is most important.

72 – NEXT STOP, VERNON!

"Around 1819, the Danes, Russians, and Germans began to experiment with electric telegraphic concepts, but it wasn't until 1832 that a man became famous using an electric telegraphic device. Do any of you know his name?"

Hands shot up, and the sergeant picked out a cadet. Yes, Rothstein."

"Samuel F. B. Morse, Sergeant. He developed the Morse code."

"Absolutely brilliant, Rothstein! Yes, along came Samuel F. B. Morse, and since that time, his method of communicating is the most recognized means of signalling in the world. Why is that ... Jackson?"

Earl paused for a second. He knew a bit about this subject.

"Because it's cheap to use. You can send it with anything ... auto horns, railroad whistles, flashlights, tapping pencils, flashing mirrors. Nearly anything, Sergeant."

"Perfect, Jackson! Absolutely right! The possibilities are endless. It is cheap to use and it consumes less power than voice transmitters."

The Sergeant walked away from the blackboard. "Write this down! Samuel Morse was born in Massachusetts in 1791 and was the son of a minister. He graduated from Yale College in 1810 after studying art. In 1811 he went to London, England to further his knowledge of art and afterwards became a great American artist.

"It was on his way back from England when dinner-table conversation centred around electric communication devices. He instantly had an inspiration.

"Morse had quite a few problems getting people to like his ideas of communication, but eventually he became very successful.

"Right, gentlemen ... and I use that term loosely ... we're going to learn Sam's method of how letters and numerals are represented by two symbols - the dot and dash, and the long and short flash. You can never be too old or too young to learn this art, and practice makes perfect!"

Sergeant Bentley had the minds of all cadets in his hands. All, that is, except Lyons. The NCO's method of instruction was perfect and his audience wanted to take in all the knowledge the sergeant could impart. Lyons just wanted to get his hands on a Nineteen Set.

Continuing, the sergeant said, "There are two telegraphic codes! We are going to use the International Morse Code. The other method is sometimes called the Continental Code, the Ralistilegraph Code, or just plain American Morse Code.

"Now we're going to go back inside to start using our Morse code keys. Are there any questions?"

Bergie asked, "How many words a minute will we learn, Sergeant?"

"Good question. I'll be happy if each of you learns to send and receive thirteen to fifteen words per minute. Any other questions? Yes, er ... Lyons."

Lyons remained seated and after slowly pushing his glasses further up to the bridge of his nose, his face took on an egotistical cast. "Er, yes, Sergeant. Perchance, could you expound upon as to which person possesses this terrestrial sphere's uppermost adroitness in this moderately parched topic? Correspondingly, in the final analysis, what is it?"

Checking his seating plan to confirm the cadet's name, a *gas pain* appeared on Bentley's face. Obviously, he was not pleased with Lyons' *question*.

Cordell Cross

"Stand up, Lyons."

Lyons quickly stood, perspiration forming on his twitching upper lip. He knew better than to toy with sergeants. It was the relaxed atmosphere that made him ask the question in such a manner. Closing his eyes for a second, he muttered, "Damn."

"Did you understand the lesson you received before pop break? Particularly the part about … brevity?"

"Yes, Sergeant, I did."

"Then ask the question like a signaller would. Don't question me like you scrutinize the face of the condescending, smug, overbearing, egotistical, arrogant pampered *infant* you see in the mirror each morning. Do you understand me … Lyons?"

"Yes, er, yes, Sergeant."

"Well, I'm waiting, Lyons?"

Lyons wiped his upper lip. "Who holds the world's record for sending Morse, and what is it?"

"I didn't hear my rank … or your question!"

"Sergeant - who holds the world's record for sending Morse, and what is it?"

"Much better, Lyons. The world's record of 75.2 words per minute was set 02 July 1939 by a fellow named Ted R. McElroy. I believe he was English, but I could be wrong. Now sit down and shut up."

Being checked over by his peers, Lyons quickly sat down. He had learned a good lesson, one he would not forget. He knew that while this sergeant was fair and friendly, he could also be very firm. He now felt like the reflected vision the sergeant had described.

After a short ten-minute break, the cadets of 21 Platoon returned to their seats in the lecture hut. Sergeant Bentley arrived about twenty seconds later because he had been *talking* with Lyons, out of view, at the end of the hut. Lyons came in with him and both parties had smiles on their faces.

"You've got that right, Sergeant." Lyons said.

"You bet, lad. Just have some consideration for my experience. Even I make mistakes. No, on second thought, I don't."

Sergeant Bentley returned to the front of the class. "Right! Gentlemen, write down the numerals 987654312 and divide them by eight."

Cunningham's hand went up. When it came to figures, the *banker* always insisted on exactness. "Er, Sergeant, er, the last three figures. Did you say 312 or 321?"

"I said, three, one, and two. Who's got the answer?"

Cunningham was ready. His hand went up again.

"All right, go for it … Cunningham."

"The answer is 123456789. Wow, that's mint, but what's this got to do with Morse code?"

Bentley smiled. "Absolutely nothing other than I wanted to wake you people up … and to make certain you ask questions if you're not too certain what you're told. Remember lads, this is signals. Lives depend on your accuracy. Now open your books and go to page fourteen … the actual illustration of the international Morse code."

(a) di-dah .- (b) dah-di-di-dit -... (c) dah-di-dah-dit -.-. (d) dah-di-dit -.. (e) dit . (f) di-di-dah-dit .. -. (g) dah-dah-dit --. (h) di-di-di-dit .... (I) di-dit .. (j) di-dah-dah-dah .--- (k) dah-di-dah -.- (l) di-dah-di-dit .-.. (m) dah-dah -- (n) dah-dit -. (o) dah-dah-dah --- (p) di-dah-dah-dit .--. (q) dah-dah-di-dah --.- (r) di-dah-dit .-. (s) dit-dit-dit ... (t) dah - (u) di-di-dah .. - (v) di-di-di-dah ...- (w) di-dah-dah .-- (x) dah-di-di-dah -.. - (y) dah-di-dah-dah -.-- (z) dah-dah-di-dit --.. (1) di-dah-dah-dah-dah .---- (2) di-di-dah-dah-dah .. --- (3) di-di-di-dah-dah ...-- (4) di-di-di-di-dah ....- (5) di-di-di-di-dit ..... (6) dah-di-di-di-dit -.... (7) dah-dah-di-di-dit --... (8) dah-dah-dah-di-dit ---.. (9) dah-dah-dah-dah-dit ----. (0) dah-dah-dah-dah-dah ----- (period) di-dah-di-dah-di-dah .-.-.- (comma) dah-dah-di-di-dah-dah --..-- (question mark) di-di-dah-dah-di-dit ..--.. (colon) dah-dah-dah-di-di-dit ---... (semicolon) dah-di-dah-di-dah-dit -.-.-. (hyphen) dah-di-di-di-di-dah -....- (slash) dah-di-di-dah-dit -..-. (quotation) di-dah-di-di-dah-dit .-..-. (error) di-di-di-di-di-di-di-dit ....

After waiting for his cadets to review the various symbols, Sergeant Bentley said, "Repeat after me. The duration of a dah, is three times larger than a dit."

The class responded. "The duration of a dah, is three times larger than a dit."

"Again!"

"The duration of a dah, is three times larger than a dit."

"And again!"

"The duration of a dah, is three times larger than a dit."

"One more time!"

"The duration of a dah, is three times larger than a dit."

"Good, fellas – very good."

The sergeant picked up a pointer and unrolled a chart attached to the top of the blackboard. "When I point to a letter, you will transmit it back to me. Eventually, your timing will be the same."

Sergeant Bentley was right. It would take a while for his cadets to notice their transmission timing; however, the boys were more than keen. Time moved on quickly, so quickly that the last period seemed like just seconds had passed before they were fallen out to wash up for lunch. Naturally, none of them wanted to leave their keys, so the sergeant obliged them.

"I want you to practice in your spare time. On your way out, each of you will sign your name and pick up one dry cell, two wires and a key. You will not lose them! If you do, you'll pay for them at the end of camp! Understood?"

"Yes, Sergeant!"

The two platoons were not marched to their quarters. Instead, they were told to make their own way back in pairs and march with signals *flair*.

Platoons 23 and 24 from the other side of the hut had already returned before the Musketeers arrived back. These other cadets were covered in dust and burrs and they packed the centre washing-section trying to clean themselves up.

"What the hell happened to youse guys?" Moose asked as he squeezed in at the sink trough.

Cordell Cross

The cadet next to him stopped running a comb through his hair. "We've just had three periods of line-laying in Area 10. Jeez it's hot up there. You guys look like you've just returned from a beauty contest. How come you weren't with us?"

"We had periods on signal office duties and Morse code," Moose said, before spotting Bergie. "Hey Bergie, take a look at these poor bastards. And I thought this whole course was going to be non, er, nonchally."

Rothstein was close by and squeezed in. "Nonchalant?"

Danyluk grinned while washing his face. "Yeah, a much better choice. Yeah, *nonchalant*. Youse knows I flunked Spanish, Rothie."

"Naturally I know. French too."

Bergie said, "If you read the course package, Moose, you'll see there's a load of field work, and ... Er, get your cotton pickin' hand off my soap!"

"Aw, come on, Bergie, I'm gettin' sick of usin' sergeants' soap. I wanna smell like youse guys, er, like Attila the Homo."

"Attila the Hun didn't smell like us, he stunk like you."

"You mean that fierce warrior, my idol, used sergeants' soap?"

"Most likely, Moose. He really reeked."

As the rest of 21 and 22 Platoons occupied the sink area, Moose welcomed them in his Adonis pose.

"Hey youse pansies, Attila the Hun reeked like me! Eat your hearts out!"

A passing Irish cadet nudged his friend and whispered, "For the first time in his life, that necrophile jerk is absolutely correct."

His buddy replied, "Uh huh, but he's proud of it."

"Well he should be ... he's a BCR ain't he? They're all fruitcakes in that regiment."

An ear to ear grin appeared on the other Irish cadet. "How stupid of me. Certainly he is. If he's not a Seaforth, he's gotta be a Duke, right?"

"Right!"

At the other side of the first trough, Douglas washed while the *man* next to him hummed a song and mixed up shaving cream. The mug and brush appeared to be new.

"Wane, what the hell are you doing? You don't have a beard, and you shaved this morning."

"Speak for yourself, Dougie old pard; I've got hairs. Over the past four months, I've been counting 'em. Number 27 popped up this morning."

As Wane spoke, the foam around his mouth splattered on the mirror screwed into the wooden structure in front of them.

Brice moved closer to the mirror and checked his own chin. He couldn't even see one hair. "Twenty-seven? Are you serious?"

Wane's proud grin didn't leave his face. "Yep. Things are lookin' great, kiddo. If this keeps up, I'll be askin' out the older dames."

Only an inch away from the mirror, Douglas examined his own chin again. "You lucky pongo. Hey, I've got one too, and I think it's fighting to get out. Yeah, it is?"

"Banks smeared after-shave lotion on his hands and smacked his face. " Wanna borrow my razor?"

"You bet, and some of that lotion too."

Moose's voice boomed over the sink's partition. "Hey Banks, I've got more hair under my arms than you've got on your chin."

With his towel around his neck, Wane strolled out saying, "Yeah, we know, Moose; we've gotta smell 'em all year."

No sooner had Wane left, Lyons appeared, and Bergie approached him.

"What happened when Sergeant Bentley took you around the end of the hut?"

Don turned on the tap and held his head under the gushing cold water for a few seconds. Drying his face and hair, he replied. "Sergeant Bentley said something that made me feel like a real idiot. He said, 'You know, son, I was once your age, but you haven't yet reached my age. Is there enough brevity in that statement to make you understand?' That was it. We started walking back."

"What did you say?" Bergie asked, giving Moose a dirty look for slinging an arm over his right shoulder.

"What could I say? I said, 'I guess I was a bit of a horse's ass, eh, Sarg?' He then smiled and said, 'Nah, just think before you talk. I had a girlfriend who used to talk without thinking. Know what happened to her?'"

"I asked, 'What happened?' And he said, 'I married her. We all can't be perfect, can we?' The Sarg is a good guy."

All five laughed as they gathered up their washing kits and headed back to their bunks. The rest of the musketeers were waiting, except East. Cunningham, Jackson, and Banks locked away the Morse code sets they were practising with.

"Where's East?" Bergie asked.

Jackson jokingly assumed the position of attention. "He's saving a place for us in the lunch-line-up, sir!"

Bergie smacked Earl on the back. "Good, then let's get going. Keep it up Jackson and I'll speak to Genova about promoting you."

"Screw you, sir!"

As a worried East hustled his friends into the line-up amidst *lewd comments* from other cadets, Danyluk said to Bergie, "Did I ever tell youse what this dumb babe I was going out with thought a testicle was?"

Bergie raised his eyes to the sky again. "No, do I have to know?"

"She thought it was an examination for ticklishness. Get it - test tickle? Hah."

Between boos, Moose got pushed through the kitchen doors.

"I am absolutely beat," Wane complained as he entered his wing of the barracks, jumped up on his bunk, and kept his face buried in his pillow. It was four-thirty in the afternoon on day one and the cadets in 21 and 22 Platoons had just completed two periods on the Nineteen Set and one period on the UCL 10 line switchboard.

"In other words, I am finished, finished, finished," he added, restating one specific word in voice procedure he and the others had learned. "If we've got five days of this stuff, Saturday's exam is gonna be a humdinger."

Cordell Cross

Douglas was already sprawled out on his bunk - hands behind his head. He was also worn out and hadn't yet taken off his boots.

"I'm with ya. Who said this course was going to be a piece of cake? Danyluk, it was you, you pongo."

Moose had already stripped to his shorts. He wasn't listening to the others. He just picked up his Morse key and battery and practised Morse.

All traces of fatigue quickly disappeared as Wane and Douglas rushed to their barrack box to get their keys. They had memorized the message Moose was sending, looked it up, and replied. Within two minutes, Wane started transmitting.

Shortly, Morse code keys were the order of the day on the west side of B-25. If a stranger had entered the barracks, to him or her it would have sounded like the code room in America's Central Intelligence Agency. Maybe even all world intelligence agencies combined.

At exactly 1700 hours, East bellowed, "The mess hall has opened!"

Those words were all it took as barrack box lids slammed shut and cadets rushed to make the line-up. Not the musketeers though. Except for East, eight of them just grabbed their towels and washing kits and headed for the sinks. They knew there would be enough food left and right now, holding their heads under the taps was more important than presenting their plates.

"I'm really diggin' this Morse code stuff," a lathered Wane told Douglas.

"Are you shaving again? Jeez, you're not gonna have any skin left on your face. Once a day is enough, Wane."

Moose moved in. "Yeah, it'll be red raw and if Genova sees youse he'll wanna spread Vicks all over your ass."

"Wane smeared his aftershave. " You mean Vicks all over my face."

"No, your ass. They both look the same."

Banks was going to reply, but Moose changed the subject, asking, "Hey, I wonder if those hairy asses shave their ass?"

"Who *are* the hairy asses?" Rothstein asked.

Cunningham took a coin out of Jackson's ear and replied for Moose. "Who else. The fags in rags. The kilters."

Rothstein laughed. "Fags in rags. Why are they called hairy asses?"

"Because they sweat," said Moose. "Haven't you ever smelled those kilts? Even I know that sweat brings on hair. Wane, if youse wrapped a kilt around your face twenty-four hours a day, you'd have a beard down to your feet. People wouldn't go near youse, but you'd have a beard."

"Yeah, they'd even call you a rag face fag," said Jackson.

"What's on tonight?" Lyons asked, checking his teeth in the mirror.

"We've got a hell of a lot of studying to do, as well as our kit," Douglas replied. "Also, we've gotta call the girls."

Trying to find a hair he might have missed, Wane asked, "Where can I borrow a kilt?"

A shocked expression came over Douglas. "You've got to be joking? You wouldn't?"

Wane threw a mock-punch. "Just jokin' old buddy. I'll leave that to Danyluk."

As the *animal* wiped his face, he said, "Di-di-dah-dit/di-di-dah."
"And you too," Banks replied.

That evening B-25 took on the look of every hut it camp. It resembled a fairground on the last day. Cadets scrubbed, ironed, shined, washed, showered, studied, joked, played cards, gambled, read comics, wrote letters home, threw articles at each other, emptied the fire extinguishers, frenched a few beds, jumped over bunks, and generally did whatever boys do when 150 of them are together. Throughout, the musketeers took part in a few antics but they remembered the year before. Play came after work, and on this course, there was little time for frolic.

Following kit cleaning, the musketeers studied in pairs in the lecture huts before heading to the cadet canteen. Lyons didn't join them because he was *immersed* in a chess game with his bunkmate. As for Cunningham, he cleaned his kit, studied, but then headed to other huts instead of the canteen. As far as he was concerned, living the good life required money, lots of it, and if it was there for the taking, he'd take it.

"Last call," the canteen corporal shouted.

Every one of them had just bought another pop, except East. He'd put the money he borrowed from Cunningham into pop tickets and they weren't accepted in the canteen.

"Last call? Jeez, I ain't even had one yet! I just got back from mug-up! Give a guy a break, Corporal. One of my friends here will fork out a dime. Gimmee a few seconds, okay?"

The corporal was fair. "You've got thirty seconds!"

As East pleaded, his buddies ignored him or shook their heads indicating they too were broke. When the bar door slammed down, a dejected East headed towards the exit. But not for long.

Bergie asked, "Where in the hell are you going?"

"To the water fountain, my throat's dry. You guys just sit there drinking your refreshing ice-cold KiK-Kolas. That's okay, I don't..."

Douglas couldn't take it anymore. "We've bought you two, Jack. Here they are. Jeez, do you really think...?"

Jack ran back and grabbed the two bottles. "Buddies, friends, pals! I love ya all. Even you, Moose."

Danyluk chuckled while swallowing the last of his three KiK-Kolas. "Youse must really think we're creeps," he said, licking his lips while staring at one of East's bottles. "If youse only wants one, I'll take the other off your hands? Here's a nickel, and..."

Jack didn't waste any time. The liquid disappeared fast before he wiped his mouth. "Take a hike, Moose."

Minutes later, they were back in the *rat-house* of B-25. Although there was no hot water left, the showers felt great and when the corporals turned off the lights, a light breeze soothed the bodies of those reclining on top of their blankets.

Whispering erupted throughout the hut, and Wane leaned over. "My face feels like it has been hit with a truck."

Moose heard him. "It looks like it too. Wow, youse were even shavin' in the showers. Probably while you were having a dump, too."

"Once a day is enough," Douglas said.

"Hey, who says so, Doug? If my broads thought I was only good for..."

"I'm not talking to you, Moose, I'm talking to Wane."

"Oh. For a moment I thought youse was talkin' to me."

Bergie chuckled. "You know what thought did, don't you Moose? It went for a shit and the crows got it."

"Stick it in your ear, Bergie. Youse is only good for once a day."

Wane popped his head over the side. "Yeah, I think I'll only shave once tomorrow. Say, did you phone Diane?"

"I couldn't. The line-up for the phone was a mile long. How about you?"

"No. I couldn't get near it either. G'night Doug."

Douglas rolled on his side. "Good night buddy."

Two minutes later, Bergie's voice was stern. "Jeez, Moose will you quit playing with yourself; these bunks are shaking."

"Bergie, I'm just scratchin' my nuts. It must be the heat that's makin' them itch."

A voice from across the aisle broke in. "Just toss 'em out the window and give 'em some night air. They're big enough to be out on their own, and you won't have to go with them."

"Look after your own nuts, Lyons."

"My name's not Lyons."

"Then shove it, ya Seaforth pansy."

As Danyluk got under his sheet, at least twenty *pansies* at the far end of the building raised their voices in anger. Although other non-kilted cadets agreed with Danyluk and voiced their opinions as well, the Scots would make a point of remembering the inference of a certain cadet at the southern end. Of course, at this moment, that cadet couldn't have cared less.

"Ha, that got 'em," the *animal* said, yawning. Soon, he was fast asleep, totally insensitive to the row he'd created that got louder by the minute.

Eventually, it would take the corporal to come out of his cubicle at the north end to quiet matters down. The Scots were mad, and when Scots get mad, all hell breaks loose.

Chapter 6

Ordinarily, teenagers believe the time of 0500 hours is the middle of the night. However, on this second day of training at the Vernon Army Cadet Trades Training Camp, BCR cadets forming the band found that 0500 hours is the start of a brand new day. To make certain they understood this new rule, they were pushed, shoved and pulled from their beds by Warrant Officer Second Class Genova as he made his rounds throughout the camp.

The sneakily grinning beady-eyed all-nose WO2 said the same thing to all the cadets he disturbed.

"You, you lazy good-for-nothing - get into your PT strip with pith helmet and report to the band equipment hut! You've got five minutes!"

Making his rounds, Genova also told brass instrument players to bring their bugles with them.

In B-25 all eyes were on Jackson. After all if anyone knew what was going on, Earl would.

Danyluk stood at an open window yawning and scratching his testicles. "Earl, what the hell's happening?"

Earl didn't know. This *movement* certainly wasn't posted on their bulletin board. He just shrugged. "Don't ask me - ask the living mutant proboscis."

Within five minutes, forty bewildered BCR cadets (the BCR musketeers' included) entered the band equipment hut looking for their instruments. Outside on the road a Cheshire cat smirk widened on the face of Genova standing there with the regimental band mace.

"Quickly now, quickly! Get those drums pulled up and get into formation. You buglers make sure you've got your crooks." (Attachment that allows buglers to attain another musical range).

Even though the picturesque serenity of the early Okanagan morning is so wonderfully novel, the forty shivering city boys weren't thinking about nature. Bickering saturated the ranks and grew louder. The sweet-smelling air hadn't yet been warmed by the new day's sun, and these cadets had just been bounced from their warm beds without any notice whatsoever.

"Sergeant Major, what's all this about?" a cadet sergeant named Geddes asked. He'd been yanked from his bunk in the D&M hut.

Genova's smirk remained strong as he eyed his group of *volunteers*. "We're going to make a name for ourselves, that's what it's all about! I have donated my time and your time to wake the camp on Mondays, Wednesdays, and Saturdays. This week, we'll perform today and Thursday! Any complaints?"

Whispered protests couldn't be heard, but Danyluk's, "You've got a son-of-a-bitchin' nerve, ya big prick," was louder than the others.

"What was that, Danyluk?"

Banks replied for Moose. He couldn't stomach Genova at the best of times and this early-morning action upset him greatly. He was so incensed he felt like grounding his drum and marching off.

81 – NEXT STOP, VERNON!

"Moose said, 'It was son-of-a-bitchin' kind of you to volunteer us. Why weren't we told about this, or even questioned whether or not we'd like to do this? We know we're playing on Saturday parades and whatever, but getting up at 0500? We don't get enough sleep as it is."

High blood pressure replaced the Cheshire cat smirk. No one spoke this way to Genova, especially one of the minions. Genova knew he had the majority of BCR cadet senior NCOs in his hands because he loaned them his car and bought them beer. Back at the Drill Hall he was always Mr. Nice-guy to the senior NCOs, and they in turn repaid him with false loyalty. False loyalty in the sense that they laughed behind his back, never to his face. Geddes and some of the other higher-ranking BCR cadets were not, however, impressed in any way, shape or form by this *man*. Nor were the junior NCOs.

Genova headed in the direction of Banks. "What did you say?"

Before he arrived at Wane's position, expressions on most faces indicated Banks had better not push his luck - but Wane wasn't finished.

"I don't know about these other guys, Sergeant Major, but the course I'm on is tough enough without this horse shit. I'm informing you now that I will ask to see my platoon commander and the Camp RSM."

Genova's friends grinned but remained quiet as a round of approval followed Wane's comments.

"Banks, you see me following this parade!"

"Sergeant Major, you can count on it!"

"And I'll be with him," added Douglas.

"And me," said East, finding the situation unbearable due to the lack of something to nibble on.

Moose entered the altercation. "Bet on it."

"Absolutely preposterous and unacceptable," mouthed Lyons with his eyes open, but not yet seeing.

"The odds of this happening with a normal-thinking WO2 would be about a hundred to one," voiced the *gambler*.

Now comments flew from all directions - these cadets were furious.

Genova knew he had a problem on his hands. He'd created a predicament that could have been solved with a little bit of solid man-management.

"Band atten ... tion! Sling drums! We're going to play, *Vernon*, followed by *Sergeants,* then *Slick As Hell,* and then *Coronation*! Band, by the centre, quick ... march!"

Over the next twenty-minutes, Sergeant Major Genova led the cadet band of the British Columbia Regiment (DCO) up and down the roads of the lower camp, as well as in between the various huts.

Thankful *recognition* of this generously offered melodious presentation became most evident. Middle fingers appeared from windows, followed by fists, arms, and indecent dialogue that would warm the heart of the meanest, toughest, gangster on the face of the earth. The half-asleep recipients of this articulate display of musical *benevolence* expressed their genuine appreciation by throwing oranges, apples, toilet rolls, washbasins, mops, brushes, and bars of soap and other objects of *fond*

Cordell Cross

recognition at the band. Yes, Genova was really making a name for himself and the BCR band.

Later, after handing in their instruments, three-quarters of the band waited to see Genova but he was nowhere to be found. Finally, a corporal locked the door and told them to get back to their huts.

Immediately upon their return to B-25, Douglas, Lyons, Wane, Moose, East, and Cunningham were tossed into the showers. Like all of the other huts in camp, the occupants of this barracks were now wide-awake thanks to the benevolence of the band.

Assisting the approximately fifty cadets who engineered the drenching were Bergie, Rothstein and Jackson. Evidently, the rule, one for all and all for one, is never considered at 0520 in the morning - especially this particular morning. The six band members really didn't appreciate this touch of kindness because shortly thereafter they were jogging with Sergeant Bentley.

Sour expressions were evident as signals jogged to the upper camp. Although the sergeant displayed his usual morning after the night before *smile*, Brice, Banks, Danyluk, Lyons, East and Cunningham found jogging in soaking wet clothes wasn't the best way to start their day.

As Moose sang and huffed and puffed, he continued trying to stretch the crotch of his shorts and as a result kept losing the step.

"Highdi, highdi, highdi, ho, in driver-mech the shit all flows!" the animal sang, before saying, "These PT shorts are so wet and tight my nuts are never gonna forgive me - they're red raw. Youse didn't have to help those idiots throw us in, Bergie; I'll remember that."

Singing away, Bergie wasn't the least bit concerned. *"If ya wanna double your trouble and run out of luck; just hang around with an IBT suck!* Oh quit your bitching, Moose. You and those goddamned cymbals got us out of bed at that shitty hour. Don't you think we know you banged those garbage lids louder when you passed our windows? I saw the smile on your face."

"Bullshit youse did! I didn't smile. Wane, Doug, did youse hear that? He said I smiled when we passed his window. That wasn't a smile, Bergie. I caught my nose in between my instruments. I was half-asleep, you pongo! Look, I've got the cut on my nose to prove it."

Cunningham took two seconds out from trying to bet a North Saskatchewan Regiment cadet it was approximately 2200 paces back to the barracks - give or take twenty paces.

"If you're not catchin' your wang in those things, you're always catchin' your nose. Your wang's full of cuts too, ain't it?"

Frustration filled Moose's face. "Yeah, but not from getting it caught in my instruments. Them's war wounds."

East was in front of the *wounded one* and twice he'd been kicked because Danyluk lost the step. "Jeez, Moose pick up the step. Now look what you've made me do. I've dropped my orange and banana! Besides, cymbals ain't instruments, they are apparatuses. The only instruments you've got are your nuts and when you bang *them* together, they're even louder."

"Oh shove it in your ear, East."

Still fuming over the Genova episode, Wane said, "Doug, I don't give a damn if they send me home. That creep just sickens me. When he pulled me out of bed he grabbed me by my left foot and just yanked. I landed on my ass and I'm still sore."

Cunningham snickered. "Don't tell Genova that - he'll buy a new bottle of Vicks. At least he had the decency to pull my mattress with me on it."

"He didn't get me on the floor," said Danyluk. "I held on to the bunk. My bedding was on the deck, but not me."

After Rothstein returned the *finger* sign to a passing company, he said, "You've got an advantage, Moose. You probably had your wang wrapped around the springs."

"I'll Vicks him," Wane replied. "I'd like to buy two bottles and shove one up each one of his nostrils."

"You mean up his backside, don't you?" Lyons asked, puffing and trying to catch his breath.

"When are we going to see Lieutenant Preston?" Douglas asked.

"During the pop break. Are you coming with me?"

"Natch. I'm with ya a thousand percent."

By the time the company was fallen out, all six had decided they were going to see the lieutenant, and if necessary, RSM Gardiner. In addition, because their first period was once again signal office duties, they knew the location of Lieutenant Preston.

For some reason breakfast tasted better this particular morning, and the parade and barracks inspection came off well. Because the boys had been up so early, there could be no excuses for not brushing and mopping under and around their bed-spaces, or not having their bunks and barrack boxes lined up. A few names were taken due to dirty brass, or traces of food on shirts and pants, but overall B-25 and its occupants looked sharp.

Following the first period, Banks talked to Sergeant Bentley and requested a meeting with Lieutenant Preston. Bentley asked why at first, but didn't push for answers when Genova's name was mentioned. He arranged the gathering in the lecture room just after the pop truck arrived so the cadets could have their pop. Also, when Lieutenant Preston asked the boys if the sergeant could remain, they agreed.

Wane was the spokesman throughout, however the five others also threw in their opinions. During their talk, for some *strange* reason RSM Gardiner entered the room and saluted Lieutenant Preston. Unknown to the cadets, Sergeant Bentley had asked a corporal to see if the RSM was busy. Fortunately, the RSM was on one of his many walks and just *happened* to be in the area. Regimental Sergeant Majors' definitely have more extrasensory perception than sergeants do, and this particular RSM appeared to know the gist of the problem instantly.

Gardiner possessed the competence, confidence, knowledge and wisdom of a man's man. Just the way he looked, moved, and talked demanded regard and respect. Over six feet tall without an ounce of fat, clear glistening eyes that could pierce the deepest minds missed nothing as he scrutinized his audience. His cleanly shaved weathered skin indicated a sportsmanlike presence that had climbed the toughest mountains, sailed the mightiest seas and still couldn't find a challenge to upset his nerves of steel. Every part of his razor-pressed uniform fitted him perfectly. Not one hair was out of place in his giant moustache, and his boots and brass shone like mirrors.

"Would you mind if I handled this, sir?" the RSM asked Preston. "I've heard some scuttlebutt from cadets in other companies as well."

Lieutenants don't usually stand in the way of regimental sergeant majors and Lieutenant Preston was no exception. He thought that perhaps it would be better if the RSM sorted matters out. "Not at all, Mr. Gardiner. I'm due at a meeting with the OC anyway. Thank you."

Gardiner took off his cap, placed his giant drill cane on a table and asked the cadets to sit down. It instantly became quite obvious to the six that the immortal being in front of them was more aware of the situation than they thought.

"When one of my sergeant majors asks you to get out of bed at 0500 hours, for any reason, you will get out of bed. Is that clear? Well, is it?"

"Yes, sir," was the reply, after a few "buts" were ignored.

"I don't want to hear any ifs, ands, and buts. If ifs, ands and buts were candy and nuts, you people would be fat as hell. So let me make this perfectly clear. When you are given a proper order, you will obey it to the best of your ability. The time of 0500 hours isn't early, and Sergeant Major Genova is older than you people are. If he can do it, so can you. You had a goddamned nerve talking to him the way you did. If he had charged you, you'd be in cells right this minute, and I'd ask that the keys be thrown away."

A smile, perhaps a gas pain appeared below the immense moustache. "Now, I have spoken with Sergeant Major Genova, and he is willing to forget this incident. I think his idea of the band playing early in the morning is an excellent idea. So excellent that..."

Sighs and expressions of exasperation faced the RSM as he paused for a moment.

"...I thought it might be good for the band, because I told him that I wasn't at all happy with the sound. It would appear to me that much practice is required; therefore if he wishes to parade the band at 0500 on any given morning, then an hour-and-a-half of band practice must take place up at Area 10 starting at 0330, with him leading, of course. For some reason he didn't quite like that idea."

Grins appeared on six faces and that of Sergeant Bentley.

"So, we reached a happy medium. Without practice, this band will march through the camp at 0545 hours on Friday mornings only."

Gardiner's gas pains actually matched the expressions on the faces in front of him. That is until he spotted Danyluk.

"My God, it's you - the nudist. I see you've returned this year? Is your partner here as well?"

Moose sat to attention. "Bergie? Yes, sir, he sure is, sir. He's havin' a prune break right now. I likes prunes too."

Gardiner shook his head and sneered. "What? Er, good, that's good. Well, I certainly hope you've straightened out your act. What's this about prunes?"

Moose winked and gave the RSM the thumbs up sign after saying, "We're with youse on those round little *fruities*, sir. As for our act, we have changed our wicked ways, sir. Er, we hate building our bridges. I was gonna buy an Austin, but I got this here better deal on a Packard hearse. Also, my dames are gonna send me more prunes, sir. I'll send you some."

With a reflective look on his face, the RSM replaced his cap, picked up his cane and marched out.

"The American navy is good for broads, er sisters," Danyluk voiced as *the man* left the building. "She should be a very happy dame, er woman."

When he was away from the hut, Gardiner mumbled, "Prunes? That poor empty-headed son-of-a-bitch. How the Seaforths or the Irish put up with him I'll never know. And what's with this Austins, Packards, American navy, and sisters bit? What's he talking about … nursing sisters? Also, building bridges? That man *needs* a goddamned hearse. Probably got that way from eating all those prunes. And he's going to send me some? Lord, give me strength."

"Words like mint, great, neat, superb, damn fine man, absolutely ace," were offered by the six after Gardiner left. Shaking hands, they knew the RSM had saved the day. With tact, Genova had been put in his place.

The rest of the morning went like clockwork as the cadets in Platoons 21 and 22 practised Morse code. Although this was only day two, most of them had already learned the basics, and practice was all that was required to send and receive properly.

The timetable after lunch was excellent for signals cadets. As fate would have it, the BCR musketeers' early-morning *march* with Genova hadn't gone unrewarded because the timetable allowed two rest periods followed by a one-hour baseball game. This spare time allowed them to catch up on their kit, have a snooze, practice Morse or do whatever they wanted. Even though the barracks was warm, the old hut kept the sun's searing heat to a minimum as most cadets pressed their freshly washed garments.

Lyons' habit of reading and ironing at the same time caused him to burn a hole through the back of one of his three shirts. Tossing his UFO book aside, he shouted, "Shit, I didn't think the iron was that hot. I've got to teach Zelda to do these female tasks."

"Barefoot, pregnant and in the kitchen, eh Lyons?" offered Cunningham.

"Absolutely my friend. We are men of the world and as such we shouldn't be expected to iron."

"Not to worry," said Bergie, grabbing the garment and exiting to visit the next hut. Within minutes, he was back with a *normal* shirt approximately the same size.

A smiling and ecstatic Lyons was overwhelmed. Having been in D&M the year before, he really hadn't heard of Bergie's genius for problem solving and decision-making.

"Hey, that was extraordinarily nice of you, Bergie. What can I do for you in return?"

Cordell Cross

Moose grinned. He knew Bergie very well. Bergie hated shining boots, and at this moment, Bergie's boots were tossed at Lyons. With a straight face, Bergie replied, "Nothing really; just put a great shine on these."

Lyons' face changed but he accepted the task as he continued to iron and read his book.

"Hey chaps, listen to this. On June 24th, 1947, a clear and sunny day, American civilian pilot Kenneth Arnold was flying over Mount Rainier in Washington State, when he saw in the distance a formation of nine glistening objects. At first, he thought they were fighter planes, but as they darted towards him and skimmed the mountaintops at incredible speed, Arnold realized that they were 'Like nothing I ever seen before'. He watched them move erratically across the horizon and estimated their speed at 1300 miles an hour. When he landed, he sought words to describe the mystery objects and came up with the phrase, 'Like saucers skimming over water'. Thus the term *flying saucers* was born."

"What's that smell?" asked Rothstein.

Reaching for the fire extinguisher, Jackson said, "It must be the afterburners of the flying saucers."

A mortified and embarrassed Lyons cowered as he separated his iron from his newly *acquired* shirt and stared through the large 'iron-sized' hole.

"Shit, I've done it again."

Bergie grabbed the shirt. "Not to worry, I'll..."

Lyons grabbed it back and began walking through B-25 to the next hut. "Er, that's OK, Bergie. Thanks anyway."

Shortly the *learned one* arrived back with another clean but un-ironed shirt.

"Where'd you get that one?" Bergie asked.

"Off the line in the other hut's drying room. I left mine and hung it in a way that the hole won't show."

Bergie laughed. "That's where I left your last one. Some poor bastard's gonna get two air-conditioned shirts. I wonder where they'll end up tonight."

"Probably back here," Douglas said, kicking Wane's springs and sending his bunkmate one foot into the air. "Y'know I think there are such things as flying saucers."

Letting his iron cool, Lyons picked up one of Bergie's boots and started shining it as he continued with his book. "Sure there are, Doug. There have been too many sightings. Listen to this. In 1948, hundreds see a huge white object in the sky over Madisonville, Kentucky. Three P-51 Mustangs are sent up to investigate. One of the pilots gives chase as the object speeds away. The wreckage of his plane is found later that day. This book is loaded with incidents. Here's another one. Earlier this year, the crew and passengers of a Boeing Stratocruiser flying from New York to London watched a formation of seven craft travelling alongside the airliner for several minutes. The UFOs appeared to be six flying saucers and a larger mother ship."

Lyons put the book down while shining one of Bergie's boots. "I'll betcha they come from some black hole in space."

Cordell Cross

Moose stripped off and headed for the showers. "What the hell are youse talkin' about, Lyons? Black holes in space? The only black hole I've ever seen is when I was…"

"Oh spare us the description," Cunningham said, trying a new trick of tossing a coin that would always land heads all the time. "There are other black holes besides your kind. They're called implosive stars or something like that. They ain't discovered one yet, but they think they're there."

"I was talkin' about digging for moles," Moose shot back. "Nothing else ya creep. Keep your mind out of the gutter."

Bergie stripped off also. "Hang on, Moose - I'll join ya."

Scratching his testicles, Moose moved his naked body over to Cunningham's bunk. "They ain't discovered a black hole because there ain't any. When I say that Professor Moose *has* dis…"

"That man, stand where you are! Don't you know better than to expose your private parts to people on the highway? Stand where you are, I say!"

Moose had no time to run. He just cringed and came to attention as RSM Gardiner entered the hut from the centre doors.

"Blast, it's you again. I thought you told me you people had cleaned up your act from last year?"

"I was just heading to the showers, Sergeant Major, sir!"

"No you weren't! You were standing in front of that open window scratching and exposing yourself! Admit it, man!"

The whole side of the hut was now aware of Danyluk's difficulties, and laughter rang out from the *fags in rags* at the north end.

"Keep quiet, you people! Listen, if I see you one more time publicly displaying that prune chewing object of yours, heads will roll, and in your case two of them. Do I make myself clear?"

"Yes, sir."

"I can't hear you!"

"Yes, sir!"

The RSM glanced around. "Where's your partner. I know damned well he's involved also. What's his name?"

"Bergie, sir."

"Perky, get out here!"

Also totally naked and embarrassed, Bergie slithered out of the corporal's cubicle and stood rigidly to attention. "I'm, er, just doing a bit of ironing in here, sir."

"Sure you are. You always iron in the nude! What the hell is this world coming to? Get to the showers with your brain-dead friend!"

Bergie and Danyluk hustled to the showers as Gardiner marched out grumbling to himself.

"Christ, it's a wonder he can wear pants with that weapon of his. What is happening to this younger generation? A young woman is going to faint driving by here and then drive off the road, and then sue the government. I'm going to ask the medical officer if he can stitch that thing around the lad's waist. And as for Perky, or whatever the hell his name is, I'll..."

With the RSM gone, the balance of the musketeers and some others from the southern end of the hut decided to join Bergie and Moose. Loud chuckles erupted in the shower-room when Banks asked Danyluk if he'd gotten into the habit of pushing prunes up his foreskin.

"So that's where you're hiding them?" Rothstein said. Jeez, you could hide a couple of pounds in there, Moose."

"What the hell *is* with the prunes, Moose?" Douglas asked. "I've never seen you with any."

Not waiting for a reply, East said, "Yeah, what's with you? Have ya got a problem crapping? I had that once and prunes sure cured it."

"He's hiding them because he doesn't want us to know he's got the bung," said Cunningham. "Bergie, I'm glad you're his bunkmate. Becoming unplugged is a guessing game. It can happen anywhere. Even in bed."

Moose released the shower nozzle. "Youse all knows I don't eat goddamned prunes. I was told the RSM eats 'em mornin' noon and night. By sayin' I ate them, I thought I could get into his good books."

"Who told you he ate them?" Lyons asked.

"Two of those Seaforth creeps in the mess hall."

"Hey maybe Gardiner's got the bung," Rothstein quipped. "I counted sixteen gas pains when he was talking to us. One was a doozer."

In the next two minutes the shower room became packed. At least sixteen cadets from the northern end of the west wing squeezed in under the nozzles and started talking about life in the highlands.

Eyewinks and head motion became the order of the day. Leaving their towels on the benches in the shower room, all the musketeers and their friends left the room and stood in the sink area. All except one - East. The *beast* had been motioned to clear the *haggis-stuffers* out, and he did it with pride. This called for a bowel windstorm that could asphyxiate at 300 feet. Without a smile as he whistled *Three Blind Mice*, East unleashed a silent blast that shook the windows. Although he had the knack of a buttocks ventriloquist, he didn't disguise the source this time. Instead, he just kept showering singing the song to himself and eating pieces of an orange he'd stored on the window-ledge. It only took three seconds for the room to empty, and East knew he'd created a new camp record.

"Oh my God! That's living hell," screamed an *escapee* with his towel over his nose.

"Am I still alive; will my lungs heal up?" said another with his nose cupped in his hands.

Other fleeting comments followed, such as, "I can't see! I've been blinded!"

"Give me Hiroshima anytime!"

"Am I alive? For a moment I thought I'd died and my head had been pushed up my asshole!"

"The rotten prick! I'll betcha that's the first time he's farted in years. He's been saving it up, the swine!"

"What regiment does that living degenerate serve in? That's if he is in fact alive!"

"Phew! He says he's in the Canadian Scottish! Those poor bastards!"

"They're all the same in that regiment."

With his newfound *friends* gone, East opened the window and in two minutes the musketeers came back and there was still plenty of hot water.

Wane lathered his body as usual. "Good work, Jack. We're proud of ya, my son. A new record."

East's stuck his chest out. "I knew it was, but I could have given them the BCR Bomb."

Douglas couldn't stop laughing. "We'd be picking them up off the floor if you gave them that one, Jack. The girl-guide-grenade was enough, thank you."

When the guys from the southern end arrived back at their bunks, the north-end *mob* still held towels over their noses.

"That stench will last in their schnozzles for hours," Moose said.

"And so it should," offered Bergie. "Sheep do shit in the highlands you know? Probably in the lowlands as well. It ain't all blossoms and heather."

That afternoon two signals platoons beat two driver mech platoons in a short baseball game that was won from the opening pitch. The signals types had the edge because the driver mechanics cadets had been up to their eyeballs in grease and oil all day. They were tired and it showed.

Moose had Alma on his mind when he entered B-25 to wash up.

"Do youse guys know we can go downtown any night we want, just as long as we're back by 2130? Let's phone the dames and meet 'em at Polson Park."

A brief discussion followed and it was reluctantly decided that they had too much studying to do. Of all people, it was East who said, "If we wanna pass this Saturday's test, we'd better start cramming."

At supper, *Detective* Bergie was at his best. Instead of sitting at their usual table, he steered the musketeers to a table next to the Scottish cadets who had given Moose the *prunes*.

Bergie sat next to Moose looking right at the culprits who were probably busy discussing the number of hairs in a sporran. (Author's note: Hey, isn't that what all Scots discuss?)

"Don't point your finger, Moose. Just whisper and tell me which one told you the RSM liked prunes."

"The middle one on the far side of the table," Danyluk murmured. "His nametag says MacKay."

All faces at the musketeers' table had to grin looking at Bergie's facial cast. To someone who didn't know him, the investigator just appeared to be stroking his chin. But it went much deeper than that. Bergie was making plans for Cadet MacKay of the 72nd Seaforth Highlanders' of Canada Cadet Corps.

This time when the screen door slammed shut and nine cadets gathered in a huddle to let Bergie explain his scheme, rippled exhilarated chuckles turned into hilarious waves of laughter.

That evening as usual, B-25 took on the look of the aftermath of a ticker-tape parade in New York City. Comics, toilet rolls, newspapers, notebooks, training manuals and pieces of Part 1 and Part 2 orders littered the floors. The paper wasn't the end of it, just the start, because it was united with mops, brooms, brushes, pails, Silvo, Brasso, shoe-polish with lids full of water, shoe-rags, boots, webbelts, washing hung out of windows, spare mattresses, tables, barrack boxes and benches covered with blankets and irons. In short, whatever else approximately 150 boys can spread.

Amidst the mess, radios shrieked, Morse code keys buzzed, true-life experiences were laid open, battle-honours discussed, silent homesick tears rolled - as did dice, letters were read, *comments* brought about chases and unrestrained wrestling, towels were flicked and new-found friendships became bonded.

Although corporals surfaced periodically, officers and senior non-commissioned officers allowed the cadets their home-away-from-home liberty by only appearing for a few minutes. While strict interior economy was demanded during training hours, in the evenings and after 1200 hours on Saturdays until Monday mornings, B-25 and similar huts were also the cadets' rumpus rooms.

Shining a boot, Earl strolled over to Bergie's bunk, saying, "After morning parade tomorrow, our two platoons are out in Area 10 line-laying. The dress is KD longs, shirts, puttees, weights, pith helmets, webbelts and water canteens. We're at it all day. Pass it along."

"Do we bring our mess tins and utensils?" Bergie asked.

"No, we're bring brought in for meals."

Wane shared Douglas' bunk. The side-by-side duo had finished studying by asking each other questions on subjects they had taken that day.

Wane kicked his own springs. "Before I left for camp, that Marigold dame phoned me. She's really getting serious."

"How do you know?" Douglas asked.

"Do you remember the other day when I told ya I was late doing my route?"

"Yeah."

"I didn't tell ya why I was late. She asked me to join her at the Guardian Angel church. That Catholic church on Nicola Street?"

"You went to church with her?"

"I didn't go inside, you pongo. I waited outside for about fifteen minutes. When she came out, she led me to the bushes at the back."

Douglas sat up. "You lucky creep. You didn't tell me about that. The last time you talked about her you said she was going to be a nun. Go on."

"I think she still is. She's tryin' to make up for the lost time she'll have. What more can I say? It's a wonder I survived. She's one sexy dame."

"I suppose you got her panties? Jeez, you must have one hell of a collection?"

Wane now sat up next to his friend. "What panties? She don't wear any. She don't wear a bra either."

Douglas asked, "You mean she *never* wears 'em?"

"Never. I don't think she has any. They're a poor family, you know? I was gonna buy her a few pairs but that's like taking the icing off a cake."

Brice laughed and gave Wane a mock punch. "It's more like putting it back on. So what happened?"

"What didn't happen? It took me an hour to get the lipstick off my face. Jesus, she got down to business in hurry, and her hands were sweaty."

"Sweaty hands? Don't tell Moose about this. He'd grab East's National Geographic and head to the jon. He loves sweaty dames. Well?"

Bashful grins met. "Well, what?"

"Well, er, did ya ... er, did you get it on?"

Wane's grin widened and his face turned a shade of pink as he lowered his voice. "Do you remember what happened to you when you spent the night at that Jenny dame's house when her parents were away?"

Both faces turned the same colour midst the chuckles.

"You've gotta be joking? The same thing happened to you?"

"You bet, Doug. Hell, I'm not joking. I was tryin' to take her off her non-existent panties. I was ready, but lookin' at my watch told me it was time to deliver papers. Boy was she pissed off. It wouldn't have happened anyway; I was too nervous."

"Did ya have a rubber?"

"Sure, but the thing was in my wallet. From now on, I'm not going to keep it in my wallet. I'll get a container and carry it around my neck. Yeah, that's what I'll do."

The rest of the Musketeers were too immersed in their own activities to notice Brice and Banks laughing their heads off while heading to the showers.

After lights out, the usual liveliness and chatter took place.

As Rothstein remade his frenched bed, Cunningham appeared from the drying room with a fistful of bills. "Don't look at me Rothie, I didn't do it."

"But you know who did, you creep."

"Yeah, but if I hadda told you, he wouldn't have coughed up for the stuke game."

Jackson gave East a blast because cracker crumbs were everywhere. He even had to take his sheets off and shake them.

Lyons prattled on about flying saucers to his newfound chess friend, and Moose read a letter by flashlight under his bedclothes.

"Hey Bergie," Moose said, popping his head out. "One of my older dames, Doris, musta been to Washington."

Although Bergie couldn't care less, he mumbled. "That's nice ... how did she like it?"

"Well she really didn't say. She just mentions that she had a D and C."

Wane leaned over and whispered. "It won't happen the next time, I'll tell ya. I'm gonna train to get it done like a man."

"Same here," Douglas said.

"Er, Doug. Have you got the hots for that Jenny broad?"

"No. I haven't seen her since. Why?"

Wane lowered his voice. "Because I got *her* panties."

"You what?

A voice shot out over the corporal's cubicle. "Keep it quiet out there!"

Douglas jumped out of bed. The thought of his best friend collecting Jenny's panties was a bit much. "You louse! When did this happen?"

"When you came up here to visit Diane, Marigold went in the hospital for a nose job. Well, er, Jenny was visiting so I took her home. Nothing else happened; I just got her panties. That's all."

Douglas got back into bed mumbling, "My friend? My best pal?"

Wane leaned over again. "Yeah, ain't life great?"

"How many pairs *have* you got in your collection?"

"At last count, sixteen. Goodnight, Doug."

"Ya lucky creep. G'night. I hope you don't start wearing them."

"No fear of that. They simply go in my collector's case so I can tell my future kids about the accomplishments of their dad."

"Just your sons, I hope?"

"Natch. If I have any girls I ain't gonna tell them. I'll be too busy making chastity belts."

Chapter 7

On day three, Major Hansford took his time inspecting all platoons of Signals Company. He was looking for the small things that hadn't been taken care of, such as haircuts, unshined insteps, traces of Brasso or Silvo on webbelts, and unscrubed pith helmets.

Considering his thoroughness, the cadets fared pretty well; they should have because they were out running fifteen minutes sooner. All platoon sergeants knew the OC would be eagle-eyed, consequently both barracks and personal kit were really gone over before Hansford arrived with his entourage to inspect his *troops*.

As the OC scrutinized 21 Platoon, an anxiety-ridden 'side of the mouth' conversation took place in the centre rank of 22 Platoon. It started when one of the corporals behind the rear rank told Cadet MacKay in the centre rank to stop fidgeting.

"MacKay, leave your balls and face alone!"

MacKay did stop, however, not for long because a sticky liquid originating from underneath his pith-helmet slowly trickled over his face, into his ears, down his chin, and down the front and back of his neck. The fluid really clung to his eyebrows and eyelids.

"I can't see," he sputtered to his friend Neish who took a quick glance and started chuckling. "What is it?"

"How the hell do I know what it is, you idiot. Jeez, it's seeped all the way down to my ass and my crotch. Damn, it's itchy."

The corporal got very serious, and shouted, "MacKay, quit moving around!"

"You should change your hair tonic," Neish murmured. "How much did you use ... a ton?"

MacKay quickly scratched his buttocks, crotch, face, ears, and the back of his neck again. Now even his hands were covered with the mysterious emollient.

"I don't use hair tonic. Oh my God, this is living hell."

"Then quit sweating - everything's cool."

"It's not sweat, you idiot. I wish it was sweat, but there's no end to it. Neish, what should I do?"

"MacKay, I won't tell you again! What have you got, St. Vitus's dance?"

Neish thought quickly. "Faint."

"What?"

"Pass out, otherwise you're gonna be in deep shit."

The forward fall of MacKay appeared real. Had the cadet not been wearing KD longs, he would have scraped both his knees.

In seconds, two corporals hauled the boy to his bunk.

"Andy, look at the sweat on this kid. He probably has no water left in his body. What should we do?"

The Corporal thought for a moment. It's sunstroke, Paddy; I've seen it before. I'll strip him off and hold him under a cold shower. You rush and get the ambulance."

MacKay's heart skipped a beat when he heard the words, "cold shower." He couldn't open his eyes, but he muttered, "I'm all right, Corporal. Just let me rest. It runs ... in the family."

"Rest my ass, man ... you're sick as hell. Give me a hand to get your clothes off."

When the cold water hit MacKay's body, the naked cadet sprung back to life and nearly had a heart attack. Paddy made certain the boy stayed under and the downpour got colder by the second. It took ten minutes for the ambulance to arrive, and had it been longer, the Scot would have had pneumonia, or hypothermia.

East leaned over to Jackson and cupped the cadet's ear. "Ain't it amazing what a blob of Vaseline can do when it's stuck inside the top of a pith-helmet?"

Jackson yearned to laugh. "Yeah, especially when the sun's rays get to the helmet."

"Just look at the poor pongo," Bergie offered, as a shivering MacKay, wrapped in a blanket was carried out in a stretcher. The only smiles in 21 Platoon were on musketeer faces. They were standing easy because the OC had moved on to inspect 22 Platoon.

Danyluk tried to act serious. It was difficult but he didn't want other Scots to notice his joviality. "Like I've always said, those cold asses can't take it. They ain't got the stengma."

Rothstein had to control himself. This whole scene was hilarious. "It's *stamina*, Moose."

"Whatever."

As a smirking Genova strolled over to the stretcher, Banks muttered, "Quick, get the Vicks."

Laughter broke out when Bergie snickered under his breath and whispered, "Oh there's no doubt about that. MacKay will get the Vicks all right. Genova will make certain he does."

"Cunningham took a small black book out his pocket and attempted to work out probabilities. I'm not giving odds on that action. It's almost a done deal."

"Bergie, without a doubt, youse is a genius," the *animal* offered, gawking in awe at his buddy.

"Nah, Moose. It's just survival of the fittest. Right now, we're more fit than him."

What little wind there is in Vernon seems to elude Area 10 the highest point in the upper camp other than the range.

Named during the war, the hilly piece of ground consists of burnt grass, dust, burrs, jagged rocks, snakes and pieces of old mortar shells. The odd ancient orchard trees can provide some shade, but temperatures in the high 90s or over a hundred are the norm.

For three periods, 21 and 22 Platoons stuck six-foot poles into the ground at twenty-yard intervals. When that was done, cadets threaded single strand wire through loops at the top of other six-foot poles before attaching (screwing) them to the poles in the ground - making the poles twelve feet high.

Wire soon encircled its way around obstacles throughout Area 10. Ends of the conductor were attached to UCL 10-line switchboards and Tele 'L' telephone sets that contained voice and Morse apparatuses allowing message centres to pass on supposed vital information and reports. Following that, Nineteen Set remote training began. A Nineteen Set was installed on the highest section of ground with cables attached to remote units hundreds of yards away. This system permitted single and multi-access to a lone Nineteen Set placed in a signal-receptive area at the lower camp.

Although the cadets had only limited knowledge of the Nineteen Set and Morse code, they knew that as days progressed, this jigsaw puzzle course called *signals* would sort itself out.

A pop truck didn't appear that morning and the water from their old British-style canteen bottles tasted stale as the cadets viewed the wonderful blue picture postcard vista of Okanagan Lake. The cattle on the far-side hills appeared like dots on the dusty, burnt, brown landscape.

Walking away from the others, Douglas took of his pith helmet and wiped the perspiration from his forehead. Knowing Kin Beach was off to the right, he mumbled, "It seems so close but it's miles away. What I wouldn't give to be there right now. This is so beautiful I wonder why every person on the earth isn't here."

Soon, his friends joined him but didn't say anything. They understood Douglas' attraction just by the look on his face. He'd explained it to them all before. In his opinion, this was God's domain - so wonderful and peaceful that the Almighty must always be close at hand. He could feel His presence in the air, the sky, lakes, trees, and the awe-inspiring dusty burnt hills. The others also knew when Douglas was like this he had included himself in the ultimate perfectly completed canvass.

About five minutes later after Earl took a long swig, his face indicated the water tasted like industrial waste. "Jeez this water's horrible. By the way, we're on the parade square tomorrow morning and we've got a swim parade tomorrow afternoon. Guess who is in charge of swimming?"

Bergie knew. "Genova?"

"Exactly right," Earl replied, replacing the cork on his bottle. "None other than the prick himself."

After Wane unbuttoned his shirt, what little swirling dusty air there was instantly dried on his chest. "Maybe he'll be too busy spreading the Vicks on MacKay. I pity that poor sheep shit and heather type."

"Don't youse dare pity that creep," said Moose. "Have you forgotten the prunes? The pongo set me up."

A grumbling Lyons appeared after losing two dollars to Cunningham. Looking at the lake below, he said, "Do you chaps know that the first reported sighting of the Loch Nest Monster took place in 565 AD. I'll betcha the Ogopogo (supposed monster of Okanagan Lake) is exactly the same as *Nessie*. After all, everything is the same. Glaciers gouged out these hills and when they receded, the cracks or lakes filled with water."

"What's Ogopogo supposed to look like?" asked Rothstein. "Like a dragon?"

Cordell Cross

Lyons enjoyed imparting his *superior* knowledge. "I read that it's more than 50 feet long with a twelve foot girth. Its head is snail-like and very small compared to its body, and its neck of 4 to 7 feet long is as thick as an elephant's trunk. I think the book said its tail is rather flat and blunt at the end, and it has two small flippers at the front and two large ones at the back."

Wiping his forehead, the *gambler* asked, "What colour is it?"

"Lyons gave Cunningham a dirty look. " I can assure you it's not the colour of money. It's snail like - grey, silver and black."

"Er, super. Wanna try and get your two bucks back? Anyone else, er…"

Lyons and the rest ignored the *gambler*.

"Wow, suppose it surfaces while we're swimming at Kal Beach," East said, chomping on an apple and quite concerned about the danger.

"Then we'll feed Genova to it," Bergie replied.

Lyons chuckled. "He'd survive because the creature's gentle. If there's more than one, they're supposed to be shy retiring and harmless animals who very rarely ever visit the surface. Like Scotland, there's no doubt about underwater passages between all these lakes. The creatures probably make their rounds."

"All right let's get back here! Pop break's over," a sergeant bellowed.

In seconds, the cadets of signals practised their trade again.

After being trucked to the lower camp for lunch and to fill their water bottles, the same two platoons of Signals Company then went back to laying line in the afternoon. At that time, they were taught 'earth returns.' A single wire only carries a one way conversation, but by sticking steel spikes into the ground at each of a sending and receiving station and attaching wires from the spikes to the sets, the earth acted as a wire. In most cases, the result was much clearer than its uncoiled electrical conductive counterpart. Certainly, two wires could have been sprung on the poles, but it wasn't necessary considering the conductivity of the earth.

At 1630 after being trucked back to camp, the dirty and tired cadets were ready for the shade and hue-and-cry *serenity* of B-25.

It didn't take long for the musketeers to hit the showers with other members of 21 Platoon. Strangers already in the room left quickly when East entered and this suited the group just fine. In spite of the fact that Douglas told enquiring faces there was plenty of hot water, other cadets with towels wrapped around their waists thought twice about setting foot in the shower room.

"Er, thanks anyway. We'll, er, wait."

Outside in the sink area, expressions were heard, such as: "Why am I waiting? Because that Canadian Scottish asshole is in there."

"Don't go in yet, Bill. The living fart is showering. You know what that CScotR weirdo can do?"

"Don't go in without a gas-mask, Gary. Shit-guts is in there eating an apple."

"Tom, hold it, hold it! If you go in there, you may never come out."

"If you want to smell like an outhouse all night, enter at your own risk."

After East casually dried his body and strolled out, the stampede to enter was on. It was also on again to exit when the *beast* sauntered back in to pick up his half-finished apple.

At supper, MacKay became the point of conversation because the Scot still hadn't returned from the MIR.

"Hey, maybe he *was* sick and didn't know it," offered Jackson, attempting to cut a piece of *mystery* meat sliding around on his plate. "Maybe we did him a favour."

"Nah, they're just thorough in the MIR, that's all," Bergie replied. "He'll be back after about sixty needles and a case of Castor Oil. Why I'll betcha Genova's up there right now telling MacKay how he's gonna be looked after."

Jackson finally cut through a piece of *flesh* he had been working on. "What a bloody shame. The poor thing."

Bergie stopped trying to chew and gave Jackson a blunt glance. "Oh quit being a bleeding heart."

Earl wondered what Bergie was getting at. "I'm not talking about MacKay, Bergie, I'm talking about the meat we're eating. This poor thing must have been a hundred years old. They should have let it finish its years."

Two seconds later a pale looking drawn out Scot entered the mess hall with his friends. MacKay didn't say too much and when he sat down at a table next to the Musketeers, he appeared to grimace.

"What's the matter?" asked Neish. "How can your ass be sore?"

"How can it be sore? How can it be sore? Is that what you're asking? Your ass would be sore if you were given the number of enemas I've had today!"

The Scot then realized he'd better lower his voice. "Jeez, I'd already had fifty dumps and the orderlies were still stuffing my ass. Also, they shoved four needles into it."

Feeling guilty, Neish responded, "Wow, we didn't know you were that bad off."

The Scot liked the sympathy. "Aw, that's okay. Y'know, our Company Sergeant Major's not a bad guy. He visited me four times and brought some comics. Although he's a BCR, he looks after his men. That's what I call man-management."

Banks chuckled, whispering, "You can bet that's *not* what it's called." Dying to laugh, he added, "He'll look after you all right."

"Did you know you were that sick?" asked a buddy.

"I wasn't sick, you pongo! Someone stuck Vaseline in the top of my pith helmet. If I find the creep, I'll..."

The same *friend* asked, "Vaseline? Ain't that the stuff you smear on your body at the beach when there's dames around? Who do you think did it?"

MacKay wasn't in the mood for jokes. With mystery meat on the end of his fork, he pointed it at his bunkmate. "I've thought about that and I've arrived at the only conclusion. It's those two Royal Winnipeg Rifles types that sleep next to us. D'ya remember the first day I gave one a blast for touching my radio?"

"Yeah."

"Well? You saw the look on his face when he told me to, 'Go stuff a sheep.' Those Royal Winnipeg Rifles types are crude."

MacKay's bunkmate now felt compassionate. "Those pongoes are gonna get it. Have you got a plan?"

"You bet I have and it improved with every needle. Come closer and listen to this."

Cordell Cross

When six Scottish cadets get their heads together and whisper, retribution is guaranteed - really guaranteed.

Smiles filled the Musketeers' faces before Earl changed the subject. "There's a movie at B-3 tonight. It's called *Infantry Attack*. Anyone going?"

"If it was called *Armoured Attack*, I'd go, but we've got some studying to do," Wane said, glancing at Douglas who nodded.

East had heard them as he sat down with another plateful of *mystery* meat. "I'll go with whoever wants to go. Say, this meat is great scoff. I'm just not sure if it's beef, lamb, duck, goose, chicken, pig, veal, mutton, or venison."

"It's probably old horse," Wane quipped.

Over the next five minutes, it was concluded Rothstein, East, Jackson, Danyluk, and Lyons would go to the movie. Bergie, Banks, Cunningham, and Brice had decided they would study together in a lecture room.

Like B-25, most huts in the camp were quiet that night because half the cadets were in B-3. Before going to the movie or studying, all kit was done and Cunningham actually got to use the phone in the cadet canteen. He managed to pass the word on to the girls that they would all meet in Polson Park after lunch on Saturday.

The cool and quiet of the lecture room helped the boys as Douglas and Wane quickly got down to business, and shot questions back and forth.

"What's the purpose of the *flick* mechanism?" Douglas asked, referring to the Nineteen Set.

"To quickly change to another designated frequency," replied Wane.

"Good. How many avenues of communication does the Nineteen Set have?"

Wane thought for a moment. "Four. The 'A' set, 'B' set, 'IC' set and Morse. Say, wouldn't it be five? What about the remote system? Er, remote for either Morse or voice."

Douglas thought for a moment. "I don't think so. Okay, four is right. Good."

Brice wrote out some symbols. "What do these mean?"

...·---···

"SOS," Wane answered

After about an hour of asking each other questions, when Bergie wrote some symbols on the blackboard the *gambler* was fast on all fronts.

"Like hell I will. I ain't buyin' a pop for anybody but me."

Bergie feigned a frown. "Cunnilingus, when it comes to money, you don't miss a bet do you?"

"You got that right," the *gambler* replied, picking up his books, dice, and playing cards.

When they arrived at the canteen, Gordie changed his mind and bought each of his friends KiK-Kolas. The canteen was nearly empty because of the movie, plus the fact that most cadets were broke and never had the advantage of associating with a walking-talking *regimental bank*.

After the movie, B-25 hummed then quietly settled down after lights out. Many cadets in 21 and 22 Platoons had already gone to sleep because it had been a tough day. The silence at the northern end of the hut, however, only lasted for a few seconds. Apparently, while getting into bed, a senior Royal Winnipeg Rifles cadet by the name of Milroy discovered a substance he wasn't prepared for. At the time of his detection, a loud farting sound originated from the vicinity around his bunk.

"What the...? Jeez, some rotten pongo gone and shit in my bed! Oh my God, it's all over me!"

The lights came on in both corporals' cubicles and when the occupants arrived at the source of the predicament, they found a cadet standing in the aisle in his undershorts with his backside, feet, legs and other parts of his body covered in a brown substance.

"Stand by your beds," bellowed 22 Platoon's corporal, making certain the other platoon knew his order was meant only for his platoon.

Although some had to be awakened, all cadets at the northern end of the hut quickly stood at attention between bunks. Curious Cadets up top in the southern end sat up to watch while those in the lower bunks saw the action through the frames of other bunks.

Both non-coms gave Milroy a repugnant look, before one asked, "How old are you ... ya dirty thing? Do you shit the bed at home? Well do you? In all my years in the regular force, I've never seen anything like this!"

Red faced, Milroy didn't really know what to do or say. "Corporal, I didn't do it, honest! Someone else crapped in my bed!"

"It's your bed ain't it?"

"Yes, but..."

Although most cadets just yawned, their glances indicated absolute disgust, and all smiles were absent.

The corporal would have none of it. "That's unbelievable! Not even an animal would do that, and you've only been here for four days! Own up, you poor excuse for a..."

Almost immediately, Genova strolled into the hut and headed to the north end, asking, "What's the problem here?"

The corporal's face said it all. "Sir, this degenerate has shit his bed!"

"I did not! Someone else did it," the cadet blared.

Genova covertly slipped the unseen bottle of Vicks he held in his right hand into his right pants pocket before taking out a handkerchief to cover his giant nostrils. Staring at the cadet, he said, "Well, who did it?"

Knowing he couldn't be heard, Banks said, "You probably did, like you kept shitting yourself last year."

Hushed laughter exploded from those awake in 21 Platoon.

Milroy shrugged. "How the hell do I know?"

"You just said someone else did it! I'm asking you, who it was?"

"Sir, if I knew who it was, I'd kill the prick! I was just getting into bed and..."

Genova interrupted him. "Did anyone else see or hear anything?"

A Scot by the name of Sterling proved.

Genova glanced at the name on the end of the cadet's bunk. "Yes, Sterling!"

"Sir, I heard a booming fart just before Milroy yelled!"

Sniggering rang out but quickly subsided under the beady eyes of the CSM.

"Where did it originate?"

"From his bunk, sir! Or around it somewhere!"

When Genova put his handkerchief away, his eyes and nostrils widened as he nodded. "Oh really? Did you now? Did anyone else hear it?"

The evidence quickly stacked up against Milroy because at least twenty other cadets agreed they had heard the *noise*. Now the cadet became more defiant than ever. "Sir, I'm telling you I didn't do it! Why don't you find out who did?"

"Hold your tongue," Genova barked, placing his nose in Milroy's face. "People like you don't tell me anything! Now move your bedding outside, and get into the showers! Do you hear me?"

Disheartened, Milroy slowly backed away. "Yes, sir."

"Well, get with it, and see me tomorrow morning!"

As the Royal Winnipeg Rifles cadet piled his arms up with bedding and walked down the end set of outside stairs, Genova approached a corporal and asked, "Which one of you has an extra set of bedding?"

Cadet Milroy's platoon corporal said, "We both do, sir."

"Good. Make certain a set is placed on his bunk. Better get him a spare mattress too."

The WO2 appeared upset as he glanced at his watch and turned, saying, "Have him see me tomorrow morning."

"Yes, sir," the corporal replied.

With a shower running in the darkened hut, suppressed guffaws made their way around the northern end of B-25. Nearly all cadets thought Milroy was guilty, but the euphoric laughter of a particular group of Scots allowed Milroy's bunkmate to reassess his original judgement. Unaware he was the next *victim*, he decided he would speak to Milroy tomorrow.

Making certain he wasn't heard, MacKay whispered, "Ain't it amazing what two cups of moist mashed potatoes and some brown gravy mix looks like on white sheets?"

"You'd better believe it," Neish replied.

Just innocent grins occupied the faces of cadets awake at the southern end of the hut, especially those of the musketeers, minus Danyluk. Even though he slept on his stomach, Moose snored.

Banks leaned over the edge of his bunk. "Genova's mad because he never got to smear the Vicks. Boy was he pissed off when he walked out."

Cunningham joined them. "I told ya the odds were too close to call. Christ, he actually had a jar in his hands. It was gonna be MacKay's lucky day."

Suddenly Bergie jumped up, shook Danyluk to stop the *animal* from snoring, and went and sat on Douglas' bunk. "Wane, do you think that jar of Vicks was new?"

Wane sat up chuckling. "Probably. He wouldn't have any left from last year - Scheaffer got it all."

Bergie stood up wringing his hands. "Perfect. Good night guys."

"I wonder what plan Bergie's working on now?" Wane asked Douglas.

Before saying goodnight, Douglas replied, "It's hard to say. One never knows with Bergie."

There were still a few chuckles around Milroy as he cursed and made up his bed. This episode had been the most embarrassing moment of his life, and as far as he was concerned, someone was going to pay. He realized now that the substance placed between his sheets was not the real thing. Indeed, someone was out to get him and he had to find out who he was. It didn't take long because just when he was falling asleep, Bergie shook him and asked him to come to the drying room.

Except for the light coming from the shower room, the centre portion of the hut was dark. "I know who set you up tonight."

Milroy didn't say anything at first; he just sat down on a folding table. "You mean it was someone from 21 Platoon?"

"No, *they* were from your platoon."

Over the next ten minutes, Bergie explained how his Vaseline scheme had worked so well, but that it wasn't planned for Milroy to take the backlash.

"It was never our intention to nail you," Bergie said. "Don't ask me why they thought you were involved. What did you do to them?"

"Not a Goddamned thing," Milroy replied. "But that's about to change."

"No, don't do anything yet. Let them do it to themselves."

Bergie had Milroy's complete attention. "But how?"

"Leave that to me. Just do nothing. As far as you're concerned, it happened and that's that. Okay?"

"Are you sure you'll be able to...?"

Bergie held out his hand. "Just leave it to me. Let's shake on it."

Not too long after the meeting, Danyluk's wandering snore was joined by about twenty other snores, Milroy and Bergie's included.

As B-25 cooled and creaked from the incessant heat of the day's sun, a slight breeze entered the windows and wrapped itself around those who had kicked off their sheet and blankets. The invisible, wandering, delicate intruder felt like Heaven to the sleeping boys.

Chapter 8

"Good morning Okanagan. John Deere tractor and equipment presents Country Fiddler and the Stix. Did you know that Country Fiddler bought his fiddle at a barn sale?"

"Do I look like I care where Country Fiddler bought his son-of-a-bitchin' fiddle?" Danyluk shouted, tuning his radio after the company had returned from their morning run.

In a moment, the hit song, *Wild Goose* filled the southern end of B-25. *"My heart goes where the wild goose goes, and I must go where..."*

With decent music bursting forth from Kelowna's radio station, Moose said, "Ah, that's better. Bergie, why does the Vernon station insist on playing that fiddle crap every morning?"

Bergie finished the hospital corners on his bed. "Because we're in the country. Where the hell did you think we are - in the city?"

When the corporals made their early morning rounds, the occupants of Hut B-25 resembled bees in a hive. As sinks and showers gushed, beds were made, brushes and mops shifted everywhere, bunks barrack-boxes towels and dust covers were lined-up, and some cadets got dressed while others ironed wet clothing.

"Are those your running shoes on the shelf?"

"Yes, Corporal," a small cadet replied.

"Well, get some White It on them, man! They're filthy! Do you think you're in IBT or Driver Mechanics?"

"Perish the thought, Corporal."

"I should bloody-well hope not."

Another corporal checked the bulletin board and walked over to 22 Platoon's area, bellowing, "Is it your platoon's responsibility to line up these folding tables and benches?"

"Yes, Corporal," a group of cadets replied.

"Well then, let's get 'em lined up! You, get that webbelt off and put on your one-inch belt!"

The dress for both platoons was khaki shirts, khaki shorts with one-inch belt, hosetops, boots, puttees, and pith helmets.

The Musketeers remained in their coveralls heading over to the mess hall without Bergie. They had changed into them after taking off their PT strip and having showers. As for Bergie, he had gone to talk to Milroy's bunkmate.

As usual, East reserved a space for his friends in the never-ending line. When they arrived, East said, "Can you smell that? We're having French toast today."

Cunningham put his nose in the air. "Smells like pancakes to me."

East countered. "Cunner, we had pancakes two days ago. Fifty cents says it's French toast."

"Take a hike, East. You probably know what you had for breakfast last year at this time. Do you think I'd bet against your nose? Hey guys ... any bets? I say it's French toast this morning."

"And fried potatoes," East added.

"And fried potatoes," Cunningham yelled.

All cadets ignored the gambler so he spent his time taking coins out of ears.

Jackson finally came to life. "Guess who we're on the parade square with this morning?"

Eight faces with a few yawns indicated they couldn't care less.

"Sergeants Beckford and Simpson."

All eyes now lit up because most of the group hadn't seen the two sergeants since last summer.

"They're still with IBT aren't they?" Rothstein asked, shoving the *gambler's* hand away from his ear.

Earl knew all the answers. "Yep, but we're getting them because our timetable says our NCOs are in Area 10 setting up some sort of an exercise for our company."

As usual, East was right. When they entered the mess hall, French toast was being served, along with fried potatoes. Everyone woke up when one of the kitchen girls dropped a giant empty pot. It sounded like a bomb going off.

When he sat down, Moose said, "I don't know what the hell I was doing last night, but my balls have been sore since I got up."

No one cared because when it came to the condition of Moose's bizarre anatomy, there always seemed to be problems. Bergie, however, had just arrived and he knew the cause. "You slept on your stomach all night, didn't you?"

Danyluk *forked in* a large chunk of French toast. "Yeah, I think so, I was really tired."

"And you wore your PT shorts to bed last night, didn't you?"

Moose swallowed quickly and his face turned a bit pink. "Yeah, I fell asleep before I could take 'em off. Not so loud, Bergie, you'll ruin my reputation of sleeping *awful naturally.*"

Rothstein stretched and recoiled. "Moose, you mean *au naturel.*"

"Same diff, ain't it, Rothie? Nude's nude."

Now Lyons entered the picture. He'd been quietly reading a book about the lost city of Atlantis, but like Rothstein, horrible English sidelined his concentration.

"Actually chaps, you're both wrong. *Au naturel* simply means uncooked food, or preparing food the simplest way. Why I once knew this English professor who..."

Moose's concentration wasn't sidelined. "Oh, go screw yourself, Lyons. Get on with it, Bergie."

After giving Moose the finger, Lyons returned to his book and allowed *Sherlock Bergie-Holmes* to continue.

"...Well, you used my boot-brush last night. *And,* you tucked in down the front of your shorts because you were going to do your other boot after lights out."

"Er, youse is right, Bergie."

"Well, figure it out. You fell asleep with it down your shorts and rolled over on it, you creep. It ended up with your balls all night."

Danyluk breathed a sigh of relief. "Bergie, my buddy, my old pal. Youse has solved both of this morning's major problems."

"What was the other problem?" Banks asked, trying to keep a straight face while holding East down from going to get *fourths.*

"Now I know why my balls were black. I used a whole bar of Sergeants' soap and they're still black. For a moment, I thought I had *mung-fungi balls*. That's when your balls rot off. It's a medical term us future doctors have to use."

"Happiness filled Brice's face. He enjoyed it when Moose was in this mood. Everything the *animal* said was absolutely hilarious.

"You've had black balls before, haven't you, Moose?"

"What's that, Doug? Uh, yeah, dark blue at least, last year in camp. I'll never forget that morning I woke up. If I ever find the son-of-a-bitch who that slipped that elastic band around them, I'll hammer the pongo."

As they left the mess hall, Bergie said, "Er, you can keep that boot-brush, Moose. I'll buy another one."

Moose put an arm around his pal's shoulders. "Hey, Bergie, youse is one fine dude. There ain't a shellfish bone in your body."

"You mean selfish?"

"Yeah, how'd youse know?"

"You! Get your hand off that man and march!"

RSM Gardiner didn't pause because he was on his way to the Sergeants' Mess for breakfast. He still mumbled though. "Bloody hell, that poor licentious abnormality is at it again. I'll keep an eye on him and that Perky simpleton, or whatever his name is."

Sick parade was void of signals cadets when Milroy was marched to the company office. Half an hour later, after roll call and morning inspection, Signals Company faced the drill instructor himself - Sergeant Bill Beckford, the musketeers' platoon sergeant the previous year. Sergeant Simpson and two regular force corporals assisted Beckford, and the NCOs had the parade square to themselves.

After standing the company at ease and easy, Sergeant Beckford's eyes missed nothing.

"So ... this is Signals Company, is it? This is the company that sings songs on its morning runs. Nasty songs about other companies! Well, I'm going to find out just how good you people are! I doubt very much if any one of you have experienced proper drill!"

Although Beckford was at one end of the company, he saw a hand prove in the middle of the front rank. He couldn't quite see the cadet when he asked, "What is it, lad?"

Instantly a nightmarish gas pain appeared on Beckford's face. He recognized the diction.

"Youse can assume that, Sergeant, but some of us are not just pretty faces! We ain't shapely legs either, like those homo pongoes in IBT or D&M."

Grins appeared on all cadet faces as Beckford with his pace stick marched towards *the voice*.

"Step one pace forward, that man!"

Danyluk stepped forward and the sergeant's gas pain worsened when he recognized the knobby knees.

"Right, step back in the ranks!"

Cordell Cross

In a matter of seconds, Beckford's eyes burnt through the bodies of Brice, Banks, Danyluk, Rothstein, Bergie, Jackson, and East.

"Danyluk! Who let you out?"

"Sergeant, youse already knows. My broads did. It's tough, but what the hell? I'm here to impoverish myself."

Bergie gulped whispering, "Improve ... not impoverish, Moose. Get with it."

"I mean I'm here to improve myself, Sergeant."

When both Sergeants glanced at each other, Sergeant Simpson just smiled and shook his head.

At that point, Beckford decided to split them up. He took 21 Platoon with one corporal, and Simpson took 22 Platoon with the other corporal.

"Right! My name is Sergeant Beckford, and you will address me as sergeant, not sir. Contrary to popular belief and unlike your family, my parents were married! Today we are..."

Another hand proved. This time it was a cadet from the 14th Canadian Hussars.

"What is it?"

"Ain't that sorta like callin' us bastards?"

"Are you saying your parents are married?"

"After all, I went to their wedding, 'eh. I'm in the pictures, so I should know, 'eh?

Beckford rolled his eyes upwards. "Sergeant!"

The cadet had stood at ease. Now he came to attention again. "Sergeant!"

"That's better! Right! As I was saying, today, we will cover the basics of drill, and you people will have to prove to me that signals is indeed something special. Is that clear?"

"Yes, Sergeant!"

"Right! I will now demonstrate the..."

For the next fifty-five minutes, Sergeant Beckford had signals practice the proper method of coming to attention, standing at ease, standing easy, turns and inclines at the halt and stepping forward and stepping back. The hot gravel on the old parade square overlooking the golf course stuck to the boys' boots, and when the pop truck arrived all the platoon's bodies and voices were worn out.

"That man is without a doubt the best drill instructor around," said Danyluk, holding the cold KiK-Kola bottle to his forehead. Moose didn't realize it but Sergeant Beckford was also having a pop and standing behind him.

"You mean in Canada, don't you?"

The *animal* turned and assumed the position of attention.

"Most definitely, Sergeant. By far the best in the country."

Beckford grinned and over the next five minutes, he shook their hands and chatted about the previous summer and their cadet corps.

"So you did come back, eh Sergeant?" Wane asked. "We kinda thought you'd had enough of us cadets."

The Sergeant nodded. "Many of my colleagues didn't come back for that exact reason, but Simp and I thoroughly enjoy your eagerness and ability to learn quickly. Brice, what barracks are you fellas in?"

"Hut B-25, Sergeant. Can ya transfer to signals?"

A lost expression came over Beckford's face. These kids had initiated him to the world of cadets and he would never forget them. "No, I'm not much of a signaller. How do you like the course?"

Douglas was just about to answer but commotion at the other end of the parade square with 22 Platoon cornered his attention. Sergeant Simpson stood in the middle of it all, holding his nose. Standing in front of the sergeant were none other than MacKay, Neish, Sterling and Scott, and all of them appeared to fidget while holding on to their rear ends.

"What's the problem? Beckford yelled, not noticing Bergie clearing his throat, turning his head and drifting away. Bergie wanted to roar out laughing, but he couldn't risk it; the Scots would catch on.

"These four have just shit themselves! Christ, if this is an example of Signals Company, they can keep it! Get away from me you execrable beats! Get back to your hut and clean yourselves up!"

At first Sergeant Beckford appeared quite concerned. Then all of a sudden, a smile appeared and his sparkling eyes searched around for Bergie and Danyluk. Six weeks the previous summer had taught Beckford a lot about cadets. Bergie was out of the way, hiding behind Moose. When he stretched his neck and his eyes met Beckford's, the expression on Bergie's face said it all. The Sergeant didn't say anything; he just joined Bergie in laughter. As far as Sergeant Beckford was concerned, there must have been a good reason for *nailing* the four cadets.

Two more periods on the parade square ended at approximately 1130 and after washing up, most cadets in B-25 just lay on their bunks.

"Mail call ... read 'em and weep," the chubby corporal bellowed while entering the barracks on the musketeers' side.

"Edgington, Young, Bacon, Pembroke, Hansen, Brice, er, Moishe ... no not Moishe ... er, Moosey Danyluk, Danyluk, Danyluk, Cunningham, Banks, Danyluk, Moose Danyluk, Danyluk, SFB Danyluk ... er, what's SFB stand for?"

Shit for brains, Corporal. My younger brother, Flagpole, is a goddamned navy cadet. No sleuth and vulture."

Bergie whispered, "You mean no couth and culture?"

"Yeah, that's it. Same diff. They're all the same in the navy."

The corporal kept staring at Danyluk for a moment before carrying on with his mail call. "Smith, Rothstein, Brown, Brice, My Darling The Mouse Danyluk...?"

After trying to get a glimpse of the letter, Danyluk said, "Er, that's pronounced 'Moose,' Corporal.

Once again the corporal stopped calling, saying, "My Darling The Moose Danyluk, sounds like royalty ... like His Royal Highness The Prince Philip?"

"Corporal, youse is lookin' at royalty. As far as my dames are concerned, there's only one prince on this planet. His Royal Highness The Prince Moose. Get on with it, will ya, please?"

The Corporal gawked at Danyluk and shook his head before continuing. Five minutes later, when he stomped out of the barracks he was still shaking his head.

With a half-hour until lunch, cadets who had received letters lost themselves in news from the *outside world.*

While Wane giggled up top, Douglas pocketed the five dollars he took out of the envelope and read his letter from home.

Dear Doug:

I know it might be a little too soon to write, because you've only been gone a few days, but I have the feeling you'll need this money. I hope everything is fine and that you're enjoying the radio course, or whatever it's called.

The weather here is wonderful, so wonderful that on Saturday, Mrs. McDonald and I are going to Stanley Park to feed the squirrels and ducks. It's good to have a friend like Vera. I haven't seen too much of her lately because she's rented an old house at Burrard and Pacific streets, and with the financial help of the government, is taking in pensioners. She says her training as a nurse will greatly help her. I've also heard from your Aunt Flow. Next week we're having lunch downtown and going to the pictures. I know you don't care for her, but she asks about you.

My how time has flown. It doesn't seem like a year since you were last there. Once again the house is too quiet. Before you left I used to think it would be nice to get some peace and not have the radio blaring all of the time. Oh well, at least I'm catching up on some things that need doing.

Colonel is fine. I take him to the beach twice a week and throw him his ball. I can't throw it as far as you do and I think that disappoints him. He misses you as much as I do. He's a real pal and great company. Mickey the cat is fine too and has stopped bringing in those live birds. The last one flew all over the house and it took me an hour to get it outside.

Well, son, I'm still working nights and it's nearly time for me to catch the bus. Do look after yourself, Doug. Have a good time. You're only young once and this is the time of your life you'll remember forever. Please give my love to Wane and tell him to look after himself as well.

All my love. Mam.

PS - Say hello to Diane for me.

A lost smile slowly crept over Douglas's lips as he read the letter again, put it in its envelope, placed his hands behind his head, and thought about home. His mom was something else. If he was there, his room would be quiet and Colonel would be next to him. Everything seemed organized at home; constant hullabaloo didn't exist. Of course being in cadets was a major part of his life. All of his friends were in cadets, including his best friend, Wane, and if Wane were in Vernon while he stayed at home, life just wouldn't be the same.

Wane leaned over, chuckling and holding a letter in his hand.

"Guess who this is from?"

Douglas kicked Wane's springs. "Er, the tax department?"

"No, you pongo, it's from Marigold. Would you believe she's actually proposed?"

"What?" Douglas asked, getting up like a flash.

"She says she wants a simple Catholic wedding and lots of children. God, there's parts in this letter I wouldn't show anyone ... even you."

"Are you going to take her up on her offer? Jesus, Wane, didn't you tell me she wants to become a nun or a milkman, er, milk woman?"

Banks jumped down. "Yeah, that's what she told me. Why?"

"Why? Because milk-people get up at four o'clock in the morning, that's why. What are you going to do when she does that, look after the kids? All fifty of them?"

"I didn't say I was going to accept her proposal. Jeez, if I married her, we'd never be out of bed. Besides, she sweats too much."

After he said it, Wane knew he was too loud. Moose came over.

"Hey, whatsamatter with youse? Broads that sweat have more goin' for them. Show me a dame that sweats, and I'll show youse a real woman! Why I used to go around with this broad nicknamed Sticky-Skin Sheila who..."

A sour look came to Wane's face. "Jesus, Moose, you'd go around with any dame as long as she gives it away for nothing."

"Hey, they all gives it to the Moose for nothin'! I ain't paid yet, and I ain't gonna start! That's the trouble with youse pansies ... you're always lookin' for dames with perfect skin, perfect faces, perfect bodies. Sometimes ya gotta look beneath all that to understand the real woman. Rotten teeth, pimples, blotches, sweat, matted hair, dirty feet, chewed nails and whatever can all be cured. Underneath all that, youse could have a real beautiful dame. Think about that! Listen to this, but I won't read youse the whole letter ... *My wonderful, beautiful, and handsome Moosey: I miss you so much I'm thinkin' of comin' up there to see you. My lips and all other body parts ache for you, my darling. I'm doin' things that I don't normally do, like buying new upper dentures, wearin' undies and changin' my socks every four days. Did I tell you I had my lower teeth out as well, and I'm even at the point where I'm taking a bath once a week instead of every two weeks? As far as my hair is concerned, you're right, a comb and brush does work wonders, and I'm gonna stop using margarine on it because it gives me dandruff. No longer do I bite off my toenails and spit 'em on the floor. I now spit 'em out in the sink. My love, with your tutelage, this young exquisite model of maidenhood is beginning to take on the presence of a duchess. I've even taken your suggestion and visited the doctor to have the wax flushed out of my ears. Write to me my white knight. I dream of riding your limousine to the stars.*

Love, Doris.

PS - Here's the $10.00 you need for your course manuals. When you pay me back, I'll buy some lower dentures. It's tough gummin' steak.'"

"So, there youse has it," Moose said kissing his letter. Doris was once an ugly duckling who is turning out to be a regal countess because of me. That's what..."

Danyluk stopped *articulating* and looked around. The only person sitting there smiling was Bergie. The rest had quietly left.

Amidst the clamour and prattle of the mess hall, Douglas asked Bergie, "But how did you do it? Also, why didn't you tell us about your plan?"

Bergie kept his voice to a very low whisper. "Doug, I had no time to tell you. Do you remember this morning when you thought a bomb had gone off in the kitchen? You know, when that dame dropped the pot?"

"Yeah."

"Well, the four of them were so busy looking at her, I slipped a piece of Exlax into each of their hot chocolates. It melted so fast, they never had a clue."

Earl edged in closer. "They're going to think Milroy did it."

Bergie nodded. "Yeah, you're probably right, but I have a feeling they'll change their minds after lunch. Speaking of Milroy, here he comes now."

Looking like MacKay did when he came back from the MIR, Milroy slowly moved past the servers and joined his bunkmate's table. The four Scots weren't at lunch so they couldn't give him a rough time. Simpson had sent *them* to the MIR.

"Where've *you* been?" his friend asked.

Milroy picked at his food. "Well, this morning I received a blast from Genova and the OC and then our platoon sergeant sent me to the MIR. Christ, I've had four needles and they've been feeding me this stuff that supposed to stop diarrhoea. I tried to tell them that I didn't need it, but no one would listen to me. Y'know, it's funny, but when I was leaving, I could have sworn I saw four of those Scottish creeps in the next examining room. They were laying down gettin' needles in their asses. Jeez, were they ever pissed off. I even heard my name."

"You did see them," his buddy Harper replied. "*They* shit themselves during the pop break this morning. Great breakfast conversation, eh?"

"Change into your PT shorts, white T-shirts, socks and running shoes! You will not wear undershorts!" a corporal bellowed making the rounds. "The trucks will be here in three-quarters-of-an-hour! Pack your swimsuits in your towels and do not wear your headdress! Any questions?"

The excited cadets didn't ask questions. They wanted to swim.

Two cadets from the South Saskatchewan Regiment bunking close to the Scots, stripped off ready to change. As one rooted through his side of their barrack box, he said, "You know, Lorne, you've got to be a little more considerate. My side of the box is getting smaller and smaller, and..."

His friend interrupted him. "Ralph, will ya quit bitching; you're worse than my mother. You do the same thing, ya know."

Ralph didn't quit. "Also you forgot to lock our box. How many times have I told you..."

The cadet stopped verbalizing when he spotted a small cardboard container on Lorne's side. The container read, 'EXLAX.'

Ralph picked up the packet, held it high and started laughing. "Lorne, what the hell are ya doin' with this packet of Exlax? Are ya tryin' to join the *Scottish shit club*?"

Naked, Lorne didn't have a clue what his bunkmate was getting at. "That's not mine, you ayrab, I don't use that stuff. You had the bung, not me."

"It was on your side of our barrack box, buddy boy!"

"Bull shit it was! If it was there, it was on your side!"

MacKay and his three companions heard the conversation, and as far as they were concerned, their *problem* had been solved. MacKay quickly gathered his friends together.

"Well what do ya know. We blamed the wrong guys. It wasn't the RWR pongoes, it was those two assholes in the Sally's Slut Refuge."

Neish agreed. "Jesus, where we ever duped. Let's rush 'em to the showers."

MacKay's mouth formed a sneaky grin. "Nah, let's get 'em at the beach."

Unlike 1953 when the swim-parade trucks usually roamed down the main hill, turning left after passing Polson Park, this afternoon the vehicles took the ever-dusty upper winding road joining the Okanagan Landing route about three miles away.

The road was barren of houses, so very few PT shorts were pulled down. The musketeers' had learned their lesson and made certain they got seats, but as usual, a few of those standing and not paying attention had their shorts yanked down and feet firmly implanted in the crotches of the garments. It didn't matter how hard the 'shows' tried to pull up their pants, it was impossible, therefore complete bodies were covered by the immense clouds of dust churned upwards by the tires. These sweaty bodies acted as magnets and as such, semi-nude *minstrels* gyrated their way to the beach.

Kinsmen Beach at the north end of the eastern arm of Okanagan Lake is eternally beautiful and never crowded. Giant trees planted years ago by the Kinsmen Club provided the blessed shade cherished by the company of cadets, and the few civilians present.

Although the roofless changing shacks were insufficient to handle the large company, line-ups kept matters orderly so it didn't take much time before all cadets wearing their swimsuits formed up in three ranks. Then the swimming-staff gave their usual pep talk.

"Place your clothes and towels down on your right and sit down! When you exit the water, you will not take your shoes into the changing shacks. We want to count them to see if someone is missing.

"You have been briefed by your company staff what to do and what not to do. Remember, use the buddy system, and stay in a minimum of pairs. When you hear the whistle, hold up each other's arms! Do not swim out past the safety boat! Are there any questions?"

There were no questions and within seconds, the water swirled with excited cadets who didn't enter meekly. Rather, these boys barged in full force. The temperature at the beach was around 95 degrees, but the glistening blue water quickly took twenty-degrees off that figure.

Races, floating, games, splashing, diving, and cannonballs followed. The normally tranquil beach was instantly converted into what would resemble a disturbed wasp's nest with people representing the wasps.

At times, Douglas and Wane roamed the length of the beach looking at the well-kept cabins and houses with lush lawns partially lining the eastern and western shores. As far as their eyes could see, they found the panoramic magnificence overwhelming. The duo didn't have to say anything to each other, their facial expressions said it all. Complete freedom of the sort they could never experience in Vancouver overcame the boys. It allowed them to relax and actually sense the privilege of uniting with such God-given splendour.

Bergie, Moose, East, and Jackson left the water also, but their minds weren't roaming as they watched four Scottish cadets take two pairs of PT shorts from two towels belonging to two South Saskatchewan Regiment cadets. The towels were then neatly rolled as before. When the Scottish cadets disappeared to *dump* their *booty*, East and Jackson relieved the four culprits' towels of their PT shorts, discarding two pairs and placing a pair in each of the towels of the Saskatchewan cadets. Now the two SSR cadets had PT shorts once again. Scottish shorts.

The plan was simple. The Scottish cadets would make certain they entered the changing shack with their two Saskatchewan *friends* and casually steal their swimsuits after removal. Thus, the Saskatchewan cadets would have nothing to wear. In this case, however, four musketeers' would also be in the shack walking away with the swimsuits of the Scottish cadets. Both sets of plans worked perfectly, but unfortunately for the Scottish cadets, they would get the 'shitty' end of the stick and the Saskatchewan cadets would find nothing wrong.

At four o'clock as the cadets lined up to change, the trucks reappeared. Bergie, Moose, Jackson, and East had already dressed, so their minds only had to look after the tasks at hand, as they followed the Scottish cadets into the changing shack.

The small shack was really packed as the four stepped out of their swimsuits at the same time as the SSR (South Saskatchewan Regiment) cadets did. Without missing a blink and totally unnoticed, two Scots picked up the SSR cadets' swimsuits and flung them over the back wall. Needless to say, at the same time in the sardine tin, the bathing suits of the Scottish cadets disappeared very quickly as well; then the Musketeers took off. To Milroy, Harper and the 9 musketeers, the whole scenario was absolutely hilarious, but they had to laugh inwardly.

In the shack, four sets of bugged eyes couldn't believe that the SSR towels contained PT shorts. Nor, after considerable searching could the same sets of eyes find their own PT shorts.

When the SSR cadets casually walked out discussing the mysterious box of Exlax, and how they'd misplaced their swimsuits in the crowd, MacKay dried his feet and uttered, "Damn, we took the wrong Goddamned shorts. How idiotic can we be? Neish, it was your job to... "

MacKay paused. "Hey, where the hell are my...?"

Neish interrupted him. "That's impossible. I never took my eyes off them. I'm certain we were right, and…"

Now a nude Neish was now on his hands and knees searching the floor of the shack.

"Hey, where the hell's *my* shorts? Give 'em here, MacKay!"

The four of them became searchers. "I don't have your shorts, you idiot! I'm still looking for mine! Okay, you pongoes, who's fooling around? Let's have 'em! I said, let's have 'em, you creeps!"

"I ain't got 'em! Where the hell's mine, you pongo!"

"Someone must have them, unless we stole our own damned shorts and bathing suits!"

"I wonder if we did?"

"Maybe there's a ghost in here?"

"What, the ghost of Kin Beach? Don't be a fool. Our stuff must be here someplace!"

Only four cadets remained in the changing shack after they discovered their PT shorts as well as their bathing suits were gone. Outside, the names MacKay, Neish, Sterling and Scott were noted.

The corporal's patience didn't last long. These people were holding everyone up.

"Okay you shitters, fall in with the rest of this parade!"

MacKay's voice came over the wall. "Er, just, er, give us another minute, please, er, Corporal."

"Have you shit yourselves again? Well, have you?"

"Er, no, er, not exactly."

"What the hell do you mean by that?"

"Jeez, we've got to do something. He's going to have us for breakfast," whispered MacKay.

"Let's wrap our towels around us. That should do it," replied Sterling.

Smiling and not showing any concern, the four Scots exited the changing shack with their towels wrapped around their waists and wearing their T-shirts.

Although other members of the company thought it was extremely funny, the corporal didn't.

"Do you shitters think this is Hawaii? Are those the new-style kilts? Get those towels off your waists!"

Neish became the spokesman. "Er, we, er, don't have anything on underneath them, Corporal."

Genova appeared out of nowhere. "What?"

"We seem to have lost our swimsuits and shorts, Sergeant Major."

The Corporal assisted. "Sir, these were the four that shit themselves!"

Genova's nostrils widened. He didn't like being put on.

"No they didn't! Only one person shit himself and I talked to him this morning! Get with it, Corporal!"

"No, that was last night, sir! These four shit themselves this morning! They're in my platoon and..."

"What? These people also? What kind of a company are we running here? Are you in cahoots with Milroy?"

Neish stood at attention with the three others. "Er, no, er, we don't know what happened, sir."

Genova marched away bellowing, "Everyone in this company is shitting himself! What's happening here? You four see me in the company office after supper!"

"You people need *effing* diapers," the corporal said. "Take off your T-shirts and wear them instead of the towels! Quickly now, quickly!"

The Scots didn't argue re-entering the changing shack, but the sight of seeing the four when they returned was too much for the four platoons of cadets. With their T-shirts upside down, the boys' legs now came out of the sleeves.

Moose and Bergie doubled over and when the Scots waddled into the ranks holding up the ends of their shirts, howling couldn't be contained.

Cordell Cross

"Now your balls are air conditioned," someone yelled as the cadets boarded the trucks.

The trucks returned via the lower road completely in song. Had they taken the same route back, the cadets' squeaky-clean bodies would have needed Okanagan Lake again.

After unloading, B-25's residents had one whole hour to relax before supper. Some did their kit, others chewed the fat, read comics, cleaned their barrack boxes or gambled with Cunningham. Not the four Scots, though - they met in one of the lecture rooms.

"What the hell is going on?" MacKay asked, pleased that he now had pants on once again. "It's almost as if we're doing everything to ourselves. Is one of you guys playing the role of asshole here? Do we have a mole in our group?"

All four looked at each other. They knew it wasn't one of them.

Neish said, "It's those farmers from Saskatchewan. Either they're smarter than they look, or they're lucky. I know damned well we got the right shorts. I think they must have noticed us?"

Scott shook his head. "That's not possible. While we were doin' the *job*, Baines watched them buyin' pop at the small store."

MacKay pounded his fist on the table. "Then we got the wrong bloody towels. Jesus, we'd screw up the Lord's Prayer in a kindergarten class."

Sterling wouldn't have that. "But if we got the wrong towels, it must have been our towels. No one else was missing PT shorts but us. Also, who made off with our swimsuits?"

"It's just likely they may have had the same plan," said Neish. "I'll betcha that's it. We got the wrong towels, and they had the same plan."

Sterling continued to bite his lower lip as he balanced himself on the two back legs of his chair. "Well, what do we do now? I say we leave the whole thing alone and get on with our lives. We should be studying."

MacKay agreed. "Yeah, you're right. It's not worth it, and we're beginning to look like assholes. It's over ... right?"

The others agreed.

Neish stood up. "Don't forget ... we've still got to see Genova after supper."

Four bitter faces nodded to each other before leaving the room.

Back in the hut, the usual things happened when relaxing cadets have some time to themselves. The occupants *discussed* which regiment had the most battle honours, the best-looking badge, the best-coloured beret, the best-coloured lanyard, the best belt buckle, or the best coloured flashes, etc. The *disputes* were concluded in good fun because each cadet knew he belonged to the best regiment so what was the point of discussing it further. Particularly the Scottish cadets. As far as they were concerned, God Himself designed their uniforms, and when they wore them, it was with the ultimate blessing of the Supreme Being Himself. *Himself*, being Scottish, of course.

"And don't call us cold asses," protested Lyons' bunkmate, glancing up from his game of chess with Lyons. "Even without gaunch, when we wear our kilts, our pre-eminent properties are kept warm."

"Youse has a nerve calling them pre-eminent properties. My dog, Colossus, has a bigger set of balls than most of youse Seaforths."

"And a bigger wang, too," East mouthed. "And he's only a Chihuahua."

Lyons took his mind off the game for a moment. "Chaps, chaps, chaps! Please lower your voices and try to treat my Seaforth companion in the manner to which he'd like to become accustomed. Remember, gentleman, and I use the term loosely, the Germans called these chivalrous highlanders, 'The ladies from hell.'"

"Who *says* they did?" Banks said, jumping down. "Maybe someone misinterpreted them. The Germans probably said, "Achtung yung Chermans! Vatsch ouchts fur dosch laddys-homoschits from der schnell. Das is der faggischits in der raggischits. Ich nein to fallsch in der trensches mid dem sexisch crazy womansch's. Isch not schoot der enemy, das bugger der enemy."

As the rest of 21 Platoon roared laughing, Wane leaned out his window to laugh his guts out.

Shortly, Douglas kicked Wane springs sending his best friend's mattress flying, and East yelled, "Supper's on!"

Over corned-beef and cabbage Rothstein told Gordie that this week had gone so fast, he didn't know what had happened to the days.

Cunningham agreed. "The course timetable is well planned and we're always doing hands-on training. That Nineteen Set is a blast. The only thing wrong with this course is signal office duties. Jeez, I always feel like falling asleep when it's being taught."

"Same here," Harvey replied. "Do you remember last year when Sergeant Beckford said any subject could be made interesting? He said, 'any subject', didn't he?"

Gordie stopped calculating the odds of having more than twelve capillaries in any piece of cabbage. "He sure did, Rothie, my son. Listen, how would you like to bet that...?"

"I ain't bettin' about anything. Let's challenge Sergeant Beckford. We've got a subject that is boring as hell - let's ask him to prepare a lecture that will make SOD absolutely fantastic."

"That's a great idea," Douglas added. "We know Sergeant Beckford is a great instructor. Now we'll find out just *how* great he is."

"What if he turns us down?" East asked with his mouth full. When the *beast* discarded the current bone in his hand, his plate would hold a total of eight chicken legs. Apparently. East liked chicken better than corned beef.

The whole table stared at East who continued eating and talking at the same time, not looking up. "You (chomp) know, (chomp) like if he says, (chomp) er, no thanks, (chomp) I'm busy enough!" (chomp)

Moments later, East was literally picked up and dragged out. To them, Beckford would never said no, and he wasn't about to begin now. As for East - he'd had enough.

The whole camp was quiet after supper. Most cadets knew that tomorrow night was 'Mother's Night' therefore if they wanted to do any studying, it had to be done now. Tomorrow, the barracks would be taken apart and cleansed like never before.

That included the *gardens* around the huts, the smoking pits, windows, toilets, showers and the like.

All cadets knew IBT usually won the pennant because that course was all starch, pomp, and pageantry. It had been years since good old signals won the pennant, so this year cadets from the four platoons got together and like in IBT, a 'company responsibilities list' was made out for Mother's Night.

It was peaceful and cool at the outdoor chapel, slightly south-east of the headquarters' building, thus the musketeers had the whole plot to themselves and low camp *noise* could barely be heard.

Including Lyons' Seaforth *friend*, the ten paired up and once they began Morse code, the area sounded like a full-fledged message centre.

Wane said to Douglas: "Take this down and I want an answer in thirty seconds. Has ••••/• —/••• Marigold — —/• —/• — •/••/— — •/— — —/• —••/— •• met ——/•/— Moose ——/— — —/— — — /•••/•

Wane deciphered it within thirty seconds. and replied, Not — •/— — — /—/ a • — bad — •••/• —/— •• idea ••/— ••/•/• —

Although Moose worked with Bergie, the *animal* knew someone had spelled his name.

"Okay, which of youse tapped out my name?"

Douglas was about to answer, but Rothstein had also been sending. "There are other names that sound like Moose, you know. I sent the word Goose, not Moose."

"Can youse give me other examples?" Danyluk asked.

Harvey smiled. "Yeah, *douche.*"

"What about loose douche?" quipped East.

Danyluk was definitely not just another pretty face, nor for that matter, just another shapely leg. He *dismissed* Harvey and Jack with a wave. "Who's this Marigold dame?"

Standing and stretching, Wane said, "She's a girl I've been taking out. I thought you might like to meet her."

A suspicious look came over Moose's face. "When youse wants to introduce me to one of your dames, something's gotta be wrong. Let's just see how good lookin' this dame is. Will you answer some simple questions about her?"

"You bet I will," replied Wane. "Shoot!"

"Head?"

Wane thought for a moment. "One."

Moose laughed with the rest of them, including Banks.

"Jesus, Wane, I know she's only got one head. What size is it?"

"Oh, er, normal, er, as heads go."

"Good. I hates broads with large heads. If they've got large heads, they've got brains."

"Money?"

"Naturally she's got one, but I don't think her father lives with them."

Frustrated, Danyluk rolled his eyes. "I said money, not mummy."

"Some. She works after school."

"How many teeth are missing?"

"None."

"Hmmm, that's nice, Wane. Sounds good. Colour?"

"Of what?"

"Her teeth, of course."

"White."

"Hmm, sounds even better. Eyes?"

"Two."

"Well I hope so, eh? I mean are they crossed? Can she see? What colour?"

"They're not crossed. She sees normally. Er, blue."

"Legs?"

"Two."

"That's good; it's been a while since one-legged Olga. No, ya pongo, I mean what are they like?"

"Oh, er, really great legs."

"Shave?"

"Doesn't need to. Her face is as smooth as..."

"Get with it, Wane. I mean her legs or her ass?"

Wane grinned. "No, she doesn't shave her legs or her ass. At least I don't think she shaves her ass. The only girl I ever heard about who shaves her ass was that Dora dame you went with. Say, why'd you quit goin' around with her, anyway?"

"I gave her up because she had a neck problem. She nodded all the time. When she was sayin' no, I thought she was sayin' yes. Anyway, let me get back to this. Ears?"

"Two and no wax."

"Ah, ah! This sounds better all the time.

"Breath."

"Two, really, really nice ones. You'll like these, Moose. They're melons to the tenth..."

"I said *breath*, not breasts, you creep."

"Doesn't smell."

"Feet?"

"Two, and always clean. They don't smell either."

"I mean the size. I don't care if they're dirty. Big feet means small bazookas."

"Oh - size five, or six, I think."

"Not bad. Anybody fat?"

"What, in her family? Her Aunt is heavy, but..."

"Not in her family: on her, you creep. Is there any body fat?"

"Moose, she's still alive. I'm not talkin' about a dead body. You've spent too much time in your hearse."

Danyluk groaned. "I mean what's her body like?"

"Oh, er ... really nice. Sorry, I misunderstood you there."

"Forget it. Hair?"

"Blonde."

"No, how much does she have? I've got dames that put too much dye on their hair. It falls out too easily."

Cordell Cross

"Full head, not dyed. Doesn't fall out. No dandruff."

"Hmmm, colour of her hair other than on her head?"

"Never looked."

"What does youse mean youse has never looked. I inspect my dames."

"You have to. I've seen your broads and I don't know how they passed inspection."

"Harelips?"

"Two, and they're wonderful.

Danyluk stood up. Two harelips? Jesus, I don't mind one, but two ...er…"

"No, no, Moose. No harelips, just two great lips. Her lips are nice."

"Oh, that's all right, then. Nosey?"

"Yeah, in the middle of her back and two giant nostrils with dyed red hair comin' out of them! What the hell kind of a broad do you want?"

"Calm down, Wane. I don't go out with just any dame. I means, is she nosy? Er, does she stay out of other people's business?"

"She hardly ever talks. She's got other things on her mind."

Moose couldn't believe it. "This broad sounds too good for the human race. Are you sure youse ain't holdin' anything back?"

Seven others started showing interest as well.

"Well, er, there are a couple of things about this dame that are different. Er … she..."

All ears eagerly moved closer to Wane.

"She sweats and she's ... er, oh, how can I say it...?"

"Get on with it, man," said East, chewing a chicken leg but wishing it was a chicken breast. "I'm gettin' a boner just listening to this."

"She's... a... "

Wane cupped his hands around Danyluk's right ear and whispered.

A quizzed expression came over Moose. "She's a what? Oh, sticky fingers, eh? I once knew a dame that went into Woolworth's and stole a..."

"Moose, I didn't say kleptomaniac. I said she's a nymphomaniac! A nymph."

In a fraction of a second Wane got mobbed. Six Musketeers and a Seaforth cadet pinned him down demanding Marigold's address. Not later, but now.

It took ten minutes for Wane to write Marigold's particulars and phone number in each *buddy's* notebook. East's took longer because of the grease stains. This Marigold girl was about to get letters ... lots of letters.

Two hours later when they returned to their barracks, a commotion was taking place in 22 Platoon's area. There, lying on top of his bed in his underwear was MacKay. At least it looked like MacKay, this cadet had a blue nose and a blue chest. The rest of his body-colour appeared quite normal.

"What the hell happened to youse?" Danyluk asked.

"That Goddamned Genova thought we had colds and told us to remove our shirts. I was the first to receive the *treatment*. He started rubbing Vicks on me and my skin turned blue. It won't scrub off. It scared the shit out of Genova, so he didn't do Scott, Sterling or Neish. They took off fast. You should see Genova's fingers."

Bergie chuckled. "I'd love to."

Cordell Cross

"You guys can thank your lucky stars," said Banks. "If it hadn't turned blue, you'd have had it all over your bodies, including your asses."

"Ya don't put Vicks on your ass," said Neish. "Asses don't sneeze."

"Genova thinks they do," Wane replied. "His philosophy is all skin can breathe, therefore your asses would have been smeared. Make certain you show the OC tomorrow. That homo's got no right to touch you at all. You won't have to go on sick parade because that will mean more needles. Just ask to see the OC."

MacKay agreed, and as the musketeers laughed all the way to their area, a larger crowd gathered around the 'blue one'.

It felt extremely hot in the barracks that night. Most cadets lay on top of their blankets until lights out, then some got under their sheets.

Douglas sneaked over to Bergie's bunk. "What did you mix with Genova's Vicks?"

Bergie's eyes lit up. "Blue clothing dye. I knew the son-of-a-bitch was going to nail someone ... I just didn't know who."

Douglas smacked his friend on the shoulder. "But how did you do it?"

"He leaves his room unlocked, and the jar was in plain view. The job couldn't have been easier, and I was certain he wouldn't notice the difference. If he did, he'd probably think the Vicks company had changed its colours, that's all."

A look of pure wonderment came over Douglas' face.

"Brilliant. Absolutely bloody brilliant, Bergie!"

Bergie's smile broadened as he got under his top sheet, saying, "Aw, think nothing of it. We've all gotta help our fellow *man*, if *that's* what he is."

Barracks B-25 quietened down quickly because including the swim parade, the cadets had put in a long day. The silence didn't last for long though, because Cadet MacKay crawled between his sheets.

"What the...? Oh my God! All right, who crapped in my bed? Step forward you rotten bastard! Just look at me, I'm covered in shit!"

A South Saskatchewan Regiment cadet across the aisle just getting into bed chuckled and leaned over his bunk to talk to his partner below.

"It looks like someone's gone and give him a bit of his own medicine. Ha, look at him. He's got blue all over his chest and his face, and shit everywhere else. You would think that ... What the...? Would ya believe this? Oh my God, I'm covered in shit, too! You're a rotten bastard MacKay!"

The SSR cadet below had been lying on top of his bed. He stood up and peeled back his covers. Needless to say, his sheets were covered as well.

"Ya got mine too, eh, ya rotten prick! Okay MacKay, this is war! You've gone too far this time!"

MacKay was so upset at the thought of more needles, he yelled back, "You bet your life this is war! You two sneaky assholes have been gettin' away with everything! I know you did this! Well, my lucky friends, this is battle! Hey Neish Scott, Sterling ... we've got to get these pricks! Just look at me, I'm covered in blue and shit! Can you believe this?"

"Aye," came their reply, but nothing else, because 22 Platoon's corporal turned on the lights, and screamed, "Stand by your beds!"

Cordell Cross

Two minutes later when the cadets of 22 Platoon marched on to the parade square wearing only undershorts, socks and boots, three of them remained in a *covered* state.

While all cadets in 21 Platoon remained warm in their beds, the endless parade square shout of, "One, two three, one," emanated into their open windows.

"Best buddy o' mine - how can youse sleep at a time like this? Those poor creeps are workin' their asses off."

Smiling and rolling over on his side, Bergie said, "It's times like this that I sleep the best. Slumber well, my son, and may the pox pass over you tonight."

"Goodnight, Bergie. Youse is one great genius."

Bergie snickered into his pillow. "I know."

Chapter 9

Regardless of the year, Fridays are always special days at the Vernon Army Cadet Camp. That day means the end of a long week, and the start of a yearned for weekend.

In 1954, after Friday's Mother's Night chores and a parade and test on Saturday morning, 1400 cadets relished the coming day-and-a-half off. Even after church parade on Sunday mornings they could go back to bed because brunch was served from 0700 until 1300 on Sundays.

Yes, the boys welcomed the day-and-a-half of rest. It was the commanding officer's way of saying, "Well done! Now, have some time to yourselves. You deserve it. We're not going to give you compulsory sports or the like just to keep you locked in and busy. We know you're mature enough not to get into trouble; go and have fun and take a look at the area. However, keep your noses clean, and be polite to civilians. The more they see you, the more they appreciate the camp."

If they wanted to, cadets could swim all weekend because every half-hour trucks did 'the run' to Kalamalka Beach. They could sleep if they wanted to, have a weekend pass if adults visited them, and if pre-approved by their parents they could obtain a midnight pass on Saturday night. Yes, most weekends were *nothing* weekends where the boys could get together with their friends, girls in town, or generally catch up on all of the things time didn't allow them to do during the week.

In certain cases, if a company was *up to snuff* even Friday midnight passes were allowed. Any cadet could accept this dispensation, but generally, most would turn it down due to a heavy schedule. The boys knew they were accountable to their peers because teamwork was the name of the game. If the company lost whole points and didn't win the pennant, the chain had been broken. Someone or some people had let everyone else down. If, however, a company lost the pennant by only a fraction of a point, then sleeves had to be rolled up even higher than high the next weekend.

At fourteen, fifteen and sixteen years of age, purposeful competition brings out a youngster's mettle to strive yet harder to fulfil unfailing allegiance to 'the team' And despite any difficulties, this subjectively accepted challenge is not just gladly received - it is steadfastly met. It unites individuals and becomes the link that forges a close-knit crew.

And that's exactly what happened to Signals Company this fifth day of the week, starting when the camp bugler (a BCR cadet named Brophie) in Driver Mechanics, jumped out of bed, put on his boots, stepped out between huts, played reveille, ran into the *shack,* and leaped back into bed. He had to hop back into bed to protect himself, otherwise he would have been hit from objects heaved in his direction.

Always *adored,* Brophie's gracefully delivered tune suggested a new day had begun - that it was time to rise and shine. The time was 0530 and in fifteen minutes, six of the musketeers would be playing with the band.

Genova didn't appear in the barracks that morning. The job of getting the *bandsmen* up and reporting to the instrument hut was left to the BCR cadets themselves. The WO2 wasn't at the band hut either - therefore Cadet Sergeant Barry

Kelly volunteered to lead the parade. Barry was a big kid who had the talent to play all the instruments. He was keen on the band and most BCR cadets respected him for his musical knowledge.

"Okay, let's make it as quick as we can. If we have to do this, we'll make the circle in fifteen minutes. Everyone agree?"

Although not yet quite awake, the majority agreed to get a move on and finish the thing.

Most cadets in the camp were up as the BCR band made its rounds. Initially, no middle fingers were displayed, and the only thing threw at first was a condom loaded with water. As luck would have it, it landed on top of Danyluk's *instruments*. Although he didn't miss a beat, he got soaked to the skin.

"Ya rotten creeps," he yelled at a window just being slammed shut in the D&M barracks.

"Here I donate my valuable time to provide my fellow cadets with the kind of cymbal ring they like, and they show their appreciation by throwing a rubber at me. Youse pansies should fill 'em with water; you've got nothin' else to fill 'em with!"

Amidst a few chuckles from the drum section, a tenor drummer said, "It could have been worse. Last year, one of the Irish pipers got hit in the face with dog turds. Consider yourself lucky."

No sooner had he said it, a decomposed cabbage bounced off his tenor drum and splashed those around him. When Kelly turned his head about to find out where the appalling smell was coming from and what all the commotion was about, he got hit in the forehead with an egg.

"You crass IBT pongoes," Kelly yelled, placing the mace in his left hand while wiping running yoke away from the sweatband of his beret.

Moose laughed with the rest of them. "At least it wasn't rotten; you should smell us!"

Kelly's face said it all as he gave Moose a dirty look. The egg was rotten.

The band dispersed fifteen minutes later after members handed in their instruments.

"You smell like a garbage dump," Wane told Moose.

"I feel like one," the *animal* replied, walking with Lyons. When the cabbage bounced off the tenor drum, a good portion of it landed between the base drum and the leopard skin Lyons wore. Thus, the chubby intelligent one had the *bomb* in his face for five minutes. No one would go near him either.

"I'm ruined. From now on my world will reek like a decaying corpse."

"So what's new, you smell like that at the best of times," Cunningham said, staying ten feet away from Lyons and taking a coin from Douglas' ear.

Lyons paid no attention. "Zelda will think I'm dead."

Bergie also kept his distance. "No, she'll think you're imitating her."

That did it. "Screw you, Bergie. I've smelled some of your dames."

Moose howled his head off while placing an arm around Lyons' shoulders. "Don, just look on the bright side. We won't need Jack to clear out the shower room for us."

"You, you horrible duo ... stand where you are!"

Cordell Cross

122 - NEXT STOP, VERNON!

As Danyluk and Lyons stood to attention, the rest marched away quickly. They knew RSM Gardiner was never in the best of moods in the morning.

Abruptly, the RSM backed off five paces. "You again! Why the hell have you always got your arm around someone?"

Quivering, Moose replied, "Sir, this man asked me to wipe some crap off the back of his shirt!"

Gardiner glowered at the top front of Lyons' shirt. "Really? And I suppose you then transferred the *crap* to the front of his shirt? My God - when did you people last have a shower? You stink to high heaven! Also, you're soaked ... Do you always sweat that bad?"

Danyluk was still wet from the full *rubber*.

Lyons let Moose do all the talking. "Sir, er, this ain't sweat, it's er ... We're going to have a shower now, sir!

"I should hope so! Is this your new partner?"

"This here's Lyons. He's a friend of mine, sir!"

Gardiner backed off another two feet, sniffed, sneered, and wiped his nose. "You've got *more* friends? Where's ... Perky?"

"Bergie? He's ironin' our stuff, sir!"

"Has he got some clothes on?"

"I hope so, sir."

"Well, young man, I don't want to see you with your arm around anyone again! Is that clear?"

"Yes, sir!"

"Carry on!"

Marching away, the RSM mumbled, "That poor filthy degenerate. He and his *friend* haven't had a shower in days. Christ, he sweats. How the hell can someone like that have friends? What is happening to this world? No wonder he's always nude, his clothes probably walk away by themselves. Why in Hades do I get posted here?"

With their arms and chins up, Lyons and Danyluk marched all the way to and into B-25. The two of them didn't waste any time shedding their clothes, and Danyluk's previous prediction was wrong because the shower room *was* full. Not for long though, because the second an earnest looking East entered, whistling *Three Blind Mice* and nonchalantly placing his half-eaten apple on the window-ledge, the exodus was on. East's superficial smile and words, "Mind if I join you fellas?" went unheard, and the last *runner* out actually had to rinse himself off by lying and rolling under the taps on one of the extended stainless steel sinks.

A towelled PPCLI cadet heading to the showers asked him, "What the hell are you doing? You Canadian Scottish creeps are really a bunch of weirdoes."

Now rinsed off, the naked CScotR placed his feet on the floor and dried himself. "Oh, yeah? Listen, asshole, if you want to shower with the living fart, that's up to you."

The Patricia winced, dropped his towel, and stretched out on the sink. "The living fart? *He's* in there? Not on your life."

Cordell Cross

123 – NEXT STOP, VERNON!

Unperturbed by the waiting line-up, the musketeers showered and just chewed the fat while Lyons washed out his nostrils, saying, "If this had happened to Genova, his nose would have the stench for years."

"I wonder why he wasn't with us?" asked Douglas.

Bergie opened the window wide. "I hear he's been posted to the MIR."

Wane put on his glasses after drying himself off. "You've got to be bloody joking? They're gonna unleash that creep in the camp hospital?"

Bergie couldn't hold back his laugh. "Yeah, there's a rumour going around he's in charge of the Vicks."

Those queuing outside couldn't understand what was so funny. They thought anyone laughing while showering with East should have his head examined.

"Just joking. But I do hear he's not with us anymore," Bergie continued. "I think I heard the corporal say he's been posted to the headquarters building."

The good humour originating in the shower room tempted some at the start of the line to enter. They were a little timid at first, but to their surprise, everything was fine. The atmosphere was so neighbourly more actually threw caution to the wind and followed.

As the Musketeers dried themselves off, Rothstein jammed the window shut and motioned to East that he should leave a small *gift* just before he left. East understood, winked, and obliged Harvey.

Although Jack was the last one out, his *bequest* remained.

Seconds later, mass *appreciation* followed. The exodus began when three cadets tried to crawl out of the window at once.

"That rotten prick! Where's my towel? I can't see! Phew, even my towel stinks!"

"Mother of God, take me now!"

"I'm dead! My nose and lungs have seized! If I'm not, shoot me Henry, shoot me!"

"I feel like my head's been shoved up a rhinoceros' ass!"

"Your face looks like it."

Entering their living area, a chuckling East smacked his buddy Rothstein's back. "That'll teach 'em to be brazen, eh, Rothie?"

"Too true, Beastie ... too true."

For some reason, signals from the Kelowna radio station wouldn't come in that morning, so the Vernon station had to do. Once again, *Country Fiddler and the Stix* 'entertained' the 'ants' cleaning their barracks. The cadets thought Country Fiddler was as horrible as the announcer sponsored by John Deere.

"We've got Pearl Busby from Lumby on the line this morning. Hello, Pearl."

"Hello? Hello? Am I on the radio? Hello? Dudley, stop coughing, I think I'm on the radio. Hello?"

"Hello, Pearl. Yes, you're on the radio. I called to say that those pies you delivered were just wonderful. The station manager ate a whole pie, himself."

"Oh, thank you, Arnold. The secret is my mother's pastry recipe. Did you also notice I use...?"

Testing the tightness, Danyluk bounced a quarter on his bunk.

Cordell Cross

"Jeez, it's one of those pie dames again. Surely, something else happens in this town besides pie baking? Why doesn't he interview Hop Sing?"

"...*berries. My husband Dudley picks them down by the creek. You can search anywhere and you won't find a better berry. My mother used to say, 'Pearly' ... she always called me, Pearly. 'If you want the best berries, Pearly, you've got to...'*"

Moose turned the radio off. "There's enough pie dames in this town to equip the whole province. I'll betcha Duffy, or whatever her husband's name is, hasn't touched Pearly in years. She's too busy bakin' pies, and he's too busy pickin' the goddamned berries. Unless he's got himself some young fluff down by the creek and Pearl's gettin' it on with either Arnold or the station manager?"

Earl nudged his (and East's) barrack box into line. "Or both of them. Listen, if you want him to interview Hop Sing, why don't you write a letter and ask him?"

An inquiring look came over Moose's face. "Yeah, that's it! I'll write and ask him to interview Hop Sing! Bergie will give me a hand! That's what we'll do during pop break this morning. Right, eh, Bergie?"

Nearly ready for breakfast, Bergie changed into his coveralls. "Oh, come on, Moose? What the hell could Hop Sing say? Well, other than... *Herro Arnold. I'm grad you rikee the dame I sent over rast week. What? Oh, the station manager had her all to himself, did he? She better than pie baking bloads, eh, Arnold? He sinkee his teeth into something leal.*' Hop Sing's got nothing to offer."

Heading over for breakfast, Wane and Douglas couldn't control themselves listening to Bergie's Hop Sing voice. Shortly six others joined them. East was already in the line-up, saving their places.

Breakfast that morning was the usual - Bacon and eggs, toast, French toast, or Kellogg's Corn Flakes. Beverages consisted of hot chocolate from the night before, tea, coffee, milk, or water.

East *shoved* a big piece of bacon in his mouth and nudged his friend. "Bergie, are you sure Genova's not with us anymore?"

"That's the rumour," Bergie replied. "I don't think the OC appreciated him smearing the Vicks."

Sneaky smiles joined the total eye contact of the crouched musketeers muttering in the centre of the table. Bergie had done a good job.

At a table behind, Lyons and his Seaforth friend sat with their backs to the other musketeers. Lyons leaned back balancing on the rear legs of his chair. "Who's gonna replace the pongo?"

Bergie shook his head. "I don't know, Don, the corporal didn't say. Although, anyone is better than Genova."

They all nodded their agreement, then Lyons said, "My learned Scottish friend here, tells me although it's Mother's Night tonight, we could have a problem after lights out. He's heard that 23 and 24 Platoons are planning to raid our side of the barracks."

"Why the hell would they do that?" Douglas asked. "We're all in the same company."

McLeod turned his chair. "Yeah, but our two platoons keep winning the company's daily best platoon award. Some of them on the other side are really pissed off."

Bergie asked Lyons and McLeod to join his table and whispered. "What are they planning on doing? ... And at what time?"

"It's planned for 0100 hours. They're going to move our barrack boxes around so we will have to search for them. It could create quite a havoc tomorrow morning."

"The creeps," yelled Moose before covering his mouth and crouching. "The creeps! Can youse think up a plan, Bergie?"

Bergie thought for a moment, then grinned and glanced around the table. When Bergie grinned his special grin, it became contagious. "I've got one now. Come in a bit closer."

With Lyons and McLeod crammed in, ten heads *discussed* a brilliant ploy that would certainly put the cadets in 23 and 24 Platoons in their places. It was hard for the group not to laugh and Bergie's back must have been sore from all the patting.

After the screen door slammed shut behind them, the nine appointed Moose as the procurer.

"Don't worry, Bergie my boy, I'll get whatever youse needs. Yes, yes ... I said don't worry, didn't I? When the Moose is loose, anything can happen."

Entering the barracks, Bergie responded, saying, "That's what always worries me."

"Bullshit, Bergie; youse don't hafta..."

Jackson interrupted Moose. He'd changed quickly and read the bulletin board while Danyluk and Bergie discussed the plan.

"Bergie, you're the Cadet Company Commander this morning. Moose, you're 2I/C (second in command) and Doug, you're the Cadet CSM. The three of you are to meet Sergeant Bentley in the lecture room at 0745. Wane, you're our Platoon Commander, and Jack, you're our Platoon Sergeant. You two don't have to attend the meeting." Earl then stuck his chest out. "As for me ... well, eat your hearts out because I'm heading to the Headquarters' Building. I've been appointed Battalion RSM for tomorrow's morning's parade."

"You whiner," bellowed a smiling Moose. "Ain't youse the one who's always complainin' that Native people don't get the breaks?"

Earl grabbed his pith helmet and rushed out the door, saying, "Yeah, that's why I'm rushing to get up there. This is one time they ain't gonna change their minds."

Because they had seen the procedure all week, the cadets running the company parade that morning made few errors. Supernumerary positions were appointed from all four platoons and the morning's process of forming up for inspection came off just as well as if regular force staff conducted it.

Following the parade, the musketeers who received parade positions, regretfully had to mention that they couldn't accept this status on Saturday because they would be playing in the band. As well as informing them that Sergeant Major Genova was now filling an administration post in the Headquarters' Building, the OC called out names of other cadets who immediately took the musketeers' places.

Cordell Cross

" ... Sergeant Major Wong will be taking over from WO2 Genova. He won't be arriving until Sunday night."

After the OC's address, all four platoons were marched to the lecture rooms where the cadets received two periods of Morse code. The third period was reserved for teaching them the Smitty Harris Tap Code. This special code has no dashes and can be utilized by just tapping a pencil, finger, or any other object. It is laborious to send, and requires pauses.

(a) •• (b) • •• (c&k) • ••• (d) • •••• (e) • ••••• (f) •• • (g) •• •• (h) •• ••• (I) •• •••• (j) •• ••••• (l) ••• • (m) ••• •• (n) ••• ••• (o) ••• •••• (p) ••• ••••• (q) •••• • (r) •••• •• (s) •••• ••• (t) •••• •••• (u) •••• ••••• (v) ••••• • (w) ••••• •• (x) ••••• ••• (y) ••••• •••• (z) ••••• •••••

During their lectures, it was pointed out that in Korea, prisoners used their eyelids to communicate via this code.

The morning went fast and after lunch all platoons worked in various regions of the camp, climbing poles and laying line.

It was during the last period of laying line that East experienced a problem splicing line in the upper camp.

Humming a song while using spikes attached to leather leg-straps to get him to the steel 'foot-stays' halfway up a telephone pole, East took an orange out of his pocket and began peeling it. He leaned back as taught, knowing his safety belt would hold, however his spikes slipped out, leaving him hugging the pole with his safety belt above him. It held him but he couldn't move; he was now *kissing* the pole.

Embarrassed and also mad because he'd dropped his *snack*, East, with great difficulty reached up, grabbed a steel step, undid one side of his safety belt and then attempted to replant the spikes. It wasn't to be, because the pole was rotten and his handhold came out, the action turning his body upside down - legs wrapped around the pole.

Hugging the pole and sliding, a distraught East moved headfirst towards the ground. The *Gods of food* were with the lad though, because after shifting only a few feet, a large piece of pole snared his belt, shorts, and undershorts, pulling them towards to his ankles as he slid down. He was now suspended, inverted, bare-assed to the breeze, with his shirttail hanging over his head.

"Help," he called. "Can anyone hear me? Jeez, I can't move! Damn it! Hello out there!"

East knew he had better not move his feet because they could slip out of his pants and he'd go plummeting to the ground.

Finally, one of the upper camp's kitchen girls noticed the *beast's* predicament. Although she couldn't see his face, she said, "Are you all right?"

A mortified East who couldn't move was in no mood for small talk. "You mean other than getting cut, scraped, and my balls pierced with fifty-million slivers? Get some help, will ya?"

The girl ran off and within a few minutes, a line truck with a ladder appeared, with most cadets of 21 Platoon following.

Cordell Cross

While Sergeants Bentley and Pennington helped the *exhibitionist* down, comments ran hot and heavy.

"That's the ass that empties the shower room. I know it looks normal now, but don't get fooled! Just think, tonight we can have a shower in peace."

"It's the living fart! He probably *blew* his pants down!"

"You'll be shootin' slivers on your next date, Mac!"

"Chris, take a look at this. This is how you *don't* lay line, or anything else for that matter! Even poles."

"Tryin' to hump a pole were ya, ya dirty devil!"

"If the Scottish aren't fartin' in the showers, they're baring their asses out in the open!"

"He's not a Scot, he's in the Irish!"

"Bull shit he is. He's in the Canadian Scottish Regiment!"

"Like hell he is! It's gotta be the Seaforths! He ain't one of us!"

A Seaforth didn't like that? Take a hike, fella. Look at his ass, body, and legs. He's in the Rocky Mountain Rampluckers! They practice humpin' poles!"

A young RMR said, "I heard that! Up yours!"

"And yours," came a Seaforth response.

When Jack was finally brought down he was covered in slivers, cuts and scrapes from his chin to his (Bergie's words) "family jewels."

Yanking up his shorts and pants, he slowly got in the cab of the line truck and Sergeant Bentley drove him to the MIR.

The rest of the Musketeers didn't see it happen, but they sure heard about it. So much so that after supper they were quite concerned and ready to visit the MIR to find out what had become of their friend. Their worries ended thirty minutes later, however, when East entered the barracks eating a banana.

Instantly swarming around him, Banks asked, "Jack, what the hell happened?"

"I undid my safety belt and did a 180 on the pole. Ya wanna talk about embarrassment. There I was with my pants around my ankles when a cute lookin' dame from the kitchen walks up to me and..."

"No, I didn't mean that. Are you all right?"

East took another banana out of one of his pockets. "Yeah, other than havin' a cut wang, bruised balls, a scratched stomach, and a thousand slivers taken out of me, yeah I'm fine. I've even got a sore ass because of the needles. What was for supper? Damn, I missed it."

Douglas joined in the laughter. "He's fine. When he's looking for food, our Jack's back to normal."

East dropped his pants and undershorts, and lifted up his shirt. "Look what I'm wearing. They said it'll protect me against further injury."

Moose moved right in. "Jesus, they gave you a jockstrap? They're expensive. I had a broad once who was gonna buy me one, and..."

Jack cut him off. "No, it's called a hard cup-protector. They know how important my balls are. The orderly said, 'Your future wife should write and thank me for giving you this.'"

Cunningham slapped East's back. "What did you say?"

"I said, 'Thanks.'"

"That's all you said, just 'Thanks?'" Cunningham asked.

"Yeah. Say, what did you guys have for supper?"

Ten minutes later, Jack was with the rest of them, down on his knees scrubbing floors. All the bunks from one side were moved to the other side and the scrubbing process began. It didn't matter how hard they scrubbed the once hardwood floor, it had been scoured so many times over the years, it was just one great mass of dirty brown slivers. After they finished, it looked no different.

When one side was complete, all the bunks were moved again and they scrubbed the other side of the hut.

After the floors, the boys washed the inside and outside of the windows, washed the window ledges, washed shelves, shined the light switches, shined the fire extinguishers, washed bunk frames, raked the *gardens*, shined the garbage cans, brushed and mopped the outside steps, cleansed the toilets and washing machine, cleansed the urinal and shined the urinal brass, cleansed and shined the sinks, taps and mirrors, and brushed and mopped out the shower room, drying room and centre walk through areas.

During the process, it was Danyluk who volunteered to get a folding ladder so that he could dust and wash the light-shades down the centre of the aisle. After completing all the shades, only the Musketeers noticed Moose sliding a ceiling panel aside before crawling in. Immediately, Bergie threw up a small pack, the panel was then closed and the ladder removed. Amidst smiles and winks, the ladder was stored in the drying room.

Half an hour later, a prearranged signal indicated Moose was ready to come down. Bergie moved the ladder back while Cunningham stood at the other end of the hut screaming, "I've got fifty bucks here that says Marco Polo was *not* a homo! Step right up!"

Cunningham only needed ten seconds to divert the cadets' attention from them catching Moose climbing down, and that's all he got because no *suckers* stepped forward.

"Who says he was?" asked a cadet in the King's Own Calgary Regiment.

"He could have been, but who the hell cares," replied a Scot. "Where'd you get your information from?"

Cunningham took out his money. "Are you betting? Okay, we have a gambler here! All right, let's see the colour of your dough."

"What? Er, no. I don't give a pig's ass what Marco..."

"Good, then get back on your knees - your floor's dry."

"No bets? Fine! Next week I'll have fifty bucks that says Christopher Columbus was *not* a Jehovah's Witness."

As Gordie walked back to his own area, he heard, "Shit, he doesn't give anyone a break, does he?"

"He never does," was the reply. "That's why we're all broke. Say, do you think Marco Polo really was a homo?"

"I dunno, what regiment did he serve in?"

Cordell Cross

When cadets finally finished cleaning their hut, it was kit time. Most clothes had been washed earlier that day, now they along with puttees had to be pressed like never before. After the ironing was over with, cadets shined their boots, belts, and brass and washed their pith helmets.

At 2100 hours, the cadets of B-25 were allowed to go over to the cadet canteen. Even then, some didn't make it because they needed haircuts. Long lines persisted at the camp barbers, so many cadets received haircuts from *friends*. Of course, these *friends* charged for their butchering.

Ten cadets sat at a table in the outdoor courtyard of the canteen. Each had a KiK-Kola and it never tasted better. The day had been long and their eyelids drooped a little.

"Any problems?" asked Bergie, nudging his *best buddy*.

Moose took a swig and groaned as he stretched his legs.

"None whatsoever, except for the bats. There are bats up there. I could have been bitten and turned into a werewolf."

Harvey laughed. "You're already a wolf. Don't you mean a vampire?"

"Whatever."

Lyons found it difficult keeping his head up. His eyelids kept closing and he didn't understand what was going on. "Any gloves?"

"No, I didn't wear any."

"I meant baseball gloves, you dummy. Or how about balls?"

"I said vampire, not umpire, and I ain't talkin' about baseball bats. Yeah, there were balls …mine, and the bats didn't get at 'em."

"If it was me they would have had them," said East. "They would have smelled the wood and the blood."

"What time are we gonna pull this off?" Douglas asked.

Bergie chewed on his lower lip. "Let's see, lights are out at 2230. Give 'em, say, half-an-hour or so. I'd say 2300. Yeah, how does that sound?"

All agreed 2300 would be just fine.

At bed check, some cadets were already asleep. Those who stood by their beds were sleeping shortly thereafter, but not the musketeers. When the lights were turned out and the rest were sound asleep, East and Earl quietly moved their bunk two feet out into the aisle. Moose then stood up on Jackson's upper bunk, opened the ceiling panel and uncoiled some wire. As Danyluk attached the end of the wire to a dry cell and a Morse code key, the bunk was moved back.

Time moved slowly, but it was just as well because the Musketeers and one Seaforth could see the light still on in a corporal's cubicle in the other wing. At five past eleven it went out, and Rothie, the swiftest *sender* smiled, wrung his hands, and approached the key. "Say when," he whispered, stretching his fingers.

Bergie waited another minute, then said, "Go."

Rothstein's two fingers and a thumb went under the blanket, grabbed the key and sent a message. — — —/•• —/• — • — • — •/— — —/• — •/• — — •/— — —/• — •/ —/• — •• ••/••• • —/— • • —/•••/••• /•••• /— — —/• — ••/• (our corporal is an asshole)

130 – NEXT STOP, VERNON!

A light came on in the southern corporal's cubicle in the other wing, followed by the northern corporal's light, followed by the main lights down the other wing's aisle.

Ten cadets had to muffle their laughs as, "Stand by your beds," boomed through the windows and the centre portion of the hut.

"All right! Who's the wise guy?

The cadets of 23 and 24 Platoons standing at attention didn't have a clue what was goin on. Most stood there yawning, scratching and looking around for the guilty *creep* that created the problem.

"I asked who the wise guy is? Listen you people, if one or two of you want to punish this whole side, you're doing a hell of a job. Now, put your keys away and hit the sack! There will be no more name-calling tonight! Is that clear?"

All voices on the east wing thundered, "Yes, Corporal!"

"Good! And I want you to know that I'm not an asshole! Actually, I'm a good guy until I get annoyed! Now, get to bed!"

Two minutes later the main lights were out, including the lights in both corporals' cubicles.

Although smiling, a small amount of perspiration appeared on Rothstein's forehead when he said, "Say when, Bergie."

"Not just yet, Rothie. Okay ... Now!"

Rothstein tapped out: •• —/• — — •/   — • — —/— — —/•• —/• — •/•••   — • — •/— — — —/• — •/• — — • (up yours Corp).

The sound of the buzzer placed just above the centre air vent did its job. All lights in the other wing came on quickly after the eastern wing corporals stormed out of their cubicles.

"Stand by your beds," bellowed the southern corporal "So, up mine, eh? Did you hear that, Wally?"

Wally sure did. "Right, boots on, and form three ranks on the road! Quickly now, quickly!"

When approximately seventy cadets bitch and complain, their whining can be heard everywhere. This night was no exception as cadets all blaming each other and only dressed in undershorts, socks and boots, formed three ranks on the road. For the next hour they had the parade square to themselves. Along with the parade square came the night air and hoarse voices.

With handshakes all 'round, seven musketeers hit the sack knowing Douglas and Wane would remain up for the second *shift*.

"Right, pay attention here! You've had an hour on the parade square. If you want more, my learned colleague will happy to oblige you. Hit the sack and quit the tomfoolery!"

While Douglas wrung his hands, Wane said, "We'll give 'em five minutes."

Five minutes later, Wane said, "Go."

Douglas sent: — • — —/— — —/•• —/• — •/•   •••/—/•• /• — ••/• — ••/ — ••/   • —/— •/   • —/•••/•••/••••/— — —/• — ••/• (you're still an asshole).

Following the message, Brice said, "I left out the apostrophe in the first word."

Cordell Cross

Wane was going to reply that they hadn't yet learned those additional characters, but sounds of armed conflict joined the commotion erupting in the other wing. Whining and bitching could probably be heard at the top of Silver Star Mountain.

"Stand by your beds, you grubby little Godforsaken...! Christ, I can't believe this! Get your boots on again! Wally, take 'em out for an-hour-and-a-half!"

Banks found it hard not to laugh as he shook Douglas' hand. "We'd be hung from the highest rafters if they knew. Wow, just listen to 'em."

Brice replied, "It's hard not to listen. The whole camp must be able to hear them."

A few moments later, Jackson and East were awakened and their bunk was moved out. It took a few shakes to wake up Moose, but in a second he was up top with a flashlight. Fifteen minutes later, all equipment was down and the bunk was moved back.

Moose tiptoed over to Wane's bunk and whispered, "Were they pissed off the second time?"

Banks' face said it all. "Pissed off? You mean did the World War 3 start? Yes, it sure as hell did, and it's still going on."

All five wanted to laugh aloud, but instead they mock-punched each other and hit the sack.

Just before Moose jumped back into bed, he murmured to Jackson, "Just look at Bergie's peaceful face. He'd make a great choirboy."

One of Bergie's eyes opened, and a smile appeared. "What's all that noise?"

"It's the other side declaring war on each other and the world," replied Danyluk.

Bergie rolled over on his side. "Oh, is that all? Tell the inconsiderate creeps to keep it down to a dull roar, will ya. We've got to be up early tomorrow."

Cordell Cross

Chapter 10

Of all military tunes, Reveille undoubtedly is the one most despised. Reveille might sound fine if played during the day, but at 0530 in the morning, its first four notes, followed by four more, then five, are recognized as *living hell*.

Cadet Brophie the bugler didn't jump back into bed this particular morning - his bedding had to be rolled up Saturday morning style like everyone else's.

Over the next few minutes throughout the camp, a process began where each mattress is rolled up with a pillow inside. A blanket is laid out and its sides are folded inwards ending at the centre stripe. It is then folded up like a concertina, ending up with three folds to its front. Two sheets are then folded in two's then folded again and placed on top of the blanket. Each sheet has four folds to its front, aligned with the blanket's three folds. Another blanket is then folded like the first and laid on top of the sheets. Now, the process is nearly complete, so the last blanket is folded lengthways and very neatly wrapped around the *sandwich*, thus completing the job. This bedding is then neatly laid on the mattress and lined up with all of the other sets. Even the mattresses had to be lined up and the height of each set of bedding has to be the same. These items, like many, were measured to an umpteenth of an inch, as were the positions and spaces between tables and benches in the middle of the aisles of both wings.

While Douglas stood at the north end of the western half of the wing holding the end of a piece of string, Wane stood at the southern end holding the other end of the string. Along the line, the string was moved at times allowing cadets of both platoons to ensure their bunks, barrack boxes, mattresses, and bedding were exactly aligned. There could be no excuses for one component being out of line. All articles had to be perfectly lined up like finely *dressed* Grenadier Guards in line. The same thing happened on the other side of the hut.

Country Fiddler and the Stix weren't playing on Vernon radio this Saturday morning. John Deere Tractor and Equipment had taken a break from sponsoring the *beloved* group. Instead, the station played current hits that gave the boys a lift while doing their chores. One of the records played while the cadets on the west side of B-25 made their beds Saturday Morning Inspection style was Jo Stafford's *Make Love to Me*.

"Just give me the chance and I'll make love to youse," Danyluk said, referring to voluptuous voice of Jo Stafford. "With my good looks, charm, posture, sleuth and vulture, and your money, we could rule the world of love. Hey, did I say that? I'm gettin' good, ain't I, Bergie?"

Bergie was having great difficulty sorting out his and Danyluk's barrack box. Although he grinned at the expression on Moose's face, he was more concerned about the attitude in the other wing.

"What's it look like on the other side this morning. Do any of them look like they're in a *loving* mood?"

Rothstein answered. "Hell, it looks like a mortuary over there. Everyone has blood-shot eyes - even the corporals'. They don't know who did it and they all suspect each other."

A full grin came to Bergie's lips as he winked at those around him. "Hah, that'll teach 'em to try and mess around with the professionals."

"*That was Jo Stafford singing, Make Love to Me. A great voice and a great gal. Not as great as the gal we've got on the phone-line though. Go ahead, Daisy.*"

"*Hello Arnold. I've been trying to get on the line for weeks. Did you get that pie I sent you? Did you taste those berries? I picked them myself and I said to my husband Hubert; I said, Hubert, these are the best...*"

Danyluk held up his open arms to the air. "Son of a bitch, it's one of those pie dames again. My god, don't these women ever sleep in? Bergie, you've got to give me a hand gettin' that announcer to phone Hop Sing. These pie ladies are drivin' me up the wall."

Moose stopped complaining and his expression indicated a new thought. "What the hell am I talkin' about? I'll be back!"

After Moose grabbed his beret and stormed out of the barracks, *Wanted*, with Perry Como's voice came over the airwaves.

"Where's he gone?" asked Jackson, tying up his running shoes.

Bergie shrugged and started singing after he said, "Your guess is as good as mine. *Our Moose goes where the wild Moose goes; and we'll never know where the wild Moose goes.*"

East peeled an orange and made sure every bit of the peel went in the pockets of his coveralls. If a piece was seen on the floor, the company would lose pennant points. "Hey, you're a pretty good singer, Bergie. Do you know how to sing, *Far, far away?*"

"Stick it in your ear, East."

When Perry's record finished, Okanagan Arnold the radio announcer, returned to his microphone.

"*That was Perry Como. Boy, he's had a lot of hits. Did you know that Perry used to be a barber? I'll bet he's making more money now. Keep up the good work, Perry.*"

"*Well, we're coming up to the seven o'clock news, and ... Wait, we'll take one more call. Go ahead, you're on the air with Okanagan Arnold.*"

"*Is that youse Arnold? Okanagan Arnold?*"

"*Yes, you're on the air with Okanagan Arnold. Who am I speaking with?*"

"*It's Dudley here, Okanagan, er, I mean Okanagan Arnold. Did youse and your station manager eat those pies my wife sent to you? The ones with them there berries?*"

"*We certainly did, Dudley, and they were some of the best pies we've had in weeks. Why?*"

"*'Cause we discovered ants and gnats in our other pies, Okanagan Arnold. I've been spittin' them out of both ends all mornin'. Have youse noticed some of the berries are kickin'? The wife's out back in the outhouse as we speak. She's been there for two hour with only yesterday's newspaper to help her. The reverse bung will do that to ya every time. It's her pies what's done it, Arnie. Found dead ants all over her pillow this mornin'. Her bakin' days are over for a while, Arnie, er, Okanagan Arnold.*"

"*What? Ants? Gnats in the pies? Where? When?*"

"*This whole valley's got a plague of berry ants, Arnie. If youse has been eatin' pies, youse has been eatin' ants. How are your innards doing? Has the reverse bung hit youse yet?*"

"*Oh, er, now that you mention it, I ... er ... thank you Dudley.*"

Cordell Cross

"Hey, before I sign off here, Arne, how's about gettin' Hop Sing on the radio one of these here mornings?"

"Hop Sing ... the laundry man?"

"Yeah, he don't bake pies, but he sure knows his business. Okay?"

"Er, what? Hop Sing? Er, yeah, sure. Thanks Dudley. Here's the news."

The whole west side of B-25's cadets that had gathered around Danyluk's radio still remained there when a proudly grinning Moose re-entered the barracks. When they saw Moose's smile of accomplishment, they had to hold their stomachs even tighter.

Yanking off his beret, he said, "Did I do it, or did I do it?"

Along with the rest of the Musketeers, Bergie shook his buddy's hand. "Did you do it? You bet you did, 'cause Okanagan Arnold's not even reading the news, someone else is. Boy, when you get mad, you also get even, don't you?"

"I had to do it, Bergie. I bet that's the last we'll hear of pies all summer. Now we'll get Hoppy on the air, right?"

"Right," came the ear-splitting response.

"Breakfast's on," yelled East. "I'll save our places."

When the red-eyed cadets from 23 and 24 platoons entered the mess hall, facial expressions indicated they were still distrustful of each other. Two-and-a-half hours on the parade square not only destroyed their raiding plans, it also ruined their night's sleep.

Blaming didn't stop and one hoarse cadet in the food line-up was really upset. "I know damned well it's one of those creeps from 23 Platoon. They're the ones frenching beds and stealing our washin'. Jeez, close to three hours of doing drill in our underwear. It was cold as hell out there."

"And we never got to *do* the other side's barrack boxes," said another.

Although a nearby cadet said, "Not so loud," Bergie's ears picked up the *information*.

"McLeod, your tip was right on. How'd you find out about it?"

Lyons' chess-playing friend was totally amazed at the upset the musketeers had pulled off. He wasn't used to this kind of scheming.

"A friend of mine visiting from driver mech was sitting on the jon and heard two of them when they were doing their laundry. Check, Don."

"Damn, not again," Lyons bellowed, with his eyes glued to the board.

Bergie's mischievous grin said it all. "Well, I never thought I'd say it, but your D&M friend deserves a medal. We would have had a hell of a problem this morning if our barrack boxes had been switched."

"I still don't understand their logic," Douglas said, picking up his plate, utensils, and cup. "We're all in the same company. If they had been successful, we wouldn't have had a hope in hell of winning the pennant. We wouldn't have been organized. Did anyone find out who planned the thing?"

"I know who planned it," said McLeod. "It was a guy named Tong in 24 Platoon. Richard, er, my friend, heard someone mention his name."

Moose finished his coffee, collected his dishes, and stood up. "I'll pound the shit out of the pongo. What's he look like? Is he blonde, red-haired, how tall is he?"

Cordell Cross

Banks' jaw dropped. "Moose, if his name's Tong, he ain't blonde or red-headed. He's Chinese, for God's sake. Get with it will ya?"

"Oh yeah?" Moose sat down again. "Well, Mr. Banks, I once went out with a Chinese girl who had orange hair. Her name is Apple-Blossom Chan. I used to call her Orange-Bottom Chan, and boy did she..."

"Hold it, hold it," Rothstein demanded. "Her name is Apple-Blossom Chan, and you called her Orange-Bottom Chan. Could I be so bold as to ask why you called her that?"

"Certainly, Rothie. Youse has heard of some of these old-country customs, haven't ya?"

All eyes switched to Rothstein. "Er, well, I guess I've heard of some."

"Well, then?" Moose asked, grabbing Bergie's teacup.

Bergie stopped the cup just before it united with Danyluk's lips. "That's mine, you creep."

"Oh, pardoney meeee. Well, her mother believed if she rubbed orange peel on her daughter's ass, it would be nice and soft for her future husband."

Danyluk then picked up East's cup because Jack had gone back for thirds. He emptied the cup with two sips.

"Well?" asked Rothstein, nose to nose with Danyluk.

The *animal* wiped his lips and burped. "Well, what?"

"Was the skin on her ass, soft?"

"Hey, youse is askin' me a personal question here. Do I ask youse if the skin on your girlfriend's ass is soft?"

"A chess-playing Lyons was in his impish mood when he said, "Check," followed by, "How the hell would *he* know anyway? A guy's got to have a girlfriend to know that stuff."

Rothstein's face turned red. "Oh, yeah? At least I can tell the difference between the face and ass of my girl. With your hippo, it's hard to tell."

Both Lyons and Rothstein laughed with the rest. Then East returned, eager to say something. "I wouldn't tackle with Tong, Moose. He looks like a tough from the streets of Calcutta. I betcha he's really tough. You should see the arms on the guy. He's got muscles on muscles and the jerk grabbed the last orange even though I had my hand on it."

"Calcutta's in India," Bergie said, before returning his attention to *more important matters*. Anyway, what was the ass like?"

As East picked up his empty cup, he thought the question was for him. "How the hell would I know? I didn't look at his ass. Why would I look at his ass? What's with you, Bergie? Jeez, Earl and I are movin' our bunks if you ask questions like that. Did you guys hear that? How did Tong's ass look. Hey, who drank my coffee?"

Laughing his head off, Douglas said, "If we stay here, we're all gonna have to rub our asses. Let's go."

Outside, in addition to admitting he drank Jack's coffee, Moose said, "Youse wants to know about the ass? Smooth ain't the word, but the smell of oranges turned off my kisses."

Cordell Cross

Jack stopped in his tracks. "What, you too? Tong's got a smooth ass? Who the hell am I involved with here?"

East was pushed into B-25 after he ran away from getting Moose and Bergie's arms placed around his shoulders.

"Get away from me, you creeps. I thought you wanted to clobber him, not kiss and make up."

Earl Jackson was at his peak as battalion regimental sergeant major that morning. Sizing fourteen hundred cadets is a chore, but he handled it in a professional manner and handed the parade over to the cadet adjutant, who in turn handed it over to the cadet second-in-command, who passed it along to the cadet commanding officer.

The regular force camp commanding officer, Brigadier W.J. Megill took his time inspecting his cadets, and throughout his review, the BCR band played its one and only slow tune, *The Waltz.*

This was the first time most cadets had seen the commanding officer, and because he insisted on inspecting every platoon, over sixty cadets fainted due to the early-morning heat. Those who passed out were taken to the side of the parade and told to remain in the sitting position with his head resting on his knees.

"Does this guy take his time, or what?" Moose whispered to Lyons.

"He's infantry," Lyons replied. "If he was armoured, he'd be finished and having a beer in the mess."

After inspecting the companies, the brigadier inspected the band, accompanied by Kelly with his chest out a mile.

"Good to see the whole BCR band up here. They play very well."

"Thank you, sir."

The brigadier stopped at Lyons. "Do you find that base-drum heavy?"

"Only when it rains, sir."

"What? Oh yes, ha, ha, only when it rains. Good show - yes, jolly good show."

The inspection of the band took five minutes and although the officer spoke with nearly every cadet, for some reason he missed Danyluk.

"You don't count, Moose." Banks muttered.

The *animal* grinned slightly whispering, "Oh? Oh yes, yes, jolly good that I don't. It's a jolly good show that he missed the most important player in the band. The only one with two instruments."

"Oh, quit bragging," East mumbled out the corner of his mouth. "He ain't like you and Bergie."

"I'm talkin' about my cymbals you pongo. Go stuff it."

The brigadier's *walk* back to the dais seemed like eternity, as did his address to the cadets following the march past.

"...And as you progress through life, you will always recall these wonderful memories and your inner strength will be stronger for accomplishing the challenges we've presented you with when you were here. Why, when I was your age, we..."

The officer rambled on and on, and twenty minutes later, at the close of his *speech,* and following the advance in review order, Brigadier Megill handed the parade over to RSM Gardiner and left the parade square as Gardiner grabbed the microphone.

"Far too many people passed out this morning. It will not happen again! What the bloody hell do you think this is - cub camp? Thirty-six cadets from IBT alone, including six from the guard. The temperature at this time is only 80 degrees, not 180 degrees."

The RSM took a paper out of his pocket. "The signals barracks was a close second to an IBT barracks this morning. The reason - a pit from an orange was found on the floor of 24 Platoon. Had it not been there the signals barracks would have won. However, considering the number of people in IBT that fainted, I'm overlooking that pit. The pennant this week goes to ... Signals Company!"

The cheering from signals was *loud and clear*.

"However, I am not at all happy with your dress! The dress of all companies! It will improve immediately and by next Saturday, it will be perfect. If not, then there will be no midnight passes! Parade commander carry on!"

After the band handed in their instruments, B-25 came alive again. Cadets remade their beds after a sheet and pillowcase exchange, and following that, the same chubby mail corporal entered. "Mail call! Read 'em and weep! Wallach, East, McLeod, Adams, Zablotny, Sidhu, Lyons, Brown, Rothstein, Cunningham, Brice, M. Danyluk, Lips Danylick, Cohen, Stud Danyluk, Banks, Bergie the Jerkie, Stannard, Moose The Goose Danyluk, Moosie Loverlips Danyluk, My Lover the Moose ... "

The Corporal knew *this* barracks because he'd been here many times before. "Don't you ever get normal mail?" he asked Danyluk.

Cunningham yelled, "He don't have normal dames, so please continue!"

"Danny my Luck, Phillips, Henderson, Glover, Banks, Jackson, El Cheapo Cripps, Mouse Dandylucky... "

Subsequent to being told it was "Moose, not Mouse," the corporal stormed out shaking his head and muttering, "That kid keeps weird company. Real weird."

The hut quietened down as the boys read their letters and relaxed. Its occupants knew they had three-quarters-of-an-hour before tests and they made the most of it.

The only person not reading his mail was Cunningham. In addition to cadets getting news from home, they pocketed their money openly. This pleased the *gambler* with the million eyes. With black book in hand, Cunningham made the rounds promptly collecting his *dues*.

Although most letters were treated as confidential, bits of information from home were transferred from bunk to bunk.

"My little brother was caught smoking. Jeez, he's in shit."

"Hey, we've bought a new car. I'm gettin' the old one to work on."

"Aunt Olga's had her wart removed."

"Damn it, my sister's gone and lost my baseball glove. I hope she's got lots of dough?"

"Mom and Dad are visiting next week. Do ya wanna come with us for the weekend?"

Cordell Cross

In the bunk above Bergie, a smiling and perfume-smelling Moose shuffled his letters into reading priority. The animal knew the letters he wanted to read first. When he began, his chuckling became contagious. "Bergie, listen to this. It's from Thelma. Jesus, it stinks of perfume."

"My dear Moosehead: I... "

Bergie stopped reading his own letter. "She calls you Moosehead?"

"Hey, it's a personal compliment! Only I knows what she means."

"Thelma? Ain't she the one with three nostrils? The one who's planning to work for a fragrance company?"

"Yeah, that's her."

"It figures."

"Dear Moosehead: I just received your letter and I'm holding it next to my hearts. It was nice..."

Now Jackson got into the act. "Did you say *hearts*?"

"Will youse let me get on with this letter? Of course I said hearts. She's got two of 'em!"

"Wow, three nostrils and two hearts? How many bazookas has she got? Six?"

Bergie howled, "With Thelma, anything's possible."

Frustrated, Moose continued. *"It was nice of youse to write to me. You know, youse is the only one of all the boys I go out with, that I really like. Youse always treats me like a lady even though I don't deserve it. I never told youse this, Moosehead, but I've got sixteen boyfriends. But they don't do what youse does. They just want my body. When youse took me to your house and made hot dogs, I felt like a real queen when you let me eat ten of them. Then when we went into your hearse, I felt my hearts pumping. It didn't matter that my nostrils picked up sort of an eye-watering odour, my breasts were yours ... all four of them, and... "*

"I was close," Jackson shouted, laughing away. "Jeez, she's got four breasts?"

Moose stopped reading his letter. "No you frump ... she's only got three, but I tell her they're like four. I ain't readin' anymore."

Jackson pleaded, "Aw, c'mon, Moose? Finish it."

"Nope."

Lyons glanced up from his chessboard. "How the hell *can* he finish it? With a broad like that, after he diddles her she probably says, 'Thanks, now, er, do the other one.'"

"Stick it in your ear, Don."

That statement really got Lyons in the mood. "I'll bet you don't say that to her, *Moosehead*, because she's probably got eight of 'em."

There wasn't time for *Moosehead* to finish the letter. Moments later, the company was on the road marching to the lecture rooms south of B-3. Tests took up the next hour before lunch.

Like Sergeant Beckford the year before, Sergeant Bentley passed out test papers.

Confidently, he said, "You should all do very well on these tests. When I tell you to turn them over, write your name on the top right corner. You have one hour to complete them. Right, carry on."

Brice finished in a half-hour and waited outside for Wane.

Five minutes later when his smiling buddy appeared, he said, "I thought I was fast, but you whizzed through those. Whadoya think?"

Douglas took a very small shoe rag and wiped his boots before passing the cloth to Wane. "I don't know what to think. Either we studied too hard, or someone forgot about Brigadier Megill's challenge. The only question I got stumped on was the receiving distance of the 19's B-set. Did anything stump you?"

"I had a tough time with Signal Office Duties. That message we had to correct must have been written by Moose."

A voice from behind them indicated Rothstein was also finished. "It probably was. Tell me, what are the characters for an error in Morse? I've forgotten."

The cadets of Signals Company had recently been taught symbols for the period, comma, question mark, colon, semicolon, hyphen, slash, quotation, and short-form for the word, 'error.'

Douglas knew. "It's eight dits, Rothie. Try to remember there are no dashes when sending the error signal. How'd you do?"

Rothstein got into step. "Other than that, I think I aced it. Are we going for a KiK?"

Banks wrapped a hand around the back of each of their necks. "Hey, we can do whatever we want. It's Saturday, remember? C'mon, I'll buy - I got five bucks from home."

"How about two KiKs, Mr. Banks?"

"Don't push your luck, Dougie, or I'll get like Lingus and write it down in my little black book."

When the three arrived at the cadet canteen, *Rock around the Clock*, with Bill Haley and the Comets boomed from the jukebox in the near-empty room. Fifteen minutes later, the place was full and the atmosphere seemed like payday. Obviously, quite a few letters from home contained money.

"Thelma sent me thirteen dollars," said Moose. "That's her lucky number."

Jackson nodded. "I'll bet. What does she do on Halloween - go trick or treating as herself?"

"Screw you, Earl. She may not be perfect, but she's got the personality of a.."

"Centipede?" Lyons quipped as he handed everyone a Fudgicle. "She's probably got a personality to match all of her parts."

"What's on, today?" East asked, drinking a KiK-Kola, eating an apple and licking a Fudgicle all at the same time. "What time are we meeting the dames?"

Earl cringed and nearly spit out his mouthful of pop. "We ain't meeting the girls today. We're meeting them tonight. Jeez, I knew there was something on my mind I forgot to tell you guys about. When I was at the headquarters building yesterday, I picked up a message from Alma to Moose. Do you remember last year when they joined the Vernon Girls Softball Team?"

Bergie appeared impatient. "Get it out, man."

"Okay, okay, they're playin' baseball in Penticton, and won't be back until 1800. We're to meet them at the Arena at eight o'clock."

"Unbelievable," East said. I travel over three hundred miles and my woman puts softball ahead of gettin' a quick feel."

Rothstein burst out laughing. "That's why she's doin' it. You're just too quick. Besides, every time you kiss her, you've got something in your mouth ... like food."

"Bull shit I have! Did you guys hear that? I never chew food when I'm kissin' dames. Speak for yourself, Rothie. Ever since I cut my tongue on that dame's braces I'm a little leery, that's all."

The news that he wouldn't be seeing Diane until the dance at the Arena that night didn't sit well with Douglas. After all, the musketeers had been in camp all week. Although he hadn't seen her since the weekend past, she was on his mind daily. He could have visited town during the week, but that would be letting the B-25 team down, and that just wasn't on. "We could hitchhike to Penticton and get a ride back with them."

Bergie didn't like the thought at all. "Oh, sure, and get picked up by the military police and shipped home. Brilliant strategy, Doug. Carry on, we'll miss you."

It was Wane who thoroughly understood the look on Douglas' face. "Okay, I know you've got a plan. What is it? I mean, count me in, but what are we going to do?"

"We take the old road to Kelowna. Listen, we know the military police patrol the main highway up to the observation point. We don't take that route. We hitchhike on the road cutting through the upper camp. You know the road that runs parallel with the east arm of Okanagan Lake. Once we're in Kelowna, we switch to Highway 97. Am I brilliant, or what?"

Cunningham pocketed his deck of cards. "Er, yeah, you're brilliant, but we all know there's hardly any traffic on that road. We might have to wait hours for a ride."

Moose counted himself in and when he was serious, his slang disappeared. "You mean *rides*. So what? It's worth a try. Come on you pansies, our ladies are waiting for us. Doug's got a good idea."

"But they don't even know we're coming," East said.

Five minutes later, they had made a decision. It was the back road to Kelowna for everyone except Lyons and McLeod. Lyons' girl was at home with her friend who would be introduced to McLeod.

A proud Lyons stuck out his chest. "Her name's Elsie, but she uses the nickname *Easy*. Ask her if her father has a liquor cabinet in her house, okay?"

"Er, sure, but why do they call her Easy?"

Danyluk got back to being his real self. "Are youse a virgin, McLeod? That's a foolish question because I know what most Seaforths are like."

Embarrassed, McLeod didn't know what to say. "Well, I did have a bad case of lover's nuts once, and uh..."

"Really? Well, when youse meets this dame, youse won't have need of another case. Her rolls of fat may even help youse."

As eight cadets headed towards Kelowna, Lyons and McLeod marched down the hill.

After giving Hop Sing's an eyes left, McLeod appeared a little apprehensive. "Is she really that fat?"

After the eyes front, Lyons kept a straight face. "Yup, but fat's good for you. Just don't get lost in one of her rolls. Apparently she hates that."

"How the hell will I know?"

"You'll know ... you'll know. Don't ask me. I get lover's nuts too, but with luck, that's going to change this summer."

While Lyons and McLeod edged closer to two sets of *lover's nuts,* the *Kelowna-bound* cadets didn't tackle the dust-bowl road leading to the upper camp. Rather, they marched south on Highway 97 and then headed west on the upper camp's only paved road. Shortly they were marching south on the old Kelowna highway.

The boys noticed quite a few military buildings west of the road had been boarded up. Most of them were H-huts and their appearance indicated they hadn't been used for years.

East chomped on an apple while viewing the old dialects. "There are enough buildings up here to house another 500 cadets. I wonder why they don't increase the number of cadets coming to this camp?"

"They probably don't have a big enough budget," Bergie said, adding, "Did you guys know they ripped down over 200 buildings after the war? This camp was one hell of a size. I've also heard rumours that German prisoners of war were housed here and they were allowed to go into town unescorted."

Rothstein crumpled up his face. "You've got to be joking? They let those bastards just walk around without a guard?"

"That's what I hear, Rothie. Where could they go? Those that did take off were caught and sent to tougher institutions."

Harvey stopped and shook his head. "Our guys were being starved and shot, and we let those evil monsters walk around at will. Those who allowed that should've had their heads examined, or better still, *they* should have been locked up."

Bergie smiled and put his right arm around Rothstein's shoulders. "Rothie, German prisoners had it so good, many of them returned after the war and bought property up here. Nice eh?"

Harvey's face said it all, but he added, "Goddamned idiots, that's what we were."

"Here comes a truck," Banks yelled. "Quick Moose, show your leg and hold your thumb out."

"Up your nose, Banks. I ain't showin' my leg unless a beautiful blonde is drivin'."

Douglas spotted the driver. "How about a white-haired farmer?"

"That's good enough for me," said Moose, quickly sticking out his leg and showing his thumb.

The smiling farmer stopped. He was short, chubby, about sixty-five and wearing an old beat-up English-style cap.

"Where are you boys headin'?"

Cunningham became the spokesman because he was the closest cadet to the truck's cab. "Kelowna, sir. Are you going near there?"

"Near enough. Two can ride in the front and the rest of you can sit on the crates in the back. Hop in boys. Miss Millie will take us there."

Cordell Cross

After an eager Cunningham replied, "Thank you, sir," Rothstein and East climbed in the front, the rest jumped in the back and the old truck sputtered away.

The driver told his new *companions* East and Rothstein that he had just dropped off some apples and was returning to his farm on the outskirts of Kelowna.

Sitting on empty crates in the back, the boys smiled like Cheshire cats.

"Showin' my leg did it," said Moose. "This right leg o' mine could sink a thousand ships."

Bergie agreed, to a point. "If you took off your sock, it would stink like a thousand shits. Don't hold your breath, Moose - this beat-up old thing might not make it."

Even with dry red-hot air encircling them, the back-hills ride to Kelowna was better than what the doctor could have ordered for cadets who had been shut-ins all week. The sky was as blue as robins' eggs and those in the back gawked at the spectacular-coloured hills uniting with the indigo of Okanagan Lake.

This was the break they needed. As the truck rambled to Kelowna, anything relating to the colour of khaki was barely discussed. Instead, they talked about *women*, the world, school, paper routes, home, and unfortunately for some, even hearses.

Moose grinned proudly just thinking about *his* vehicle. "Just think, in two weeks time my older brother's gonna bring up my hearse. Alma will finally get to lie in the casket. The bar will be operational, and with music playing, all the girls in Vernon will want to meet me just to get near it."

"Where are you going to park the thing?" asked Douglas.

"On one of the side-streets just outside camp. I actually thought about parking it in the sergeants' mess parking lot, but there might be prob..."

A loud "bang" interrupted Danyluk's dreams and the truck swerved nearly going off the road. Everyone had a tough time hanging on. Eventually, when the driver gained control, he stopped, got out, viewed his left front tire, and threw his cap on the ground.

"Damn, it's that same Goddamned tire that burst last week! Sorry boys, but I don't have a spare!"

All cadets got out and looked at the tire. There were no visible treads and going over a pothole must have been all that was needed to create the two-inch hole.

"What are you going to do?" Wane asked, studying the strain on the old man's face.

"Dunno," the driver said, bending over, picking up his cap and slapping it against his right leg before putting it on. "Last week I had to hike to Charlie's house to phone Victor's Garage. Damn that tire."

Cunningham couldn't believe it. "You mean nobody picked you up? You had to walk? How far is it to Charlie's house?"

"I was closer last week. Charlie lives about eight miles south of here. As far as being picked up, there's very little traffic on this road, son."

Not much was said as the driver inspected the tire and the cadets gathered at the back looking at one another, but mainly at Douglas. After all, it was his idea to take the route.

Finally, Bergie broke the silence. "What now, old wise one?"

Like the rest of those who rode in the back, dust covered the *wise one's* face. "We could always push, couldn't we?"

"What, Dougie, push this heap of shit?" Moose asked, before quickly covering his mouth and lowered his voice. "Push this bucket of bolts eight miles? Are youse out of your cotton-pickin' mind? It's gotta be a hundred degrees up here and you wants us to push this thing. Jesus, Doug, give us a break. We'd never get it up some of these hills."

"You got a better idea?" Wane asked Danyluk.

Danyluk took off his beret, wiped the perspiration off his forehead, and then pulled his pants away from his crotch.

"Yeah, let's walk until another ride appears."

"What, and leave the old guy here?" Rothstein asked. "Hey, that's real appreciation - BCR style. He's a hell-of-a nice old fella. His name's Fred, and he's been tellin' us what he did around here when he was a boy."

A guilty look hit Moose. "I was thinkin' as Irish think, you creep."

Within minutes, with the old fella steering and the truck in neutral, eight *keen* cadets pushed Miss Millie towards Charlie's house, which as far as they were concerned could have been on the moon.

At first only berets came off, but during the second hour, shirts and hose-tops came off as well. Miss Millie was heavy and the dance was long. An hour-and-a-half later, unseen red skin accompanied both foot and hand blisters, aches and pains and bitching. Always out of breath, Moose led the grumbling parade. "Hey, tell him to stop for awhile. I've gotta get these pants off."

Bergie grunted, pushing harder. "Get your mind out of the gutter. Christ, Moose, here we are at the gates of hell and you're thinking about dames again. Give your wang a break for God's sake."

"I'm not thinkin' about dames, Bergie," Moose wheezed. "I'm wearin' my tight underwear and it's diggin' into my balls. I think my wang's nearly cut in half."

The ground at this point was rather level so Danyluk's efforts in pushing the truck wouldn't be missed too much.

"Youse guys carry on and I'll catch up to ya."

As Miss Millie rolled away. Moose stiffly walked to the side of the road and in great pain removed his pants and undershorts. When they were off, a naked Moose felt like he was in Heaven as a very light breeze massaged the *hot spots* where his skin had worn away.

With his undershorts around his head, his shirt wrapped around his waist, and his pants tucked under an arm, the unclothed *animal* sat down on the side of the road, waving away the bugs and not caring the slightest about the fact that cars or trucks could appear at any moment.

"Why should they show up now?" he mumbled. "We've been on this Godforsaken road for hours and I ain't gonna start worryin' about receivin' company when I feel like this. Damn, this feels good. I ain't gonna wear those gaunch again. Well, maybe when I'm with my dames. Yeah, just when the girls are around."

Cordell Cross

Two miles south, a military jeep slowly advanced towards Miss Millie's position. One of the vehicle's two occupants was immersed in the serenity of the countryside's unblemished beauty. "I can't get over this, Mr. Gardiner. Never in my life have I experienced such wonder. Before I was asked to command this camp, a few of my fellow officers informed me the whole area was just a dust bowl. It is most kind of you to show me the real off-the-road magnificence of the Okanagan Valley."

"It's a pleasure I knew you would enjoy, sir. Although this route is a little dusty, there's hardly any traffic, and..."

Gardiner stopped talking when he spotted Miss Millie.

"Looks like a farmer and his children have really got their hands full pushing that old bucket of bolts."

"Christ, there's a jeep heading our way," Banks yelled, after just assigning himself the position of pushing from behind the left front fender. "It's slowing down - just look the other way until it passes!"

Bergie, noticing it was Gardiner, quickly moved around to the other side. "Shit, it's Gardiner!"

As RSM Gardiner slowed the jeep to a crawl, a standing, smiling and waving brigadier gestured to a whistling farmer.

"Tough luck, old chap! Everything all right?"

"Rightly enough, thank you."

"You're lucky you've got so much help with you. Are they your family?"

"Say yes," whispered Banks.

"Er, near enough. These boys are of great help!"

The brigadier grinned. "Well tallyho and best of luck!"

The old man yelled back, "Very kind, Captain."

As the jeep moved on, Mr. Gardiner didn't say anything, although he thought it rather odd that all the boys were wearing khaki shorts and boots. "Probably war surplus," he murmured.

"What was that, RSM?"

"Oh, nothing, sir. I was just thinking that those lads are certainly going to need lotion on their bodies when they get to wherever they're going."

"Nonsense, Mr. Gardiner ... country boys can gobble this weather up and spit it out. Why when I was a boy ... I say, what the bloody hell is that?"

The commanding officer's outstretched hand pointed to what appeared to be a nude hiker with a white hat strolling while quickly putting his pants on.

When he spotted the jeep, it was too late for Moose to hide. What good are hiding places anyway when one's heart is pumping so fast it could break out of the chest cavity at any second.

The military vehicle stopped, but a dirty, dishevelled, and tired Moose didn't. Instead, he looked the other way and kept on walking, now at a brisker pace. "Son-of-a-bitch, it's Gardiner! I'm dead," he mumbled. "Oh my God, I'm dead!"

Gardiner didn't say a word. Although his mouth remained in the open position, he couldn't speak. But he could think.

Dear God, say this isn't happening to me. Lord love a duck, it's that weird head-case again! Now he's balls naked on the back roads. Jesus, what am I going to say to the CO? Of all the rotten luck. I take the CO out for a ride and we bump into this undressed sex machine. His friend Perky must be somewhere nearby in the bushes. What am I going to say? Nothing ... that's right ... I had better say nothing!

"Back the jeep up, please, Mr. Gardiner. I want to talk to the boy."

"Er, are you sure, sir? The lad may be a little shy."

"Shy? I would say this teenager is anything *but* shy if he had the guts to walk naked on a public road. You! You, there! Are you from this area?"

Danyluk stopped now knowing the RSM hadn't said anything. *Perhaps he hasn't recognized me because I've got my shorts on my head,* he thought. Still looking away, his parched throat replied, "No, I'm here for the summer."

Gardiner had to think fast. "He's probably from the nudist colony down by the lake, sir."

The brigadier said, "Are you with the nudist colony?"

Moose's mouth was bone-dry from fright. "Er, youse is right, sir."

Gardiner flinched when he heard the word, "youse."

The brigadier continued. "Well it doesn't give you the right to walk around half naked on a public road! We saw you put your pants on!"

Danyluk nodded, ignored the comment and started walking again as the jeep sped away. When the vehicle was out of sight, he yanked on his khaki shirt and ran for the truck.

"Why me? Son-of-a-bitch, why me? Doesn't that man ever take a day off?"

"Mr. Gardiner, I can't get over how brazen these nudists are. What gives them the right to think they can walk around naked on public roads? Are all of these so-called naturalists hung like horses? And where do they get the khaki clothing?"

"No, I think *he's* one of a kind, sir. They probably buy the clothing in war surplus shops."

"Well I should bloody-well hope he *is* one of a kind. He'd scare the living daylight out of any decent woman."

Then the brigadier smiled. "Lucky young bastard, though, isn't he, Gardiner?"

Mr. Gardiner swallowed and feigned a smile. "Why's that, sir?"

The officer slapped his swagger stick against his thigh, mentioning, "RSM, boys weren't hung like that when I was young. Not that my build doesn't always drive the ladies wild, but, er, every additional bit helps, (snort, snort) eh what?"

Reservedly, Gardiner expressed a gas pain and nodded, saying, "Er, undoubtedly, sir."

"Bloody teenagers. If they like wearing khaki so much, we should put them all in cadets. That would straighten them out, wouldn't it, RSM?"

Gardiner rolled his eyes upwards. "Huh? Oh, yes, sir; cadets would do them the world of good. The little ... er, the big bastards would then learn how to become real proper gentlemen."

Although Danyluk was out of sight, the CO turned around as if to confirm what he had seen was real. His question to the RSM now totally forgotten.

"What? (snort) Quite true, RSM, quite true."

Cordell Cross

Danyluk caught up with his friends fifteen minutes later as the others pushed Miss Millie up a hill. Like the others, the *animal's* boots were ruined, his hair was matted in sweat, and his body was both dirty and burnt.

"Where were you when we needed you and what the hell have you got on your head?" yelled Bergie.

Pushing and grunting, Moose now had the back of his shoulders against the rear of the truck's flat deck.

"My gaunch. I was sittin' stark naked in the middle of the road! What the hell did youse think I was doin'?"

"Wow, did Gardiner see you?" asked Jackson.

"Did he see me? Even if he had his frigging eyes closed, he could see me pullin' up my pants! Shit, he couldn't miss me. I know I'm dead! I know the minute we get back to camp I'll be called to his office. Why me? Why is it always me?"

"Because he knows your name!" Bergie said.

Rothstein didn't agree. "Look at it this way, Moose. If you *must* go to his office he won't recognize you, you'll have your clothes on."

Like the rest of them, Cunningham howled. "Were you really balls naked in the middle of the road? You mean both Gardiner and the CO saw you that way?"

Moose tried to smile. "What else? But I had my pants on by the time the jeep came close. I don't think Gardiner told the CO he knew me. Megill thinks I belong to the nudist colony down by the lake. Believe me, right now I wish I did. Hey, how long have the nudists been there, anyway?"

Bergie joined Danyluk and started pushing. "Oh, about four inches. You'd be the new leader."

"Screw you, Bergie."

"And you, ninth wonder of the world," added Douglas.

Frowns turned to grins. The group needed Moose and Bergie to help them forget their plight.

"Say Pops, how much further is it to this here Charlie's place?" East asked, his lips parched and cracking like the rest.

"It's only about four more short miles. How are you youngsters holding out?"

East began massaging his own shoulders. "Holding out? It'll be a wonder if I ever hold anything after this. My muscles are shot!"

Gordie mouthed, "Sure, go ahead and embarrass yourself by calling those veins, muscles."

"Up yours, Lingus."

"It's Cunnilingus to you, *Beastie.*"

Laughter reigned again after a puffing and grunting Moose retorted, "Only four short miles? Is that all? Hey, I'm startin' to enjoy this. This is just what the doctor ordered, partner. I hope Charlie's got a daughter. It'll be the last bit I get up here!"

The contented old man didn't hear Moose's last remarks and it took three more hours to move Miss Millie the *four* short miles.

Cordell Cross

Chapter 11

Charlie's *residence* was set back in fifty acres of uncut grass, pines, and aged fruit trees laden with apples, pears, and cherries. The antiquated house, barn, and two other wooden buildings appeared as if they had been assembled in the back hills of Arkansas at the turn of the century and left to rot. The weather had stripped off all evidence of paint, and broken windows had been replaced with sheets of clouded plastic.

Relics of farm machinery and tools remained throughout the property, rusting away at their place of breakdown. The only thing resembling anything in shape was a small sawmill about a hundred yards from the house.

When the truck halted after two hundred metres of Charlie's winding pot-holed *road*, its occupants, including the old farmer, all looking at the ground sat down in the shade against aged bug-covered trees. The musketeers were totally beat, burned, bleeding, dirty and hungry. Threads of smeared sweat and dust covered their faces, necks, and upper bodies. They didn't have the energy to talk and each boy's heavy breathing impeded all signs of a smile.

It was obvious Charlie wasn't around but five of his friends were. Two affectionate dogs appeared with three curious cows that badly needed milking. Both canines were of the Heinz variety source. A small black mixed cocker spaniel sat wagging her tail next to a shiny grey-coated wolfhound - part lab and two parts of whatever. They joined the cows in licking the arms, faces, and legs of the noble eight and their patriarchal leader.

The dogs knew Fred, and vice-versa.

"These are Charlie's dogs. The black one's Daisy, and the other's Bum."

East tried to lick his lips before he spoke, but there was no saliva left in his mouth. "Why do they call him, Bum?" he asked, now finding Bum's head resting on his legs.

The old man took off his cap. "Cause he raids the chicken house for eggs. That's why he's got a shiny coat. Old Charlie hardly ever has an egg 'cause Bum's got 'em first."

Tired half-closed weary eyes viewed the aged man and a few smiles appeared.

"And these are Charlie's cows. Normally he's milked 'em by now. I don't know where the hell he is today. That's Jugs, that one's Bigtits, and the other's name is Supercups," he said, pointing to a cow licking Douglas' hair. "His son, Elmer named them."

Although it was difficult talking, Wane said, "Hey, Moose, the cows are named after your broads."

The whole group needed that line, including Danyluk. He coughed and laughed with the others.

"Yeah, and they even look like 'em," Douglas added, trying to evade Supercups' tongue.

Again, Moose roared with his pals, but not before he replied, "I wish they did. Do youse thinks I'd turn down broads with bazookas like these? It's been so long, they're startin' to look good, but just a bit *coyote* ugly."

Cordell Cross

"What's coyote ugly?" Rothstein asked, biting into an apple to get moisture in his mouth.

Danyluk managed a grin and also started on an apple. "Coyote ugly is when you wake up with your arm around a strange dame that makes Hilda the witch look beautiful. You know if you move she'll wake up, so you bite your arm off instead."

That did it. Howls echoed around the fifty acres and tired eyes became whole again.

Bergie leaned his head back against his tree and joined in. "Sounds like the girl our RSM goes around with. We hardly ever see him because she's so ugly. When he's at her house he can't leave because she always wants to kiss him goodbye."

At that moment, if anyone normal had arrived to see the looks and hear the laughter of the eight 'crazies' they would have left quickly thinking the *funny-farm* gates had been left open.

"She sounds like Jack's girl," Jackson said throwing a rotten cherry that hit East's left cheek. "The grass around the neighbourhood dies the minute she walks out of her house."

"Screw you, Earl. At least I've got a girlfriend," East shot back before changing the subject. "Hey, did you hear about the homo judge at the Three Little Pigs trial. He said, 'Come, come, come, Big Bad Wolf; you couldn't have blown down that whole house by yourself. What's that? You did? Case dismissed, meet me in my chambers.'"

When Fred stood, his stomach was sore from laughing. "C'mon you fellas. Go freshen up at the well and I'll take you inside the house. Also, help yourself to all the fruit you want. Charlie lets it rot or gives it to his animals."

After East wound up the well-bucket at the back of Charlie's house, each tried to grab the four banged-up tin mugs sitting on the top of a circled stone-walled well. The clear cold water tasted wonderful, but the shock of receiving a full bucket of water against his upper-body almost gave Wane a heart attack. The boys didn't know they were so badly burned.

"Jeez, go easy, will ya," Wane screamed at Jackson, who had received a full bucket from Cunningham a second before.

Soon, the dust and dirt of the trip was washed away and the eight lay in the tall grass; boots off, socks off, berets off and shirts still off. The trees supplied enough shade and the first evening breeze coming from the lake a mile away felt like Heaven on earth.

Danyluk lay on his left side throwing blades of grass at Bergie. "I know I'm burnt to a crisp and I've got blisters on my hands, arms, upper legs and feet. I also know I'm on the RSM's shitlist, but do youse wanna know somethin?"

Bergie lay on his back, arms outwardly extended, eyes exploring the sky. "What?"

"This ain't that bad. I feel like I've put in a full day's work and now the world can go and hide and just leave me in this field. Gettin' this break from camp routine is like playin' hooky for the day and goin' to Third Beach in Stanley Park. I feel free."

Bergie felt the same. His shiny black hair was clean and combed. Filling his lungs with fresh air, he replied, "Oh yeah? What if Genova appears and screams, 'Form up in three ranks?"

"I'd say, 'Go and screw yourself Sergeant Major! Youse can do it on your own, or get someone else, but just go and screw yourself. Do youse hear me?"

"I'd say the same," growled Rothstein.

The rest chuckled listening to the banter of Bergie, Danyluk, and Rothstein. Everyone knew Moose wouldn't talk that way to Genova, but it was funny watching him scowl. He always managed to keep a straight face when he was in the mood to be tough.

Fred appeared on the back porch, making certain his feet weren't caught in the holes left by missing floorboards.

"Hey you fellas, c'mon in the house!"

The main room of Charlie's house was large, clean, and even cosy considering old paintings or ancient photographs covered holes or cracks in the stained orange-patterned wallpaper. Four chairs and three old couches with springs coming though sat against the walls, one of which hosted a cobblestone fireplace. The way the furniture was placed left a big open space in the middle of the room.

The floorboards of the shanty were in the same condition as those at Camp Vernon and they held up a heavy old highly polished table on which sat an Edison Phonograph windup wax-cylinder machine. There were no curtains on the windows, just roll-up blinds. The kitchen was separate and a wood-stove, sink, well pump, wooden table and six wooden chairs stood next to an icebox by the back door.

Off the main room, two small bedrooms held steel-framed made-up beds with mattresses sagging in the middle. A set of stairs inside one of the bedrooms led to the attic containing three more bedrooms with old bunk beds and night tables. As below and because the house had no electricity, each upstairs room contained a paraffin lamp.

"What the hell is this?" Jack asked after opening up a creaky closet door.

Inside, a leg of pork hung on a hook. There were no clothes, just the full hind leg of the animal.

"He's ageing it," said Fred. "It's been smoked and it's hung there for quite a while."

"It looks it," replied East, wincing. "Will he eventually eat it?"

Fred smacked his lips. "Sure will, and it'll taste good."

Heading back down, Douglas asked, "Er, Fred, who lives here with Charlie?"

Fred nudged the eight into the main room and they sat down.

"Charlie's 79 and he lives here alone. His wife died about eight years ago. They had a wonderful but sad life; she gave him four sons and three were killed in various accidents. His remaining son, Elmer, who's about 45 works with Charlie at their sawmill. You saw the mill when we pushed Miss Millie by it. Elmer lives about six miles down the road. He's married with six children of his own. Four boys and two girls.

Douglas stood up to peruse a photograph hung on the wall separating the bedrooms. A man and a woman posed with four smiling teenage boys.

"Is this Charlie and his family?"

Fred walked over and the other cadets stood to look.

"Yes, that's them. They ranged in age from thirteen to seventeen, there. This picture next to it is a typical bath night. The bathtub was brought in from the shed and pails of water were heated in the fireplace or on the stove. The children were younger then, but how two boys managed to fit in that tub at a time is beyond me. Charlie and his wife used the water last.

A lost smile came over Fred's face. "The other picture is Charlie in his uniform when he was overseas in World War One. Beth ran the farm then; she was quite the woman. They don't make 'em that way anymore. She..."

Fred stopped speaking because he heard a Model 'A' Ford chugging up to the house. After the key was turned off, a pleasantly plump grey-haired gentleman about five foot eight stepped out - his arms full with bags of groceries. Grinning, Charlie knew he had a visitor on account of the truck being there.

"So you blew the tire again, eh Fred? Ya cheap bugger, when are ya gonna buy four new ones?"

Fred appeared on the front porch first, followed by the slowly appearing cadets.

"I wouldn't be here if these here lads hadn't helped me."

Still smiling, Charlie stopped in his tracks as the last of the boys came out the front door.

"What the...? Eight lobsters? Where in the world could you collect eight lobsters? Undoubtedly at the camp, eh? Well, welcome boys."

Jackson and Wane helped Charlie by taking two bags of groceries each. After placing them on the table inside, Fred introduced everyone, saying, "This is Gabby, and this here's Bitchy, and…"

The boys accepted their new nicknames and introduced themselves when they shook Charlie's big hand. They also learned his last name was Stevenson.

Charlie's face and clear gun-blue eyes indicated long-past memories when he asked, "Where are your shirts?"

"Out in the back field," replied Bergie.

"Well, go get them on, boys. The mosquitoes will be out when the sun starts to go down. It looks as if you've done enough damage to your bodies for one day."

As the cadets walked through the house to head out the back door, Jackson glanced at his watch. "Jesus, it's seven o'clock already! We've missed the girls and everything. They don't know where the hell we are and they'll be at the dance without us!"

Bergie ended the panicky moment. "What would Sergeant Beckford do if he was in this predicament? Let me tell you. He'd say, 'There's not a goddamned thing I can do, but get on with the situation at hand.'"

Although Danyluk screamed, "Alma's gonna kill me," he reluctantly agreed with the rest. When they put on their shirts and met with Fred and Charlie, a plan was devised. It was impossible for them to return to camp that night, so their host wrote down their names, packed Douglas and Wane in the back seat of the old Ford and drove Fred home.

After dropping Fred off at his farm, Charlie stopped at the only country store in the area, picked up more supplies, made a telephone call and drove back to his house.

"What did the orderly officer say?" Wane asked, taking some of the bags and placing them between him and Douglas.

The old man pushed the starter. "What could he say? Actually, not too much, but he mentioned church parade. I gave him your names and told him a weekend pass wasn't planned, but now it was needed. You're staying with relatives in the Kelowna area. Hey, I was in the army too, you know. These things do happen, and you'll just have to miss church parade."

Both wide-eyed cadets mischievously looked at each other and grinned. He was right, they would miss the *beloved* parade.

"Mr. Stevenson, sir, you're a Godsend," Wane said.

Smiling when changing gears to take on a hill, the driver replied, "My name's Charlie. Like I said, I was in the army too. *And* I remember the church parades."

With the cows milked, and the dogs fed, their new host barbecued nine steaks and eighteen massive baked potatoes. For obvious reasons, the food never tasted better. To wash everything down, each cadet drank at least four glasses of fresh cold milk. Fruit followed the milk and soon all stomachs were full.

Throughout dinner, Danyluk boasted that he had milked the cows better than the rest. The others tended to agree saying he had more experience with cows' parts, particularly teats.

"What's this word, *teats*? I call 'em tits. Get with it, youse guys. Did youse see the way Jugs kept throwin' me kisses and blinkin' her big eyelashes after feelin' each gentle stroke of these hands? Even with blisters, they're soft. It's gotta be the lemon juice. All the girls love the feel of 'em."

"I don't doubt it," Earl commented. "You had two teats going in each hand. That's not normal."

Bergie snickered. "It's normal for him. He's used to it because of that weird broad. Acne, he dates. She's got four teats, ain't she Moose?"

Moose gave Bergie a disgusting look. "Her name's Anise, and I'll have youse know she's got five, and they ain't teats."

"Ain't she the one that sent the letter; the one with three?"

"No! Is youse writing a book?"

"Er, sorry, Moose, I should have known."

East didn't agree. "Well Jugs couldn't have liked those hands that much 'cause she kicked the bucket over."

"She was excited, that's all," a contented Moose replied. "All the dames get excited when they feel the velvety caress of these big *grabbers*."

After washing their dishes, Charlie and the boys sat on the back porch. The sun had long gone down and it was dark - pitch black dark. When their eyes got used to it, the boys noticed that daytime images had hesitantly bowed to nighttime profiles, changing the setting entirely.

Charlie's porch became the best seats in the house and the clearing out back the stage that permitted a giant moon and a billion heavenly bodies to light up the evening sky. Glittering falling stars were accompanied on their long journey by a symphony of far away train whistles and chipmunks saying *goodnight* to nearby owls, crickets, coyote howls, and the enchanting harmony the wind makes rambling through branches of steadfast trees.

The *orchestra* and *scenery* mesmerized the cadets. No one spoke but each knew what the other was thinking. Nature put on this majestic play only for the chosen few. That small number who discard the likes of radios, newspapers, the hubbub of city life with its daily brainwashing and advertising trying to churn out the Joneses. Yes, this rewarded a full day's work and the setting could not be matched. The performance granted all those who were heartfelt to sit back and enjoy their blessings. To behold.

Over supper, Charlie had told the boys about his family and when asked, he explained that he really hadn't gotten over his wife's death.

"I never will. Beth meant so much to me." His face lit up. "We met at the rides at the Picnic Fair. She was wearing a beautiful pink..."

The old man stopped in the middle of his sentence and the thrilling look on his face slowly faded. Douglas thought he saw a watery sparkle in Charlie's eyes as a sigh and a long pause followed.

"Life is a cluster of memories, boys. Like photographs, some are sad or wonderful, some happy, funny, or common. At certain times, the mind turns on the projector and chooses past images. Depending on your mood, at times it's damned hard to take. We humans take so much for granted. Our race always lives for tomorrow and unfortunately it's only then, tomorrow, when you realize you had already captured the brass ring. It wasn't necessary to go after the silver, or gold. Value and cherish the present, because in the future, you're going to miss it intensely."

Charlie was a pioneer with the spirit and wisdom of a man who had enjoyed and suffered. He knew what life had to offer and what "this good earth" could give. The boys in turn expressed *their* feelings; the beliefs of youngsters not ready for life's daily obstacles, but lucky enough to slowly learn what was coming as they grew older. That whatever they put in to it, they'll have an opportunity to enjoy, with of course the heartbreaks of prescriptions signed for everyone at the beginning of time. Formulas that can never be changed. Blueprints that have to be accepted and their resulting consequences faced.

When talking with the boys, Charlie told them about the hard realities. That life is happy but also sad. That death is a part of life and its accompanying grief had to be acknowledged as much as the wondrous joy of birth. He explained that life's process is never-ending; sickness and pain had to be acknowledged for life to go on.

The boys listened intently and nature's stage allowed them time to think about it. Of all people, Cunningham broke the silence. He had his chair on its back legs and his feet on the porch railing. Not taking his eyes off the stars, he kept his voice low. "Even with what you've been through, you're a lucky man, Mr. Stevenson, sir. A lucky, lucky man."

Charlie smiled but didn't say anything then. Instead, he walked into the house and came out with a guitar and sat down again.

Cordell Cross

"I know that, son. Enjoy life while you're young. Step out and step back if you have to, but try not to repeat your mistakes."

For the next hour, Charlie Stevenson strummed his guitar and sang a few songs and a small number of hymns. His repertoire wasn't the greatest but the lonely tunes and words couldn't have been sung better, or more suitably chosen for that matter. Charlie sang with the feeling of a hundred country singers that had experienced life and witnessed the same play. The only difference tonight was a young audience joined in. Though not admitting it to themselves, the songs made them appreciate *Country Fiddler and the Stix* a little more. After all, they *were* in the country, and it had its own music.

It was nod-off time after each of them drank a cup of hot cocoa. Following trips to the outhouse, Charlie lit some lamps and showed them to their rooms. He also left a small jar in each room.

"This is a home-made sunburn remedy. Smear it on yourselves before you hit the sack."

Bergie and Danyluk took the downstairs bedroom at the front of the house. Jackson, East, Cunningham, and Rothstein each took bunk beds in the 'pork-leg' room upstairs, and Douglas and Wane shared the room next to them. Some bunks were made-up but for those that weren't, their host provided sleeping bags.

The eerie silhouettes of the smoking lamps provided a few funny moments but the boys were tired and small talk just wasn't on the menu. It had been a tough day.

Since Wane had the upper bunk, he leaned over as usual.

"That salve makes me smell like a hen-house."

"Same here."

"Say Doug, did you notice that the cows and dogs sat in on the music session? They were in a semi-circle in front of the porch, and one of the dogs even howled a bit."

A lost smile came to Douglas' lips. "Yeah, when the cows arrived, the dogs left the porch and joined them. I guess he entertains his *family* every night. Kinda nice, eh? He said when he dies, he's left enough money for them to be well looked after."

Wane returned his head to his pillow. "I've learned a hell of a lot today. It's funny how these things happen, isn't it? Who would have guessed we'd end up here?"

Brice rolled on his side. "We've all learned a lot, and I think he enjoyed it as much as we did. Jeez I'd like to live here. Goodnight buddy."

"Goodnight, Doug."

Just as they were dozing off, a scratchy song absorbed the house. With the voice of a tenor emanating from the Edison Phonograph, the boys fell asleep listening to the *Lord's Prayer*.

Charlie didn't go to bed right away. Instead, he returned to the porch and sat in his favourite chair. With a dog at each side, he wiped the moisture from his eyes, lit up his pipe and quietly said, "Goodnight my dear Beth. Thanks for sending them. You always seem to know when I need company. Tonight was like old times."

Chapter 12

Moose Danyluk didn't hear the rooster calling the new day. He didn't have to because Jugs' tongue explored his face and the sound of an accompanying cowbell woke him up. Jugs had climbed the few stairs and placed her head in the boys' window.

"Son of a bitch, I'm covered in cow drool! Bergie, get your head out from underneath the covers and get a load of this!"

When Bergie's blurry-eyed head emerged, he also got his face *washed* and two wet dogs jumped on his stomach.

Wiping his face with his sheet, the *animal* said, "Phew, we should have these in camp. Everyone would be most willing to get out of bed before reveille and the run to the upper camp. What with the cow drool and lotion, I must smell like shit."

Bergie sat up petting Bum and Daisy. "Mornin' Moose. Christ, these dogs are soaked," he said, trying to clean off his hands on Danyluk's shirt that he picked off the floor. You always smell like shit anyway, but right now, my nose detects bacon, eggs, pancakes, and coffee. Am I dreamin'?"

"No, you ain't dreaming," offered East entering the room. "Jesus this place stinks; what did you do?"

"It's the combination of lotion, cows, dogs and Moose," Bergie replied.

Jack snickered. "Charlie's been cooking for twenty minutes, and the rest of the guys are already up. They've gone for a dip. Are you guys going?"

Danyluk jumped out of bed without his usual morning erection. "Trust youse to be up when the food's on."

"I'm helping him cook."

"What else is new?" Moose said getting dressed. "Whaduya mean, *dip*?"

East threw two towels. "Get your asses in gear. There's a swimmin' hole out by the sawmill. Bum, Daisy and I have already had our swim; the others are there now."

As far as the eight were concerned, no words could describe the wonderful country morning scent. The lukewarm rays of the new day's sun *polished* the enchanted fragrance released by the sweet-smelling Okanagan blossoms.

When Moose and Bergie arrived with the two dogs, they witnessed that a small creek had been partially damned by beavers; the customary glistening newly formed lake churned with the crisp exuberance of five bare bodies.

The duo knew better than to get in slowly. Instead, each holding their breath, they dove.

"Son of a bitch! Talk about awake! Yeehah, this is cold," Danyluk bellowed trying to catch his breath and dunking again because of Rothstein's Tarzan act. Holding onto a rope and swinging from an overhanging tree, Harvey nearly landed on him.

"It's about time you two creeps got up," Jackson yelled.

Pushing *Tarzan* away, Moose said, "Hey, I had to get up! I got a face full of Jugs' cow drool! She got on the porch and put her head through our window!"

Wane was on Douglas' back having a horse-fight with Cunningham and Jackson. "I told ya Jugs has got the hots for ya! You're her kind of animal."

"Oh yeah? Well, she got Bergie, too, you pongo!"

Jackson howled. "Did she, now? Why that fickle bitch! She's a two-man cow! Bergie, I'll bet you're jealous as hell!"

Bergie placed a finger to his lips. "Quiet, do you want to hurt her feelings? The three of them are behind those bushes."

A "yoo-hoo" from Danyluk didn't entice them over.

When the boys arrived at the house thirty minutes later, Charlie bid them good morning and asked if they had a good night's sleep.

"Never better," they replied in unison, except Moose. He still complained about the assertiveness of Jugs and described her actions to Charlie.

"Really? That's a new one on me. She's normally more reserved than that."

"She wants to be his girl, er, cow," Cunningham joked, snickering. "When soft hands grab soft teats, true love has no bounds. She also knows he has what it takes to please her. She saw that down at the lake."

Amidst the chuckles, Danyluk's smile widened and his face turned a deeper crimson. He knew he'd never live this one down. For that matter, so did Bergie.

It was Charlie who came to their rescue. "I can't tell a lie," he said. "She's done it a few times before. Jugs was really small when we bought her so we bottle-fed her on the porch. Whenever guests appear, she's there. I see your burns are healing?"

The lads all agreed and Wane asked, "Sir, what's in that potion? Would I be wrong saying a little chicken shit?"

"You don't want to know, but near enough. Now boys, let's have breakfast. Who's hungry other than Jack?"

"Oh, so you found out about his love of food, eh?" Rothstein asked.

The old man laughed wiping his hands on his apron. "Show me a teenager who isn't always constantly hungry and I'll show you a fibber."

Following the fantastic meal and chatting with Charlie, the boys helped with the dishes and those who had used sleeping bags hung them on the porch to air out.

Fred arrived at ten o'clock as the group were getting an escorted tour of the property.

After the normal greeting, Charlie said, "You fellas carry on while Fred and I try to fix this damned tire."

It was noon when the boys returned. The dogs had guided them through the hills and along the trails of "God's Country". Although their boots were scratched and their khaki shorts bore the stains of their experience, spirits were high and a million questions were asked over lunch of sandwiches and milk.

At two o'clock it was time to say farewell. If the cadets had had their way, they would have stayed until the end of summer and Charlie would have agreed, but the camp beckoned.

After handshakes of gratitude and pats on all backs, the boys loaded themselves in the front and back of Miss Millie.

As she drove out of sight, loud voices and waves heightened the melancholy smile on Charlie Stevenson's clear-eyed face as he stood with his dogs.

Cordell Cross

Charlie didn't move for a moment as he lowered his hand and stared at the bend in the road. Then after lighting up his pipe, he said, "You missed your eggs this morning didn't you, Bum? For once, I actually beat you to them. Oh well, c'mon Bum, Daisy, I've saved you guys some of last night's bones."

"No, you owe me a buck each! You too, Cunnilingus," yelled East with a hand outstretched. Apparently, Cunningham had tried to get away with paying him only eighty-seven cents.

It was Monday evening after a full day's training as East tried to collect for his part in getting their boots back into shape after they arrived back on Sunday afternoon. East had a knack with boots, and when he was offered seven dollars, (a dollar from each musketeer who pushed Miss. Millie) his shoe polish, brushes and rags came out quickly. He finished at midnight and although his work of art was appreciated, it wasn't fully paid for.

"Fork it over, Moose! Do I look like I give a fat rat's ass if it comes out of your *Sick Cadets With Only One Ball Fund?* If I don't get a buck, you'll have *no* balls!"

Moose opened an envelope. "Okay, here, cry baby. I just wanted youse to wait until my next set of donations came in."

A grudging Cunningham passed along thirteen cents as well.

East now had seven dollars. Grinning, with his eyes gleaming, he said, I'm rich! I'm rich! I'm rolling in dough! God, it feels good to be normal again!"

"You may be rich, but you'll never be normal," Cunningham retorted.

"Go screw yourself. I'm gonna start loan-sharking like you do. Who's for goin' over to the canteen?

"Are you buying?" Rothstein asked.

East stuck out his chest. "Hey, do I look stupid?"

"Yeah."

"Oh. All right then, I'll buy us all one KiK-Kola each."

That's all he had to say. The rush was on."

The day had been a routine day. Two lectures on the Nineteen Set, two lectures on Morse code and two lectures on the UCL Ten-line switchboard.

Throughout the day the musketeers had thought and spoke about old Charlie. The ride back had been uneventful and when they had arrived in the barracks, they washed and ironed their clothing and each shined two belts. After supper, all of them except East and Cunningham had attended the movie, *The Cruel Sea* in B-3. East couldn't because he was too busy shining boots, and after Cunningham had learned that a cadet in D&M had received fifty dollars from home, he skipped the movie and eased the cadet of half his wealth.

Sunday night after the movie, they had hit the sack and slept like babies until the sergeant stormed into the barracks at 0530 and *kindly* asked them to join him in PT, which of course they all *voluntarily* did.

Now it was Monday evening and not only was the canteen quiet, so were the musketeers. Sure IBT was playing baseball with Driver Mech and most cadets had run out of money, but there was something happening amongst the group of eight. The boys hadn't said much all day. Separately, each boy was concerned about

Charlie. He seemed in good health, but he was getting on. How long could he last? What would happen to the place? They had had a grand time, offered generously by a stranger. An old man had donated his time to explain the turning of the world so they could enjoy themselves. Moreover, in that short period each of them knew they had made a fine new friend. The age barrier didn't count, and none of them looked at it as a barrier. Instead, it was as if Charlie was in his teens and they were in their seventies. Yes, age didn't matter at all - it was Charlie Stevenson's hospitality and kindness that did.

"Let's buy him a plaque and send him a big letter of thanks," Douglas said, knowing the rest were thinking the same thing.

Wane agreed. "And invite him here. We could show him the camp."

"I wonder how often he sees his son's family?" Bergie asked staring blankly at some carved initials in the wooden table. "I know he works with his son, but I got the impression the family doesn't visit very often even though they're only a few miles down the road. Why doesn't he mention it to them?"

Rothstein cleared his throat. "Because he's proud. I don't know about you guys but when I was with Charlie, I felt I should be visiting my grandfather more often. I've only got one left now, and we hardly ever visit him. He used to phone all the time, but not anymore."

Rothstein's statement got them all thinking. Douglas' grandparents' had died in England, but the other seven boys were more fortunate - some grandparents were alive.

In the ensuing silence, inner pacts were made that wouldn't be forgotten, and by the time they left the canteen, a decision had been arrived at. A giant letter of thanks would be sent to Charlie with a card and a plaque. In addition, he would be invited to spend a day with them at the camp.

After lights out, Lyons came over and sat on Bergie's bed.

"I'm sorry I didn't see you guys on the weekend. How'd it go?"

Bergie had to turn his head away. "Jesus, Lyons, you reek of booze and union. What the hell have you been up to?"

Unnoticed by the rest of the musketeers, Lyons had been under the influence all day. That's why he hadn't been seen or heard. He was now attempting to *re-surface*.

Staggering back to bed, Lyons said, "I'll have you know, that's the smell of expensive cognac, old chum. Cadet McLeod's new girlfriend's parents have a liquor cabinet. Nice one, too."

Week two in camp went by slowly even though the cadets were kept busy. Money was tight and nighttime exercises in Area 10 dragged out the day. Map Reading had been introduced and using the man-pack Fifty-Eight sets, mobile sections responded to flashlight beacons by plotting their grid references and reporting them to field headquarters. The exercises usually ended by 2200 hours and the cadets were allowed a late mug-up. All cadets were usually asleep by 2300, but getting up at 0530 and putting in such a day made signals a very weary company indeed. When Friday finally rolled around the cadets were looking forward to

Saturday's pay parade, the dance at the arena and one-and-a-half well earned days off.

The shower room soon filled after completion of the Mother's Night responsibilities. That is until East entered, whistling *Three Blind Mice*. All cadets in the company knew the tune well. They should have, because it was the warning that at any minute wind would be released – the type of wind that could rip paint off buildings. Everyone knew of the rumour it could literally blind those brave enough to hold their breath, grimace, and wait for the aftershock, which was another *dazzling* release of wind.

During the stampede from 'ground zero' comments of those quickly exiting the room fell upon deaf musketeer ears.

"One of these days I'm gonna stuff a cork up his ass!"

"It wouldn't be of any use, Ernie. He kills even when he burps!"

"Jeez, can you imagine what his mother went through when she changed his diapers?"

"She musta wore a gas mask"

"A gas mask wouldn't work - the glass would probably melt."

"So would the rubber or leather, I betcha!"

"Hey, maybe he's an alien."

"All Irish are aliens, you creep. Get outta the way!"

"He ain't Irish, he's with the Westies!"

"Should be in the goddamned artillery!"

"If they had him in the trenches during WW1 they wouldn't have needed mustard gas. One fart and the enemy would have immediately surrendered."

"The bastard got me again. This is the second time in a week I couldn't rinse off."

Newcomers arriving and quickly leaving couldn't believe it either. "My God, everyone in the world has shit at once and it's in there!"

When East started whistling the BCR song, *We come from the west by the sea,* his friends knew it was safe to enter.

"What time are we meeting the girls' tomorrow night?" Cunningham asked patting a self-satisfied East's back.

"Ya liked that one, eh, Lingus?"

"One of the best, Jackie my boy."

"Seven, at the arena," replied Jackson. "They're in Lumby playing ball until five."

As usual, Wane lathered shampoo all over his body. "I'm amazed they didn't stay at the dance last Saturday when we didn't show up."

Moose picked up a giant bar of sergeants' soap and sudsed up. "Hey, don't be amazed. Alma told me they're loyal. They coulda picked up a hundred guys that night, but they went home instead. We're damned lucky to have 'em. Jeez, I hate this soap. Bergie my boy...?"

"Forget it, Moose; purchase your own. By the way, didn't you forget something?"

"Now what?"

Cordell Cross

"Last Sunday we were supposed to get a tour of Hop Sing's."

"Bergie, I couldn't find any priest's collars. I nearly had one, but the guy was wearin' it."

Cunningham immediately reached for his towel. "Bergie, why the hell did you have to mention Hop Sing?"

"It came to my mind, that's all. Why?"

"Why? Because Danyluk's gettin' a boner."

In seconds, Moose was alone in the showers, but not for long. He didn't mind though, because Bergie left in such a hurry he forgot to take his sweet-smelling soap.

As soon as East left, five cadets who hadn't rinsed earlier, joined Moose.

"Hey, Rhino, er, what regiment...?"

"Are youse talkin' to me?"

"Yeah."

"It's Moose to youse."

"Sorry, er, Moose. What regiment is whistling asshole in?"

"Hey, watch your mouth, he's a friend. Youse means the gentlemen that farts?"

"Uh, yeah."

"The Seaforths."

"See, that's what I told you guys. That's what I thought all along," the questioner stated. "The poor bastards."

That night Danyluk and East slept on the floor - their mattresses and bedding already shaped in Saturday Morning Inspection style. By doing this they thought, or at least East thought he'd have a little extra time to himself in the morning. Like the rest of the BCRs, both boys were worn out because starting with band practice that morning, and studying after Mother's Night, their day had been a tough one. Little did East realize just how tough Saturday would be after the bugler blew reveille and Danyluk turned on his radio to the sounds of Hank Williams singing, *Your Cheatin' Heart.*

"Good mornin' youse creeps! Let go of your wangs and start brushin' your fangs!" Moose yelled, using one of Sergeant Simpson's sayings from the year before.

Their Platoon Sergeant didn't have to appear this morning. The cadets knew they had little time, so everyone was up quite quickly, including the corporal at the musketeers' end of the barracks. His *gentle-hearted* voice thundered over his cubicle walls before he stormed out.

"Oh, for Christ's sake! Who the hell would...? Goddamnit, this is war! Stand by your beds you rotten little bastards! I said, stand by your beds!"

Most cadets were quite used to the command, so few thought little of it as they obeyed. However, the tone of the normally composed corporal was quite different this morning. So were his lips, fingernails, and toenails. He hadn't yet seen his cheeks and lips, but he sure as hell had noticed his red-painted nails. If he had seen his face, his opening address might have been a little more resolute.

"Of all the *effing* military creeps in this camp, I end up with you people," the corporal shouted coming out of his cubicle.

Cordell Cross

The junior non-com didn't have to walk very far before stopping in front of East who was bent over in laughter.

"So it was you, eh?"

Like the others, East thought the corporal looked like Minnie Mouse because his rosy-red cheeks heightened his big red lips. Unfortunately, the midnight stalker who had painted the NCO had also *nailed* East's cheeks and lips, and now the corporal's rosy red face was in East's feminine kisser.

"You, you non-masculine prick! If you want to play your silly little games, don't ever play them with me. No breakfast for you, you poor excuse for a living garbage can! Get dressed quickly and get out on that parade square! The rest of you carry on!"

As the half-naked corporal stormed back into his cubicle, only the cadets in the immediate vicinity noticed four perfectly formed sets of lip-prints on his back - one set slightly protruding from his undershorts. Someone had been very artistic with lipstick.

Oblivious to the laughter going on around him, East stood there with his mouth wide open. He hadn't yet noticed that *his* toenails and fingernails had also been painted, and that he had lipstick, rouge and powder all over his face.

It was obvious how the corporal had found the "guilty prick" so quickly. As well, a tube of lipstick, a jar of rouge, a powder-pouch, puff, and a half-full bottle of nail polish were on Jack's shelf for all to see.

Comments from the whole side came hot and heavy.

"Aw, they're breaking up because their pyjama party didn't turn out. The pongo probably farted and the blast blew the corporal out the window!"

"I told ya to watch out for those BCRs. If they're not dropping the soap, they're painting their nails, and doin' up their faces."

"That's the creep that wears hair-curlers to bed. All the mothers in Vernon warn their children about him."

Although initially laughing, musketeer moods changed as East quickly dressed and rushed into the sink room.

One look in the mirror was enough. "Oh my God! Okay, you assholes ... I don't know who did it, but I'll find out!"

Someone commented, "If he's the bitch, then Danycluck must be the butch."

"Hey, I heard that," Moose yelled. We'll get the pansy that did this to him.

Another voice said, "Now Danysuck's one-track mind is tryin' to protect his *boy*."

Jack spent a whole hour on the parade square before the main Saturday Morning Parade. He was scheduled to spend another three hours there in the afternoon, but over breakfast, Douglas and Wane spoke with the corporal.

After the initial argument, Douglas spoke plainly. "Listen, corporal, if he had done it, would he have left the lipstick, rouge, powder puff, and nail-polish on his shelf? Doesn't it seem odd to you that his lips were covered in lipstick and *his* nails were painted as well? He was set up and you know it."

"I don't give a damn! A minute ago, someone whistled at me. I can't get this shit off, and I'm on duty in the headquarters building this morning! I must look like a whore out on the job!"

Now Wane got into the act. "You don't give a damn? What's that supposed to mean? Is this like the French army in the First World War ... find someone to punish even if the poor pongo's innocent?"

The NCO thought for a moment, fiddled with his fingers, hid his hands, and then calmed down. "Okay, what the hell would you two do?"

Douglas and Wane also relaxed. "Well, you've got our whole side of the hut believing you've found the guilty one," Douglas said. "Leave it at that and we'll come up with the real culprit. Give us a few days, and get off East's back. If he had done it, he would have owned up to it."

The junior non-commissioned-officer nodded and then smiled. "All right, Brice. Tell East to get over here. I guess I owe him an apology. But I pity the guilty party when I get my hands on him, or them!"

The two cadets glanced at each other before returning their attention to the corporal. Banks cleared his throat before saying, "Er, Corporal, when we find out who it is, we're not gonna hand him in. If it's all right with you, we'll look after the matter our way. You'll hear about it after we've finished with him. Agreed?"

"Or, *them*," said Douglas.

The corporal agreed and handshakes ended the *parley*.

McLeod was asked to move to another dining table that morning. He was told he wasn't under suspicion, but this was a musketeers' meeting. Douglas and Wane couldn't attend because they were talking with their hut NCO.

As usual, Bergie chaired the assembly. "That's something *we* would do. We've been beaten at our own game. Whoever set up Jack did it because of the shower room farts."

"I'll bet it's those Seaforth *fags in rags*," Rothstein said.

Cunningham wasn't so sure. "It could have been anyone pissed off with East's shower-room antics. Even someone on the other side of the hut."

Danyluk eyed everyone at other tables before returning his attention back to the heads huddled in the middle of the dining table.

"It was funny at the moment, but if they get away with it this time, they'll try it again. What are we gonna do, Bergie?"

Before Bergie had a chance to speak, Lyons broke in. "Chaps, as you all know, I'm also a police cadet, and..."

"A police cadet and you drink?" Jackson asked, quizzed.

Lyons gave Earl a dirty look and waved him off. "In *our* studies, we find that criminals usually talk about their exploits the same day. We've got to find out today, not tomorrow. They might not talk about it again."

Bergie agreed. "Yeah, I get it. Sorta like what we do when we pull our pranks. We keep our mouths shut."

Lyons' chest came out. "Exactly, old chum. I propose we borrow some Tele 'L' sets, tape down the send-switches and plant them above the upper air-vents in the drying room, shower room and toilet area. We can run wires through the ceiling down to the luggage area beneath the hut. Three of us will have to monitor the sets. It will be a long day, but I think we'll find out who he or they are."

"Why don't we monitor the sets up top?" asked Moose.

Lyons had worked out his plan. "You should know it's too hot up there. Besides, I have no intention of becoming bat-meat, old amigo."

Earl chuckled. "The bats wouldn't bite you. If they did, they'd all be pissed."

Lyons laughed with his friend. "You mean *pissed as a bat?*"

"It's *nit*, but that's close enough."

Now Danyluk had other questions. "But what about the dames? What about the dance? I can't miss another dance - Alma will kill me."

A grinning Lyons was prepared for these queries as well.

"McLeod and I have no plans, and I propose we pay Johnston fifty-five cents an hour. That will stop him from harping about that Spanish fly caper. He'll be the third."

With five minutes left before they had to return to the hut, Wane and Douglas entered the mess hall with East and his red-painted nails. Nothing had worked at getting the "shit" off and to make matters worse, East's stomach was rolling and he couldn't take his eyes off the kitchen area. Once pulled away, the plan was made known to them and quickly approved.

Wane put an arm around Bergie's shoulders. "Brilliant, Bergie my boy."

"It's not my strategy, it's Lyons'."

Instantly Wane shook Lyons' hand. "Don, I've gotta hand it to ya. After the liquor-cabinet jaunts, I never knew your brain had any thinkin' cells left."

"Actually, old comrade, my brain has never worked better. Did I tell you that cognac helps build the white cell count? Why I can remember the time I... "

Lyons never had the chance to finish. The group lifted up him and East and dragged them through the end door. As he left, East kept his hands in his pockets but his nose remained aimed at the food counter.

As Saturday morning parades go, this Saturday's parade was a definite improvement over the first Saturday's parade. The BCR cadets forming the band played well and the cadet battalion's standard of drill had clearly improved due to the amount of practice taught during the week by the drill cadres. Cadets weren't fidgeting as they did in the first week. Feet came up six inches off the ground and slammed down twelve. Daylight didn't show between the arms and when the cadets stood at attention position, all fingers touched their pants - middle fingers at the centre seam. Although it was hot, very few cadets fainted.

As the commanding officer made his personal inspection on the old parade square, boots, helmets, and uniforms gleamed and an expression of pride was most evident on his face. In all, he talked to about thirty cadets.

"So, Barton, how are you enjoying it here?"

"Er, fine, sir.

"Where are you from?"

"Winnipeg, sir. Well, a small town near there."

"Winnipeg, eh? Considering your winters, this weather must be the extreme. What do you think of it?"

"It's too hot for me, sir. I like the snow and cold. As my dad says, 'It keeps a man's pecker up.' This weather keeps it down. Probably the saltpetre, eh, sir?"

"Er, what? Yes, (snort) yes, er I would it imagine it could be. Er, good turnout, Barton."

"Thank you, sir."

Marching towards the band, the CO leaned towards his Adjutant, whispering, "Are we putting saltpetre in their food?"

"I think there's a small amount dished out, sir."

"How do the boys know about it?"

"I think Barton answered that question, sir."

"What? Oh yes, how silly of me (snort). Er, what about in the officers' mess?"

"I, er, think we get double the amount, sir."

Marching towards the band, a hideous expression showed on the CO's face.

"And how are you ... East?"

"Fine, thank you, sir."

"Your lips and cheeks appear to be a little red this morning. Anything wrong?"

Always truthful, East answered as nonchalantly as ever.

"No, sir. I just had a little trouble getting the lipstick and rouge off, that's all. Our platoon corporal is probably having the same problem, sir."

"What?"

Quickly moving on after noticing East's red-painted fingernails, the CO decided he'd better not say anything else ... except to his Adjutant as they returned to the dais.

"Make a note to cut out the saltpetre. Is that clear?"

"Yes, sir. And the reason, sir?"

"For goodness sake man, just look around you. It appears to be having a reverse effect. Also, is there hot water in the showers?"

"Absolutely, sir."

"Are our platoon corporals screened as to their sexual orientation? Are they, er, normal?"

"The finest in the army, sir."

"Good. Get that Goddamned saltpetre cut off. Er, Mr. Gardiner, are we having any problems with the sexual attitudes of certain cadets in Signals Company?"

Gardiner did not need that question. All week he had been trying to decide what to do about Danyluk's *jaunt* on the road. Thinking that the CO was referring to Danyluk and *Perky*, the RSM cleared his throat and transferred the position of his large drill cane.

"Er, (ahem) there are times when we experience, er, should I say, an emphatic display of intemperate conviction these lads have with their bodies, sir. I have discussed the matter with the MO and a psychiatrist, and they both say it's perfectly normal for certain teenage boys to exhibit such self-satisfaction. Er, probably similar to that civilian teenager we saw on the road last week, sir."

"That exhibitionist! People like him should be locked up in a carnival for life. Bloody nerve." The CO shook his head. "Hell, (snort) I hope they don't revert to wearing silk stockings and the like, Mr. Gardiner."

"I don't think it will go that far, sir."

"It better not, RSM. Or silk panties, bras or anything else for that matter."

"Not to worry, sir."

Driver Mechanics won the pennant for the best company and its cheers were loud even while marching off the parade square. Signal Company was a close second and *hand-signals* to the 'grease monkeys' indicated they would have a tough time winning it again.

After exams, a sheet exchange, their first pay parade, and a mail call, the cadets in Signals Company remade their beds and planned their move against the "shit disturber."

Moving quickly, Lyons, McLeod and Johnston obtained the Tele 'L' sets and went to work setting them up. A display of a burnt out ceiling-bulb allowed Lyons to sneak into the attic. His action went unnoticed and when he emerged, he had the sneakiest look on his face. As far as he was concerned, this was a challenge like never before and as a police cadet, he would solve the mystery.

"Everything okay?" Moose asked, whispering.

As Lyons left for the storage locker below the hut, he murmured, "Never been better, old chum. I fed the lines down a wall. The sets are operational right this minute."

The rest of the Musketeers had decided they wouldn't shower in their own barracks before lunch. Instead, they changed into their PT strip and headed over to the next hut. Bergie had suggested this move because he knew other cadets wouldn't talk if East's friends were in the immediate vicinity.

Johnston didn't have the opportunity of making much money that day. He was, however, smart enough to make a minimum deal of three dollars should the mystery be solved sooner. As it turned out, the guilty party let the cat out of the bag just before lunch while ironing in the drying room with the door closed. Lyons monitored that outlet and his ears became the ears of an elephant as he wrote down every word.

"Did you see the look on that asshole East's face? I nearly bust a gut it was so funny. I thought he'd fart himself to death. Neish, you did a great job on the corporal. Was he mad, or what?"

Neish let out a robust laugh. "MacKay it wasn't all me, you know? I had a lotta help from Scotty. He used the small nail-polish brush to put the lip-prints on the corporal's back. It actually looked like someone had kissed his ass."

"Yeah, and that was one tough job," said Scott. "Just doing those lip-prints took two-and-a-half hours because the son of a bitch kept moving."

"Hey, we all have to kiss our corporals' asses now and then," mouthed Sterling.

"I mean literally, you crud. Mac that will teach that East asshole for screwing around with our clothes at the beach."

"Do you think his buddies are wise to us?" Sterling asked.

"They haven't got a clue," replied MacKay. "I also lay odds that the living *stench* won't fart in the shower room again, either. And I say that not knowing if the guy really is living."

Cordell Cross

"You mean East's asshole won't fart," quipped Neish, still in an 'up' mood, snickering.

Lyons heard the door being opened and then he heard Sterling ask a question just before he left. "What's on for tonight? Are we going to the dance at the arena, or to the movies?"

"It's the dance," replied Neish. "And don't forget we're going regimental. The broads love us when we're wearing our kilts. Cindy's got ten hands."

"Only ten? How many do you have?"

"Fifty."

The door banged shut, then opened again and Lyons heard Scott call Sterling back.

"Remember nothing more is to be said. It's over, all right?"

"You bet! Do you think I'm a fool? Great idea Jock had, eh?"

Just before the door shut again, Scott said, "The best!"

Lyons sat back. "Ah ha, so a fifth one came up with the idea, did he? That makes him as guilty as the others."

While the company lunched, they removed the wiring and put the sets away. Just seeing Lyons and McLeod enter the mess hall indicated to the others that they'd finished their task and that the truth was finally known, but this wasn't the location to discuss it. That took place in the indoors Protestant chapel after lunch. Rothstein didn't attend because he had other tasks.

Like all would-be ministers, Bergie stood at the pulpit (a lectern) reviewing *his* flock. "So it's MacKay, Neish, Sterling and Scott, is it?"

"And MacElvoy," replied Lyons. "They indicated Jock came up with the idea. I don't think he participated, but, well, we must include him."

Moose stood up quickly. "Youse can bet your life we should. He's as guilty as the rest."

"Any ideas on retribution?" asked Bergie.

Douglas stood. "Do you guys remember last year when the OC decided to hold a surprise personal kit inspection?"

The rest nodded. They remembered it very well because East got caught with some rotting food in his and Earl's barrack box.

"You bet I do," Jack replied. "Earl and I really got nailed for that."

Jackson shoved East. "Don't remind me, you slob. That was all I needed - getting down on my hands and knees for two hours scrubbing the kitchen floor."

Douglas' grin became infectious after his next question.

"Well, I propose that we ask the corporal to ask our OC to hold a surprise kit inspection tomorrow morning. Those Scottish creeps will be at the dance tonight ... they'll be tired. We simply do our thing during the night. What say?"

It was obvious Bergie loved the idea, so did everyone else. A decision was quickly made and they prepared their plans. The infamous four plus one, were about to be generously *compensated* for their mischievous efforts, or as Moose said, "Around here, youse don't screw around with the musketeers."

Following the meeting, it was quiet in the barracks. Many cadets had already left for downtown. The Musketeers didn't have to meet the girls until seven, so they prepared their kit, wrote, or read letters. Cunningham, however, was in gaming spirit as he walked the aisles of both sides shuffling a new *marked* deck. Presently, he got a stuke game going full tilt in the drying room.

Wane lay next to Douglas on the lower bunk. "Did you get any money with your letter?"

"Yeah, five bucks. How about you?"

"Nope. I'd be broke if they hadn't paid us. How's your mom?"

"Not bad. I think she likes working nights. It gives her a chance to go shopping with her sister."

"The sister you don't like?"

Douglas paused for a moment, taking a deep breath and letting it out slowly. "Well, I don't really dislike her - it's her attitude I can't stand. She's always boasting about the money she has. She brings her used clothes and really makes a big deal about giving them to my mom. The clothes ain't bad, but Jeez, she never stops boasting."

"Do you talk with her?"

"Yeah, but only when she starts the conversation. ' My, aren't you growing. You're just about as tall as your cousin Fred or your cousin Norman. Both of them have new cars and they're really busy on the waterfront. Douglas why don't you think about working on the waterfront when you leave school? Look at this lovely ring your uncle Fred bought for me. Have you ever seen a diamond this big? Did I tell you about our recent expensive holidays?'"

Wane kicked his own springs. "One of those, eh?"

"Yeah, and it never stops. Whenever I see her, it's too soon. How's your dad?"

"Good. He still keeps putting in for a transfer up north. Why the hell he wants to work in Vanderhoof, I don't know."

Wane suddenly stopped, grinned, and took an envelope out of his shirt pocket. "I just got this from Marigold. Wanna hear it?"

"Sure."

"My darling ever-so-sweet Wane:'"

Douglas interrupted. "Ever-so-sweet? When did you turn out to be a savage like Moose?"

"Hey, maybe my earlobes taste good, I don't know. Let me get on with this thing.

'I know I promised to write every day, but I simply can't because I've been getting so many letters from other cadets at Vernon, especially a cadet called Field-Martial Danyluk. He says he's the top cadet at Vernon and he's from a very rich family in Vancouver ... a family that loves to give, rather than to receive. Apparently, the Danyluk family trust fund runs most of the charitable organizations around here. What a dear boy he must be because he puts all of his time into collecting for the family trust. Right now he's collecting for the Short Arm Inspection Fund ... a fund that evidently solves problems before they begin - whatever that means. I guess it must be for those poor soldiers and cadets who have short arms and need physiotherapy. It's a funny thing, but when I decide to go collecting from house to house as he suggested, most people laugh at me. How cruel can human beings be? Anyway, I keep my chin up and tell them they won't laugh when it's their family's turn for a short-armer. Some people just don't care, do they? One fat fellow even said

he was once given a short-arm inspection. I said, 'It must have helped you? Your arms look normal now' He nearly died laughing and slammed the door in my face, saying, 'Darlin' I haven't had crabs in my life.' Imagine, talking about seafood when I'm concerned with disabilities. How heartless. Anyway, I collected sixteen dollars from my friends and sent Field-Martial Danyluk a post office money order made out to F. M. Danyluk. If you know him, does the letter M stand for Marshall? His letters are so charming and intelligent. I think I could fall for him if you weren't around. Tell me, do girls ever get short-arm inspections. I know my arms are normal, but what about Edna's? Do you remember Edna? She was the girl I introduced to your friend Johnston. The girl with short arms, short legs, and no neck. Boy, was she ever sick after she went out with him. Also, her breath smelled like horseshit. I think the last time I saw her she was getting into a funeral hearse with some tall ugly skinny guy. At least I think it was a hearse. Poor thing, she was still unwell at the time.

Well, my sweet dear, I still think you're the only one for me, but Field Martial Danyluk sure has a way with words. I'm going out collecting tonight and I'll think of you as I always do. But I must say this Field-Martial Danyluk sounds very nice. Love and Kisses, Marigold. PS - FMD says when he gets back, he's going to give me a ride in his "Trailing Pagoda". Is that a Chinese car?"

Wane had read the letter in a low voice but even after he finished, bellows of silly laughs continued wafting around their bunk space. Both boys enjoyed the letter so much, they actually kicked Wane's bedding and mattress off the upper bunk. When they explained the situation to the rest of the musketeers, the only person not laughing was *Field-Martial Danyluk.* That's because he was in the jon with East's National Geographic magazine.

While the Musketeers roared their heads off over Marigold's letter, two other people in the headquarters building weren't laughing. The RSM had been called into the COs office and ordered to take a chair.

"Sir, if I knew who it was, I'd strangle ... er, I'd straighten the matter up instantly. That, you can be assured."

"RSM, this is a very serious situation. This isn't the first report I've received. Why, just yesterday, the Adjutant received five telephone calls about boys in B-25 sticking their bare bottoms out the windows facing the highway. A certain female civilian almost drove off the road. It's horrible I tell you. To make matters worse, some teenage girls from Vernon drive by and stick their bare bottoms out their car windows towards the hut. It's got to stop."

A light lit up in Gardiner's mind. "Hmmm, B-25, you say, sir?"

"Yes, B-25, the signals hut. They're even drawing eyes, noses and mouths on their rear-ends. What's happening over there? Scottish cadets lift the front of their kilts as cars go by. With eyes drawn on their stomachs, and mouths drawn on their legs, I don't have to tell you what their noses or tongues are. I've spoken with the OC, and on Monday morning he's going to lay the law down. I want it stopped, Mr. Gardiner - is that clear?"

Gardiner stood up, replaced his forage cap, placed his stick under his left armpit and came to attention as only *he* could. Saluting, he replied, "Very clear! I'll see it doesn't happen again, sir." That said, the RSM turned and marched out of the commanding officer's office.

Cordell Cross

Marching down the main road, Gardiner mumbled to himself. "Do I know who the guilty bastards are? You bet I do. It's that Buffalo character and his sidekick, Perky.

With the RSM only seconds away from entering the barracks, Moose came out of the jon, took off his undershorts and threw them on his bunk. "Look at my ass! Jesus Christ, the minute I sat down I knew someone had put shoe polish and honey all over the toilet seat. It was smothered in it. Don't these creeps realize this is signals? Shoe polish pranks are only pulled during the first year. I wouldn't…"

Jackson, ironing at the window cut off Danyluk.

"Hey, fellas, it's those broads in the Ford. They're bare-assin' us again!"

Moose didn't have to be told twice. Instantly pushing open the window as high as it could go, his sticky black derrière proudly responded to the girls' *challenge*.

At the same time as the sneakily grinning Moose pushed his bare ass out the window, Rothstein saw the RSM enter their side of the barracks. He couldn't leave Moose in such a predicament so he gently cupped his hand over Moose's face, shoved the upper torso of the *animal* out, and closed the window on Moose's upper legs. Moose was now half-outside and half inside and regardless how strong his stomach muscles were, he couldn't quite sit up to re-open the window. A frontal buff-bare Moose Danyluk was now upside-down joining the tarpaper on the outside of the shack.

Wane witnessed Rothstein's action and quickly threw a blanket over Danyluk's now protruding wiggling legs and feet. The blanket worked well, except it didn't quite cover Moose's feet, so Wane stood in front of them.

Jackson *welcomed* the RSM so that all could hear - even the gooey-*assed* cadet stuck to the outside of the hut.

"Good afternoon, Mr. Gardiner!"

Moose's toes instantly stopped wiggling, as did his yelling, however horns from passing cars made up for the cries of the silent nude contortionist.

As usual, Mr. Gardiner played with his moustache while asking, "Why the hell is that entire horn racket coming from the highway?"

Rothstein had to think quickly. He remembered there was a soccer game going on at the sports field. "The citizens of Vernon are cheering on our soccer teams, sir."

Gardiner's piercing eyes perused the near-empty side of the hut. "Where is everybody? Especially 'Buffalo' and 'Perky?'"

Only Bergie knew his *nickname* and since he was ironing in the corporal's cubicle, he didn't say a word. The rest also played dumb as Lyons replied, "I think the ones you're referring to live on the other side of the hut, Sergeant Major."

As he marched past Banks towards the centre section and the other side, a confused expression hit the RSM's face and he mumbled, "Is my mind playing tricks? I could have sworn those two boys lived in this side of the hut."

This fraction of a second bafflement that Regimental Sergeant Major Gardiner was never famous for, allowed Wane to open the window and let Danyluk and the blanket fall to the ground. The "ow" was loud and in addition to a sore head and shoulders, the *mooner* now had skin scraped off his feet and legs.

Cordell Cross

Covering his head and body as best he could with the blanket, Moose crouched and ran around the other side not knowing the RSM was there. It was his intention to quickly get under a shower, but he never made it. When he entered from the centre doors, he ran smack into the RSM's back.

"Christ, how many of you are there?" Danyluk mumbled turning tail and fleeing down the stairs again.

Although Gardiner turned quickly, he wasn't swift enough to see the face of the fleeing 'monk' wearing a blanket that didn't quite cover a sticky bare black ass.

Gardiner was now hot on his trail. "That man stop! Stand still, that man!"

Youth has its advantages when one's existence is at stake. With his pursuer gradually gaining ground, Danyluk's legs never moved so fast in his life as he ran on the south road around the back of the next hut and up into the unlocked furnace room.

Although Gardiner passed the furnace room, he never thought of entering. Instead, he marched into the IBT hut, but Danyluk had disappeared into thin air.

"Stand by your beds!"

The few confused cadets remaining in the hut immediately stood to attention by their beds wondering why the RSM was sweating and breathing so hard.

"Ok, where's the black-assed cadet wrapped in a blanket?"

With their chins up, not a word was spoken. They didn't have a clue what the RSM was talking about.

Finally one cadet who had heard of the expression *black-asses*, spoke up.

"Is he armoured, Sergeant Major, sir!"

Gardiner wasn't in the mood for jokes. "How the hell would I know if he's armoured? Where is he? Speak up!"

Danyluk's knees shook when he heard the RSM through the walls. He now knew the Regimental Sergeant Major was in the eastern wing so he made a dash back to his own hut, entering from the end north door of the west wing.

Throwing the blanket aside and heading for the shower room, he screamed, "Get me a scrub-brush and some scrubbing powder, quick! Bergie, give me a hand!"

Bergie ran for the items but was adamant on *other* matters.

"Here ya go, but I ain't scrubbin' your ass!"

"A fine friend you are," Moose replied, applying two sudsed up scrub-brushes to the cheeks of his black *posterior* and feeling each stroke take its layer of skin.

"Jesus, this hurts!"

It took five minutes of scrubbing and whining to get Moose looking normal again. Bergie's help came in a manner that has never been adopted after. He used *East's* new powder puff to spread powder on the red raw buttocks of his *best friend*.

"You owe me all the favours in the world after this. You know that, don'tcha? If someone took a picture of me doing this I'd never live it down."

"Bergie, ol' pard, ol' pal, I'll give youse the world if this works."

Ten minutes later when Gardiner stomped back into the barracks, a gleaming Moose Danyluk and his buddy Perky, were sitting on the centre outside steps shining their boots. Moose was wearing PT shorts, socks, and running shoes.

Powder had also been used to erase the red scrape marks on the front of his legs and upper feet.

The RSM's confident smile showed beneath his giant moustache. He knew damned well he wasn't losing his memory. These two did indeed live on this side of the barracks.

"Where the hell where you two when I was here a few minutes ago?"

Holding a boot in each hand, both lads came to attention, and Bergie spoke first.

"Good afternoon, Mr. Gardiner. I was at the canteen, sir."

"Er, and I was with him, sir. Youse can bet on it."

Gardiner gave both of them a suspicious look, took off his forage cap, wiped his brow, replaced his cap and put his cane on a folding table. He knew he finally had Moose.

"Oh you were, where you? Turn around and drop your shorts, soldier!"

Danyluk felt the piercing eyes of the RSM. "I beg your pardon, sir?"

"You heard me! Turn around and drop your pants!"

"But Mr. Gardiner, sir, you're always telling me to pull them up. This is embarrassing, and totally out of ... Your order is against the Jehovah's Convection."

Gardiner winced again. "Embarrassing my ass. You've never been embarrassed in your life. You heard me, do it!"

Moose did as ordered and the RSM's face turned from triumph to bewilderment. The man, who was never wrong, *was* wrong. He was staring at a lily-white ass.

Red-faced, Gardiner swallowed while hastily reaching for his cap and cane. "Er, you can, er, pull them up."

"Is this some kind of a new inspection, sir?" asked Bergie. "Should I drop my shorts also?"

"Hold your tongue! I thought your friend had been up to some tomfoolery. My apologies, Cadet, er... "

Chin in the air, Moose replied, "Danyluk, sir. Youse can be assured I will drop my drawers for my country anytime, sir. Jehovah's Convection or not."

The RSM didn't waste any time in leaving. "I've noticed that, Cadet Danyluk. Er, your country would like you to keep them up. Carry on."

"I'll be here when my country needs me, sir. Youse can bet on it."

When Gardiner was out of sight, those remaining in the hut surrounded Moose. With his heart back to normal, he joined the others in merry-making and their laughter must have been heard at the golf course.

"When I was upside-down, my wang was nearly up my nose. I ain't never been so humiliated in my life, you creeps. Fifty drivers must of thought I was doin' callypsothepics, usin' the window as a brace. One broad even screamed, 'Keep it up; I'm in room 204 at the Allison Hotel.' The dizzy dame thought I had a boner. Can youse believes that?"

"It's callisthenics, Moose," said Jackson.

"Whatever."

Wane's grin widened. "Yeah, we can believe it, eh guys?"

Cordell Cross

Everyone nodded and laughed at Cunningham when he counted his winnings saying, "If it had been hard, it would have been partin' your hair."

"Or diggin' in the dirt and propping up your head," quipped East. "I'll even betcha your nuts were strokin' your chin?"

Moose roared with the rest after he said, "Nope, they were stuck in my eyes."

"We could have let you be caught," Rothstein offered.

Moose gave Rothstein a mock punch. "On second thought, Rothie, you did the right thing. My thanks goes out to all of youse buddies. Even you, Bergie."

Brice smacked his friend on the back. "Moose, it's the Geneva Convention, not the Jehovah's Convection."

"Hey, I go around with a dame who's in the Jehovah's Convection and it's difficult as hell to get her to drop her drawers. Whatever it's called, it's unfair to us men."

A smiling Bergie shook the animal's hand. "She's a Witness. You owe me, Moose."

When Moose gently sat down on a barrack box, he indicated every move was painful. "Bullshit she was a witness; she ain't even here. Bergie my boy, the Moose always pays his debts. There's three things I'm gonna tell ya. One - youse is gonna get what's comin' to ya. Two - youse is gonna be looked after. And three - youse is gonna get what youse deserves. That's how grateful I am."

Bergie slumped on a bed. "Now that worries me."

At that moment in the Headquarters' Building, the Adjutant approached the RSM's desk. "Mr. Gardiner, we've just had complaints of nude signals cadets doing sit-ups out their windows."

"When, sir?"

"About ten minutes ago, RSM."

"That's impossible, sir. I was there ten minutes ago and no such thing was taking place. The hut is quiet. I have a feeling it's the other hut facing the highway, the D&M hut."

The Adjutant made notes. "Right! I'll mention that to the CO."

After the Adjutant left, Gardiner put his feet on his desk and murmured. "You do that, my boy. You just do that. I don't have an *effing* clue what's going on. Bloody hell, I actually asked the poor brain-dead simpleton to drop his pants. How revolting. For once in his life, the kid was innocent. Why do I get posted here?"

Cordell Cross

Chapter 13

At 1845 that evening, a giant line-up wound its way around the Vernon Arena. Perfumed glossy-eyed fidgety and eager teenage girls held hands and shyly chatted with *their* polished, squeaky clean macho *soldiers*.

The girls were proud of their make-up, sheer-white blouses, loose twirling skirts that came down to their knees, bobbysox, and two-tone shoes. The boys in turn wished camp orders had allowed them to wear KD longs. Instead, it was khaki shirts, khaki shorts, webbelts, boots, puttees, and hose-tops. Once inside, berets could be left at the coat-check or rolled and placed in their right epaulets. The Scots of course wore their kilts with *conviction*.

Even though it was nearly seven o'clock, the merciless sun hadn't let up as the musketeers with midnight passes in their pockets, strode up to the arena. The march down the hill with the usual eyes left at Hop Sing's had been uneventful, except for East stomping on a giant wad of gum as a passing Provost jeep told him to keep moving and march.

East still fumed when the girls ran towards their heroes. "Jeez it's hot. I can't dance with this shit all over my sole. Oh hi babe."

In seconds, ever-waiting sweaty arms were wrapped around bashful young ladies who appeared to have spent at least two hours preparing their make-up and clothing. After greeting, the couples rushed into line.

"I really missed you last week," Diane said to Douglas after they kissed and he put his arm around her waist and shuffled in the now slow-moving queue.

Diane's eyes gleamed. "We waited and waited until about nine and then walked home. God, I was worried about you. I sat on a lawn chair until two-clock wondering what went wrong."

Douglas squeezed her and kissed her left cheek. "I really missed you too, but as I explained on the phone, we couldn't do anything about it. The truck got a flat tire and we ended up pushing it to a farmhouse nearly at Kelowna. We thought that if we could make it to your game we could get a ride back. Nothing worked, except..."

"Except what?" she asked, picking an imaginary piece of lint off his shirt.

Douglas' face became melancholy. "Well, we met an old farmer who was a really great guy. He went out of his way to look after us, and sitting on his back porch at nighttime, the setting was like Heaven on earth. The only thing missing was you."

Diane smiled. Douglas Brice, you've gone and fallen in love with an Okanagan nightfall again. It is beautiful, isn't it?"

He grinned and touched the tip of her nose with a finger. "Yes, but not as beautiful as you. You're right, because the lights of the city and the noise at the camp doesn't allow us to witness it, or feel it. I'll tell you, Diane, it was wonderful."

Diane knew every picture in his mind. "I know how you feel; you don't have to tell me. Is mother nature my only competition?"

Douglas gently turned Diane around so he could face her. As he held her in his arms, he said, "Sweetheart, mother nature made you, didn't she?"

Cordell Cross

"Hey, move it up front," yelled Moose wondering why the queue had stopped moving.

"Alma, youse and I are really gonna do this place up tonight. I've had a hellova bad day and although this heat is driving me nuts, youse changes it for the better. Is that perfume you're wearin' called *Tonight For Sure?*"

In a low shy voice and not looking at her *man of admirable exploits*, Alma softly replied, "Maybe."

Moose's eyes lit up as he brought his arm up from her waist to her shoulder and pressed her close to him. "That's my favourite girl."

A handbag across his back made him think twice.

"Oops, I mean that's my *only* girl!"

"I'd better be, Moose Danyluk, or you're dead!"

"Youse knows I was only jokin' Alma!"

Four couples back, Debbie stiffly moved Wane's hand from her buttocks to her waist, saying, "There're people around us, you know?"

Wane knew something was bothering her. "Debbie, what are you mad at?"

"I'm mad at you, you skuzzball. You haven't called me all week, and I had to hear the flat tire story from the other girls. That's what's wrong."

"But sweetie-pie, there's a hundred cadets at the phone when I get there. The best I can do is pass on a message."

His girl turned her eyes away. "Moose always manages to call Alma."

"Yeah, but he spends hours in the line-up just to do it."

"So, *I'm* not worth hours?"

As Wane cupped his hands around her ears, he knew he had to say something right for a change.

"Baby-face, I spend every hour of the week just thinking about you. I'm wild about you, Deb … you know that? I can't sleep because I'm always thinking about you. You're always on my mind. You're numbre uno."

That did it. "Numbre uno? Oh, Wane, you're so romantic. "Numbre uno. I'm so sorry."

As Wane moved his hand back to her buttocks, he said, "Have you bought any new panties?"

The couple in front were romantic in their own way. East still had boot *problems.*

"Blast, now I've got another wad of gum under my other boot. The whole world is gnawing gum and laying it for me."

"Jack, my big strong flame, don't worry about it. After we each eat four hot-dogs, it'll be off your mind. Aren't you hungry, my turtle dove?"

East was both hot *and* hungry as he put on his hurt look. He didn't have too much money with him. "Well, maybe after four or five hot-dogs and a couple of hamburgers, I'll be all right."

"And some pop and chips, my big heartthrob?"

"Yeah, those too, babe. How much money ya got?"

"Lots, my broad shouldered, brave and handsome gladiator. Should we have french-fries too?"

"Yeah, but not if they're greasy, Sweetie. Grease makes me burp.

Cordell Cross

"See, my big sweet handsome hunk, your mind's off your boots already, isn't it?"

Hey, yeah. I guess this bein' in love removes the world's problems, don't it?"

As the musketeers entered the packed fiery arena, distant thunder hinted at why it was so hot.

Checking his beret, Douglas said, "It's going to pour tonight. I hope it starts while we're heading back up the hill."

"You'll get soaked if it does," Diane replied, straining her neck to find the others in the throng.

"Who cares? We were sweating just marching down. Christ, it's hotter in here than outside. I'm soaked now."

"Welcome cadets and young residents. We've got a great show for you tonight. During the first half you'll be entertained by *Buggerlugs and the B-Bops*, and during the second half, we'll play your favourite records."

As Alma and Moose pushed their way through the boisterous crowd, Danyluk was on cloud nine. "Hey, Alma, Buggerlugs and the B-Bops are from Vancouver and they're great. They never work on a stage; instead, they like being surrounded by their fans. This Buggerlugs fella plays a mint piano."

"I like their outfits. Do they play rock and roll?"

"Alma, that's all they play."

Moose words rang true. The minute the announcer mentioned the group's name, Buggerlugs and his group opened up with five rock tunes in a row. The floor was immediately crammed with jiving teenagers and it didn't matter if they knocked each other while dancing, this music was *Real George*.

It was during the last song of the first set that Buggerlugs wished he'd used a stage. With his arms full of hot-dogs, hamburgers, pop and chips, Buggerlugs' top fan, Jack East, with gum on both soles, came to a grinding halt and dumped a full container of pop and two *oozing* hamburgers over Buggerlugs' head, lap and keyboard. Although the B-Bops kept playing, a livid Buggerlugs stood up quickly.

"What the...? For Christ's sake! What's with you, man?"

Mustard, relish, ketchup and onions had now mingled with Buggerlugs' Brylcreem.

Mortified, East didn't know what to say as he used a napkin to clean off his *idol*. Even then, two wieners shot out of their hot-dog buns and ended up on the entertainer's piano.

The crowd around the piano recoiled at first then howled laughing. Even the B-Bops couldn't take it; they were bent over as well. Not necessarily because of what Buggerlugs looked like, but because of the look on East's face. His mouth was open and he was totally in shock.

When he came around, East profusely apologized trying to explain about the gum on his boots. "...And I keep sticking to the floor."

"I don't doubt it with all that crap you're eating. Now how about getting me a wet cloth."

After a few wipes, and probably still fuming, a "covered in shit" Buggerlugs went back to work, as East's girl dragged her *lover* towards to the food stand again.

Cordell Cross

"You've got to stop wasting your food like that. People are starving in this world, you know?"

East had a hard time picking up each foot. "Yeah, and I'm one of 'em. Damn, I can't walk right with this sticky gum all over my boots."

"Why don't you take them off and check them?"

"Good idea. I'll be right back."

Jack's girl yelled, "Whaduya want and I'll buy it for ya?"

"Three hot-dogs, three hamburgers, chips and a large pop."

"Okay, Sweetie."

As East disappeared into the crowd, a heavily perspiring Cunningham and his girl, Maggie, jived the night away. Each time she twirled under his arm, or he tossed her over his hips or through his legs, she asked him his sort of *romantic* questions.

"But why *is* an ace one or eleven?"

"Don't ask because that's the way it is. Depending on what the dealer's got, sometimes it's necessary to hit a soft fourteen. That's an ace and a three ... remember that. It's important."

"So a face-card and an ace is Blackjack, eh?"

"Now you're gettin' it. That's my partner."

As usual, the Scots danced the only way they knew. With their kilts twirling up around their waist half the time, their immediate audience got bare-assed with each move. Quite a few of the Scots had three *ladies* each and the girls giggled with each other, taking note of the hard-faced smiles or smirks on their boys' faces as they *mooned* those in their vicinity during the jiving. Needless to say, the non-Scottish cadets without dates couldn't understand why the girls mobbed these *haggis-bashers*.

"It's unfair, I tell ya. Glen, what do we do? Look at that short skinny asshole in the kilt. He's got four dames dancin' with him."

"Pete, it's common sense. When we get home, we'll join the Seaforths. Yeah, that's what we'll do."

"Hey, yeah, or the Irish, right?"

"Are you out of your mind? Only the band wears kilts in that regiment. You wanna get broads, don'tcha? Their kilts are just brown."

"Yeah, you bet I do."

"Then get with it. It's the Seaforth Highlanders or nothin' you dummy."

"Couldn't we just borrow a couple of kilts?"

"Hah, just try it; they're like gold. Also, ya gotta be trained how to bare-ass the dames. Have you ever seen a Seaforth without a broad?"

"No."

"See then? There's a knack to it. I betcha they take two periods of bare-assin' each week. They do it dancin' around big swords or sumpin."

"Are you *serial*? Jeez, the lucky creeps. We learn about the Bren gun and they learn how to bare-ass dames, dancin' over blades."

Buggerlugs and the B-Bops had to be congratulated considering East's *drenching* during the first half of the night. They bowed to a very appreciative and elated audience and afterwards signed autographs. Buggerlugs even signed one for East.

Cordell Cross

The second half of the evening was a little more passionate as the romantic sounds of *Ebb Tide, Hey There, Little Things Mean a Lot, and, I Went to Your Wedding*, reverberated throughout the old ice-skating building. Slow-shuffling couples clung to each other not caring about teenage problems, their summer jobs, the camp on the hill, or tomorrow. Their space on the floor was now their little piece of the globe without the intrusion of adult-caused dilemmas. Oh yes, there was uncertainty, but it was about themselves, their inner feelings, their first step to a world of mutually explored wonderment with each other.

After the lights dimmed, this was their night and their time in the universe of mixed-up feelings. A time of fast-beating hearts, eyes meeting but really not seeing, silent kissing, nibbling, or hands being guided to or from faces, waists or more *padded* parts.

At least that's the way it was for the majority. In the dark, some people still had their everyday problems.

"Jesus, fella, will you get off my feet? My toes are flattened already, you pongo," East yelled, nearly choking on his hamburger.

"Well, put your socks and boots on, Mac, and quit wipin' my girl's hair with your burger. Why the hell are you eatin' on the dance floor, anyway? It's dark in here and we can't see your chow."

East had managed the knack of resting his arms over the shoulders of his girl - a hamburger binding his hands. He had found the floor too slippery to wear socks, so he had taken them off as well. Being slightly flat-footed, sometimes when he stepped sideways, nearby cadets unknowingly stomped on his unclad feet.

"'Cause I'm hungry. Go take a hike."

"Hungry? I don't doubt it. You've shared your goddamned groceries with everyone in here."

Someone said, "It's that weirdo Westie that farts in the showers! Now he's in his bare feet."

East recoiled. "I heard that!"

"It's surprising considering the noise you make when you eat or fart. It's a wonder you're not deaf."

"Oh, yeah?"

"Yeah!"

Moose and Alma slowly slid between the vocally battling couples and soon everything got back to normal, except for the odd: "Get that burger off the back of my head," or, "Debra, what are you wipin' your hands on the front of my shirt for?"

"Sorry, Lyle, but you've got mustard all over your shoulders."

"Well darlin' it's all over your hairdo as well, but I don't wipe it on the front of your dress."

"You'd better not!"

"Hey babe, are you wearin' perfume tonight?"

"Yes, I certainly am; can't you notice it?"

"Nah, all I can smell are fried onions. What's your perfume called, *Wimpey's Night Out*? Hey, where are you goin' - what did I say wrong?"

Cordell Cross

Yes, romance was in the hot air and it didn't matter what form it came in, it was love, even love at first bite.

Throughout the evening, Douglas and Diane had stayed to themselves dancing, or sometimes sitting high in the stands staring into each other's eyes or observing the herd below. It felt wonderful being together. At times they said very little, but when they did talk, neither one could shut up.

After *Ebb Tide*, the last record played was Doris Day's *Secret Love*. It wasn't planned. Rather, it was probably just thrown in by the disc jockey. But for the chock-full house of teens, that particular song answered the unspoken call. Only lonely singles sat out the tune. The darkened floor quickly filled with slow-moving ever-devoted young romantics, captured by an unaccustomed enchanting spell in this spine tingling fresh new stage of their lives.

When the main doors opened, the hot air entering was as warm as that inside. Thunder was nearer now and everyone knew the Heavens were about to open.

While the boys stood kissing their girls goodbye, a loud horn reminded the girls it was time to go. Diane's dad had arrived, as did other family members.

"Do you want a ride, son?"

"Thanks anyway, sir, but there's ten of us and we're gonna walk up the hill together."

"When are you coming to the house for dinner?"

A sneaky grin hit Douglas' face. "Whenever I get an invite, sir."

The cadet's statement started all three laughing. He'd been invited nearly every night but he couldn't get out of camp.

Douglas asked, "Is the invitation still open?"

"Always ... you know that."

"How about tomorrow then?"

"Great, Doug, you'll like Sunday's roast. Diane's cooking it."

Large drops of rain accompanied waves and blown kisses, and Douglas Brice got his wish - he'd get soaked marching up the hill.

Before they left the arena's parking lot, they had to find Earl. Nobody had seen him since a dispute on the dance floor ten minutes earlier. After five minutes though, Earl and his girl appeared. There was a bit of blood on his nose and he was slightly nursing his right hand.

"What the hell happened to you?" Wane asked finding it difficult to see Earl's face because of the attention his friend's nose was getting from the girls.

"Some civvy guy called me a wagon-burner. He's Chinese, so he didn't like me calling him a rickshaw puller. I think he's gonna have a bit of difficulty pulling his rickshaw because now both of his eyes are black."

"How'd it start?" Douglas asked.

When Earl smiled there was blood on his teeth. "He was going to grab East because his girl got her hair wrapped around the *beast's* burger. I just grabbed his hand and said, 'There's no damage, leave it be.' He didn't like that, so we went outside."

East hadn't even noticed the disturbance. "Hey, why didn't you tell me, you creep. I would have handled him. Jeez, people are picky around here."

Earl licked his teeth. "Jack, let's make a deal. No more food on the dance floor, okay?"

Jack noticed the nodding going on around him. "All right, all right."

Shortly, the girls were gone and the musketeers took on the hill.

Halfway, after finalizing their plans for the *Scots*, Moose covered his eyes. "Son of a bitch, this storm is blinding me. We're gonna catch the death of cold by the time we get to the camp. Also, the wind is picking up."

Loyal, regardless of the weather, all ten gave Hop Sing's an eyes right. Two minutes later, they didn't have to undergo the body-piercing scrutiny of the provost sergeant. It was raining so hard, he stayed playing solitaire in his military police hut.

Only one corporal walked the darkened hut, and he quietly told them to hit the sack.

The boys shivered a bit after shedding their saturated clothing and crawling into bed. Someone had suggested a shower but all the hot water was gone.

With its windows closed, B-25 became a shield from the howling wind and ceaseless rainstorm hammering its roof and walls.

Normally chit-chat would have taken place, but not this night. Each bunk's three blankets were used as the clatter of teeth indicated a hut of *soldiers* were damned cold and needed immediate well-earned sleep. As for the musketeers, at 0230 the majority of them had to get up to get even.

Sergeant Bentley wasn't alone when he entered the hut at 0630. Joining him were the OC and four platoon commanders, two of which headed for the other side. Although Bentley, the OC and the lieutenants wore raincoats, they were still soaked through.

The sergeant did all the *talking* after shaking the coats and handing them to a smiling corporal looking forward to the upcoming commotion.

"Stand by your beds!"

Throughout the side, confused cadets sat up rubbing their eyes. This was Sunday morning and it was cold. On Sunday mornings, they were allowed to sleep in until church parade. Even the kitchen stayed open until 1300.

"Stand by your beds! Quickly now, quickly! You, turn around until your future wife's plaything goes down. Put your goddamned underwear on, man!"

As a red-faced Danyluk faced the window for a few moments, the *visitors* walked the aisle. When he was *normal*, he put on a pair of PT shorts and stood by the end of his bunk.

"It's pouring out there today, so company dress for church parade will be KD longs, shirts, sweaters, boots, puttees, and regimental head-dress."

Some cadets grabbed their towels from the end of their bunk and started heading for the showers. No one wanted to miss the hot water in this weather.

Sergeant Bentley said, "Did I say to move? No, I did not! Stand to attention! Right! Today we're going to have a surprise personal kit inspection. You will open your barrack boxes, leave them open and stand by your beds! You will not touch any article. Is that clear?"

"Yes, Sergeant," echoed throughout the musketeers' side of the hut, and at that exact moment the same thing happened on the other side.

Puzzled expressions captured the faces of most shivering cadets. This was the first day after a casual Saturday. The inside of most barrack boxes looked like the interior of a ragman's shop, or even worse.

While individual platoon corporals ensured items weren't touched, the OC made his rounds with Sergeant Bentley. Naturally, the musketeers' boxes and most of the others in their platoon were *up to snuff.*

Names were taken and comments came loud and heavy during the inspection, however, the *fun* began when the OC stopped at MacKay and Neish's box. Actually, all cadets at their end of the hut wondered where the fish and urine smell was originating, so were the *owners.*

The inside of the barrack box appeared fairly normal, however the stench was abominable as both the OC and Sergeant Bentley took out their handkerchiefs to cover their noses. The officer commanding even used the end of his swagger stick to *gently* move certain items. Rot might have set in had he used his hands on the garments.

Bellowing into his handkerchief, the sergeant pointed to Neish, then to MacKay and his lower bunk.

"Empty everything out on *that* bed!"

Visibly retching, MacKay and Neish obeyed, not noticing that nearly all clothing items had been turned inside out. Their underwear, KD longs and khaki shorts all had large brown *marks* in appropriate places. Additionally, the butt-ends of shirttails and white T-shirts possessed the same dark chocolate-coloured *crease* stains.

As the startled boys bent over to move the garments, thick brown crinkled *stripes* appeared on the backsides of the very underwear wore.

The OC couldn't take it any longer. "I have seen and smelled enough! Two days in the guardroom should rid these animals of living this filthy way of life! My God, what kind of homes do you people come from? It's a wonder you're not sick. Then again, maybe you are with those blotches all over your bodies?"

Both boys didn't know what the big red itchy blotches were. They did know, however, that their faces, neck, arms and torsos were covered.

Although excuses came hot and heavy, they fell upon deaf ears.

Sterling and Scott's box was no better. To their astonishment, the "shit stain spots," as Danyluk later put it, covered all their clothing. To make matters worse, the bottom of the wooden receptacle held bowls of mouldy porridge with spoons still stuck in them, rotten fruit, pieces of decayed meat, putrefied sandwiches and malodorous halves of hard-boiled eggs.

"Two days in the guardroom as well, Sergeant Bentley! And I want those four out of here now, with their barrack boxes!"

The musketeers had left MacElvoy's box untouched. When he had opened it with the others, he quickly disposed of a note saying: *Own up to the corporal you nailed him and don't do it again. If you don't, you're going to have one hell of a problem! Also, don't mention this note to your buddies ... Leave well enough alone.*

Cordell Cross

In addition to the now famous four, twenty-six names were taken during the inspection. Their barrack boxes were loaded with dirty clothes, and had just been neglected. These cadets were confined to barracks for the one day and had two hours extra duty in the kitchens of the lower camp.

After the NCOs and officers marched out, small groups gathered to *discuss* how some cadets could be so filthy. The musketeers, however, didn't congregate. They needed the hot water of the showers.

On cold or rainy days, East always shared the hot shower-water with those courageous enough to enter. It was here that the musketeers listened with glee to those brave souls.

"The dirty bastards. Are all Scots like them?"

"The Irish are worse!"

"Who says so?"

"Er, are you Irish?"

"Yeah, what of it?"

"Er, nice regiment. The Scots are worse!"

"We'll never get the fish smell out of our end of the barracks. It's still there. All those guys ever did is shit themselves!"

"Two days in the guardroom is like two days in hell. They'll wash everything ten times over when they come out!"

"There's no shortage of toilet paper, what drives guys to do that?"

"All Scots are the same! At home, they're too cheap to buy asswipe, so the habit stays with 'em."

"Hey, that's it! Maybe they're airing out their asses when they dance with the dames."

"And to think I slept near them. It's a wonder I ain't got scurvy. (gulp) What's scurvy look like?"

"Why? Did she go around with one of them?"

"Scurvy ain't a dame, you dummy. It's a disease."

"Oh! Like pewmonia, eh?"

"The word's pneumonia. What regiment are you in?"

"The Rocky Mountain Rangers ... The best!"

"The Ramsuckers, eh? It figures."

Yes, East's retribution had taken place. Although well organized, it hadn't been easy. Shortly after midnight when the corporals' lights went out, Danyluk and Bergie reluctantly left their warm beds, donned dry clothes and gloves, and confronted the rain. For fifteen minutes, they collected stinging nettles and pea-weed from the field just south of the hospital. In addition to an open can of sardines, they taped the reeking pea-weed below the springs at the extremity of MacKay's lower bunk - unseen and just inches from his barrack box.

While Bergie and Danyluk completed their task at the ends of both sets of bunks, Jackson and East using the soft undersides of the stinging nettle leaves, ever-so-slowly stroked the faces, necks, arms, legs and torsos of the exhausted danced-out four *really* sleeping cadets.

Cordell Cross

While the peaceful dreamers were being *blotched*, Douglas, Wane and Cunningham stood in the drying room removing the latch-pins so certain barrack boxes could be opened. This allowed Lyons and Rothstein the opportunity of painting brown shoe polish *pleats* in pertinent regions of the clothing, before returning the garments and replacing the pins.

Because Lyons' buddy was a Scot, he was relieved from any of the assignments. McLeod was loyal enough to the Scottish cause not to join in, but as far as he was concerned, MacKay, Neish, Scott and Sterling were not the norm for Highland *or* for that matter, Lowland *warriors*.

Although some cadets did return to their beds following the inspection, the musketeers remained up, shrewdly got rid of the sardines and pea-weed, had breakfast, washed some clothes, and ironed them dry. With their ironing done, scrubbing pith helmets, and shining boots and brass took up what spare time was left until a wet corporal marched into the barracks yelling: "Church parade! Form three ranks on the road. Wear your regimental head-dress, and yes you may wear your ponchos."

Even though other faiths did not have to attend the weekly services, everyone had to form up in the rain until the roll was called.

"All those who are not Christian may now fall out! Just a minute, what are your names?"

The corporal noticed Cunningham walk off with his arm around a turbaned Moose Danyluk's shoulder. Both cadets kept their head turned away from the NCO.

Straight-faced with the rain blinding him, Cunningham assumed the position of attention and confronted the corporal.

"Who me?"

"Yes, you. With a name like Cunningham, you've got to be Christian."

"My name is not Cunningham, Corporal. It's pronounced, Cu-nningh-am. Our large family is a sect of the Maharani Far-ine-ah, Corporal - the Goddess of predilection and propensity. The Maharani guided the Beggars of Sagacity higher in the Mountains of Antediluvian before the great cataclysm. It is said she is obeisant only to the powers of Deus Himself. Thus my family..."

Normally composed, this corporal had spent too much time in the Junior Ranks Club the night before. "Did I ask for your pathetic life story? Here I am getting soaked, and you start a *effing* speech! Take that shit and peddle it elsewhere! You're probably one of those weirdoes that knock on doors in the early hours, and tries to convert... "

Cunningham appeared to be very upset, as were all others standing in the rain.

"I beg your pardon, Corporal. I do not make fun of your conviction, whatever it may be. I take umbrage with your remarks and I will write a letter to my parochial exalted mistress, explaining your unmerciful ill regard for the Beggars of..."

The corporal appeared to have second thoughts." Er, perhaps I was a little harsh on you. Carry on with the vagabonds. But as for you, Danyluk, get than turban off and fall back in the ranks. We have no Sikh cadets in this company. Since when did you become Sikh?"

Cordell Cross

As Cunningham briskly marched away, a flustered Moose became upset at himself for being discovered.

"Er, since this morning Corporal when I went on sick parade. As you can see, I cut my ear shaving and my religious doctrines are... "

"Are you going to start giving me that hobo crap also?"

"Youse knows I won't! I simply..."

"Get back in the ranks!"

Within minutes, as the Protestants marched to B-3, the Roman Catholics marched to the outdoor chapel behind the headquarters building. Large Marquee tents had been joined together to facilitate the assemblage.

The expressions on the faces of wet cadets from all companies joining one-another indicated pure *exhilaration* at the thought of the next exciting hour.

During that hour with the rain pounding the canvas, Moose Danyluk listened *reverently* as a far-sighted and hard-of-hearing priest rambled on about the inferno of Hades. Well, not quite that conscientiously because when he started snoring, his attention always had to be rekindled by elbow-jabs from Jackson. Actually, Jackson seemed to be in the middle of the action because two cadets behind never stopped arguing.

"No it wasn't!"

"Yes it was."

"Like hell it was!"

"Was, too. I'll betcha two-bits."

"You're on."

One of them finally tapped Earl on the back. "Hey, who painted the Pristine Chapel?"

Earl just gave them a dirty look. Then the other one said, "It's called the Christine Chapel, you ayrab. Yeah, Mac, who painted it?"

Seated in the second row, Danyluk didn't know what had happened after Jackson shoved him to get his head off his shoulder.

"What the hell?"

The padre was most accommodating. He thought Danyluk was involving himself with the sermon, but the Moose had closed his eyes again.

"Yes, my son, that's what it is called when you stray from the path our Lord set out. Very good indeed. Are you following that path?"

Another jab from Jackson got Moose back on track.

"Christ, will you leave me..."

The padre was ecstatic; for once he had a willing *subject*.

"Exactly, my son. Christ will indeed *lead* you on that course to Heaven. Did the rest of you hear this boy? Being young, sometimes all of you hide your innermost feelings about the proper way of living. Not this mature lad here. He isn't afraid to speak up. Very good, my boy. Stand up and tell us your name."

With a little help from Jackson, Moose stood up. He didn't know why he was standing and as far as he was concerned, he'd rather be curled up in bed. When he tried to sit down again, Earl propped him up and whispered, "Answer the priest."

Rubbing his crotch, the *animal* was now half-awake.

Cordell Cross

"What's he wanna know?"

A cadet behind unwittingly assisted by patting Danyluk's shoulder. "Who painted the Sistine Chapel."

"Michelangelo, sir!"

As one cadet behind collected twenty-five cents from his friend, the priest appeared as if a halo had been placed over his head. His face took on a look of pure veneration.

"My, son, my son, my son; how utterly wonderful. After all these years, the artist still lives to beautify the lives of us sinners. You are indeed a paragon of puritans ... the mortifier of the flesh. Let us all stand and applaud this gentle being of truth and kindness who is not afraid to voice his beliefs."

Now fully awake, Moose appreciated the applause from his *flock*. When seated, he whispered, "Hey, Earl, thank God he asked me a simple question. Jesus, from the look of admiration I'm getting from him, you'd think nobody else knew the answer. This here guy really likes to talk about paint."

After the sermon when the hymnbooks were being handed in, a few voices were heard.

"Suck. What are you, a religious freak?"

"Another signal's suck, eh"

"The living, walking-talking penis has found religion."

"He talks about screwing dead bodies and then hides behind his religion."

The priest certainly didn't feel that way; he made a point of shaking *the artist's* hand. "My child, thank you ever so much. Your presence and interpolation has made an old soldier, very, very happy. Michelangelo, you are indeed a credit to your faith.

It was chest-out time for *Michelangelo* Danyluk.

"Youse can ask me any paint questions any time, father. Did youse knows that Hector Rassmusen painted the Nine-O'clock Gun in Stanley Park. Did youse also know that Wilbert Freephinger painted the public washrooms at Victory Square? I know 'em both and if you wants to meet 'em, just ask me. This dame I know ... her name's Beatrice Rackington ... I call her Ratbottom ... Anyway, she painted the hell out of my hearse. Charged me a lot too. I nearly shit myself and..."

Jackson had to pull Moose away because the priest's brilliant expression of adoration faltered.

Marching back to the hut, Moose said, "Hey why did youse stop me from tellin' him about my buddy, Marty Forgers?"

"Who the hell is Marty Forgers?"

"He's the guy that got drunk and fell on his paint brush while paintin' a picture of a nude broad on the side of the Barn Restaurant. He got a week's detention in reform school and four stitches. Hellova guy, Marty ... He can cup his hand under an armpit and make it sound like he's farting."

Earl grinned. "Were you going to tell the padre that story?"

"Sure, he could use it in one of his sermons."

Cordell Cross

The rain never let up as the musketeers went their own way that Sunday afternoon, and throughout the day Moose remained on cloud-nine because he knew *Haggis* Patterson was taking pictures of Hop Sing's sacrosanct establishment.

It had been a while since the group had split up, but this day individualism was in the air. While Lyons and McLeod raided their *sweethearts'* liquor cabinets, Jackson, East, Cunningham and their girls went bowling. Rothstein, Bergie, Moose and their *beloved-ones* took in an afternoon movie.

At Diane's house, Douglas, Wane Diane and Debbie danced, played charades, cards, and darts and *wrestled* in the basement. Diane's parents were home but they remembered what it's like being young and left the teenagers alone.

For the boys, this was the afternoon of afternoons. No one yelled or screamed. Officers, sergeants, corporals and the military police didn't pass along despotic military *comments*.

As soon as they arrived, the lads quickly replaced their khaki clothing with civilian clothes and were treated like kings. It was nice having Debbie and Diane serving pop and sandwiches and other goodies.

The two cadets felt great being away from the barracks and relaxing in Diane's cosy and spotless wooden house.

One floor above the basement, the front door opened into the living room with a smaller dining room at the end, off the kitchen. A hallway led from the kitchen to a bathroom and two modest bedrooms. A basement sawdust-fed furnace heated most of the house, but even with the rain and wind, it wasn't on. Instead, a sawdust-fed kitchen stove just heating the first floor was aflame and the mouth-watering aroma of Diane's roast filled the house.

The house's antique furniture and rugs blended in well with the more modern household furnishings spread throughout. Knickknacks from far and wide adorned each room, and a finely polished cabinet revealed a prized gun collection.

Two rooms in the darkened basement allowed the young couples to separate an hour before dinner. If the upper door opened, its squeak would warn them of close-at-hand adult intrusion and get them dancing again. The phonograph was left on so that both parents knew hanky-panky was kept to a minimum. As the machine's turntable continued dropping 78 RPM records, devotion consumed all *couch-talk* moments.

With impish smiles on their faces, Diane lay partially on top of Douglas - his hands inside her sweater, caressing her smooth back.

"I like it when you wear this short sweater."

A soft melodious, "Why?" ensued.

"Er, because, er, jeez, you're shivering."

"I'm not shivering; you're tickling me. Did you notice something else?"

"Should I?"

Diane's voice was barely audible. "Doug, I'm ... I'm not wearing a bra."

He gulped. "Er, yeah, I..."

Diane didn't allow him to finish. Placing a fingertip on his lips and delicately kissing him, she gently moved her position, ensuring his hands left her back, but not the confines of the garment.

Cordell Cross

Douglas' mind went wild. Nothing could describe his elation. He loved Diane beyond the description of mere words and at this moment, nothing, absolutely nothing, or no one could enter his world.

In the next room, similar but different behaviour took place.

"Wane, stop that!"

"Can I have these?"

"No."

"Aw, c'mon, Deb? C'mon babe?"

"No, Wane. You probably show them to the other boys."

"No I don't, baby. You know I wouldn't do a thing like that. This is personal - just between you and me."

"Well, I don't care. I'm not walking around here without panties anymore. Besides, it's cold outside. I have to walk home, you know? Why do you want them, anyway?"

"To remind me of my one and only girl. I'm in love with you, you know?"

"It's still no. They're expensive. You must have six pairs already."

"Seven in fact. I'll give you mine, they're warmer."

"You probably borrowed them from Moose."

Wane's tone changed. "Debbie, sweetheart, if I borrowed these from Moose, I wouldn't let Witch Hilda wear them."

"Oh, Wane, you're so romantic when you're serious."

"Deb, you're my numbre uno."

"Oh, my darling Wane. Whatever I have is yours."

"Anything, babe?"

Yeah, but you're not gettin' these panties."

When the door squeaked, both couples quickly straightened their clothing and hair and resumed dancing. It was difficult for the boys, but the girls understood.

After a delicious roast beef dinner with engaging conversation, Diane's parents and the four settled down to a night of Dragnet, The Shadow, People Are Funny, and The Battling Bickersons. These radio programs were broadcast from Kelowna and except for Dragnet and The Shadow, the audience of six laughed loud throughout. At eight-thirty though, it was time to go head into the ever-pounding rain.

After thanking their hosts and accepting a ride, the boys stood on the front porch with their girls while Diane's dad warmed up the car.

Wrapped up in her boyfriend's arms, Diane whispered, "Will you call me? Can we get together this week?"

Douglas kissed her. "You know I will. I think we've got an evening off even though we're getting prepared for Glenemma. We're there the whole of the fourth week."

"You mean I won't see you at all during that week?"

He grinned. "This coming week, but not the next. That is unless you want to come out to Glenemma. Hey, maybe you could sneak in with the food truck."

Both youngsters laughed as they held each other tightly.

Cordell Cross

"Don't tempt me, Douglas Brice. You know me when I get an idea in my head. I'd be there."

That same evening when Wane and Douglas returned to camp, B-25 appeared like it had barely survived the biggest earthquake to hit the Western Hemisphere. Totally a shambles and with a deafening noise - approximately 180 cadets did everything possible to keep it looking that way.

Although Douglas and Wane were cold, there was enough hot water to make them feel warm again. The rest of the musketeers had showered after returning earlier from downtown and taking in Sunday's B-3 movie, *Fix Bayonets,* with Tyrone Power.

After taking showers, the boys were surprised to find everyone in their *crew* busy. Well, nearly everyone; Lyons and McLeod were asleep, Danyluk sat writing his charity donation letters, East ate a chicken leg and shined boots, Bergie fixed his bed springs, Rothstein chuckled reading a comic, Cunningham hid in the drying room with his dice and *suckers,* and Jackson sat on the floor ironing his shirt on a blanket.

Wane and Douglas lay on Douglas' bed totally oblivious to the wind, rain, and bedlam surrounding them. They had an hour before lights out and they had already done their kit.

"Wane, I know I keep saying this, but that was the best day yet. Come hell or high water, I'm going to marry Diane."

Wane grinned. "We noticed it was kind of quiet in there. What were you two doing? C'mon Doug, own up."

"Oh, just talking about life. You know ... what's ahead for us, and that sort of thing. How about you two? It was quiet in your room as well."

"I can't tell ya, Doug, but Debbie knows a hell of a lot more than Marigold. I asked her how she knew all those things and she said it comes natural."

"What things?"

Wane didn't answer. Instead, he got up and walked over towards East. "If I told you, Doug, you wouldn't have fun learning them. Jacky, my boy! How are ya?"

East glanced up from his *task.* "Forget it, I've got the corporal's boots to do. He's paying me two bucks. Do your own boots, Wane."

"Two bucks? Shit, I was only gonna pay ya two bits! Oh well. Say, what's with the eggs?"

Two farm-fresh eggs balanced themselves on top of East's barrack box.

"I got 'em from the kitchen at mug up. Do you remember the lecture Sergeant Beckford gave us last year? The one about usin' the sun's heat as a stove?"

"Yeah."

"Well, as soon as it stops raining, I'm gonna use the bottom of my wash basin to cook these. Neat eh?"

East put the second of the corporal's boots on the floor before saying, "His boots are startin' to look better than mine."

"Hey Wane," screamed Danyluk, coming out of his very *serious* writing session. "How do ya spell *unprogressive?*"

Wane correctly spelled the word, then added, "Er, what, er, why are you using *that* particular word?"

Cordell Cross

A passing Irish cadet asked East the time.

"It's 2200 - that's ten o'clock to you creeps."

Danyluk cussed and made a few necessary changes to his letters. "Because I'm running the 'Unprogressive Testicles' Fund, this coming week. Youse knows, balls that don't grow any bigger than a peanut?"

Moose's words triggered some comments from Bergie.

"If I find the creep that undid my springs, he'll have the reverse of *unprogressive* testicles. Why didn't you just call it the small balls fund?"

Danyluk closed his ten letters and started licking. "Hey, youse is lookin' at a class organization here. I can't use 'small balls.' All the broads will think the money's going to East."

Like Humpety-Dumpety, eggs have a really totally unreliable way of rolling. When they start moving, they do it their way. That's exactly what happened when East glared at Moose, jumped up and unknowingly kicked his barrack box, sending both eggs into one of the *generous* corporal's boots.

East's face nearly touched Moose's. "Screw you, Moose! Jesus, did you guys hear that? Do I talk about the size of your balls, Moose Danysuck? No I don't! At least my balls are normal sized! So there!"

The *animal* bent over in laughter. "Now Jacky, don't get your normal-sized nuts in a knot. Haaa, I was thinkin' about using your nuts as a model in my next role brochute, er..."

Once again, Rothstein came to his rescue. "Brochure?"

"Yeah, brochure. But I'll have to use one hell-of-a large camera just to find 'em. Thanks Rothie."

East strolled back, picked up the NCOs boots by their tops and put them in the corporal's cubicle.

"Stick it in your ear, Moose!"

"Lights out in ten minutes, a dripping wet corporal bellowed, just back from the Junior Ranks Club. He paused at East's bunk. "Did you finish them?"

"Yeah, they're in your cubicle. I should be chargin' you three bucks."

The corporal opened his wallet and paid Jack. "A deal's a deal. Here ya go my boy. Thank you."

Just after the lights went out and the corporal had returned to the junior ranks club, East suddenly I realized his eggs were missing.

"Okay, Moose, fork 'em over."

"Fork what over?"

"My eggs, you pongo. What are you going to do - use *them* as models?"

"I ain't got your eggs; go stick your head in the jon. You've probably glued them under your crotch."

After a few moments of accusing everyone in the immediate area, a furious East hit the sack, but not for long. Jumping out of bed, and heading for the other wing of the barracks, he said, "It'll betcha it was that Irish creep that asked me for the time. Jesus, what kind of a regiment is that? They must teach 'em to survive at any cost. Stealing *my* eggs, eh? Well, nobody steals BCR eggs."

Cordell Cross

Moose grinned and rolled over on his side. "Go get him, Beastie."

Although the rain eased off a bit, the wind wrapped itself around B-25 that night, shaking a few windows and rattling doors. With most of its occupants asleep, cadets in the other wing drowned the hut's normal creaking sounds out.

(Slap) "Wake up, you asshole. Where's my...?"

"What? Huh? Who the hell are you?"

"Uh, sorry, wrong guy. Sorry about that."

(Poke) "Arise you creep and pass over my... "

"What the...? Is this a nightmare or is the shower monster really talkin' to me?"

"Er, sorry ... I thought you were someone else."

"That's all right, but please don't fart ... I'm sure I've got a wife in my future and I'd like to have kids. I also wear glasses."

Finally, Jack arrived at the right bunk. (Cuff) "Ah hah! Okay, you Irish ignoramus, fork 'em over."

"What? Fork what over? Who the hell are you?"

"I'm the guy who give you the time."

"I don't read Time, just National Geographic."

"Oh, smart guy, eh?"

"Listen, Mac ... I'm tryin' to get some sleep here. What the hell do you want?"

"My eggs, you creep. Those are BCR eggs."

"I ain't got your legs. Have you got an artificial ass, too?"

"I said eggs, not legs. Let's have 'em."

"Listen, Fartface, you Dukes have been out in the sun too long without your helmets. Go buck a fuffalo; I'm tired and I ain't got time for small-talk."

Two seconds later the same boy yelled, "Hey, get out of our barrack box! Hey James, some BCR ayrab's in our barrack box."

"Where's my eggs?"

"In your *effing* nest, you creep. Now, bugger off!"

"I ain't leavin' until you hand 'em over you hackled dill pickle. They were both extra large; one was brown and the other was white!"

"Musta been a mixed marriage, eh? Someone call the hospital or Sunny Farms."

"Turn on the lights! Hey, it's that Westie farter from the other side! So that's how he does it. He eats two eggs before he goes to bed!"

"Let's have 'em! I ain't leavin' here without them!"

"Listen you BCR bastard from Beatty Street, go and..."

"Oh yeah?"

"Yeah!"

Chapter 14

Although the trees, soil, and local inhabitants relish the breaks, Mother Nature doesn't let it rain long in Vernon. At 0600 on Monday morning of week three, the massive dark clouds had disappeared and the sun's early rays lit the way for a gasping Signals Company to jog throughout the upper camp and sing off key.

The Sergeant was in full form. "Let's hear it! *Oh you can't get to Heaven.*"

The chorus sang, *"Oh you can't get to Heaven."*

(sergeant) *"In IBT skates."*

(chorus) *"In IBT skates."*

(sergeant) *"'Cause IBT skates."*

(chorus) *"'Cause IBT skates."*

(sergeant) *"Are full of snakes."*

(chorus) *"Are full of snakes."*

(sergeant & chorus) *"Oh you can't get to heaven in IBT skates, 'cause IBT skates are full of snakes ... Lord thanks ... for the signals course!"*

"Not bad ... now one more, me hearties! *Oh you can't get to Heaven.*"

(chorus) *"Oh you can't get to Heaven."*

(sergeant) *"In D&M kit."*

(chorus) *"In D&M kit."*

(sergeant) *"'Cause D&M kit."*

(chorus) *"'Cause D&M kit."*

(sergeant) *"Is full of shit."*

(chorus) *"Is full of shit."*

(sergeant & chorus) *"Oh you can't go to heaven in D&M kit, for D&M kit is full of shit ... Lord thanks ... for the signals course!"*

"Following falling out, B-25 started becoming habitable again. After the boys showered, they made up their bunks, aligned everything that needed aligning, brushed and mopped the floors, hung clean towels, cleared the shelves except for running shoes, shined the fire extinguishers and garbage cans, and then tackled the sinks, showers, drying room, urinal and toilets.

Prior to breakfast, all cadets pitched in straightening up the outside areas.

After queuing up at the mess hall, cadets had the choice of bacon, eggs, sausages and toast, corn flakes or French toast. To quench their thirst, hot chocolate, coffee, tea, milk, Freshie, or water was available in the centre area of each dining wing.

"What happened to your lip?" Lyons asked, joining East who had already started digging in on his first helping. East's lower lip was swollen and red.

"Some Irish guy decked me after I accused him of stealing my eggs."

Lyons had been asleep during the *hunt*, so he wasn't aware of the eggs episode.

"What, here in the mess hall? When did this happen?"

A couple of Irish cadets entered and *displayed* their middle fingers to East.

"Same to you, you pongoes," Jack yelled before returning his attention to Lyons.

Cordell Cross

"Last night, you creep. The guy stole 'em after he asked me for the time. When I went to get them back all hell broke loose. There he is now - the guy with the black eye."

Lyons glanced over. "Jeez, what happened to him?"

"I hammered him, that's what. The son-of-a-bitch stole my eggs. The other one's his bunkmate. After he got me, I gave him a fat lip."

As the rest of the musketeers arrived, Lyons said, Wow, I'd hate to see what you'd do if someone stole your whole meal."

Bergie grabbed the salt and pepper. "It's the principle of the thing. Ya did all right, Jacky, my son. Did he eat 'em, or what?"

East quickly finished his first course, and stood up for seconds. "How the hell could he eat them ... they were uncooked?"

"He's Irish, ain't he? They don't cook anything."

East chuckled with everyone before feeling his sore lower lip and wincing. "Yeah, he's Irish, and I'm gonna watch those two like a hawk."

At exactly 0800, a gleaming Signals Company formed up on parade on the south road outside B-25. Normally cadet supernumeraries would have conducted the parade along with the OC, however, this particular morning the officer in charge had other things on his mind as he left his company standing at attention.

"As you know, four cadets from this company were sent to the guardroom because of their filthy living standards. This will happen again if interior economy is not maintained in Signals Company. At this time, both cadets are back with us, and I see a considerable change in their personal habits. A significant transformation indeed!"

All heads turned towards the four immaculate, but militarily tranquillized red-faced Scots. Their personal cleanness, dress, deportment and the cleanliness of their barrack boxes and bunk spaces undoubtedly had improved immensely. Two days in the guardroom under the *delicate* and considerate care and attention of regular force Red Caps Provost (Military Police) had greatly changed the boys' outlook on life.

"Good to have you back with us!"

All four Scots appeared apprehensive.

"Now, it has come to my attention that certain members of this company are sticking their bare bottoms out the windows and distracting passing traffic."

Snickering spread throughout the ranks.

"If you think this is funny, we'll see how amusing it is after eight hours on the parade square. Keep quiet!

"Furthermore, some of you have been outside doing nude callisthenics, using the window ledges as support."

Sincere straight expressions faced the OC, however on the insides of those kissers, laughs, chuckles, chortles, giggles, sniggering, cackles, yells, and yes, even screams of pure exhilaration vied to be let loose.

"I've even heard that certain Scottish members *arch* full frontal and rear attacks from the windows! Well, let me tell you, it will stop immediately, along with rooftop sporran parades! Is that clear?"

"Yes, sir!"

Cordell Cross

"Gentlemen, and I certainly use that term loosely, this is Signals Company, not IBT or D&M. Don't you realize that?"

"Yes, sir!"

"Good! You will make certain it doesn't happen again! Signals Company, standat ... ease! Stand ... easy!"

The OC took a small paper from his pocket.

"This morning I have something else to say. It's unusual when bad news is accompanied with good news. It would appear that a certain corporal of ours who served in Korea, has been *Mentioned in Dispatches* for his bravery during that police action. The commanding officer will be here in a few minutes to present the commendation to Corporal Francois."

As cheers and whistles erupted along the road, heads strained to view the brave Corporal Francois who was nowhere in sight. Obviously organized, the non-com had put on his boots and experienced the fright of his life. Had he known about the award, he would have left his boots on, however the *immediate* request for his presence had him appearing without boots and with one sock on and one sock off. His extra boots were in the NCOs quarters and he didn't have time to retrieve them.

Although the road was *paved*, the good corporal's expression indicated both his *soul* and *soles* were sensitive. Not smiling, he approached the OC and saluted.

"Good God, Corporal Francois, where the hell are your boots, man?"

Corporals are only one rank below Gods (sergeants) but their training to attain three stripes pays off handsomely at times.

"Er, it's happened to me again, sir ... ever since the minefield rescue in Korea. I can't even wear a sock on my left foot when the *pus* starts oozing."

Needless to say the pus *was* oozing, but it was quite difficult to detect that this pus came from a couple of Mark 4 Class 'A' Eggs, *for the use of*. When the material from Mark 4 Class 'A' Eggs, *for the use of*, intermingles with toes, the result looks most horrid to say the least.

"Corporal Francois, I humbly apologize, my lad. Had I known of your condition, I..."

The officer turned to a grinning Sergeant Bentley who became very serious the second his eyes met the OC's.

"Sergeant, will you please advise the RSM that the presentation cannot be made this morning. He can notify the commanding officer. Just say, er, certain conditions negate the matter at this time."

Trying hard to keep a straight face, Bentley saluted and marched away from the concerned OC. Because sergeants *are* Gods, they can clearly distinguish the difference betwixt egg-yolk from a Mark 4 Class 'A' Egg, *for the use of*, and flesh ulceration discharge.

"Corporal, please go inside while I send for an ambulance. Is that all right?" the officer commanding asked.

A meek, sore-footed and gas-pained Corporal Francois hobbled to the doorstep and said, "Actually, sir, I'm beyond the hospital stage. They've helped all they can. After a warm soaking my foot will be fine. I just need a little assistance with a few things. Could I, er, request, er, Cadet East for about fifteen minutes, sir? He can be assured that's all the time I'll need him for."

"You certainly can, my boy! Where's Cadet East?"

Ordinarily cadets are not like sergeants, but there are times when they also possess the same perceptible senses, even if only for a second or two. Since this was one of those moments, a knee trembling East kept his mouth shut.

"That's him there," offered a black-eyed Irish cadet.

The OC spotted the now popular cadet. "Are you hard of hearing, Cadet East? The corporal needs you!"

"Sir!" Eyes to the sky, East came to attention, stepped one pace forward, turned to his right and sore lip or not, headed for *irrefutable hell.*

"I wonder if *Jack* going to be Mentioned in Dispatches?" Danyluk whispered.

Bergie grimaced. "Do bears shit in the woods?"

A puzzled expression came over Moose's face. "Er, yeah, I think they do, Bergie. Why do youse ask?"

Bergie's eyes met the sky as well. "Forget it."

Signals training continued hot and heavy during Monday and Tuesday of that week. The company had to be completely knowledgeable for the upcoming Glenemma trip. Moreover, at 0900 on Wednesday morning, On Job Training (OJT) was introduced at the camp level. This exercise allowed all camp personnel to grasp the extensive calibre of academic accomplishment signals cadets had achieved thus far.

Although posted on the bulletin boards, the officer commanding read the schedule.

"Cadets from 21 Platoon will be posted to all telephone stations including the headquarters building, supply stores, camp hospital, transport, and training cadres.

"Cadets from 22 Platoon will install additional temporary telephones throughout the camp, and provide certain communications for the D&M convoys.

"Cadet personnel from 23 and 24 Platoons will lay line for IBT camp exercises and conduct signals exercises for the various command posts in those companies.

"Now pay attention here! Individual OJT training duties and timings have been posted on the bulletin boards. Know your tasks and be on time. These duties cease at midnight on Friday. The next time we will parade as a company will be on Saturday morning. This Friday's mother's night for signals has been cancelled and the company will not compete for Saturday's pennant. Now, if you have any questions, see your platoon sergeants."

Following the fall out, most cadets rushed to the bulletin boards. Jackson had reviewed 21 Platoon's board earlier, but additional information had now been added so he made the necessary notes. This information was supplied to the balance of the musketeers at a meeting called in the Protestant chapel, a quiet place where they wouldn't be interrupted. For some reason East and Rothstein didn't attend.

Standing at the altar, Earl displayed his finest tutorial pose, achieved at great expense the year before.

"Those Scots certainly look dapper this morning. Their dress and bed-space compares to our platoon. Do you think we should ask them to move to the better end of the building, and join us? After all, they've received great training from the Provost."

"Youse has got to be bloody joking?" Danyluk yelled, standing up but sitting down just as quickly. "They're the enemy, until they quit their pranks!"

Using his knowledge of instructional technique also learned the year before, Jackson scanned the group to ensure he maintained eye contact. He did, and his suggestion didn't sit well.

"Er, sorry about that. I don't know what came over me. Well, let's get on with this thing. Moose, you're on the camp switchboard today from 1000 this morning, until 1600 hours. Tomorrow and Friday, you're on the same job from 0800 until 1600 hours. Rothie, will follow Moose all three days from 1600 until 2359.

"Bergie those same timings apply to you and me. You start today at 1000. We're telephone orderlies for transport.

"Cunningham and East..." Earl paused for a moment. "Where's Jack?"

Wane knew. "Where else? Since Monday, he's been washing out the shitters in the officer's and NCO's quarters, *and* peeling the hard-boiled eggs in the kitchens. If he's doing well, he might..."

Wane didn't have to finish, because East entered, blisters and all. He appeared tired as he threw himself into a pew and closed his eyes.

Bergie smacked his friend's back. "Ah, here's our lavatory and egg man, now. Where's your tools?"

Eyes still closed with head facing the ceiling, East replied, "What tools, you creep?"

"Your plunger, mop and knife of course. The four of you have been inseparable since Monday."

"You appear *flushed and a little shucked*," offered Douglas.

"Take a hike you pongoes. If I ever see another toilet or egg again, it'll be too soon for me. Let's get on with this thing."

Earl continued. "Well, I don't know about the eggs, but *you* of all people, will need a shitter. Jack, you and Cunningham are partners. He'll brief you on the timings. Gordie, you're day shift and the two of you are telephone orderlies for the number one kitchen. Wane and Doug, you're doing the same at the camp hospital. Doug, you work days. Lyons and McLeod, you're gonna love this. You're telephone and radio orderlies for the Provost Sergeant. McLeod, you're working days.

After he was finished, Earl sat down and listened to Danyluk's bitching.

"Son of a bitch, can we switch jobs?"

Earl shook his head. "No, it's extra duty if we do. Why, what's the problem?"

"Youse all knows me. I would be better suited in the *unwell* building with those nursing sisters. I could play tunin' the radio with all those big bazookas. Doesn't our officer know I'm gonna work in a sick people's place when I finish school. Shit, us famous ginnyolistics don't work on phones, we work on dames."

With Rothstein not around, Jackson came to Moose's rescue. "Gynaecologists in a hospital?"

"Yeah, thanks, Earl. It's totally unfair."

Moose didn't get the chance to protest further, within seconds all were up and looking forward to their On Job Training. All except Moose, that is, and in the long run, perhaps the OC should have posted him to the *sickly people's place.*

There are four entrances to the headquarters building at Camp Vernon. The structure somewhat resembles a cross. After passing the famous cannon, one enters the main entrance from the camp's principal road. Heading south along a typical hallway, offices, washrooms sit left, and right. The switchboard room is located halfway on the right hand side next to the RSM's office. The building is also accessible from a back entrance at the end of the hallway. Also at the end of the main hallway, corridors head east and west. East leads to the inner sanctum and eventually to the CO's office and west to the orderly room. Both the CO's office and the orderly room also have separate entrances to the building.

At exactly 1000 hours, Danyluk knocked on the door of the switchboard room and introduced himself. It didn't take long for the female operator to acquaint him with the systems and procedures and she was quite happy because cadets taking OJT allowed permanent workers the opportunity to take some valuable paid-time off.

After a one-hour lesson, Moose was ready to take over.

"Are you sure you're up for this, Cadet Danyluk?"

"Mrs Martins, youse can rest assured your job is in good hands. We signals types take pride in our work."

"Fine, thank you. This will give me time to catch up on some shopping. By the way, the RSM has gone to lunch."

"He has? Er, wonderful. Don't you worry about a thing, Mrs. Martins. When Moose is on the job, nothing is left to chance. Goodbye."

After the switchboard operator left, Moose put on his headset consisting of two earphones and a microphone and proceeded to read a magazine. But not for long. A buzzer sounded, and a light lit up.

Placing a jack in the appropriate spot, Moose Danyluk was ready to take on the world.

"Vernon Army Cadet Trades Training Camp; Signalman Danyluk at your service."

A male voice responded, "Adjutant, please."

"One moment, please." Moose took the other end of the jack, placed it in the Adjutant's slot, and pressed the appropriate ring switch. In a few seconds, the connection had been completed. When a red light came on indicating the conversation had finished, both ends of the cord were disconnected.

"This is a piece of cake," he muttered, carrying on with other calls. He knew if he had been using a UCL Ten-line switchboard, after the call he'd have to say, "Are you finished, finished, finished?"

Soon, cords headed in all directions, but Moose was used to this because of his training on the UCL portables. Also, throughout, he had the opportunity to talk to his buddies when they answered various calls in transport, the kitchens, Provost shack and the hospital, etcetera.

"How's it going, Moose?" asked Douglas.

"Not bad, Dougie. Did youse knows there's five outside lines comin' into this switchboard?"

"Keepin' ya busy, eh?"

"Nah, it's a break from the routine. How about youse?"

"Pretty good. These nursing sisters sure look nice."

"Youse lucky creeps! I ... sorry, gotta go."

(Author's note: Caller's names have been changed to protect the guilty.)

"Vernon Army Cadet Trades Training Camp; Signalman Danyluk at your service."

A deep male voice followed. "Commanding Officer's secretary please."

Danyluk employed the necessary jacks but no one answered.

"I'm sorry, sir, neither the CO or his secretary are in their offices. Does youse wish to leave a message?"

"Does ...? Wha ... what was that?"

"Does youse wish to leave a message?"

Moose heard the party at the other end cover the mouthpiece and laugh. "Er, yes I does. This is Colonel Boe Stanwhine. Tell the CO's secretary that General Hugh Jass will arrive Friday at 1800. There will be a party of..."

Another red light went on. "Sir, can youse hold on a minute, I've got another call?"

"Oh, all right."

Moose put two calls on hold and went back to the first party. "Sorry, Major, what was your message?"

"Colonel..."

"Sir, I thought you said, 'General?'"

"No, it's Colonel Boe Stanwhine. I'm calling on behalf of General Hugh Jass. He will be arriving on Friday at 1800 hours with a party of six. One in the party is an MP, and..."

Moose didn't know the term MP stood for Member of Parliament. When the red light came on again, he said, "One moment please, Major Boe, I'll be right back."

Danyluk handled two waiting calls then took a new one. "Vernon Army Cadet Trades Training Camp; Signalman Danyluk at your service."

"RSM please."

"He's at lunch right now. Would youse like to leave a message?"

"Yes, tell him RSM Gattling will be visiting with General Hugh Jass, but he won't be arriving until Saturday at 0800. Have someone pick him up at the railway station. Goodbye." (click)

Danyluk went back to the first call. "Er sorry, Sergeant Major. Now, let me get this straight. General Gattling is arriving at 0800 on Saturday and..."

The Colonel spoke too quick for Moose. "No, you idiot. I'm Colonel Boe Stanwhine. General Hugh Jass will be arriving on Friday at 1800 hours. He has a party of six of which one is a senior MP. Have you got that?"

"Er, yeah. What else. Oops, hold on a sec. Vernon Army Cadet Trades Training Camp; Signalman Danyluk at your service."

"This is Brigadier Ben Danbough. The CO please."

"Sorry, the CO's at lunch."

"OK, tell him that I'll be joining General Hugh Jass on Friday, but I'm coming by plane on Thursday. Have me picked up at 1400 hours. As well, RSM Gun Gattling has changed his plans and is coming by bus on the same day. Have him picked up at 1300 hours." (Click)

Back to the first party again. "Er, sorry, General Gun. Now, is there anything else?"

"Colonel, please."

"No, Major, if I was a Colonel, I wouldn't be on the switchboard, would I? It's *Signalman* Danyluk here. Being a Colonel would be nice, and it's probably in my future, but please carry on about the party."

"Christ ... is anyone else around there?"

Moose was now getting flustered. "Outside or inside? There are two thousand outside, and nobody inside. Do youse wish to leave a message?"

"Yes, have the General picked up and make certain rooms are booked. If Brigadier Ben Danbough and RSM Gun Gattling attend, it will be a party of eight, including the MP. They'll require rooms as well. Make them good ones, and have food and beverages laid on for both parties. Goodbye." The voice trailed off. "Jesus, what kind of a camp...?" (click)

Another red light. "Vernon Army Cadet Trades Training Camp; Signalman Danyluk at your service."

"This is Lieutenant-Colonel Stan Dansayess. I'll be joining Brigadier Ben Danbough, which *enlarges* the party by two, because Mrs. Danbough will also be joining the Brigadier. Have you got the picture?" (click)

Moose sat back in his chair staring at the notes he'd made. For the *millionth* time in his life, he didn't have a clue what was happening. Not only that, calls kept coming in hot and heavy. When he finally figured he had it all worked out, he used a dictionary and typed the following message:

Incoming message date: 21 July 1954 - Time: 1230

For: Commanding Officer - VACTTC

Info: RSM Gardiner

Subject: Visiting Dignitaries

A number of telephone calls were received and information passed is as follows:

Start 1. General Dangatt and his wife visiting camp Saturday at 0800. To be picked up at bus station. He wishes a good party to be laid on for eight people with plenty of food and beverages, including wine, and he wants books in his room.

2. A senior military policeman will be accompanying the general.

3. Major Boe is arriving Thursday by plane. Time of arrival is 1300. His wife is joining him along with RSM Benbough and his wife, who is *enlarged*. (probably

means pregnant.) Lay on books, beverages and plenty of food. They also want to have a party.

4. Brigadier Yuessdance and his wife have will arrive by train on Friday at 1800. He wants a huge party for eight with books, beverages, food and pictures.

5. RSM Stanrifle is joining Brigadier Yuessdance. The RSM may bring his wife. He wants RSM Gardiner and his wife to meet him upon arrival at the station. Both RSMs and wives will join party.

End.

Danyluk placed the message in the out-box.

When Rothstein learned the *tricks of the trade* and relieved Moose, there hadn't been a call in over an hour, and Moose sat with his feet up reading a Canadian Army Journal.

"Signalman Rothstein, there will be busy times, and times when youse can catch up on some sleep."

Both boys laughed when Danyluk said, "The job ain't bad, but the pay's the shits. Have fun, Rothie."

Rothstein sat down, put on the headset, and said, "Thanks Signalman Danyluk."

"You're most welcome. Oh, yeah, there's coffee at the end of the hall. Also, don't forget that Gardiner's office is next to ours. I left our door shut so he wouldn't see me."

When Harvey took over, a few other *matters* went wrong.

"Vernon Army Cadet Trades Training Camp; Signalman Rothstein at your service."

A pleasant female voice came forth. It was the camp doctor's wife. Doctor Dan Deebelly and his wife had just been married prior to the young physician coming to camp.

"Camp hospital, please. Doctor Dan Deebelly."

"One moment, please," said Rothstein.

When Rothstein made the connection, he didn't check to hear the conversation. By mistake, he'd forwarded the call to the kitchen. A still-tired East had his feet up and was eating a banana. "Ya, go ahead."

"Hello darling ... are you busy?"

Always being the gentleman East thought his girlfriend was calling and acted accordingly. "Nah, what are you up to?"

"Sugarplum, I'm hot for you. I'm showered, powdered, and lying in the nude waiting for you. We'll have a naked candlelight supper. I want your body next to mine, our hearts beating together, our tongues intertwined. What time are you off shift today?"

East didn't feel his feet hit the floor. He also didn't realize he'd chomped on another banana, with the peel still on.

"Er, wow, Jesus, you're gettin' a little forward ain'tcha?"

"Babykins, I thought you liked me like talking like this."

"Er, yeah I do. Well babe, I'm on duty until 2359 and..."

Her tone changed. "Just a minute, who is this?"

Cordell Cross

"It's me, Hamburger Jack; the only man in your life. Who do you think it is? Hello ... hello ... hello baby? Are you still there?"

Meanwhile, back at the switchboard, the light and buzzer sounded again.

"Vernon Army Cadet Camp; Signalman Rothstein at your service."

"Listen, *Signalman Rothstein*, this is Mrs. Doctor Dan Deebelly. When I ask to be put through the hospital, I mean the hospital. Now, put me through, now!"

At the hospital, Wane's conversation with an inexperienced teenage nurse probably changed the course of a new marriage. Just Wane and the nurse were on duty because everyone else was at supper.

"You're nineteen and already a nurse?" Wane asked.

"No, I'm really a nurse's aide. I'm still a private soldier and I won't be a nurse until I'm twenty-one - then I'll be a lieutenant. What are you planning to do when you graduate?"

Wane stuck his chest out. "Who, me? Well, I ... er, I'm, er, planning to become a surgeon. Yeah, that's what I'm going to do. How do you like them apples?"

"A surgeon? Oh how wonderful. Let me see your hands. My they're soft. Yes, you do have the hands of a surgeon. But have you got the manners?"

A quizzed took over Banks' face. "Manners?"

"Yes, doctors have to have that sophisticated and nonchalant manner about them. Even when Doctor Deebelly is on the phone, he's cultured and dashing."

Although there was a significant age difference, Wane anticipated a new pair of panties coming his way.

"Hell, I can do that. That's easy. Why..."

The telephone rang.

"Listen to this," Wane said, placing a stethoscope around his neck while picking up the phone. Instantly, his voice became that of a *sophisticated medical practitioner*. With the nurse's aide snickering in the background, Banks answered, "Camp hospital - doctor speaking; please make it short, I'm very busy this afternoon."

"Darling, I just spoke to someone called Hamburger Jack? I thought it was you. God, I feel embarrassed. Do you realize I told him I was hot, nude, and waiting for him. His voice sounded like yours. Oh, how humiliating."

Like East, Wane was momentarily *mixed up*. He thought Jack was on the switchboard and as far as he was concerned, Debbie was on the other end of the line. He winked at the youthful nurse's aide who was leaning over the desk giggling while she listened to him.

"Oh hi, sweetheart. There's no need to feel embarrassed. If it's not hamburgers, it's hot-dogs - he's harmless. Are you wearing any new panties?"

"I'm not wearing *any* panties. When do you get off shift? I've been yearning for you all day. God, I'm hot for you."

Wane couldn't believe his good fortune. "Well, I'm hot for you, too, my beloved, but OJT is tough and..."

"Please, sweetheart, you know I'm not yet familiar with your medicinal terminology. What medical term is OJT?"

Wane's chest stuck out a little more. "What, OJT? Er, it means, er, Obstetrics, Jaundice and Tonsillectomies. I'm in the camp hospital, ya know?"

Cordell Cross

A giggle came through the earpiece. "Oh, as if I didn't know that? Seriously, darling, when do you get off, I want your thumping body on mine."

"Huh, you do?" Wane cleared his high-pitched throat. "You do? Jesus, that's a switch ... you're normally nervous when I take your panties and..."

"Well, I'm over my trepidation now. Dearest, we've been married three whole weeks. Can you take some time off and come and give it to me. Baby wants a little sweetener in her tea."

"Huh? Married? Debbie, I never knew you felt like this? Why didn't you tell...?"

Once again, the young *bride's* voice changed. "Debbie? Who the hell is Debbie?"

Wane now knew he had problems. "Er, if you're not Debbie, just who are you? I'm available and..."

"Who am I? I'm your wife you louse! Just wait till you get back to the motel. Where's my mother's num...?" (click)

Activity over the wires was alive and well during supper break, and even afterwards for that matter. When four calls came in at once, Rothstein inadvertently pulled two jacks by mistake. Realizing his mistake, he tried to correct his error and made matters worse by re-plugging them into the wrong ports. One conversation went like this:

"Provost unit, Sergeant Gabriel here."

"Sergeant Gabriel, this is Mr. Hadley at base supply. Are you familiar with the shortage procedure if a few protractors have gone missing?"

"Yes, I am. It happens when we've got 1400 cadets at camp. You simply need to complete ... I think it's form 2923, in quadruplicate and send it through the normal channels. Let me see if I can find some copies. Hold on a sec, okay?"

"Okay, Sergeant."

Here's where Rothstein made his error. He interrupted a conversation between the Technical-Adjutant at transport who was ordering spark plugs from a local auto firm. The Tech-Adj ended up with Sergeant Gabriel. As well, the fellow from the local auto firm ended up with Mr. Hadley.

"I'm back."

"I didn't know you were gone."

"How many are we talking about?" asked Gabriel.

"About 1200. It's a long summer and..."

The Sergeant sat erect in his chair, quickly butting his cigar. "Did you say twelve-hundred?"

"Give or take a few. I don't know how many come in a box."

"What do you mean you don't know how many come in a box? It's your *effing* job to know how many come in a box!"

The Tech-Adj couldn't believe his ears. Here he is trying to give a local firm some business and all hell breaks loose.

"Jesus, have you had a rough day or what? It's not my *effing* job to know; it's your *effing* job. Anyway, let's make it an even 1300."

"Thirteen-hundred? Do you want the commanding officer on your ass? What's the matter with you idiots?"

"Who do you think you're yelling at. The CO has nothing to do with this. Clean up your act or we'll forget the whole thing."

"Like hell we'll forget the whole thing! You'll be charged!"

"Not by you I won't. I'm taking my business elsewhere."

"Listen, you sham artist ... the only place you're going to is the glass house!" (click)

The other conversation was much more congenial.

(Click) "You need not worry, it is 2923. We're totally out of them." Mr. Hadley said. "I'll get some from..."

"How soon do you need them?" asked the auto clerk.

"As soon as possible. I like to keep up on things."

"I should say you do. Let's see now. Two thousand, nine hundred, and twenty three, times ... Yes, we've got them in the warehouse."

Mr. Hadley just couldn't be more appreciative." The warehouse? Don't go to any trouble. I'll send a driver down to pick them up."

The clerk smiled. "Not at all ... not at all. When two thousand, nine hundred, and twenty is the figure, we deliver, promptly. Give me fifteen minutes, all right?"

"Such service! Are you certain it's no bother?"

"A bother? You must be joking? By the way, who do we bill?"

Hadley thought the last question was a doozer. Laughing, he said, "Mr. Hadley at base supply. The CO's good for it. I'll also buy you a drink. This is just wonderful. I've heard that you can be such a mean son of a bitch. That must be pure bunk. Thank you very much."

"The drink is not necessary, and you're most welcome. Those rumours were probably started by our competition."

"Competition? Er, the RCMP, eh?"

"What? Yeah, them too. Thanks again." (Click)

Yes, it was a busy day for certain cadets of signals. A day that wouldn't be forgotten by many at Camp Vernon.

At midnight, not too many of the boys in B-25 were asleep. They had really enjoyed this day because it was different from the norm.

It was East who started off the conversation. "Some dame phoned me today and wanted my body. It was probably one of the kitchen girls putting me on. Jesus, she sounded nice. I got a boner just listening to her voice."

Moose laughed. "Youse has never had a true boner in your life."

"Up yours, Moose. At least mine don't last twenty-four hours."

"Yeah I know. More like twenty-four seconds."

"It's gotta be the weather," said Wane. "The doctor's wife phoned and started coming on to me. It's a wonder the guy can walk. If his dame had her way, he'd be screwing her twenty-four hours a day. It's a funny thing about these doctor's wives, they don't mind getting their feelings off their chest. Mrs. Deebelly said she was showered, powdered, nude, and waitin' for me to hump her."

Douglas sat up. "She said that?"

"Dougie, she wanted me to sweeten her tea at the same time. Whatever that means."

"Brice lay back again. " Wow that never happened on my shift. Come to think of it, the doc does look a little pale."

"Pale? I should say so. It's a wonder the guy's wang is still attached to his body. Anythin' exiting happen to you, Bergie?"

"No, but Earl tells me the Tech Adj fumed after he tried to give some guy an order for spark plugs. The guy told him to *eff* off, so he's writing a letter to get him fired."

Lyons finished putting on his nightshirt and cap. "If you think he was mad, you should have heard the Provost Sergeant talking to old Mr. Hadley who works at the supply stores. Apparently, the elderly geezer's been stealing protractors and selling them on the side. When the Sergeant went to arrest him, Hadley was in the middle of an altercation with a local mechanic who had just delivered 2400 spark plugs and said he wouldn't take them back. Gabriel has charged Hadley with selling spark plugs on the black market as well. All hell broke loose. Apparently when Hadley was being taken away, his last words were: 'They were right, Gabriel, you are a rotten son of a bitch.'"

Cunningham, who had been silent throughout, said, "A lot of things happen in this place that we don't know about. I mean ... it's not as organized as we thought. There's problems happening everywhere."

Rothstein jumped out of bed and stood in the aisle.

"Organized? Let me tell you it's not organized. Especially the headquarters building. The commanding officer and adjutant stormed into Gardiner's office today complaining about some party he was throwing for a visiting RSM and his pregnant wife. Gardiner took it for a while before saying, 'Well, why the hell shouldn't I? It appears everyone else in this joint is throwin a party; what's wrong with me attending one? According to this memo there's three parties going on this coming weekend, and I've been invited.'"

"You mean there's mix-ups even at the headquarters building?" McLeod asked.

Rothstein crawled back into bed. "Mix-ups? Ten people have been tasked to find out who these people are coming from Ottawa. The CO's never heard of them. He's pissed off because they all want him to throw to party. He stood in the hallway screaming, 'Who the hell is General Dangatt and who's going to pay for the food, liquor, wine and movies? Not me, I'll tell you. Do you hear me, Mr. Gardiner? Also, I'm against expectant women visiting the camp during training hours.'"

If Danyluk had not been asleep, he may have recognized some of the particulars and joined in the conversation. Unfortunately, the *cause* of the problem kept snoring.

Discussions continued on both sides of B-25 for at least an hour. It would appear the actions of numerous cadets that day changed the way of life for many more NCOs, officers and civilian employees. Many, many more.

At 0100 hours as snores wafted out through the windows of B-25, the smile on the round yellow old man above appeared to widen. Although he'd seen it all before, the enthusiasm of this year's youngsters undergoing training had nearly made him change his orbit.

Cordell Cross

Chapter 15

Because signals cadets attended On Job Training courses on Thursday and Friday, PT was cancelled which gave the cadets more time to prepare their kit and to get B-25 in shape.

When the Corporals came out of their cubicles at 0630 each of the two mornings, the occupants of the hut thought it was the middle of the day. The extra one-hour's sleep had changed their outlook completely.

"Rise and shine; it's Thursday and the camp will stop running if you people aren't up to par this morning. Let go of your prongs and put on your thongs! You, Danyluk, get some decent music on that radio!"

A naked Moose was once again dancing with his skinny silver-haired girlfriend (mop) with *her hair* spread all over his shoulders. Needless to say, *her leg* rubbed his crotch.

As Bergie straightened their towels, he said, "Don't dance too close to her Moose. Remember the time you got your wang full of slivers?"

Danyluk paid no attention to his friend. "Excuse me, my sweet, but I must take my leave and attend to our entertainment. Besides, I believe your deodorant is starting to fade. What's the matter, Corporal? Don't youse likes Back-Hills Willie singin' *I hope your horse throws you into my heart?*"

The Corporal had returned to his cubicle but his voice boomed over the top. "I said, get rid of that country shit, Danyluk!"

Moose changed stations and shortly, *Sh-Boom*, with the Crew Cuts entertained the occupants of 21 Platoon, and when   *Sh-Boom* finished, the announcer ruined Moose's day.

"It's six-forty on a glorious Okanagan morning and would you believe we've got a lady from Vernon on the line. Go ahead, Doris."

A feeble voice replied, *"Is that me? Am I on the air, Ogopogo Ole?"*

"Yes, Doris, this is Ole, and you're on the Ogopogo Ole Show. Go ahead, dear."

"Have you heard of bumble berry pastry, Ogopogo Ole?"

"No, I can't say I have. What is it, Doris? Has it got something to do with the bees and the birds, my dear?"

"Ha ha, oh Ole you devil; if I wasn't married to Eggbert I'd be in Kelowna as fast as you could say 'liftupmydress.'"

"And I'd wait for you, precious. Now, tell us ... just what is, bumble berry pastry?"

"Well, first of all, you take two cups of flour..."

"Two cups?"

"Yes, that's what I said ... two cups. Then you slowly mix in butter, sugar, water and..."

"Don't tell me, Doris. You then mix in bumble berries. Am I correct?"

"Why, yes. Ogopogo Ole, you are one smart young man. If I wasn't married I'd be there as fast as you could say, 'upwithyourpetticoat.'"

"Can youse believes this crap? One of the local pie broads is off the pies and on with the pastry. She's even tryin' to get it on with Ogopogo Ole? Does this crap never end?"

Cordell Cross

"Anyway, you mix in a little baking soda ... just a wee bit mind you, and then you put it in the oven for forty minutes. It is so sweet when you taste it, you won't want to..."

"Is it as sweet as you, Doris?"

"Tee hee hee. Oh Ole, you are such a brash young thing. If Eggbert ever stops being jealous, I'll be there as fast as you could say..."

"Stickitinandmixit," Danyluk screamed. "Don't these old dames ever quit? Where's that Vernon station again. Ah, here we are."

"... that's right Okanagan Arnold, but make certain you use only mountain berries. You see, it's them there berries that make the pie what it is. We, that's my sister and I. We grow our own berries. My husband Norbert, God rest his soul, left this world two years ago. He..."

"He ate too many of your son-of-a-bitchin' pies. That's what he did! Youse killed him off without knowin' it - ya pie murderer. The poor pongo probably got your goddamned pies for breakfast, lunch, and supper. I can't take this anymore ... who's goin' over for breakfast?"

Bergie was ready. "I am, but aren't you going to call Ogopogo Ole and Okanagan Arnold first?"

A sneaky smile began broadening across Moose's face.

"Bergie, are youse suggestin' I should call Ogopogo Ole? I think it's long distance."

"Just reverse the charges."

After Danyluk left the building, Bergie tuned the radio back to Kelowna and cadets from 21 Platoon gathered around.

It didn't take long to hear Moose's voice.

"It's six-fifty five on the Ogopogo Ole Show. Here's another call from Vernon. Hey, isn't anyone listening here in Kelowna? Go ahead, Eggbert. Eggbert? Where have I heard that name before?"

"Youse heard it from my wife Doris. I had our portable radio out in the outhouse. How are youse, Ogopongo Ole?"

"That's Ogopogo, Eggbert. Er, fine, you're one lucky man, Eggbert. I'll bet you just love Doris's bumble berry pastry?"

"Er, youse is right, Ole. Say, are we on the radio now?"

"You bet you are, Eggbert. Carry on."

"Well, Ole, the last man who flirted with my wife got carried to the hospital as fast as I could say 'pumpedyafullofholesdidn'tI'? Didn't even finish his pastry."

"Huh? Gee, Eggbert, er, did he like your wife's bumble berry pastry?"

"He had a hankerin' for a little more than the baked goods. While he was a eatin' the pastry I said, 'Clean it up fast, Clem. As a matter of fact, gobble it up before I can say, I'magonnashootyerwangoff.'"

"What...?"

"Youse heard me, Ole. He ain't had any since, and I ain't talkin' about pastry. Doubt if he ever will. Ya see, Ogopongo, he didn't move fast enough. I got him before he could say, 'Sheeitisthatyergun?' Ya see, I'm the possessive type, Ole, an' I think I'm a gonna visit ya there at that there radio station. How's that grab ya? Been married forty-two years to Doris, an' she ain't sharin' her pastry or anythin' else anymore. It ain't healthy ... youse knows what I means?"

Cordell Cross

"Ah, (ahem) er, you know, er, Eggbert. I, er, don't like pastry anyway. Never did like it. Er, Thanks for calling. (Click) Here's the news to seven-o'clock."

When 21 Platoon went over for breakfast, Moose's back was sore from all the patting. In addition, for some *unknown* reason, Kelowna radio only played records for the balance of the morning.

During the day from 0800 till 2359, signals cadets were everywhere. Besides being up the poles, they operated in transport, the hospital, the kitchens, provost shack, headquarters building, supply stores, classrooms and company offices. They even linked up remote Nineteen-set units from the training office to Glenemma - the field training area approximately forty miles away. In addition, Nineteen-sets and Thirty-Nine sets were set up in some D&M jeeps, which allowed inter-vehicle, as well as camp/convoy intercommunication.

Camp Vernon's communication system never worked better, and not too many of Day One's mistakes were repeated ... except at the headquarters building. The cadet attending the switchboard found the apparatus to be a little more complicated than the UCL Ten-line switchboards he was used to.

"Vernon Army Cadet Trades Training Camp; Signalman Danyluk at your service."

"This is Brigadier Joe Kaulways. I'm completing my progress report reference camp training, and..."

"One moment, sir. I'll put youse through to the training officer."

"Thank you."

"Youse is welcome."

"What?"

"Youse is welcome."

Instead of putting the other end of the cord into the training office slot, the jack ended up in the kitchen's orifice. As usual, Signalman Cunningham was showing the cooks how to play cards for big money. The problem for the cooks' was Gordie's advice.

"You'll have to lose a *bit* to learn. But don't worry, I'll give you the chance to win it back as soon as I answer this phone call. "Signalman Cunningham, Good morning."

"What the hell did you say."

"Er, Signalman Cunningham, Good morning, sir."

"Ah, that's much better. This is Brigadier Kaulways. Is the supervising officer there?"

"No."

"Er, oh. Where is he?"

"Don't know."

"Surely his assistant is there?"

Gordie knew the head kitchen lady very well. She kept providing him with new gambling suckers.

"Certainly, just a minute." (Click - call put on hold.) "Er, Gert, er, some officer wants ya."

"An officer wants me? I wonder why?" (Click) "Good morning to you."

Cordell Cross

"Good morning. It's Brigadier Joe Kaulways here. I'm completing my report and need the chronicled framework of your systemized individual organizational programming."

Although Gert was usually on the ball, she was a little hard of hearing and didn't have a clue what the man was talking about.

"Huh? What was that? We must have a bad connection. You want sizzled pork chops with your...?"

"No, no, no. I require the unencumbered multiphase imputation of your implied methodology as it refers to yield. How's is working?"

Now Gert got it. He was talking about fried cucumbers in the field.

"Good, but not today. We're getting prepared for lunch right now. It's beef stew and..."

"Er, that's nice, but, er, work before pleasure. Let's forget about lunch. I'm more concerned about the incrementalized technological feasibility implementation. Is it labour intensive, and if so, what are the numbers?"

Gert turned up her hearing aid. The word 'feasibility' sounded like feedability.

"It works fine. We're putting through about eight hundred a day. It's tough but we carry on the best we can. Need more staff though."

"More staff? I increased your numbers by eight."

"Ain't seen 'em. We need 'em on the early shifts."

"Well I'll certainly talk to the CO about that. Where the hell is he utilizing the extra personnel?"

"Dunno, probably in the officers' mess."

"That's outrageous, against all regulations, and totally unacceptable. I'm going to pass that along to Major-General Phil Myplate-Phurst. Thank you for informing me. Now, have you adopted the relevant analytical infrastructure of SP guidelines that we finalized and forwarded?"

While the Brigadier was referring to Signals Personnel, Gert thought he was talking about saltpetre

"Oh yes, and we've lowered the amount substantially. Your figures were way out of line."

"Like hell they were! You can't do that! Who told you to do that - we're short as it is?"

"It came directly from the commanding officer. I don't think it affects the officers' and sergeants' messes though."

"I'll bloody bet it doesn't. It sounds to me like everyone is working in those messes. What about the GCS upgrades?"

"To Gert, GCS didn't mean General Commission Standards, it meant Grilled Cheese Sandwiches. Margarine had recently been substituted for butter. "It's marg now. And, they don't like 'em."

"What only marginal? Damn, why is it not working there? They're applicable every place else, and working fine! What the hell do you mean, they don't like them?"

"Dunno. Probably the same reason why the BLTs ain't movin'.

Cordell Cross

"What? The BLTs aren't moving. What are they doing? (Battalion Lieutenants in Training - not bacon, lettuce and tomato sandwiches.)

"Well, we prepare them as you know, but they just sit around. Everyone ignores them. Well, not everyone, because one did disappear yesterday."

"Disappeared? What the hell happened?"

"East had it."

"Where? East? He went east? That's AWOL."

To Gert, AWOL meant, a white with onion and lettuce, no cheese, hold the mustard - not absent without leave.

"We've got lots of those too."

"Lots of AWOLs? What the bloody hell is happening at that camp? Doesn't the CO do anything? Headquarters hasn't heard all this is happening!"

Gert got tired of standing and sat down. "Since the change, the CO (cheese and onion) is just as bad as all the rest."

"Yes, I'll bet you're right! I'll be there on Monday with Major-General Myplate-Phurst! Don't worry, we'll sort matters out!"

"It should be a nice trip. You'll like it here in the Okanagan, and..."

"One last question. Any problem with the MPs?"

Obviously, the Brigadier had heard of the *dilemma* between Hadley and Gabriel.

"No, none whatsoever, Gert replied, thinking MPs meant mashed potatoes. But we've cut back on those as well. We send the overflow to the officers' and sergeants' messes."

"I should have guessed! More personnel graft, eh? See you Monday. Goodbye." (click)

"Yes, far too much Kraft. Perhaps a local cheese would be more suitable ... Er, goodbye."

Gert turned to Gordie. "He hung up on me before I was finished. Nice fella but he sure likes usin' short-forms for words."

"Officers always do that, Gert. Got any more money left?"

"A bit, but when I play you, my luck seems to run out."

While Gert was talking with the Brigadier, other problems were happening elsewhere.

"Switchboard."

"This is the Quartermaster, Major Will Hovel - get me Major Lyon Seighnothing."

Danyluk checked his list. "He's in training, one moment please. If he's not in his office, I'll try and find him."

"Fine."

Instead of training, Danyluk erred again and put the call through to the sergeants' mess bar, where the bar steward was busy for a moment.

"Sergeants' Mess bar, one moment please," the bar steward said before finishing his task. "Good morning."

Hovel assumed Seighnothing was on the line. "Good morning. Will Hovel here ... what are you doing over there?"

"I just came in to clear up some things. Why?"

"You're not sneaking a drink, are you?"

"Me? Never!"

"Listen, I've been reviewing the records and we seem to be going through a hell of an amount of water purification tablets. They're only to be used in the bottles (water canteen bottles in the field) or jugs of water.

The steward winced. Hired for his brawn, not brains, he understood the importance of proper hygiene. "You've got me there. Are you telling me we're supposed to be putting them in all bottles?"

"Come on, man, where else can you use them? Well, if you're not putting them in the bottles, where the hell are they disappearing to?"

"I've got no idea. Never seen one, but I can assure you we'll start using them."

"You've never seen one? We sent two cartons to you yesterday."

The steward looked around his bar. "You did?"

"Yes we did. You've been ordering two cartons a week. At this rate, we're going to run out. Are you saying someone's stealing them?"

"Must be. We've never put one in a bottle."

"My God, man, are you saying people are drinking without the protection of a capsule?"

"Er, yeah, must be. Pretty bad, eh?"

"Bad? It's a wonder no one's come down with dysentery or other stomach ailments. Listen, you start using them. I'll tell the clerk you're going to come over and pick up a box. In the meantime, I'm going to find out who's been stealing them. Okay?"

"Yeah, please let us know. Should I pass along this information to the messing sergeant?"

"Why?"

"Well shouldn't he know? Right now he's out in the field, and I think..."

"Jesus, he's in the field without...? I'll tell him and the messing officer ... I'm going to Glenemma today. Just make certain one tablet goes in every bottle. I said, every bottle, got it?"

Okay, I've got it!"

While speaking, the steward wrote a note to himself.

"Every bottle it is."

"Good. Say hello to the little lady for me." (click)

"What little lady? Hello? Shit, he's hung up. He must have meant Kathleen, who's on the bar at night. I'll tell her about the tablets when she reports for duty."

After the call, all the sergeants' mess bar stewards started using water purification tablets in every bottle ... even beer. Needless to say, at lunch, and thereafter, Korean veterans and other *men of the world* couldn't understand why there was a sudden change in taste of their daily supply of liquid *nutrients*. Especially RSM Gardiner. He held his glass up, peering into it.

"What the bloody hell have you done to this scotch?"

"It's the same scotch you always drink, Sergeant Major."

"It is? Tastes like leopard piss. Must be my mouth."

"Must be, Sergeant Major; I've never tasted leopard piss. We don't serve it."

Cordell Cross

"Don't get smart. Gimmee a beer instead."

The steward served him a beer.

"Jesus Christ; what did I have for breakfast this morning? My taste buds have all quit at once! Everything tastes like leopard piss! Oh well."

Meanwhile later at the switchboard, Moose's partner, Cadet Rothstein, unfortunately made the same mistake.

"Switchboard, I'm Signalman Rothstein."

"Yes switchboard, this is Major Bea Cute, the head nurse. Put me through to the adjutant, please."

"One moment, please."

Like most medical personnel, head nurses really aren't concerned who answers a phone. To them, it's simple - they've asked for the person they want, therefore they'll be connected to the correct party. Major Cute had just finished conversing with the medical officer about the importance of cadets using foot powder. With the weather hot, the boys would benefit from using lots of it.

In the kitchens, however, a notice from the adjutant was being circulated about the shortage of salt tablets. If salt tablets were in short supply, then all kitchens would use extra salt in the food. The kitchens were advised that the MO would call and inform them of the proper *dosage*.

Needless to say, Major Bea Cute wasn't put through to the adjutant. She ended up with the head messing sergeant who just returned from the field. "Good afternoon."

"Good afternoon. This is Major Bea Cute, the head nurse. I've discussed the matter with the medical officer and we're of the same mind. Each cadet should have at least a quarter of a container per day."

The Sergeant's face took on the look of pure shock. "A quarter of a container for each cadet? That's far too much?"

Nurse Cute definitely did not like this *man's* attitude.

"Where did you earn your medical degree? The weather is extremely hot and these lads need the protection. They sweat, you know?" (While she was referring to feet, he was referring to bodies.)

"Major, they might sweat, but in my opinion you're overdoing it. Are you certain the MO told you this?"

Medical staff literally hate interference. "The health of the cadets is *our* primary concern ... not yours. Need I say more? It is *our* opinion that each cadet should get a whole container, but we understand the cost. I don't wish to discuss the matter further. Each cadet will receive a quarter of a container. Is that clear?"

"Yes, ma'am, perfectly clear, but where the hell am I supposed to get that much?"

"That's your problem, not mine and watch your language. We've got some here, but I suggest you get it from base supply. Use it! (click)

Sergeants don't just issue orders without approval. Remember, they are Gods, therefore Sergeant D. Pockets covered his God-like *rectum* and telephoned the adjutant. After all, it was the adjutant who informed everyone that the medical officer would make the decision.

Cordell Cross

"Switchboard."

"Adjutant, please."

(Very busy voice) "Adjutant here."

"Er, yes, sir, it's Sergeant Pockets. Reference your memo regarding the salt tablets, I've just heard from Major Bea Cute and I think she's prescribed too much salt for the meals. I..."

"Sergeant Pockets, I'm a busy man. They're the health specialists - do what you're ordered to do."

"Would you issue me a memo authorizing their decision, sir?"

"Most certainly, I'll send it over now." (click)

After the Sergeant hung up, he shook his head while writing a memo to all kitchens.

From: Sergeant D. Pockets

To: All kitchen personnel

Info: Base Foods Officer

Amount of salt used in food preparation.

Due to a shortage of concentrated salt tablets, the adjutant, as authorized by the medical officer, has declared that each individual will receive at least a quarter of a carton of salt per day. Effective tomorrow, please prepare your meals accordingly. This includes all messes.

That evening while certain cadets of Signals Company *protected the world* by being on duty, people sitting back and watching the *action* in the sergeants' mess would have *wet* themselves.

Sergeant Beckford entered the mess, picked up the liar's dice, rolled a few hands with Sergeant Simpson and lost.

"Okay, Simp, what'll it be?"

Simpson perused the liquor on the shelves. He also analysed lovely Kathleen.

"Kathleen, my sweet, what do you recommend? How about something exquisite? Beck's paying for a change. No, I'll be fair with you, Bill. Make it two Lemon Heart and coke."

While Kathleen served them, Beckford put the Liar's dice away. "You're a fair, fair man, Simp. Cheers buddy. Through the lips and over the gums, look out stomach, here it comes."

Both non-coms touched their glasses and drank before proceeding to spurt it out. Beckford had the manners to turn the other way, but Simpson sprayed it all over Beckford.

"What the hell are you trying to do, kill us?" Simpson yelled at Kathleen who had picked up a bar cloth and handed it to Beckford.

"Jesus Christ, woman, I asked for Lemon Heart Rum and Coke, not camel piss and rosewater."

Kathleen's feelings got hurt quickly. "Don't yell at *me*. What's the matter with you sergeants tonight? Everyone's yelling at me, even the RSM."

Beckford straightened up. "Oh, the RSM's here? Where is he?"

"He's in the men's room looking at his tongue. For some reason, every drink tastes the same to him. He's tried rum, rye, bourbon, scotch and beer. Even when I gave him a glass of ice-water he nearly threw up."

She'd no sooner spoken when the RSM came out, licking his lips and putting away his handkerchief. "Ah, Beckford, Simpson. How are you boys tonight?"

Simpson did the talking. "Good, sir, how are you?"

"Not worth a damn. I think I must be running a temperature, or my flavour glands have gone. I had a late supper and the whole goddamned thing tasted like salt. Now when I'm really thirsty, I come into the mess and my beer and everything else tastes like leopard piss. I think I'll go on sick parade tomorrow morning. It's horrible when one can't luxuriate in the rapture of a delicate cold beer. Still, I have the feeling that I've experienced this situation once before. I just can't remember when."

"We may be coming down with the same thing," said Beckford. The rum and cokes we just tasted are bloody horrible. Tasted like bog-water."

"Bog-water?" Gardiner yelled, placing an arm around Beckford's shoulders. "That's it, Becky … you've put your finger on the problem. As the world's most professional beer *savourer*, I now know what the problem is. Young lady, are you putting water purification tablets in the beer?"

Kathleen's face turned red. "Is that what they are?"

"Yes that's what they are! They've been put in the booze as well. Who ordered you to do that?"

"The head bar steward, sir."

Gardiner went and picked up the telephone. After a few minutes of ranting, and raving, he regained his composure and rejoined Beckford and Simpson.

"Would you believe it was Major Will Hovel who ordered the head steward to doctor up our booze? That son of a bitch has been trying to become an honorary member of this mess for years. The fact that he's continuously been turned down has gotten to him. Just wait until the CO hears about this. Kathleen, my lass, get some fresh bottles out. Gentlemen, and I use the term loosely - the next round is on me. Belly up to the bar, my lads."

No one really knows why commanding officers changed following the upcoming weekend. It may have had something to do with the steady stream of personnel entering his office, and Gardiner's final words following the meetings.

"Sir, with all due respect - all your officers are *effing* screw-ups!"

All the conferences started quite amiably, but excuses and denials came from all sides. The commanding officer's waiting area was packed, and perhaps the following minutes of a portion of the confidential meetings might be of help.

1. CO: "Now, Mr. Hadley, you state you never discussed the deficiency of 1300 protractors with Sergeant Gabriel, nor did you order 2,923 spark plugs. Is that correct?"

2. Hadley: "Bloody true it's right! I think the sergeant drinks on the job! He's a closet drinker, sir!"

3. Gabriel: "I caught you with those spark plugs, Hadley."

4. Hadley: "You also ordered them you son of a bitch! You're not going to make staff-sergeant at my expense!"

5. CO: "Gentlemen, please act a little more civilized. Speak up Mr. Largeanempty? (garage man)

6. Largeanempty: "Hadley phoned us and ordered nearly 2400 spark plugs. He said to bill him ...that you, the CO, would make it good!"

7. "CO: "What? That I was good for it?"

8. Hadley:"Like hell I did! Sir, I wouldn't..."

9. Largeanempty: "Yes you did! We gave you our last *effing* spark plug, you con artist."

10. Gabriel: "And what did you do with the 1300 protractors, Hadley you thief?"

DETERMINATION. The *meeting* dragged on for hours. No decision was made, and the matter was brushed under the carpet. On to the next meeting.

1. CO: Now, Doctor Deebelly, why, for Heaven's sake are you putting in for a transfer? We're only halfway through camp."

2. Deebelly: "My wife has left me, and I've got to go and fix things up. She's accusing me of committing adultery with a woman by the name of Debbie. She wants a divorce."

3. CO: "You mean you're married to two women?"

4. Deebelly: "No, just one."

5. CO: "Well, why does Debbie want a divorce?"

6. Deebelly: "No, not Debbie; my wife wants a divorce."

7. CO:" How does the other woman enter the picture? Are you just fooling around with her?"

Cordell Cross

8. Deebelly: "No! Hell no! I've only been married three weeks. The last Debbie I knew was in university and I haven't seen her in..."

9. CO: "So, you call all of your women, Debbie?"

10. Deebelly: "No, I only know one girl by the name of Debbie."

11. CO: "And she followed you here, eh?"

12. Deebelly: "Well, she might have, but I haven't..."

13. CO: "Well, Deebelly, your request is denied. I suggest you start keeping it in your pants. What the hell's the matter with you young pups? Married three weeks and getting it on with other women? A divorce? That's out-bloody-rageous. Get out of my office!"

14. Deebelly: "I'll phone the surgeon general if I have to."

15. CO: "You just do that. I'm phoning him now. Listen, mister, it would be more applicable if you started worrying about your career, not other women. Leave my office at once, you charlatan!"

DETERMINATION. Deebelly should not be promoted. He's a conniver. Probably married to two women at the same time. Check and see if he earned his medical degree properly.

Doctor Deebelly went AWOL. Although the matter was later sorted out, Deebelly never did get promoted. Retiring early, he and his wife got jobs on a Russian fishing vessel operating out of Vladivostok. The Sea of Japan is a long way from Vernon, therefore Deebelly's wife loves it. Sometimes she earns extra money working as a car cleaner on the Trans-Siberian Railroad. Whenever she hears the name, Debbie, she pees herself.

On to the next meeting.

1. CO: "Now, Adjutant, why the hell did you ask for so much salt to be put in the meals? Surely to God, man, you must have more brains than that?"

2. Adjutant: "Sir, I thought ... er ... that is ... I left it up to the medical staff. We're short of salt tablets, and..."

Cordell Cross

3. CO: "Then you recommended it, Major Cute?"

4. Cute: "Sir, I assumed the adjutant knew I was talking about foot powder."

5. CO: "What? But you phoned Sergeant Pockets and he works in the mess halls. You wanted foot powder put in the meals? How the hell did the salt come up?"

6. Cute: "Er, no, sir, I phoned the adjutant, not Sergeant Pockets.

7. Adjutant: "Oh no you didn't. Sergeant pockets doesn't work out of my office."

8. Sergeant Pockets: "Major cute phoned me, sir."

9. Cute: "That's bullshit! I spoke with the adjutant."

10. CO: "Watch your language; this isn't the camp hospital."

Determination. No decision.

This *meeting* also dragged on. It was so hot in Vernon, clear heads and cool minds just didn't prevail. The adjutant and Major Cute were cautioned. Rumour has it that Major Cute works in a Chinese restaurant owned by Sergeant Pockets. The adjutant delivers the restaurant's food. Although they all suspect each other, they've partially patched up their differences. Sergeant Pockets prefers them to call him, sir, which they of course do. Now on the to last meeting.

1. CO: "Now, head steward, why the blazes did you order, Kathleen, and others, put water purification tablets in the water, beer and liquor at the sergeants' mess?"

2. Kathleen: (pointing at head steward.) "He told me to do it."

3. Steward: "Yes, but only after I was ordered to by Major Hovel."

4. Hovel: "Pure unadulterated lies - all of it. Why the hell would I contact him in the first place? I've never spoken with the lad."

5. Steward: "Sir, your nose is going to grow. You were quite emphatic that I utilize the tablets. Perhaps your memory is going ... You telephoned me about the thousands of missing tablets."

6. Hovel: "Why the hell would I phone you about missing tablets? Gardiner's got something to do with this ... I just know it!"

7. RSM: "Don't put the blame on me, sir. I can't help it if you can't become an honorary member."

8. CO: "You're saying there's a ritual when these tablets are used, RSM? He wants to use them, but didn't pass the ceremony?"

9. RSM: "Er, no, sir! As far as he's concerned, if he can't drink in the sergeants' mess, no one else will. Many of my NCOs wish to string him up. It's because of him, we've run out of toilet paper in the sergeants' quarters."

10. Hovel: "That's ridiculous. I have my own mess."

11. RSM: "You can say that again, sir."

12. CO: "So, Hovel, it's you who's been stealing the toilet paper? Are you behind the missing protractors? Did you order the spark plugs? I'm going to charge you with..."

13. Hovel: "I demand redress. This is absolutely ..."

DETERMINATION. Hovel charged.

Rumour has it he now kills chickens for Sergeant Deep Pockets' Chinese restaurant.

That Saturday morning, the second in command of the camp took the parade. The commanding officer was busy Friday, Saturday, Sunday and Monday, sorting out: Women who were or weren't pregnant, parties, liquor, food, wine, pictures, motion pictures, and books. Additionally, names such as Colonel Boe Stanwhine, General Hugh Jass, RSM Gun Gattling, Brigadier Ben Danbough, General Dangatt, General Gun, Major Boe, RSM Benbough, Brigadier Yuessdance, RSM Stanrifle, a senior military policeman, and a Member of Parliament were discussed, along with improper arrivals and departures. Heads did roll ... even his.

Yes indeed, if one actually understood Murphy's Law, one would arrive at the conclusion that Murphy was truly an optimist, indeed.

Cordell Cross

To make matters worse for the Commanding Officer, Brigadier Joe Kaulways arrived on Monday morning with Major-General Phil Myplate-Phurst. The two were most shocked and surprised that the training officer, Major Lyon Seighnothing wasn't prepared for them after what his assistant had told Brigadier Kaulways on the telephone.

"What the bloody hell is going on here, Seighnothing? Your assistant personally told me on the phone that everything had gone wrong with the GCS upgrade, and..."

The Training Officer couldn't believe his ears. Was it possible his assistant was out to get his job? "Get my assistant in here!"

Beautiful Captain Fran Knevver entered. "You wish to see me, sir?"

"Yes, Captain, sit down. This is Brigadier Kaulways and Major-General Myplate-Phurst. Why did you give the Brigadier all that improper information?"

"Sir, I've never spoken with Brigadier Kaulways."

Kaulways stood up. "The hell you haven't! Are you calling me a liar, young lady?"

"Er, no, sir ... but ... I've never talked to you in my life."

"What, you have the nerve to sit there and inform me you never mentioned to me that MPs were working in the officers' mess. That the BLTs were just sitting around and one had gone AWOL. That the GCS upgrades were only marginal and that they weren't liked. That the officers' mess had the extra staff I provided for the incrementalized technological feasibility implementation. Are you telling me your commanding officer is not utilizing the staff supposed to be completing the relevant analytical infrastructure of the SP guidelines? Just what the hell are you telling me? I got all this from you!"

Captain Fran Knevver thought the Brigadier had been out in the sun too long without his helmet.

"Sir, I don't know you and I've never spoken with you. If you're saying *I* told you all that, then I can only offer four words. Bull shit I did, sir!

"I beg your pardon, Madam? Who the hell do you think you're talking to? We were on the phone for twenty minutes! What the hell is happening around here? I drag the general all the way from headquarters and you deny telling me any of this. That's the reason we're here for Christ's sake. You even knew I was bringing him. Now listen, Knevver ... do you even contradict the fact that you told me your CO was horrible."

Knevver calmed down and crossed her legs. "I said no such thing. As a matter of fact, I'm going to *report* this to my commanding officer."

Now Kaulways fumed as he stood up. "Bloody true you will! Get the commanding officer in here now!"

Seighnothing knew about the other *meetings*. "I'm sorry, sir, he's busy with General Hugh Jass, Brigadier Ben Danbough, and Colonel Boe Stanwhine."

Myplate-Phurst's face look puzzled. "What? Hugh, Ben and Boe are here also? Jesus, what's happening? Is the chief of staff here as well?"

That afternoon the training officer and his assistant were ordered to take seventy-two hours sick leave. Questions about the chronicled framework of systemized individual organizational programming, and unencumbered multiphase imputation of applied methodology as it refers to yield, went unanswered.

(Author's note: You're asking why they went unanswered, aren't you? It's quite simple - Gert wasn't there.)

It was quiet in B-25 after midnight on Friday. Most cadets slept except those returning from late shifts. The day had been tough for both shifts and as Jackson slipped his feet down between his sheets, he heard a loud, 'rrrrrrrip!'

"Oh, for cryin' out loud! Who the hell frenched my bed?"

Rothstein burst out laughing. That is until he got between *his* sheets and … 'rrrrrrrip!'

Harvey stood in the aisle yelling, "All right, who's the dirty pongo that did the frenching?"

Shortly it was discovered that all night-shift BCR beds had been frenched. Also, after straightening out his bedding, East's head flopped on two fresh eggs that just happened to be in his pillowcase. Wiping the yoke from his ear, the *beast* fumed.

"I don't need this tonight, or any night for that matter! This is war!"

"I agree," yelled Lyons encountering an iron-burn hole in the front of his nightshirt. The opening just happened to be in the genitalia area.

"Well, it needed airing out anyway," quipped Banks.

"I'll have you know I wash this garment daily," Lyons replied, leaving the shirt on and getting into bed.

Wane quietly laughed. "Who says I'm talkin' about the shirt?"

Within ten minutes, the sounds of crickets, a lonely train whistle, and the odd car on the highway were drowned out by snores. Moose's snores of course, were the loudest.

Chapter 16

Although Signals Company did not have to compete for the pennant, the *shack* had to have the appearance that its occupants were responsible.

After the blowing of reveille, B-25 came alive as cadets took clothes off the window ledges and clotheslines, ironed, shined, showered, shaved, washed, brushed their teeth, combed their hair, dressed, cleaned out their bunk-spaces, aisles, drying room, washing area, shower room, toilets, outside area and steps.

Normally these tasks would have been completed on Mother's Night and the hut would have only required a touch up, but not today, because the boys didn't participate in Mother's Night. They were allowed that night off, and although the hut didn't have to be completely up to snuff, it had to be close to it.

With Danyluk's radio blaring out *Little White Cloud that Cried*, and Lyons receiving a blast from the corporal for letting his *member* hang out of his air-conditioned nightshirt, cadets stepped over each other getting prepared.

"Lyons, I've already told you, I don't want to hear your excuses! Do yourself a favour and quit taking advice from Danyluk!"

Moose didn't like the remark. "I never told him to cut a hole there! You don't see me wearing clothing with my wang hanging out!"

"Danyluk, we usually don't see you wearing clothing of any kind! Turn that music up!"

The BCRs had to hustle a little bit more because members of the band had to report 15 minutes earlier than the rest.

In spite of the fact that there wasn't much time, over breakfast, a closely-knit crew, minus Bergie discussed the frenching of beds, placement of eggs and *windowing* of the nightshirt.

"It had to have been done before 1600," Earl said, showing signs of being really upset. "Any ideas of who the culprits are?"

Blank stares indicated no one had a clue. "I don't think it was the Scots because they've been keeping a low profile," Douglas said. "How about the Irish?"

East shook his head. "Nah, the Irish are becoming good friends. They've been showing their human side lately."

Moose laughed. "Don't get fooled, Jack. We're talkin' about Irish, ya know?"

"I know, I know," East replied. "But seriously, they are more down to earth. I don't think it was them."

A grinning Bergie rushed into the mess hall, grabbed a breakfast, and quickly sat down. "I know who did the dirty work," he whispered, as all heads huddled in the centre of the table.

"I've been talking to a few of the cadets on our side and they told me it's the two blonde cadets at the end. Have you guys seen those two very quiet creeps in 22 Platoon at the other end of the hut? Their bunks are right by the door. They're both blonde and..."

Douglas couldn't believe it. "Bergie, you've got to be wrong. Those two are Royal Canadian Chaplain Corps cadets. They're both going to be missionaries in a few years. Haven't you heard the sermons they've given to Cunningham about the sin of gambling?"

"Oh, those two creeps," said Cunningham. "One of them keeps calling me, 'My son.' I said, 'Get off it - you guys are the same age as me, for God's sake.' Then one of them replied, 'It isn't necessary to use the Lord's name in vain, my son, and age hasn't got anything to do with God's good work. Come and read the bible with us. We read every night in the outdoor chapel from 2000 to 2100 hours.'"

Wane agreed. "Yeah, they wouldn't say *shit* if their lives depended on it. Why do you think it was them?"

Bergie gulped down his food. "Because I was told they were hanging around our area for at least twenty minutes. They made a point at looking at the names on our bunks and writing them down. It's them I tell you - it has to be. No one else was in our section of the hut except our own guys."

"Those bible thumpers," yelled Danyluk, before lowering his voice. "I suppose the bible allows anyone who's that close to the Lord to french beds, and distribute eggs. What do we do, Bergie, old buddy?"

East tried to get up for thirds, but was held back by Douglas and Wane.

"Yeah, I'm still gettin' yellow yoke out of my right ear." He then pushed his *restraints* away. "Listen you pongoes, I'm only going back for more coffee. They let him go and he came back with more pancakes.

"Guys, I couldn't say no. They're so damned good; I may even go back for more."

Bergie leaned forward again. "Well, I think it's them and I've got a small idea which will teach them a lesson the Lord doesn't offer. It will call for co-operation by those that got their beds frenched.

"And who got yoke in the ear, eh Bergie?"

"Yeah, Jack. Yoke in the ear as well."

Moose's nose nearly hit his Bergie's. Wringing his hands, he said, "When do we do it?"

Grins covered all the faces at the table, even East's, and although his cheeks were full, he asked, "Yeough, phendo vegough its?"

Bergie winced. "Jeez Jack, swallow your food before talking. " The *five of you* will do it tonight."

Bergie's information was partially true. The two blonde Chaplain Corps cadets at the end did write down many names they copied off bunks, but they didn't do the dirty work. It happened to be two Scots who were blonde and living at the far end of the other wing. Sterling and Neish didn't want to be seen, so other buddies pitched in for them. For the first time, Bergie assumed and forgot about Sergeant Beckford's advice to "never, never, never assume."

Lyons looked at his watch. "We'd better get out of here, the band's got to report, and we're still in our coveralls.

Although grabbed by his upper arms, when East was picked up, his right lower arm managed to lift a pancake off his plate. Fortunately, it was swallowed before the screen door slammed shut behind them.

Cordell Cross

As Saturday morning inspections go, this Saturday's was one of the best because training really started to show. Unfortunately, the commanding officer didn't get to witness the ceremony, but the second-in-command did, and he was absolutely thrilled. "I only wish movie cameras were here. I can assure you that all people across this country would see the results of your effort and feel the same pride that I have for all of you. Well done, indeed!

"Your dress is superb, your drill is excellent, and considering you have only been here for three weeks, your personal deportment is exemplary. Only six cadets passed out this morning. Well done!

"I also wish to congratulate the British Columbia Regiment cadet band, as well as the pipes and drums. You fellows have to wear two hats; therefore, my one hat goes off to you. Keep up the good work.

"This week, the pennant goes to ... E-Company. Very well done indeed IBT."

After the usual *talk* by RSM Gardiner, companies marched back to their quarters where cadets remade their beds, attended a pay parade, bedding exchange and received their mail. Weekly examinations followed at 1030 and then the rest of the weekend was free time.

The usual chubby corporal went from hut to hut delivering the mail.

"Mail call, read 'em and weep! Patterson, Warrington, Parr, Prouse, Querin, Thompson, Court-Martial Danyluk, Danyluk, Danyluk, Danyluk, Danyluk, Dany ... er, Daniels, Drabb, Snivel, er, Snidel, Brice, Banks, Danyluk, Moose, Moose, Moosey ... er, just a minute Danyluk, why are you collecting Moose's mail?"

"Because I'm Moose as well."

"Oh! Why don't you get your own friggin' post office?"

"I'm thinkin' about it, Corporal!"

"Danyluk's OB fund, Danyluk's TB fund, Moose and his TT fund...?"

Once again the corporal paused, asking, "Just what the hell is OB, TB and TT stand for anyway?"

"One ball, three balls, and tiny testicles, Corporal!"

"Oh!" The corporal then carried on. "Goose Danyluk, Danyluk You Son Of A Bitch..."

"Corporal, I represents youse usin' that kind of language when passing out my money ... er, mail!"

Rothstein said, "Moose, you mean 'resent.'"

"Yeah, I resents it, Corporal. Thanks Rothie."

The NCO smiled. "That's what's on the envelope, lover boy!"

"Er ... then will youse please get on with it!"

When the corporal left the hut still shaking his head, half-an-hour of silence followed as the cadets of Signals Company read their mail. While some cadets shared information and others went outside to read, one took money out of an envelope and spared no hesitation in broadcasting the contents of the accompanying letter.

"Bergie, listen to this. *'My Darling Goose...'*

Danyluk's bunkmate stopped reading his own mail.

"Don't you mean, Moose?"

"Er, I'd really not like to get into that, Bergie."

"I understand, Moose."

"Thanks, Bergie. Er, *My Darling Goose:*

It's Wednesday here in Vancouver, and shit, it's raining like cats and dogs. Not just outside, but also in my heart. Shit, it's been over a month since we shared that wonderful evening in your station wagon and I still can't get the stench out of my clothes. Yes, even after laundering, they smell odd. My older sister, the one who's going to university says I smell like embalming fluid, but I told her exactly what you said, that it's your special aftershave called, Knights of the Cavern. She said Nights in the Cadaver would be more appropriate. Shit, I don't know what cadaver means and I think she's just jealous.

Here's a cheque for $19.67 my darling. I collected it while cleaning out the Stanley Park Riding Stables, or as you would say, shovelling shit. When I told the female patrons it was for the poor boys born with jellybean testicles, they gave all they could. The men just laughed saying, 'Life's a bitch ain't it?'

Shit, I wish all men were like you; strong, noble, smart, rich, and gifted in oh so many ways. Although your hands haven't exactly got the velvet touch, your other (part) makes up for them, my love. Shit, you know what I mean, don'tcha?

Well it's finally happening ... I'm talking your advice and getting rid of my second full set of lower teeth. It's sure going to feel funny not being able to rip the caps off beer bottles. Also, my mother will have to start getting used to our can opener again. Shit, what I don't do for love. Now when we kiss, your lips won't look like raw liver.

You've made so many changes to my life, darling. Last Christmas when you bought me those nose-hair clippers, I thought I'd never forgive you. But now I know my nose didn't need the braids. I hope you don't mind, I'm using the clippers in my ears. Shit, now they're even lookin' better.

Love and new kinds of kisses ... Fatima.

While Moose read his letter, Bergie had stood up. He was just too astonished to lie there and listen. Every letter Danyluk received amazed him more and more, but this one took the cake.

Bergie's stood there with his mouth open. He couldn't believe what he had heard. "You're not going to tell us that Fatima has two sets of lower teeth, are you?"

"Er, yeah, but that's gonna change."

"Jesus, Moose, I know I've said this before, but what the hell kind of women do you go out with? When you met her she even braided her nose-hair?"

"Well, it wasn't that bad, Bergie. They only came down to her chin."

East took an apple out of his barrack box and entered the conversation. "Yeah, but her chin's fifty-feet long. I had to part the braids when she smooched me at the dance. Then after we kissed, although it was only pierced, I thought my lower lip had been ripped off. When she asked for a bite of my burger, she nearly took my hand off."

Those within earshot howled at East's description of Fatima.

Wane put his letter aside for a second. "Ain't she the dame with the strong lookin' lower jaw?"

"Yeah, that's her," replied Moose. "Nice bazookas, eh?"

Banks lay back again. "I couldn't tell 'cause her jawbone covered them. She said, 'Do you like my necklace?' I said, 'Fatima, I can't even see your neck.'"

Cordell Cross

Lyons came over. "Are you fellows talking about that last dance at the Georgia Auditorium? The military dance?"

The group nodded.

"Yes, I remember dancing with her. I had a small unopened flask of brandy in my inside tunic pocket. When the dance was over it was empty. Because of her jaw, she couldn't lay her head on my chest. I thought I heard the grinding of metal and glass followed by a sucking sound. She didn't spill a drop, either."

A proud Moose replied, "She never does. She can spit a beer cap thirty feet. That's my Fatima for youse."

Harvey Rothstein hadn't been listening to the banter. He'd been quiet while Danyluk was reading. Letter in hand, he jumped off his bed and stood in the aisle by Bergie and Moose's bunks.

"Hey fellas, we've got a letter from Charlie Stevenson."

Harvey had been tasked to write to Charlie on behalf of the musketeers, and after a collection, to send a VACTTC (Vernon Army Cadet Trades Training Camp) plaque.

The group of them wasted no time in gathering around Harvey, before Douglas said, "Read it to us, please, Rothie."

"Hello boys:

Your wonderful letter and plaque brought tears to an old man's eyes. Thank you very much.

Yes, it was a marvellous weekend and I thoroughly enjoyed sharing it with you. I haven't had that much fun in many years.

To tell you the truth, I was sorry to see you all leave. This antiquated farm hasn't seen that much frolic in a long, long time. Well, at least not since my children were your age. When I told Elmer my son about it, he laughed as hard as I did. Then a funny thing happened. His face took on a different expression ... like he remembered the times on the back porch and at the swimming hole. We talked about his mother, her wonderful sense of humour, her baking, bath-nights, and our annual trips to the fair, etc. Although he hated the barn dances when he was young, he says he now misses them and that urban sprawl has ruined the togetherness of family life. My, how wonderful it was to sit down and listen to him tell stories about what he and his brothers got into. Allen, our second youngest was very similar to you, Moose. He enjoyed life to the maximum and never let things upset him.

Before Elmer left, he took hold of my hand and said, thanks Pop. Would you mind if the kids visited more often and even spent some weekends here? I don't know if I can drag the wife along ... but ... the kids are off school for the summer and.... He couldn't finish, he just waved and drove away and I'm having a hard time writing this letter because my memories of many long lost wonderful years keep returning.

Boys, the word, life, really has no definition. It would take volumes to determine the boundaries of its extent, yet we humans individually bear page after page of both exhilarating and mournful chapters. That's how unknown it really is. Without meandering on as I did when you were here, take an old man's advice, and start your own editions. Don't worry about the ending and make certain you won't have to rip out any of those pages.

By the time you receive this letter, the weekend will be upon us. I've asked Fred if he'd like to come with me and visit the camp next Saturday and he is just as anxious as I am. We're actually going to bring an old friend of yours ... Miss Millie. That damn tire blew again last Wednesday

Cordell Cross

and Fred's been cursing ever since. I told him to quit being a cheap old bastard and spring for a new one. He says he'll have to spring for four. So look out, Miss Millie may be sporting four new tires and you won't have to push her anymore. Moose, you probably won't like that, because I know you enjoyed the experience, as I know all of you did.

Well lads, I'm actually having two eggs this morning. I beat Bum to the chicken house again. It's a tough job to do because I have to get up earlier than him. He's been pouting all morning as if I'd taken away one of his God-given rights.

Look after yourselves. Whether you know it or not, the group of you certainly changed my life. Days aren't so long anymore.

Fred and I will be there at noon next Saturday.

God bless you all. Charlie, Fred, Bum, Daisy, Jugs, Bigtits, and Supercups."

Following Harvey's reading, there was an atmosphere of composure in the musketeers' area. Each in his own way understood the 'between the lines' significance of Charlie's communication. The picture had changed for the better and perhaps a new generation of children would learn to openly love and understand the old storyteller, their grandfather, and in doing so, embellish and hold dear their own chapters in the *voluminous book of life.*

Smiles of confidence weren't evident as cadets left the lecture rooms following Saturday morning's examinations. Those who normally completed them in twenty-minutes took an hour.

The signals staff wanted to know if the boys were ready for the field exercise in Glenemma and as such had laid the questions on hot and heavy. Even signal office duties, the most boring of subjects, had its own section of twenty questions.

Beckford had earlier turned down the musketeers' request to try and teach an engaging and refreshing lecture on SOD, saying, "I've got to decline because the subject reminds me of watching paint dry."

On the way back to B-25 prior to having lunch, Harvey Rothstein couldn't get over the tricky questions.

"Doug, how the hell were we supposed to know the magnetic strength of the Nineteen-set's hand-cranked generating unit? We've never been taught that stuff."

"I know, Rothie. Wane and I didn't get it either."

Danyluk skipped to get into step. "I put down two heffalumps and four attract-cinepeths. I also mentioned that more power could be gained by using a reverse klyceptor connection. I betcha they mark it right."

Rothstein's face turned into one of pure admiration. "Moose, that's brilliant. How did you know the answer?"

"I didn't. I just copied Cunningham's answer. He said if they wanna bullshit him, then he's gonna bullshit them. I just joined in on the bullshit. Sounds right, though, don't it?"

Although East was always weary of Gardiner being around, he chomped on an apple anyway. "Did anyone get all nine problem personalities that play a role in each of our lives?"

Bergie indicated he got them all. "Yeah. I know a certain person who *is* all of them. The Always Agreeables, the Bullies, the Fence Straddlers, the Con Artists, the Cry Babies, the Silent Sams, the Negativists, the Know-it-alls, and the Dictators."

Cordell Cross

"Wow, who's the person you know who is all of those, Bergie?" Moose asked.
"You."

Danyluk stopped in his tracks. "That's horse-shit! I ain't always agreeable."

"You are when Alma's around."

"Er, well ... I have to be. But I ain't a cry-baby."

"You're always crying when Gardiner finds you."

"That's different! He's always there! But I ain't a dictator."

"Oh yeah? Then how come we share a barrack box and I always end up with a quarter of the space?"

"Er, well if I'm a dictator, you're a know it all."

"Moose, you don't even know the meaning of the word."

That's all Danyluk was waiting for. He'd done his homework and got all nine, as well as the meanings.

"Really Bergie? Five KiK-Kolas says you're wrong."

A grin appeared on Bergie's face. "You're on."

Moose's chest came out. "The know-it-alls: Those who are condescending to the less intelligent mortals around them. Often overbearing and pompous, they want others to acknowledge that they know more about everything worth knowing."

Bergie's smile quickly disappeared. "Er, double or nothing says you don't know the meaning of a con artist."

This time the smile had transferred itself to Moose's face.

"Make it ten KiK-Kolas and a Fudgicle and youse has a deal."

"All right. If I lose, I owe you ten KiK-Kolas and a Fudgicle. If you're wrong, you don't owe me anything. How fair can I be?"

Danyluk put an arm around Bergie's shoulders - his face only inches away from his friend's kisser.

"The con artist: One who picks your pockets while pretending to pat you on the back. These two-faced connivers are the slicksters of the workplace who are loyal to no one and will do whatever it takes to get ahead."

Bergie winced throughout Moose's explication. "I've been set up! You are a con artist, you KiK Kola mutation!"

Philanthropic in victory, Moose bowed. "Thank youse. Everyone gets a KiK Kola on you, even you. The Fudgicle is for me. That's how maggynim ... er meganim..."

"Magnanimous?" Rothstein offered.

"Yeah, thanks Rothie. That's how maggynanimous I am. How's that sound?"

Bergie couldn't get over the offer of such generosity.

"Hey, that's my buddy. You're not so bad after all. Hey, just a minute ... we're in Glenemma next week! Where the hell am I gonna get ten ice-cold KiK-Kolas and a Fudgicle?"

"That's your problem, you *cry baby*."

The group still laughed as they entered B-25 to wash up. Afterwards, lunch never tasted better. In addition to vegetable soup, shepherd's pie, roast pork, and a grand selection of sandwiches, coconut-cream pie topped off the dessert menu.

224 – NEXT STOP, VERNON!

Throughout, East's eyes were as big as saucers. He made certain he covered the *carte du jour* from top to bottom.

During the meal, further plans were made for the two blonde cadets and afterward just small talk ensued.

East slapped his stomach after eating seconds of shepherd's pie and said, "Dolman in 23 Platoon was rushed to the Vernon hospital this morning. He's got a hernia and they're gonna operate on him. What's a hernia, Moose?"

Using his knife, Jackson flicked a pea at a cadet sitting at another table. "It means he's got an ingrown hair on his knee."

"Is your name, Moose?" East asked.

Earl ducked from a return shot. "No, but I've probably got a better answer."

Danyluk put on his serious *doctor-type look*. "I'm not sick people trained yet, Jack, but I think Earl's partially right. It's a problem he's got with his hair. Youse has heard of a hairnet haven't you?"

"Er, yeah."

"Well, when the roots are sore, it's a hernia. They probably wet his scalp down, shave it, and pull a few."

Bergie took a still overflowing fork out of his mouth and slowly turned his head towards Danyluk.

"What the hell did you just say?"

Moose chomped on his sandwich, not looking at his friend. "Does youse thinks I'm wrong?"

"Wrong? Christ, you're 180 degrees away from the problem. If there's going to be any shaving, it'll be around his wang and nuts."

"Oh, so a hairnet's put around his wang, is it, Bergie? Well, I knew it had sumpin to do with hair. I was partly right, wasn't I?"

Bergie sang a portion of his reply. *"No, you're not partly right*. It's some sort of a rupture in the lower gut." He pointed towards his groin. "In the abdomen. They'll open him up, push whatever's ruptured back in, sew it up and then sew his skin back together. Hairnet? ... Jeez."

"Well they gotta shave him, ain't they? You said that!"

"Yeah?"

"Well, that's hairs, ain't it? Why would they shave him if he didn't have any crotch-hairs, like Jack here?"

East dropped his fork. "Screw you, moose. Did you guys here that? I have no crotch-hairs? Up your nose, Danysuck. Jeez, that's humiliating. I was growin' crotch-hairs before you started searchin' for your first dame. Get a grip, moose."

"Oh, youse started growin' them at six months, eh?"

Danyluk's ear-to-ear grin got the whole table roaring, except East. Jack still hadn't got over Danyluk's statement.

"He says I've got no goddamned crotch-hairs. Listen Moose, my crotch-hairs were growin' when you were wearing diapers."

Danyluk didn't let up. "I never wore diapers. Diapers stop a wang from growing."

East grinned. "That I believe. Ya probably wore dresses until you started tripping over it, didn'tcha? Anyway, I was growin' crotch-hairs before your first chest-hair popped up."

"I ain't got no chest-hairs."

"See what I mean?"

"Moose brushed Jack's comment aside, and returned his attention to Bergie. "Let's get back to the hernia question. How in the hell can a hair rupture?"

Bergie cringed. "A hair don't rupture, you pongo. I didn't say they were gonna open up one of his hairs. Jeez, will ya get with it?"

"Well why the hell are they gonna shave him, Mr. Smart Guy?"

"So they don't get any hairs inside the cut. Hear me out here. If you had to have an operation on your armpit, they'd shave you first."

"Horse shit, Bergie. Sometimes youse just don't make any sense. They're gonna shave around my wang and nuts when they operate on my armpit. That don't make any sense at all!"

"Not your wang hairs, your armpit hairs, you dolt!"

Moose sipped his tea. "Oh, I getcha."

"It's about time."

When everyone was finished and they were heading back, Danyluk got in the second last word. "They won't have to shave Jack if he gets a hernia in his armpit. He ain't got hairs there either."

East thrust off the restraining arms of Wane and Earl.

"Listen, you ignoramus, will you...?"

East's voice trailed off as the screen door slammed behind them.

After giving Hop Sing's an eyes right, McLeod asked Jackson if he had picked up the midnight passes.

"Yep and I'll pass 'em out at the bowling alley."

The hill was full of cadets that afternoon. It almost appeared as if the whole camp was heading into town.

"Christ, it's hot," said Cunningham. "How the hell do the residents of this place stay cool? If I put an egg on the sidewalk, it would cook in seconds."

East nudged the gambler. "Do you have to mention eggs? When I hear the word, egg, I almost want to throw up."

"Sorry, Jack."

"That's okay, Lingus."

Bergie indicated he was fed up with the heat as well.

"These people are used to it. It's hot in the summer and cold in the winter. I'll betcha they just open up their icebox and put a fan by it. God, that sounds nice. What I wouldn't give to be sitting in front of an icebox with a fan blowing all that cool air at me."

"What if there was a fish in the icebox?" Rothstein asked.

"I wouldn't give a damn. In this heat, I'd sit in a fish-packer's hold."

Harvey acknowledged Bergie's *dream*, with a smile. "What about the smell?"

"The fish would simply have to get used to it," Lyons quipped.

Cordell Cross

Bergie turned. "Very funny, Don."

A passing Provost jeep stopped, and the Corporal scowled at Danyluk. "You! Yes you! Get your arms up, and march!"

"I'm doin' the best I can, Corporal. I've got a hernia in my armpit!"

"Oh, then that's all right then," the corporal replied, as the jeep carried on.

Wane smacked Danyluk on the back. "Good shrinking, er, I mean good thinking, Moose. He knows as much about hernias as you do."

Danyluk nodded proudly. "We won't have to march down this hill next week – on Saturday mornin' my brother's bringin' up the hearse. We'll be ridin' in style. Just think, it'll be cold pop and smooth music in the trailing pagoda. Charlie and Fred will get a real tour of the camp."

"Moose, just how big is this *trailing pagoda*?" Douglas asked. "I mean, how the hell are you going to squeeze us all in?"

Danyluk had it all worked out. "When the pagoda's empty, there's room for nine in the back. Three can fit in the front."

Brice still remained inquisitive. "Uh huh, and where are you going to store the coffin?"

"Youse means the casket?"

"Er, yeah, the casket."

"I ain't worked that out yet, but I'm thinkin' about it."

McLeod asked, "Did you guys read today's newspaper?"

"When the hell do we get time to read the paper," Banks asked, wondering where McLeod got the time. "Where'd you see The Vernon News?"

East agreed. "Yeah, I ain't had time to finish readin' the National Geographic."

"You mean you read that thing?" Bergie said. "Moose just looks at the pictures."

"Stick it in your ear, Bergie!"

McLeod continued. "I read it in the mess hall. Some guy down south in the Unites States is getting rave reviews for his singing. Guess what his name is?"

Danyluk scratched his beret. "Bing Crosby?"

"No, the guy's name is Elvis Presley. He sings rock and roll."

Other passing cadets wondered what was so funny as howls echoed off the nearby hospital.

East had a fit. "Elvin Prestley? The poor bastard. Whoever named him Elvin, really didn't do him a favour. He'll never make it big with that name."

"No, not Elvin Prestley, Elvis Presley," McLeod replied, laughing with the others.

Jackson couldn't believe it either. "Elvis Presley? Elvis? His name's really Elvis? Who the hell could make it with a name like that? Moose Danyluk would be better."

"Hey, yeah. I can dance and sing, can't I, Bergie? I'll bet youse I could be big."

"Keep your wang out of this. We're talkin' about popularity," said Wane.

"So am I, ya creep. Don't youse think I could be a star?"

"Moose, in your own mind you are a star. It's the way you prance and yodel."

"I am? It is? Jeez, thanks Wane. You're Real George."

McLeod continued to expound on his newfound knowledge, saying, "Well, according to the paper, Elvis is the guy's name, and he's making it big."

Unchained Melody played on the jukebox as the group entered the air-conditioned bowling alley, and shortly even the girls chuckled about the name, "Elvis."

An hour-and-a-half later, a vote was taken as to what their next move would be. Jack and his girl voted to head for the nearest restaurant, but the majority decided Alma's basement was a much better idea. When she mentioned her parents were shopping in Kamloops, in addition to the basement - the whole house became *available.*

Teenagers have a way of slowly disappearing when there's a space where they can be alone. Soon after entering Alma's house, it didn't take long for each couple to display this characteristic. The time was 3pm and knowing her parents wouldn't be returning until around 5:30pm, the first heads started resurfacing and raiding the icebox at five.

Cunningham, of course didn't vanish. He and Maggie stayed playing cards at the kitchen table. An hour later when East and *company* started helping themselves to what food there was, Maggie had to get dressed quickly. Strip poker is a personal game; therefore, the game was suddenly changed to Caribbean stud poker. Either way, whether it was strip poker or Caribbean stud poker, Gordie never lost. His philosophy of never giving a sucker an even break had no bounds.

East wasn't the least bit phased when he saw Maggie. After placing his head in the icebox, he casually asked, "Whatsamatter, are ya hot, Maggie?" Jack's girlfriend just smiled before her head disappeared in the icebox with his.

"Er ... yes, Jack," Maggie replied, turning her back as she replaced her blouse.

"Christ, the least you could do is knock, Cunningham said, upset and quickly putting his shirt on. Actually, the *gambler* was probably more upset that the game had been stopped. After strip poker, he'd planned to play stuke with Maggie for money.

When East and his partner emerged from the icebox, he got the more important things off his mind before paying attention to Cunningham.

"I've got the meat and cheese; you bring out the bread, butter, and pickles. Gordie, why should I knock? I've seen ya without a shirt before. Shit, we don't find it that hot, do we honey?"

"No, darling. Say, grab some of that corn on the cob and hand me the potato-salad."

Soon, all shyly-smiling couples sat in the kitchen snacking on what was left. All, that is, except Lyons and his girl. They were in the attic singing army songs. Although Alma's dad hid his liquor, Lyons' 'living firewater schnozzle' had found it. As Bergie said, "When it comes to the smell of cheap or expensive port or brandy, Lyons could be up to his neck in hippopotamus shit, but he'd know there was booze around."

When Alma went up to bring the 'drunkards' down, she found three-quarters of a bottle of port gone, and got quite upset.

"Listen, you creeps, my dad's going to think I'm secretly drinking his special stock. What am I going to do? Moose get up here and look after your friend!"

Moose joined her. "Let's fill it with water and hope for the best."

Cordell Cross

Up top, they found that Lyons' couldn't stand and his girlfriend was nearly as bad.

"Ssay, that's a waste a good washer, er, good spirits. How's about we shing, *Rolls me over in the clovers.* Moose, you lead .. *Oh thish is number three and she's sittin' on my knee, roll me over, lay me down and do it again.* Sing, Moose ... I ... *Oh, thish is number ten and she's doin' me again, roll me over..."*

Alma became frantic. "God, Moose, get them out of the house. If my dad sees those two he's gonna have a bird."

"Alma, Don can't even stand! Where the hell am I supposed to take him?"

"Although she's havin' a fit, 'cause I'm grabbin' a little tit, roll me over, lay me down an.."

"I don't care; just get him out of here ... Now!"

With great difficulty, Moose threw Lyons over his shoulder and headed downstairs. When the rest saw him, they couldn't believe their eyes. Every muscle in the figure propped up before them was limp, except for his mouth.

"Oh, thish is numumumber four, and I got her on the floor, roll me over, lay me down and do it again .... Sshay, where's the bottle? Hey, let's all have a few swigs; I share my aqua vitae with my buddies, don't I, Moosie ol' pard?"

When Lyons laid a big wet kiss on Moose's forehead, the place erupted. Banks laughed so hard he had to open the window.

"Get him out of here, Moose," Alma yelled as she threw a pair of boots, a set of puttees, a belt, and a beret in Danyluk's direction. In the meantime, Diane took Lyons' girl to the bathroom, and Douglas and Wane made some coffee.

"Alma, I'm goin' I'm goin'! Don't just stand there, Bergie, give me a hand. This guy weighs a ton."

Getting down the back stairs was hilarious. Lyons tripped and took his two *handlers* down with him. Luckily all three landed on the grass.

When they got him to his feet again, Bergie said, "There's a small park just around the corner; we'll prop him up sitting against a tree. He can sing there."

"Yeah, put a tin cup by him and maybe we'll make some money," Cunningham said.

"Good idea. We can dress him there as well, but I ain't concerned about his singing," replied Moose. "When the hell did youse start liking his singing, Bergie?"

"Forget it, Moose."

Luckily, there were no military police vehicles in the vicinity of the grounds where they attended to Lyons. While the others cleaned the house, Douglas poured coffee after coffee down his friend's throat, shirt, pants, legs, hosetops, puttees and boots. It wasn't Douglas' fault. Lyons shook so much, when the cup touched his lips, coffee ran everywhere.

Lyons still wasn't sober in the queue for the movie and neither was his girl who hung on to her *man* with both arms. Neither said anything - they couldn't. Port has a way of slowly interfering with ones vocal chords. In Lyons' case, his vocal chords were only part of the problem. The three-quarters of a bottle gradually interfered with his eyes, nose, lips, tongue, head, shoulders, legs, arms, and soon, his gastric juices.

Cordell Cross

Promptly, with only minor complications, the group took up the back row of the packed boiling hot theatre. Poor planning more than anything else placed a pale-faced Lyons and his sickly girl in the middle sitting next to Moose. Actually, Moose had hesitated in the aisle hoping someone else would volunteer to sit next to "the drunk" but unfortunately, the others knew better and planned their moves *accordingly*.

After the news, *Calamity Jane* started - the first of two feature films. The music and action was wonderful and had everyone's interest until Lyons with his head back started snoring loudly.

A cadet sitting with his girl in front of Lyons turned around. "Hey fella, how about giving us a chance to hear what's happening?" The green ribbon on his epaulet indicated he was in Driver Mechanics.

When Moose shook the snorting *corpse*, it stopped snoring and started singing again.

"So this is number one, and her dress is all but gone; roll me over, lay me down and do it again. Roll me o ... ver, in the clo ... ver, roll me over ... Hey, Moosie, let's you and I shing, Fartin' an' a startin'! You lead. *Oh fartin' is no good for startin' - unless the girl of your dreams is a hag. I just had a big bowl of chilli, and..."*

With a hand over Lyons' mouth, Moose did the best he could to stop his friend competing with the songs on the screen. Eventually, to prop him up, he had to put one arm around the *star entertainer's* shoulders; his other hand remained covering Lyons' mouth to stop him from singing.

Finally, the cadet in front stood up and glared at the duo. Lyons' head was now resting on Moose's shoulder.

"Jeez, will you two homos give us a break? We paid to get in, ya know?"

When the cadet sat down again, Danyluk released his grip around Don and tapped the cadet on the shoulder not caring or knowing that Lyons had fallen forward - his mouth now breathing down the girl's back. To say the least, Lyons' breath wasn't pleasant.

"Listen, you D&M pongo, who are you callin' a homo?" whispered Danyluk.

"You, you asshole. Who the hell else do you think I'm talkin' to?"

Other voices were heard in the third row down. They thought the cadet behind them was causing the trouble.

"For God's sake, you loudmouth, will you shut yer face, we're tryin' to watch the picture!"

Although the cadet's girl had detected the foulness of Lyons' breath, she didn't know his gas-pained eyes-closed face was only one inch from her head. The discovery didn't take long though because when Lyons loudly belched, her scream brought the audience to its feet.

Danyluk quickly pulled Lyons back and gave him a swift smack. In spite of the fact that his eyes opened, Lyons didn't have a clue as to what was going on around him. This helped somewhat because the theatre manager appeared and a row had erupted between the cadet up front and those in front of him.

"It wasn't us. Why don't you open up your eyes?"

"Are you calling me a liar?"

Cordell Cross

"No, I'm saying that we're not the problem. It's these homos behind us."

"We didn't hear them, we just keep hearing you. Quit the singing."

"It wasn't me you IBT skuzzball. *Smiley* behind me was singin'."

"Bullshit, my girl says it was you."

"Listen, Creepface - I don't sing at the best of times."

"Who are you callin' Creepface?"

Throughout, Lyons sat in a dream-like state. Eyes wide open, and even grinning, but not moving. Actually, the grin was a gas pain.

Realizing it couldn't have been Moose or Lyons, because they were quiet, the theatre manager warned cadets in other areas where *vulgar* arguments were now taking place.

"It was them."

"Who, us? We were neckin' ... I think it was those six."

"Like hell it was. Up your ass, you Engineer slob."

"Same to you, you Strathcona pongo."

Eventually things quietened down and the movie continued, as did Lyons. When Danyluk moved his arm to get some popcorn, the boozer's head fell in Moose's lap. A normal person wouldn't have felt the *encroachment*, however Danyluk isn't *built* like a normal person. Lyons' chin got him square in the testicles.

"Aggghhh! Jeez, Lyons," was accompanied by a push that sent Lyons hard against his semi-conscious girlfriend who was about to sip her drink. She also didn't have a clue where she was, and the ice and cool liquid never touched her lips. Instead, it landed on the head and shoulders of another person to her left in front.

Rothstein acted quickly. He wrapped his arms around Lyons' girl, placing his face in hers as if they were kissing. When the tall, stocky, infuriated, and soaking wet civvy teenager stood up and turned around, he realized it couldn't have been them. His conclusion was it must have been a grinning East who was engrossed in the movie.

Kneeling on his seat and grabbing East, the foul-mouthed *newcomer* got a chocolate bar in his face, followed by Jackson's fist. When the *foreigner's* civvy friend tried to get into the act, Cunningham planted one on him, sending him into the row in front. East never had to throw a punch. He couldn't have anyway - his hands were full of goodies.

While all this was happening, Don's face ended back in Danyluk's lap and Moose wasn't fast enough ... Lyons threw up.

The voice was loud ... really loud. "Son of a bitch!"

When a screaming Moose stood up quickly, some of the stomach-material headed to his front and started an action that could be described as the commencement of the Third World War.

While the unbearable stench covered a radius of five metres, the fanfare of agony covered much more. Total pandemonium erupted in the four rear rows of the theatre as the lights came on. Even McLeod, Wane, Douglas, and Bergie who tried to maintain their cool throughout got *involved* in the conflict. Banks got a black eye and Douglas almost got his nose ripped off.

Laughs filled the hill that night. Not because the girls were mad and went home on their own, or Moose and Lyons looked like they'd entered a pie-eating contest and won, or the musketeers had either cuts, bruises, bloody noses or black eyes. The evening had been fun. In that noisy half-hour, the heat, discipline, routine, and rigors of camp were washed away. It wasn't planned and it should never have happened, but it did and their camaraderie was never closer.

Lyons never let up. Sober but still staggering and held up by Moose, he said, "Let's all sing a song."

Danyluk couldn't get over the suggestion.

"Oh shit, not again."

"Yeah, again; let's sing, *We came to Vernon!*"

Don didn't have to ask the second time. In seconds, the song started and finished just outside the camp. Other cadets climbing the hill joined in as well. (Author's note: The tune is, *And The Band Played On.*)

"We came to Vernon to learn us a trade, and the camp was hot; We de-moustached the sergeants, and shaved all the rest, and the camp stayed hot.

"We frenched every bed and planted some fish, unaware what our future could hold; But some guy named Gard'ner, stepped on our toes, and we all got told.

"If you little bastards just try one more prank, you'll soon see why; You'll be out on the road, with a full effing load, or you'll say bye, bye.

"So stand by your beds as stiff as a board, I've got a short story to tell; I'm not your mother, your father, your brother, and it's just as well.

"It's been thirty long years and I've seen it before, and that's no gas; Thousands who stood where you're standing now got my boots up their ass.

"If you want to continue to act like creeps, I'll oblige you in so many ways; And as you all know, I'm a man of my word, in your ill-numbered days.

"We came to Vernon to learn us a trade, and the camp was hot; We got down to studyin' and figured it out, and the camp stayed hot.

"We're not goody-goodies, or yes men, or fools; we've studied what ol' Gard'ner meant;

"We're proud of ol' Vernon, though it's too goddamned *hot, and our bodies have got all the dents."*

Whether Lyons was right or not, the song eased the pain brought on by the previous altercations.

Had they passed the Provost shack the lot of them would have been booked, so they took the back route. This move didn't please Moose because he never got the opportunity to peek inside Hop Sing's window. He understood, however, that the key would have been thrown away if they were *inspected.* Once the military police had got past the smell, one look at their clothes would have meant *hard labour* for the balance of camp.

Inside B-25, the lone corporal walking the aisles didn't hesitate in offering his advice. He'd come from the next hut over and would be replaced by two Signals Company corporals when they left the Junior Ranks Club at 0100.

"What the hell did you do, go looking for food in the Vernon garbage dump?"

He checked their name tags. "You two, Lyons and Danyluk ... hit the showers and take your clothes with you! The rest of you get in there as well!"

Cordell Cross

232 – NEXT STOP, VERNON!

When East checked to see if a tooth was loose, blood came out with his finger. "Not a bad idea, Corporal. Any good food there?" he asked, referring to the garbage dump.

As Moose and Lyons passed two Irish cadets getting into their beds halfway up the aisle next to the entrance to the washing area, one paddy pinched his nose and whispered to the youngest of the two, "Ya see, O'Flaherty, BCRs not only look like shit, they smell like shit."

"Those two reek worse than shit," his friend replied, waving a comic to move the stale air. "Are all BCRs like that?"

"Yep, and if you associate with 'em, you'll smell the same. They're nearly as bad as Seaforths."

"You mean Seaforths and BCRs smell the same? Which group is worse?"

"It's hard to tell. Seaforths spray perfume on their kilts. At least that's what we were taught at our armouries. Dirty lot, eh?"

"Doogan, you can say that again. Thank God we're in the Irish - the purest of regiments."

As the Irish cadets spoke very softly, more cadets who got *messed up* at the theatre joined the shower room *conference*. Throughout, East remained in a benevolent mood allowing them to share the hot water.

Shortly after the showers stopped, snoring filled B-25.

Chapter 17

Some of the musketeers were still hurting when they got up at 0230 to *take care* of the Chaplain Corps cadets.

Bergie held his meeting in the drying room. "I've changed my mind on how we pull this off. I think all of us are going to be needed when we move the second one."

McLeod had included himself in this caper, and the whole nine agreed.

"We'll move the top one first," said Bergie. "Doug, Wane, Gordie, Moose ... you'll have got to be really silent when you do your jobs. Just act like nuns inspecting a whorehouse?"

"I didn't know nuns inspected whorehouses?" Banks said, grinning.

Bergie was in no mood for questions. "You know what I mean. Okay, let's get to it."

While Rothstein, East, McLeod, and Jackson collapsed two folding tables, Douglas and Wane silently entered the south-end corporal's cubicle on the other side of the hut. The door creaked a little, but not enough to wake the snoring NCO in his wide single bed against the wall.

Ever so slowly, the boys took hold of the end of the bed and moved it towards the middle so Wane could get around to the other side. When that was done, they waited.

At exactly the same time as the first corporal was being looked after, Gordie and Moose were in the second corporal's cubicle at the northern end of the same side, moving *that* sleeping NCO's bunk out from the wall. When they were finished, Gordie was on the enclosed side, with Moose in the open. Now, they also waited.

Back in their own wing at the far northern end, Rothstein and East held the table high next to the sleeping Chaplain Corps cadet's upper bunk. Cautiously, Bergie and Lyons pulled the mattress, cadet, and bedding onto the table. When the boy was lowered, Bergie and Lyons took an end and Rothstein and East took the other end gradually moving the blonde religious *type* through the washing area to Douglas and Wane. Within twenty seconds, the table with the sleeping cadet was in the corporal's cubicle next to the snoring corporal. The ensuing stage was tough, because if the corporal woke, all hell would break loose and the musketeers knew it.

Luck was with them with this *peaceful* NCO because he had shifted onto his side, his face in Wane's direction. On the other side of the bed, Douglas lifted up the corporal's upper sheet and blanket and Bergie and Lyons picked up the cadet's lower sheet and moved him next to the non-com. Nothing went wrong; it took fifteen minutes for them to take the cadet's upper sheet and blanket off him, and his lower sheet out from under him. He was now on his back, with his head placed on the corporal's pillow. With that done, Douglas covered the cadet with the corporal's upper sheet and blanket.

With phase one concluded, they silently closed the door moved the lad's bedding back to his bunk. A few snickers were finally let out, but not until they reached the washing area. Afterward, Douglas and Wane made up the cadet's bed as though he had just threw back the covers and left.

The succeeding *move* wasn't as easy. Although the cadet occupied a lower bunk, he was curled up on his side. Attempts at trying to move him onto his back almost woke him up. Bergie solved the problem by taking a running shoe off the shelf and letting the dangling lace tickle the sleeping cadet's left ear. That did it. He scratched, shifted, and remained on his back. Within seconds, he was transferred to the table and taken into Gordie and Moose's cubicle.

Making the last movement was not easy and did not go according to plan. The corporal lay sleeping on his back in the middle of the bunk and had started snoring. Bergie had to make a decision and he made it quickly. Motioning to the *carriers*, the table with the sleeping lad was taken out, turned around and brought back in. As Danyluk lifted the corporal's upper sheet and blanket, the cadet's upper sheet and blanket were taken off him and he was lifted by his lower sheet onto the corporal's bunk, but at the bottom - his feet next to the corporal's face. The next ten minutes were used for taking out the cadet's lower sheet. When that was completed, the NCO's bedding was laid over him. It was difficult because they had to leave the cadet's head out, but at the same time cover the corporal's feet. Nevertheless, all went well and neither woke up. Two minutes later, the cadet's lower bunk was remade to look as if he had decided to throw back his covers and visit the jon. It took half-an-hour to complete both moves.

In the drying room, chuckles, pats on their backs and handshakes ended the execution. The happy but still-in-pain musketeers went back to bed eagerly awaiting Sunday morning.

Some alarm clocks are loud; others just make a low noise. In the corporal's cubicle at the south end of the eastern wing, the alarm's sound would wake the dead, but not necessarily sleeping cadets.

When his alarm clock started, the drowsy eyes-closed corporal sleeping on his side, face away from the clock, couldn't quite figure out what the weight was on his left shoulder. He also couldn't completely sense why his head wasn't on his pillow.

Turning on his other side, the weight remained and his arm was hindered from turning the loud chime off. His eyes opened, but at least four seconds elapsed before he concluded a nose was sticking in his face. At 'Mark,' plus one second, his new bed-partner, owner of the nose, was propelled onto the floor with the force of an elephant hitting the water after a ten-story jump, and the cry: "What the...? Jesus Christ," was enough to wake up the whole camp, never mind his cadets.

By the time 'Mark' plus three seconds evolved, the alert corporal was standing wide-eyed on his bed, fists in the boxing position with a dazed blonde cadet standing, scratching, and holding his injuries created by the launching.

"What the hell are you doing in here? How long have you been here? How did you get into my bed? Who are you? Speak up you rotten little bastard!"

The uncomplicated reply was typical. "Huh? Er, good morning, my son, er, Corporal. Why did you move me here? You must have been lonely, eh? Leviticus, 23-27 states, 'When a bullock or a sheep or a goat is brought forth, then it shall be seven days under the dam: and from the eighth day and thencefore it shall be accepted as an offering by fire onto the Lord!' Today, Corporal is the seventh day."

Cordell Cross

At the opposite end, the other corporal was still a little intoxicated from the night before. When his clock went off and he felt, smelled, and saw feet in his face, he thought he was in the wrong place at the wrong time. Too many experiences of angry husbands haunted him, therefore 'Mark' plus one second allowed him to grab his clothes and jump out the window. Once free where he could get into his pants, he realized his predicament. It was the right place and the right time, and he'd just jumped out of his own room.

This corporal's sleeping cadet was rolled onto the floor and given a *slight tap*. (Author's note: Military terminology for a hard thump.)

"What are you, some sort of a homo? Where are you from? What ... What the hell were you doing in my bed? How long have you been in here? Where's your mother? Christ, if Gardiner hears about this I'll be demoted and become the laughing stock of camp! Never mind camp ... the world!"

Just like his friend, the cadet remained cool and replied, "Did you carry me here? Such language isn't necessary, my son. I've heard of these things happening. You must be under pressure to be close to someone. Are you aware of Daniel 4-11? 'Thus were the visions of mine head in my bed: I saw and behold a tree in the midst of the earth, and the heighth thereof was great.'"

"I don't give a shit about that! Where are you from?"

"I'm from 22 Platoon, Corporal. Men act in strange ways when they are lonely. If you needed someone to talk to, all you had to do was ask. Both of us would be glad to converse at any time. In Kings, it says, 'James slept with his fathers and...'"

"I'm not your goddamned father. Who the hell is James? Both of you? There's more like you? Listen, kid..."

It took an hour to sort matters out, and this was done on the hill overlooking the golf course. Both the cadets and the corporals apologized to each other.

Needless to say, after returning to their barracks, two red-faced corporals were certainly hazed by cadets in their platoons. Hazed to the point where extra duty was handed out.

Naturally, both NCOs believed the perpetrators were on their side of the hut, probably in either 23 or 24 Platoons but the subject was hushed up for obvious reasons. Nothing was said when the religious cadets returned to their bunks because the west-wing's inhabitants weren't aware of the *fun*.

That afternoon Bergie got tipped off that two Scots from the other side had frenched the Musketeers' beds, not the religious cadets.

Bergie felt both guilt and blame. This was the first time the close group had taken action against innocent parties. Although they wouldn't admit their mistake to the Chaplain Corps cadets, they would make up for their error. In addition, during breakfast conversation the two events turned out to be in their favour.

"Damn, we got the wrong ones," said Jackson. "Bergie, I thought you said you don't make mistakes?"

"I'm only human, you creep. I feel sorry for those guys, but they're taking it well. Our problem is how do we fix our Scottish friends? Two guys named Robertson and Fowler frenched our beds."

Cordell Cross

A blurry-eyed Lyons glanced up from his chess game with McLeod. "We don't. We leave it alone."

"What do you mean we don't?"

Lyons' head went down again as he made a chess-move.

"The only thing we have to do is somehow get news to the corporals."

"News?"

"Yeah, the names of the six guys who *really* moved the *monks*."

The word "monks" got the whole table chuckling and the grin still covered Bergie's face when he asked, "How do we do it?"

Lyons pushed the chessboard aside. "I'm afraid I'm not up for chess this morning, old chum. My *war* injury is getting to me."

"You mean your liver's acting up," quipped McLeod.

Lyons ignored him. "All we have to do is wait for one of the corporals to visit the jon. When he's in there, two of us will change our voices and have a small conversation."

Lyons slowly rose from the table. "Easy, eh what? Right now I need more coffee."

"Brilliant," replied Bergie. "Don, you may be the battalion lush, but you've still got **your** brain cells."

Moose finished his plate. "No he hasn't. He emptied them all over me last night."

"Are you saying my brains are in my stomach?" Lyons said, hesitating.

"Yeah, nearly. Like my dad always says: 'Moose, your brains are at the wrong end.'"

Bergie didn't agree. "No he doesn't. He says, 'Moose, you've got two heads and you think with the wrong one.'"

Picking up his cup, Lyons replied, "Moose, as you know, we're not all built alike. I think your dad's right. He must be a very smart man."

Danyluk's chest came out. "Thanks Lyons. Youse can bet he is. Kinda, like father, like son, eh?"

"Er, yeah. In your case, I guess you can say that."

"Youse is Real George, Don."

"I know."

After breakfast, they put their plan into action. It called for at least one musketeer to be washing his face, waiting until one of the corporals entered the jon. When that happened, he would get Lyons and Bergie and they would *spill the beans*.

Musketeers changed every twenty minutes and it was during Douglas' watch when the corporal from the north end of the east wing entered and didn't stand at the urinal. Douglas rushed out and informed the *actors*, who in turned strolled in pretending to do some washing.

Bergie started. "What a riot, eh? Did you hear about how Neish, MacKay, Sterling and Scott in 22 Platoon got the corporals on the far side?"

Lyons played his part well. "No, what happened?"

"They talked two of their friends in 23 Platoon to give 'em a hand in moving a cadet into each corporal's bed. Ya should have seen it … it was funnier than hell."

"Who were their friends?" Lyons asked.

"Robertson and Fowler. Apparently, the six of them worked all night to pull the caper. They got away with it too. The corporals haven't got a clue so rumour has it that the six are gonna do it again."

Bergie winked, finding it hard not to burst out laughing. "This damned machine is broken again, we'll have to wash these clothes by hand."

"Yeah," said Lyons as the two left the room. "Did you say they're gonna do it again?" His voice trailed off.

The broad smile didn't diminish as the corporal wrote down the names of Neish, MacKay, Scott, Sterling, Robertson and Fowler. It also never left his face as he printed *22 and 23 Platoons*, finished his business, and washed his hands. As he entered his wing wringing the same hands, he mumbled and sang, *"Oh no they're not. Horace, you made a mess of me. Oh, Horace, de de de dee de dee."*

It is a known fact that Chaplain Corps cadets are laid back. They're above the norm and closer to the *Man Himself* so to speak. For two blonde Chaplain Corps cadets in 22 Platoon, this wasn't the case at all. Although calm on the surface, they wanted a little revenge but required some assistance. That comfort came in the form of a note written by Rothstein.

'Neish, MacKay, Scott and Sterling from your platoon moved you, with the help of Robertson and Fowler from 23 Platoon. Have fun. A friend.'

"Mark, may I quote Isaiah 18-6?"

"Paul, if you didn't, I'd wonder why? Please go ahead."

"They shall be left together unto the fowls of the mountains, and to the beasts of the earth: and the fowls shall manner upon them, and all the beasts of the earth shall winter upon them."

Mark smiled peacefully. "Yes, absolutely perfect, my son. In Glenemma of course?"

"Of course," replied Paul.

For some, Sunday *deportment* has a way of catching up on them. After a corporal yelled, "Form three ranks on the road for church parade," this Sunday's behaviour of a few was quite *novel*. Also, it was the same corporal from last weekend.

Following the roll call the corporal ordered, "Fall out the non-believers!"

At least eighty percent turned to their right and started strolling away.

"Get back in the ranks! You, you with the blanket over your head! What's your name?"

"Cu-nningh-am, Corporal."

"Oh Christ, not you again. Okay, bugger off!"

"Thank you, Corporal. Come, my flock."

"Flock? Wait a minute. What's with you three with towels over your heads?"

"They're studying my faith," Gordie said. "That's sibling Da-nyl-uk, sibling Be-rg-ie, and neophyte-sibling E-as-t."

"What? More Goddamned beggars? You should do your recruiting at the freight yard! What's with the neo ... er, the nefit, er...?"

"The neophyte-sibling?"

"Yeah?"

"He hasn't yet mastered the oath of predilection and propensity. My Goddess says that…"

"Okay, okay, puleeeze don't give me that bloody induction crap again! Why is your sibling *nibbling* on my parade?"

Gordie rolled his eyes upwards. Here he was trying to help East out and the *beast* is chomping on a chicken leg under his towel.

"Er, he has informed me that … er…"

Although the gambler's mind worked a mile a minute, he was lost for words.

The Corporal's menacing grin moved into Cunningham's face. "Yes, go on? He has informed you of what?"

"Er, that it is an offering prior to taking the oath of…"

The NCO's hand came up. "The oath of the chicken? Hold it! I want you and your other tramps, er beggars of profanity *and exploitivity* to get rid of your coverings and join the rest of us simple human beings in church. You've got exactly ten seconds."

"But, Corporal, I…"

"Eight seconds!"

With the prophet of predilection and propensity cursing East, the four of them made it back with two seconds to spare.

"That's better! It's good to have all you little buggers, I mean little beggars, with us!"

Having said that, the corporal marched back to the centre of the company. "Fall out the non Christians!"

Moose tried it again. In the middle with his arms around Rothstein and Isaacson's shoulders, he made it to the *shack's* door.

"Oh, no, no! Not you *sibling* Da-nyl-uk. Father Anthony has personally asked that you assist him during mass. When he asked for *Michelangelo*, every Catholic in the company volunteered your name."

"Finks! I've been framed," Moose bellowed.

This time when the Protestants marched to B-3 and the Roman Catholics marched to the outdoor chapel, the *gambler* took his cards. He was certain the Lord wouldn't mind him making a buck or two. As it turned out, he was right. He made twelve dollars. Two of which came from tapping the bottom of the collection plate with one hand, while relieving it of a deuce with the other.

Chapter 18

The plains of Glenemma lie between two heavily treed mountains approximately forty miles north of Vernon. The area is ideal for training cadets whether it be D&M, Signals, map-reading or company, platoon and section tactics.

The land is owned by the Okanagan Indian Band and for years it has been leased on and off by the Department of National Defence, under the condition that it be looked after.

To cadets and staff, Glenemma is the only place in the world where there is more dust than at camp. When cadets write home to mention that their intake of VD (Vernon dust) has advanced to GD (Glenemma dust) wise parents know field exercises are in progress.

The cadets of Signals Company were confined to camp after church parade on Sunday. Many things had to be looked after, such as receiving extra ponchos or ground sheets, extra webbing, canteen-bottles, as well as preparing their radio sets, batteries, and ancillary equipment for the trip. Additionally, although the girls were still upset about Saturday night's activities, they reconsidered their views that their *soldiers* were rogues after receiving sweet-talking telephone calls from their boys.

All signals cadets had undergone lectures on how to build hootchies and how to survive and stay clean in the field. They looked forward to the break of Glenemma, therefore at 0530 on Monday morning when the sergeant bellowed, "Stand by your beds," most cadets were up, showered and dressed.

At 0845 when the convoy of trucks left camp and rolled down the hill, loud and enthusiastic singing erupted in the backs of the vehicles.

"Oh Provost, oh Provost we're leavin' ya now. But that doesn't mean we're takin' a bow.
It just means you won't be checking our kit. And that suits us fine, ya big bags of shit."

Even with the tarps off the trucks, signals cadets sung every military song written heading north along route 97. The boys weren't the slightest bit worried about civilians hearing their musical *works of art*.

With the musketeers sitting together with twelve other cadets from 21 Platoon, the forty-minute drive allowed them to experience the marvellous scenery and fill their lungs with the sweet-smelling air only reserved for *explorers* encountering a complete sense of freedom.

"Doug, we're actually going back to the place of the borrowed lantern. Mint, eh?" Wane said, putting away a letter he'd been reading.

"And the only *shitters* in the world that devour people," Wane's best friend replied.

Danyluk had been quiet that morning, but when he heard Douglas, it brought back *fond* memories. "If I end up in the shitter this year, all of youse are goin' in with me. Do you hear me, Mister Bergie?"

"I keep telling you Moose, it wasn't me. It was East."

Jack nearly choked on his apple. "Bull shit it was! Did you guys hear that? I didn't cut your shitter chair - it was Jackson! Jesus, give me a break, will ya? I've had to put up with Cunnilingus' bitching since yesterday morning!"

A still-upset Cunningham glared at East. "Ya ruined my religious act, ya pongo. Just because the towel covered your face doesn't mean you can gnaw on a chicken leg. Whatsamatter with you, East?"

"I was hungry."

"Hungry? You had ten breakfasts before the parade?"

"Get off my back, Lingus!"

Earl interjected. "And don't blame me for cuttin' the shitter chair, Moose. I've already paid my debt; remember? Bergie cut the damn thing, not me! It took a week to get the smell outa my nose!"

The gambler grinned. "That's because you were bunking close to East. If I had been with you guys last year, I would have cut East's chair."

"Take a hike Cunner! Maybe you'll go for a ride in the shitter this year!"

"I'd better not, Jack. One never knows when he'll need his banker. Also, his banker might start callin' up some past loans."

"Er, well ... I didn't say *I'd* push ya."

Lyons put down the book he was reading and wiped his brow with the hankie he kept up his right sleeve.

"Chaps, chaps, let's not quarrel in front of these other regimental-type peons."

Picking up his book and pushing his glasses up his nose, he said, "Listen to this: *"Henry Ziegland thought he was a dead man. Standing before him was an angry young man, gun in hand, telling him that he was about to kill him. The gunman was the brother of Ziegland's ex-girlfriend, who had just committed suicide after Ziegland jilted her. The brother was out for revenge.*

"The gunman pulled the trigger. The bullet grazed Ziegland's face and buried itself in a tree. Ziegland fell to the ground and stayed still, as the brother, thinking he had accomplished his mission, turned the gun on himself and blew his brains out.

"The murder that never occurred happened in Honey Grove, Texas, in 1893. Over the next 20 years, Ziegland put the incident from his mind. One day in 1913, he decided to cut down the tree on his land under which the shooting had occurred. It turned out to be a tough job, so he used dynamite.

"He drilled a hole in the tree trunk, filled it with explosives and set the fuse. The explosion blasted fragments in all directions - and send the old bullet through Henry Ziegland's head, killing him instantly."

Lyons put his book down again. "Now that's what's called getting your own back, isn't it, chaps? Retribution may take years, but it comes."

Moose nodded. "Hey yeah. If it takes me twenty years, I'm gonna get my own back, Bergie."

Bergie shook his head and his face assumed a holier-than-thou look. "It might take you thirty years because I'll be watching you. Besides, you don't believe in that unexplained ghost crap, do you?"

Indeed, Danyluk was a strong believer. "Yeah I do. I also believe in predesy, er pred, er preyd ... "

"Is *predestine*, the word you're looking?" asked Rothstein.

Moose nodded again. "Yeah, thanks Rothie. My ultimate end has already been decided and I can't change it. Ain't that right, Doug?"

Douglas didn't have the chance to answer because Bergie did. "If, for once in your life you're right, then I can assure you, your destiny is in the shitter."

"Yeah, they won't have to bury you," said Wane, "They'll just find a shitter that's six feet deep, throw you in, and cover you with dirt. Or, if you're lucky, Moose, they might cover you with more shit."

A questionable look came over Moose's face. "What the hell do youse means, if I'm lucky? How can I be lucky if they cover me with more shit?"

Wane winked at Douglas. "Increased maggots."

Danyluk still wasn't satisfied. "Yeah, go on? So how are maggots involved with this?"

"Do you want your body to just lie there, or do you want it to be eaten immediately?"

A Seaforth cadet sitting on the other side of the vehicle whispered to his buddy. "These BCR assholes really take the cake. Just listen to 'em."

His friend replied, "I can't. I'm starting to retch."

Jackson interjected. "Moose, ya wanna to go to Maggot Heaven, don'tcha?"

"No I don't want to go to Maggot Heaven," Moose moaned. "What's the matter with ordinary Heaven? I'm a Catholic for God's sake! Maggots don't get last rights!"

"That's right, but they get last dibs," said Wane. "Or in your case, last ribs. If you live the life of a maggot, ya go to maggot heaven. The way those grubs breed you'll have fifty-million female larva to screw."

As the truck filled with laughter, Danyluk gave Wane the finger.

Lyons added: "That's the real meaning of exterior economy. It'll be a simple funeral with no frills. Even the tombstone's message will be uncomplicated. Here lies Moose - it's still up and being used."

Brice leaned over and whispered to Wane, "If Moose believes in ghosts, we should have a ball this week. Wadoyasay?"

Still chuckling, Banks murmured, "I'm with ya. The old Glenemma ghost is about to appear." He then returned his attention to Moose. "Don't think about it, or your mind will disturb the Glenemma ghost."

Moose ignored him, but East didn't. "Glenemma ghost? What's with the Glenemma ghost?"

Leave it to Rothstein to come to Wane's rescue. He sensed Wane didn't know what to say, so he volunteered an explanation.

"Er, In 1904 a white phantom first brought terror to Glenemma. Initially, it appeared as a naked blonde-haired woman walking across Round Lake..."

"That's my kind of ghost," said Danyluk, grabbing his crotch.

Rothstein hadn't finished. "But it can change sexes, and..."

Moose let go of his crotch. "Damn! Er, sorry, Rothie, please carry on."

Rothstein now knew Moose couldn't be fooled, but he had Jack East's attention. "Anyway, one day at 3 am a local Native fella's horse turned lame just as he arrived at Glenemma. He got off the horse, let it go, and started to walk. After a few paces, he heard someone ask in a high-pitched voice if he wanted a lift. He turned to see a dark figure sitting on a stagecoach drawn by four jet-black horses. He got in the back and ten minutes later, he was home. Although he couldn't see the driver's face, he thanked him and offered to send him a chicken for his trouble. The apparition wrote down a name, an address on a note, and handed it to him. It was signed, Mort."

Jack looked puzzled. "The ghost's name was Wart?"

"Not Wart, you pongo ... Mort," Rothstein replied. "Anyway, when the guy tried to deliver the chicken to a nearby farm, a woman came to the door and said Mort was her husband, but that he had been dead for three years. Mort had been a stagecoach driver. When she looked at the note, she said it was definitely her dead husband's handwriting."

East was almost in Rothstein's face. "Yeah, go on, Rothie, go on."

"There's not much more to tell, other than Mort wanders Glenemma's plains and he changes form. The local natives say that Mort can be nice, or..."

Jack was hooked. "Yeah ... or ... or, what?"

"Treacherous."

East sat back wide-eyed. "Bloody hell! Jeez, I don't wanna meet this Mort character, so I hope he doesn't offer me a ride."

The *new believer* didn't see the straight-faced winks as the trucks pulled off the highway into clouds of Glenemma dust.

After five minutes of rambling on a narrow dirt road containing potholes nearly as big as the vehicles, the convoy emerged into the plains of Glenemma and continued north along the western boundary route.

When the transport finally stopped, the ride, heat, and dust had already taken its toll. Some cadets were bruised from bouncing around in the backs of trucks, and others that had the misfortune to sit up front with drivers who didn't warn them, rubbed the tops of their heads.

When the tailgates opened, each platoon sergeant gathered his *brood*, forming them up in three ranks with their backs to the sun. Twenty One Platoon was lucky, they would stay in that area, but the other three platoons were marched to other confines in Glenemma's expanse.

"There should be a sign here saying the wonderful area of Glenemma welcomes you," Bergie said to Moose who was standing next to him but couldn't be seen because of flying dust and dirt thrown up from the departing trucks' tires.

"Is that youse, Bergie?"

"No, it's Mort! Of course it's me, you pongo! Where are ya?"

Danyluk moved toward the source of the voice. "I'm right here," he said, coughing. Good 'ol GD covered the *animal's* face, teeth, and total body. "I'd almost forgotten what this stuff tastes like," Moose added.

Bergie wore a bandanna covering the lower portion of his face. He offered a second piece of cloth to his friend. "Tie this over your nose and mouth."

Although Sergeant Bentley couldn't be seen, he could be heard. "Twenty- One Platoon, pay attention here! Just fall out until the dust settles then we'll get organized!"

Ten minutes later, the cadets of 21 Platoon sat in a semi-circle in front of Sergeant Bentley. The copse of trees allowed some small respite from the sun's searing rays.

Cordell Cross

"This is your new home for the next five days! How many of you were here last year?"

Approximately half the Platoon's hands went up, and Bentley nodded.

"Now, most of you have read the brief we issued about Glenemma. You've also studied the map. Additional maps will be issued following our talk!

"Those who smoke will stop doing so immediately! If I find anyone smoking, you'll curse the tobacco industry for the rest of your days. Also, you will not light fires. Is that clear?"

"Yes, Sergeant!"

"This portion of Glenemma is our platoon's bivouacking area! Twenty Two Platoon is on both sides of the centre plains, 23 Platoon is at the southeast boundary, and 24 Platoon is bivouacking at the southwest boundary. I..."

Moose's hand went up.

"Yes, Danyluk?"

"Does that mean that 23 Platoon is close to Round Lake?"

Bentley grinned. "They're closer than we are, but they're on the high ground above the lake. You needn't worry; all platoons will swim at the same time. Twenty Three won't have first use of the lake."

"Thanks, Sarg."

"Right! Now pay attention here! I want your hootchies put up properly. Don't cut any live trees and make certain foul ground markers are used when building your ablution facilities. Do not build anything near old foul ground symbols.

"There is livestock in the area ... just leave them alone. The animals won't bother you! Insect repellent can be obtained at the MIR tent. The messing area is on your maps and exercise instructions will be distributed after lunch!

"As you've read, this will be the last served lunch until lunch on Friday. Five-in-one rations will be issued this afternoon. Remember fellas don't over eat. Throughout our stay, each pair will only be issued with two five-in-one ration packs.

"There might be a little rain on Wednesday, so make certain you construct your hootchies properly. The objective is to keep you and your equipment dry.

"Now, this is a signals exercise, not an Instructors' Basic Training exercise. Most of the time you'll be in this immediate area and you're going to be very busy. Our OC is not too concerned about your dress, however don't get burned, and..."

Bentley paused and smiled. "What's the rule?"

The cadets recited. "Cleanliness is next to Godliness, unless you're in IBT or D&M! Those two components may become diseased, but signals - never!"

The Sergeant laughed with his platoon.

"Not bad! Now remember, every hootchie must be *at least* a hundred yards away from other hootchies. There will be two cadets to a hootchie and you've already arranged yourselves into pairs. Our area is large and we'll be spread throughout.

"Section corporals, carry on with your people! The time is now 1000 hours; we'll be ready for lunch at noon. All radio equipment will be arriving at 1100. Individual pairs will pick up your equipment at that time. Pick-up location is on the map. The OC and our platoon commander will be inspecting the platoon area at 1330. Any questions?"

There were none.

"Okay guys - let's get to it! Remember the lectures you've had on surviving in the field! Your maps will also show you the location of our platoon's first-aid post. Corporals, take 'em away!"

Twenty One Platoon's area covered approximately eight-hundred yards by six-hundred yards. After the *pep-talk*, the junior NCOs split the platoon in half. While one group headed east, the other went west. Half-an-hour later, bivouac areas were prepared, washing stands erected, latrines dug, foot routes and vehicle in and out routes were cleared, and locations for telephone lines and certain command relay units were plotted on maps.

As far as the musketeers were concerned, Wane and Douglas would bivouac at the extreme west of the platoon's southern front line. Bergie and Danyluk built their hootchie at the extreme east of the front line, Rothstein and Cunningham built in the centre at the front, and Lyons and McLeod, erected their hootchie west at the northern extremity - six hundred yards north of Douglas and Wane. East and Jackson set up theirs east at the northern extremity, six hundred yards behind Danyluk and Bergie. Other pairs from the platoon were placed centre rear and spread throughout.

As 21 Platoon went to work, comparable positioning took place in other platoon areas.

At exactly 1100 hours, a siren from the mess-tent indicated the communications equipment had arrived. Individual pairs of cadets from 21 Platoon made many trips with Nineteen sets, batteries, portable radio sets, Tele-L sets, UCL Ten-line switchboards, portable poles, wire, and ground return spikes. Two three-quarter-ton trucks (beeps) moved equipment to the far-flung 23 and 24 Platoons. Cadets from 22 Platoon split and placed in the centre eastern and western boundaries of Glenemma were close enough to carry their equipment.

The company exercise would be conducted by A-set transmission, using voice and Morse, as well as line transmission using voice and Morse. Platoons would use B-set voice and Morse transmission where possible, including line transmission using voice and Morse. Additionally, Company Headquarters would lay line throughout the total area and a relay-Nineteen-set was taken to high ground. It was installed to allow communication with Camp Vernon. Two cadets from each platoon assisted at the Company Headquarters level.

Most of this equipment would be set up in the afternoon, following the OC's inspection after lunch.

When the siren notified the area it was lunchtime, the hungry winding line moved to the loud clinking of mess-tins. Naturally, 21 Platoon's cadets were first in line, followed by 22 Platoon. It took ten minutes for the southern lot to arrive, bitching and dusty because of the *hike*.

While the food was served, not one cadet heard Glenemma's permanent messing sergeant accuse one of his young staff members of stealing a jar of honey.

"Listen Davis, I am organized. I always keep the honey in the same spot ... the place where this Bible is now. You took it, didn't you?"

Cordell Cross

Davis didn't have a clue what the sergeant was talking about. "Took what? What Bible? That Bible wasn't there half-an-hour ago. It's not mine."

"I'm talking about jar of honey."

"Sarg, what the hell would I do with a jar of honey?"

"Then if you didn't take it, who did? Also, whose Bible is this? This is the first time I've seen a Bible in a mess tent. Bloody thieves, that's what we've got around here."

"Remember the time we climbed that mountain?" East asked, digging into his beef stew, mashed potatoes and corn bread. His other mess-tin contained two pieces of chocolate cake.

Danyluk nearly choked. "Don't remind me. My feet haven't been the same since - or my wang."

Speaking with his mouth full, Bergie said, "That's because you put foot powder on your wang, you ignoramus. Do you guys remember that? Because his wang was red raw from bouncing around in his pants, our own *animal* here put foot powder all over it."

"It worked, Bergie! Youse knows that!"

"Don't bullshit us Moose! Sergeant Beckford wondered why you were at the water-trailer every ten minutes with your pants down! Some Westie cadet even said you use your prick like an elephant uses its trunk!"

Food shot out of Danyluk's mouth as he laughed with the rest. He remembered the incident very well.

"Well, I thought it would do the job. How did I know it would burn?"

After flicking a yellow jacket out of his stew, Bergie said, "It did the job all right. I had to listen to your complaining all night long. People in our area must have thought we were a couple of weirdoes. 'Bergie, my wang's on fire! Bergie, I smell like a ton of shit!' It's no wonder those two Lord Strathcona cadets moved their hootchie in the middle of the night. One of 'em said, 'I can't take this anymore. That BCR man and wife team never let up. Christ, how they got in the service, I'll never know?'"

"I was complaining because my shitter chair broke, you pongo! You're the one that cut it!"

While Moose and Bergie *entertained the troops*, Douglas washed and rinsed out his mess-tins and utensils, strolled over to a nearby tree, sat down, leaned back and read his letter from home.

Dear Doug:

I received your last letter and I'm really happy you're having a fine time on the course, even though you can boil eggs on the ground. It's nearly that hot here, but the radio says we're in for a little rain.

The way you describe Charlie Stevenson and his farm reminds me so much of the farm we stayed on for ten days after we arrived from England. I think maybe all farm people are that friendly. They stay away from the hustle and bustle of city life and don't have to put on any sort of a front. Lord knows, if I didn't dust and clean this house twice a week it would get filthy from the smoke and grime coming in from outside. Perhaps we should have stayed in Whonnock, I don't

Cordell Cross

know? I do know that I had your education to worry about, and the both of us just weren't ready to accept that way of life. Then again, you might have, but I couldn't.

A letter came from England a few days ago. Norman, Joan and Raymond are fine. My how your nephew Raymond has grown since the last picture they sent. Your brother borrowed or rented a car and they spent a few days in Blackpool and had a wonderful stay. I've saved their letter for you to read.

I think I told you the time I took you to Blackpool during the war when you were a baby. We stayed with a friend of mine with a daughter your age and they lived in a flat near a large lake. One day when the four of us were on the roof sunning ourselves (the two of you were in your prams, and she and I were hanging laundry) a plane came over. It sounded like one of ours so we waved and waved. When it turned out to be German, we panicked, but we had no need to worry. Although the pilot could have dropped his bombs on us, he didn't. He dropped them in the lake, turned, flew low over our building, dipped his wings and left. He had seen us wave, and in his own way, he waved back. I know you're still not fussy about Germans, but remember there are good and bad in all nationalities. That pilot must have had a family and understood the senselessness of war ... thank God. Do you remember me telling you that story?

I know I'm repeating myself, but it's quiet here without you. I'm not saying I enjoy the loud songs on your radio, or miss having to nag at you to clean up your room. It's just not the same when you're away for such a long period. I believe Colonel the dog and Mickey the cat feel the same way. Mickey brought home a mouse yesterday and although I hate mice, after I used the broom, he dropped it and I put it outside. Shortly, it took off back to its home where ever that is. I hope it's not under the house.

Well, son, it's my day off and although I'm a little tired, I think I'll go shopping. I've enclosed three dollars for you to buy some of that delicious KiK Kola you keep mentioning. It's so hot here I think I may just buy a bottle myself, just to see what it's like.

Please give my love to Wane and Diane and try to stay out of trouble. I think I know what it's like when a thousand boys get together.

I'll write again next week. All my love ... Mam. XXXX

"A letter from your mom?" Wane asked, sitting down next to Douglas.

Brice gave Wane a small smile, smacked him on his right knee, returned the letter to its envelope and put it in his back pants pocket.

"Yeah. I also got three-dollars to buy KiK Kola. I wonder if the pop truck's gonna come out here?"

Wane shrugged. "Dunno. Bergie doesn't want it to show. He doesn't have the money to buy all that pop and a Fudgicle for Moose. How are things in Vancouver?"

"Pretty good, I guess. My mom sends her love. She also mentioned something that happened during the war, and..."

Over the next few minutes, Douglas repeated the story his mother had told him. After he finished, both boys were quiet until Wane eventually spoke.

"You normally don't hear of those things happening. I mean the odds are probably one-in-a-million. He must have been a pretty decent guy, but ... but just look at what those bastards did. We've both read Rothie's books and seen it in newsreels. Humans didn't run that country or those camps - monsters did. Bullies and brutes, every one of them. My dad says, 'Steel doesn't absorb tears.'"

More silence followed before Brice replied, "Your dad's right. I told Rothie the world could never shed enough tears for what happened. I still can't understand it. Where were the protests? The so-called leaders of what was left of the free world must have known what was going on. We learned at school that Hitler in his book warned the world what he was going to do. Wane, that just took place yesterday when we were in diapers. The slaughter only stopped nine years ago."

Both stood up and started walking back to their hootchie. "Nobody cared, Doug. You and I have discussed religion. As long as it's around, the same thing can happen again. I was Christened a Protestant. What the hell's a Protestant? I believe in the same God as the Jews and the Catholics, and if I'm not wrong, all other religions believe in the same God. My dad says they're just different clubs, and every club wants to be the big one. That way there's more money."

Douglas chuckled. "You mean it's my club or no club?"

Wane was really into it now, and he wasn't about to drop it. "Exactly! That son-of-a-bitch Hitler was a Catholic. I don't know, but do ya think the Pope told him to stop the slaughter?"

"I haven't got a clue, Wane, I..."

Douglas stopped speaking and thought for a moment. "I hope he did. All religious leaders should have. Not just religious leaders - everyone. But, for some reason I don't think the brass of countries or religions cared that much. I've spoken with Rothie ... Jews have been the whipping boy from day one. During the war, they just never had their own main country to speak up for them. Oh, sure, they're British, Canadian, American, and Russian ... pick a country and it's got Jewish citizens. But in all of those countries' most accepted *clubs* ain't Jewish. When their club had its own country, the Egyptians or the Romans enslaved the people, or whoever had the biggest army did. Although there are Jews all over the world, they didn't belong to ... as you put it, the *big one*."

"Until now, eh?" Wane asked.

Douglas grinned and put his left arm around his buddy's shoulders. "Let's go have a wash. Their club's strong now, and they have their own homeland back. But look at the damned mess going on over there. Wouldn't it be wonderful if the people of the world could unite like the cadets in our company? We've got Protestants, Sikhs, Jews, Muslims, Catholics, atheists ... you name it, and..."

Wane couldn't resist. "...and Cunningham's Beggars of..."

"Haaa, them too. And guess what? Other than Cunningham's *Beggars*, we all respect one another as human beings and race and religion's got nothing to do with it. Remember...?"

Wane said, "Remember," at the same time as Douglas did. He interrupted further. "Doug, I know what you were gonna say. You were gonna say, 'Remember what Sergeant Beckford said last year. 'If someone's gonna kill ya, and a person comes to your rescue, do you say, 'Thanks, but before you help, what religion or race are ya?' Or if you're sick or injured with only minutes to live, do you say to the doctor, 'Uh, thanks, but what religion or race are ya?'"

Douglas nodded. "And what did Beckford say after that?"

The words, "Not bloody likely!" yelled by both boys, echoed around the area.

Cordell Cross

When they arrived back at their hootchie, Wane threw himself on his blankets. "Adults can be pretty dumb, eh? Say, how the hell did we get on this subject?"

"The German pilot," replied Douglas. "Maybe we should have interesting conversations like this more often. It beats listenin' to Danyluk's letters."

A wide grin came over Wane's face. "Speaking of Danyluk, do you remember how he filled in that personal questionnaire? For *race* he wrote down, 'Sometimes, but I'm not as fast as I used to be. I like the mile, but I prefer the 440.' For *religion* he wrote, 'If I can persuade the girl, then I'm of *her* persuasion.'"

Hilarious laughs filled their hootchie, and then Douglas said, "He does that on all questionnaires. When he got to *Mother's name*, he wrote, 'Mom.' For *Father's name*, he put down, 'Dad.' For *sex*, I think he said, 'Love it, when it's free.'"

Wane took a letter out of his pocket. "What a guy. By the way, if you think Moose's letters are steamy. Get a load of this one I just received from Marigold. It starts, *My Darling Wane: I miss...*"

Ten minutes later more insane laughter came from the lone hootchie.

Meanwhile at a UCL Ten-line switchboard station somewhere within the centre bounds of Glenemma, two Chaplain Corps cadets also chuckled to themselves.

"Quit worrying, Paul. We didn't steal the honey ... we simply exchanged something for it. The Bible we left cost more than this product, so that's not stealing."

Mark's reasoning comforted Paul. "Perhaps you're right. It will also do them more good than honey. Okay, let's sit down over our plan one more time."

After the Officer Commanding completed his inspection, the cadets of Signals Company still had their work cut out for them setting up for the communications exercises that would last most of the week.

As Glenemma was being criss-crossed with wires and poles, numerous pairs of cadets sat in their hootchies studying codes, deciphering material and procedural instructions.

This exercise didn't last eight or twelve hours a day, it would last twenty-four hours a day, every day, starting at 2359 this night.

Although the enemy (Evil Force Mobile = EFM) was imaginary, precise instructions detailed the (Friendly Force = FF) response for EFM's every move, and EFM did indeed emit radio signals which were monitored.

A great amount of planning at the regular force level had gone into the exercise and regular force instructors scrutinizing the airwaves and lines demanded skilled cadet proficiency.

That afternoon at 1830 hours, UCL Ten-line switchboards, Tele-L sets, and Nineteen sets went into action for a test. Earlier, after a selected supper from their five-in-one rations, both Douglas and Wane had a one hour snooze.

Wane had the headset on and was reading a comic when a message came across. It was a B-set transmission, sent after tuning and netting calls. "All stations one; puddle and nix; I say again, puddle and nix, out!"

Wane wrote down *puddle and nix* on his message pad and passed it to Douglas who looked it up.

Cordell Cross

"Puddle - we're to report to grid reference 650349 in fifteen minutes for a swim parade! Nix - everything is to be switched off! Wane you old pongo, we're goin' for a swim!"

Over the next fifteen minutes cadets in all forms of dress emerged from every nook and cranny in Glenemma, heading for their own platoon's checkpoint. Except for different grid references, the four platoons had received exactly the same message.

The two platoons close to Round Lake were already there when 21 and 22 Platoons arrived. The small lake appeared as a beautiful blue oasis beckoning those who desired its wondrously laid open delight.

Not a ripple was exposed on the appealing water. Water that could wash away the layers of sweaty dust and dirt accrued under the day's merciless sun. Soon, the lake's cool liquid would agitate and surge, obliterating the mesmerising mirrored representation habitually capturing the reflections of angelic pale-green pastel likenesses of the nearby rolling hills.

When the company was complete, Major Hansford gave the normal safety speech. The buddy-system would be used; fifty-feet out was the maximum they could swim, and towels and footwear would be lined-up, indicating to the staff that someone was missing if the items were left unattended.

With instructors tasked as lifeguards, four platoons of screaming eager boys ran into Round Lake. Their dress remained mixed. Half were unclothed; others were fully dressed except for boots, and still others were only partly dressed. One totally-bare cadet just wore his pith-helmet to keep the sun off his face. Some, when they thought their clothes were washed, took them off and laid them out to dry. Seconds later, buff bare, they slap dashed back to *paradise*.

Swimming, splashing, diving, and jumping off shoulders, tossing, horse-back fighting, and mud-flinging ensued over the next hour. As well, boisterous vocal endorsements accompanied this much-appreciated physical activity.

At 2000 hours, refreshed and ready to tackle the world, the cadets headed toward their platoon areas. Each of them welcomed the break and they thanked their staff for the respite.

With Hank Williams' *Your Cheatin' Heart*, blaring from Danyluk's portable radio, the walk back allowed the cadets of 21 Platoon to chat with friends they hadn't seen since lunch.

"Me and Bergie are splittin' up the night shift," Moose told the others. "Startin' at 2359 we're workin' in three-hour intervals. It gives each of us a chance to get some sleep."

The remaining musketeers had basically arrived at the same schedule, except Lyons and McLeod. Lyons had suggested that night and day shifts should remain the same, which meant McLeod would be permanently on nights. Lyons would work during the day while his partner was sleeping.

"I might look dumb, but I ain't continually workin' the night shift," offered McLeod. "If you want to work it that way, I'll take two nights and you take two nights."

Lyons finally agreed, but not before murmuring, "Seaforth creep," under his breath.

McLeod heard him and mumbled, "BCR pongo."

"How far is your nearest shitter?" East asked Cunningham silently sitting and fingering a two-headed coin.

The *gambler* had remained constantly upset because the various pair-locations discouraged any gambling.

"We've got three in our area," East continued.

"We've all got three," replied Cunningham. "That's the way this thing was planned. Shitters are spaced evenly between stations. Why do you ask?"

"East's response got Wane and Douglas slyly winking at each other. "Because I sure as hell don't want *Mort* disturbin' me when I'm takin' a dump."

Rothstein laughed. "Mort ain't gonna bother *you*. He doesn't have a gas-mask."

"Oh yes he does," Wane whispered to Douglas.

Douglas chuckled quietly and whispered back, "Did you bring the sheet?"

"Two of 'em," Wane replied, before hearing a particular tune on Danyluk's radio. "Moose, turn up that song, please! Rosemary Clooney's singin' *Hey There*."

After the sun retired, a billion stars filled the sky and daytime scents normally burnt upon release gained strength and managed to waft through the region on a soft warm breeze. To the boys, the perfume of evergreens, mountain blossoms, and nearby farmers' new-cut hay united with air as pure as the "Maker," could create it.

Throughout Glenemma, pairs of cadets discussed the upcoming exercise, life at home, their schools, cadet corps, girls, movies, records, books, dress-styles, the universe, and their future. The ease of Glenemma even helped homesick cadets that were too ashamed to let it show. It comforted all the cadets because it was a break from the routine of the camp's methodical procedures. Something that would go unappreciated until the boys were older, then they would look back on it all.

At 2359, silence broke like the resounding noise of a tree cracking open in the frozen north. The humming of Nineteen sets, ringing of Tele-L sets, and crackling of UCL Ten-line switchboards joined the vocal and Morse messages being sent to every portion of Glenemma.

While Wane slept, Douglas operated their Nineteen set, deciphered messages and passed along important information.

"One-Four Alpha, message over." the voice called.

Brice pressed the pressel-switch. "One-Four Alpha, send your message, over."

"One-Four Alpha, relay to One-Three Alpha, move puppy to green now, over."

Brice continued. "One-Four Alpha, move puppy to green now - Wilco, out to you; One-Four Alpha for One-Three Alpha, message over."

"One-Three Alpha, send your message over."

"One-Four Alpha, relay from One, move puppy to green now, over."

"One-Three Alpha (pause) move puppy to green now. Roger. Relay to One, puppy (pause) has seen fleas, over."

Although unnecessary, Douglas checked his book. He knew what was happening. "Roger One-Three Alpha, puppy has seen fleas; Wilco, out to you; One-Four Alpha, message over."

"One-Four Alpha, send your message, over."

"One-Four Alpha, relay from One-Three Alpha reads, puppy has seen fleas, over."

The voice from Douglas' headset was blunt. "Roger One-Four Alpha, puppy has seen fleas, out."

Sixty seconds later, Douglas Tele-L set rang. "Cowline," was all he said after picking up the receiver.

The cadet's voice on the other end was serious. "Cowline, this is Paintbrush … Angle Softly, out."

'Angle' in another book meant a flick mechanism move to the company net for one transmission. 'Softly' meant *lice* (platoon of EFM) at grid reference 987564.

He made the switch and was fortunate he only had to wait a few minutes until the air was clear. "One-Four Alpha, over."

"One-Four Alpha, send your message, over."

"One-Four Alpha, lice at 987564, over." (nin-er, eight, sev-en, etc.)

"One-Four Alpha, Roger lice at 987564, out."

Douglas switched back to his platoon net; checked page ten of a book, then wound the small *hand-crank* on his Tele-L set and picked up the receiver. The voice said, "Switchboard. Who do you need, Cowline?"

"Paintbrush, please."

It took a few seconds until a second voice said, "Paintbrush."

"Paintbrush, this is Cowline. Angle Softly message passed, out."

As the night wore on, messages that were more complicated got passed along and there wasn't time for cadets to sleep on the job. Signal Office Duties meant logs had to be kept up and carbon copies of all messages filed. The area buzzed with muffled voices and Morse. Fortunately, Douglas had to use Morse only once and he had to slow down his transmission because whoever was at the other end hadn't mastered any sort of speed.

Twice during his three-hour shift, he woke up Wane to deliver hand-written messages to nearby stations and platoon headquarters. When Wane returned the second time, he said he got lost twice. "It's pitch-black out there, and I nearly ended up in a shitter. When I saw this shape about fifty yards away, I put on a female voice and said, 'Halt, who goes there?' I did it just for fun, but Doug, do you know what the reply was? Do ya? He said, 'Is that youse, Mort? Are youse lookin' for your chicken? Jeez, Mort, er, buddy, friend, you've made me pee myself. Cripes, I'm gettin' out o' here. Er, see ya, er Mort, or whatever your name is.'"

Douglas kept tapping out a Morse message, but roared laughing with Wane, who crawled back under his nice warm blankets.

"Doug, if he hadda been taking a crap, he would have fallen in."

At 0300, Wane relieved Douglas and was just as busy. Twice between 3am and 6am Wane sent Douglas with hand-written messages. One to platoon headquarters and the other to company headquarters. It was while he was at company headquarters, Brice had the opportunity to have a coffee and see the large map showing friendly and enemy troop movements. Four cadets plotted the programmed progression of both forces, as well, six cadets operated the various

Nineteen-sets, Tele-L sets and the UCL Ten-line switchboard. Two platoon lieutenants sat at folding six-foot tables, writing and receiving various messages before directing the plotters. With messengers coming and going every two minutes and communications in full swing, cadets were far too busy to sit around.

At 0600 there was a short break, which allowed the cadets to make breakfast. Even then some work had to be done, so while Wane cooked, Douglas took care of the communications.

At the two *Bible-thumpers* hootchie, a map had been drawn indicating the precise locations of MacKay, Neish, Sterling, and Scott. This knowledge was gained when each cadet visited platoon headquarters with messages. A glance at the posted chart revealed the names and grid references of various stations, and they accurately memorized the information.

After glancing at the map, Mark passed it to Paul. "They're in pairs which will make it easier for us. Sterling's with Scott, so I'll get the one who's off duty during the first shift tonight. You handle either MacKay or Neish ... whichever one isn't working from 0300 to 0600, okay?"

Paul checked the destination on the map and grinned. "Corinthians 1-15 ... But he that is spiritual judgeth all things, yet he himself is judged of no man. How true, eh Mark?"

Mark winked, nodded, and exposed his ear to ear smile.

"The land of milk and honey is about to share some of the Lord's blessings with those who would become His servants after receiving their baptism. Henceforth the servants' bodies shall become the partaker of milk, honey, and *bugs*. Light on the milk, even on the honey, and particularly heavy on the bugs."

Shortly, both boys' stomachs were sore from laughing.

At the same time as the Chaplain Corps cadets made their plans, two corporals sat in their tent doing exactly the same thing.

"Chris, we've got to get those little bastards that set us up. I was embarrassed as hell when I woke and found a cadet in my bed."

"George, you weren't the only one who was embarrassed? At the Junior Ranks Club, Dave Castle looked at his watch and said, 'It's nearly time for bed, Chris - who's your cadet partner tonight?' I almost thumped him out. I would have if the PMC (President of the Mess Committee) hadn't been there. That idiot Castle is so typical of the Postal Corps' breed. Their sense of humour is sick."

George went into deep thought and a few moments later his face indicated he'd arrived at a conclusion. "Chris, have you ever heard of exercise, Animal Husbandry One?"

Chris's face lit up. "Have I? You bet I have. I was in Korea too, ya know? But there's six little buggers to take care of ... we'll need assistance."

"George stood up and poured himself a coffee. " Don't worry; some of the other guys will give us a hand. We'll talk to them this afternoon, okay?"

"You bet we will," Chris replied. "Uh huh, right on. Animal Husbandry Two will do the trick just fine."

Chapter 19

The cadets of Signals Company remained busy all day Tuesday at Glenemma. Totally engrossed in their work, there wasn't any time to talk when they passed each other delivering messages.

The previous night's experience, however, never left Moose's mind. "I'm tellin' youse I didn't see him, but I heard him. Bergie, it was Mort - I guarantee it was Mort. His voice had a hollow high-pitched sound to it. He said, 'Halt! Whoa... youse mare.'"

Bergie kept cooking their bacon. "What? Whoa, youse mare? Come off it, Moose - Mort wouldn't talk like you. Also, if he runs a ghost stagecoach, he must have more than one mare."

"Bergie I don't care what youse believes. I couldn't get my wang back in my pants fast enough. I pissed myself, and I ain't goin' to the shitter alone again at night."

"Well I ain't joinin' ya, that's for sure. Oh, quit being a chicken-shit, Moose. That stuff about Mort is just pure crap. Go get us some water from the water-trailer."

Sleeping on and off during the day, Douglas and Wane reversed their shifts that night. Wane took the midnight until 0300 shift and prayed a message wouldn't have to be hand delivered. If one did, it would be late because Douglas was making his *rounds* with a bed sheet. Rounds that *just by chance* took him first near Jack East's station, where Jack was on duty.

East sat eating an apple and tapping out a Morse code message; the lantern near him was *alive* with flying insects attracted by the light.

Standing thirty feet away behind the lantern, Douglas wrapped himself in the sheet and moaned in a high-pitched voice, "Aaghhh-eeeeaaast!" before quickly moving behind a tree.

That's all it took. Jack had glanced up in time to see the white *apparition* and the resulting uproarious and quite extraordinary *fart of fright* was enough to wake Jackson from a deep sleep. It was one of Jack's best.

Coughing and gasping, Jackson said, "Jesus, what the hell's happening? Jack, are you tryin' to kill me? My God, the trees, grass, and birds around us will be dead tomorrow."

East stood, holding the seat of his pants. "Ja, Jackson ... I just saw M... Mort. He call, call, called my na, name."

Dressed only in his undershorts, Earl timidly kept his voice low. "Where?"

Another *imposing* release of anal air followed. "Over th... there."

Earl couldn't see beyond the *living* lantern. "I don't see anything. What did he say?"

Jack had turned white. "I ... I think I'm gonna shit myself."

A puzzled look appeared on Earl's face. "Mort said that? He thought he was going to shit himself?"

"No, I ... I think I'm gonna shit myself."

"You're what? Jack, get to the shitter and..."

Earl didn't have time to say anything else, they were being called on their Nineteen set and their Tele-L set. While Jack stood there holding his rear, Earl had to go to work.

Douglas didn't stay around. He moved close to Bergie and Danyluk's hootchie next and the conversation he overheard nearly had him rolling on the ground. The *bizarre couple* were bitching at each other once more.

"Moose, I don't want to hear about it. Put the damned thing in your pants and go scratch somewhere else. Don't mention it again. Have you got that? I'm busy here."

"You're heartless, Bergie. What if it hadda happened to youse?"

Bergie pressed the pressel switch. "Roger, One-Seven Alpha, out!" He then released the switch. "Moose, it wouldn't happen to me. These Goddamned things always seem to happen to you. How could a mosquito crawl up my foreskin and bite me; I don't have a foreskin, and besides, I wear gaunch. Christ, it's a wonder every mosquito in Glenemma is not up your foreskin; there's enough room for them. Quit complaining, will ya?"

"If youse had got bit on the end of your knob, I'd show some sympathy."

Bergie took off his headset. "What the hell do you want me to do ... find the bitch and swat her? All right, all right, I'm gonna show you some sympathy." He cranked and picked up the Tele-L set. "First aid station, please. (pause) Hello, first aid station ... Listen, a mosquito just bit my buddy here. What should he do? Yeah, I know, but that's gonna be difficult. Why? Because the bite's on the end of his wang, that's why! Listen, same to you fella! Hello ... hello!"

A scratching Moose asked, "What did they say?"

Bergie replaced his headset. "In your case their suggestion makes sense. They said, 'incise the swelling and suck out the poison.' When I told them where the bite was, they thought I was joking and told me to 'eff off.' Listen, Moose, do what you did last year when you put foot powder on your wang. Go to the water trailer and let the cold water run on it for awhile. That should ease the itch. There, I've been sympathetic. Now, get out of my life, I'm busy."

Moose took Bergie's advice and found the water-trailer. Because of his experience the night before he wasn't happy about being alone under the moon, but when he took off his pants, the water felt great. Shortly, he started singing low.

"There are lice, lice, as big as any mice; In the stores, in the stores.

"There are lice, lice, as big as any mice; In the Quartermaster's stores.

"My eyes are dim, I cannot see; I have not got my specs with me.

"I have, not, got, miyiyiyiyi ... "

Moose stopped singing because he thought he saw a white object moving towards him from about thirty yards away. The form was between Danyluk and his hootchie.

"Er, is, is that youse ... Bergie?"

"Aaaaaghhh! Mooooooose," came the reply.

A pair of KD long-pants, a pair of undershorts, and a running water-tap was the only evidence that Moose Danyluk had visited the water-trailer. His feet couldn't move fast enough as he hightailed it in the opposite direction, totally lost in the darkness of Glenemma, wearing only a shirt, socks and running shoes.

Shortly, Moose's voice echoed in the night.

"Can anyone help! I don't know who youse are, but I've fallen in your shitter! Son-of-a-bitch ... Bergie, where the hell are youse! I can't stand this itch, now I'm covered in shit! Help me, somebody!"

"Is that you, Moose?" a nearby voice called, getting closer.

Danyluk recognized the sound of his friend. "East, old pard, you're a blessing in disguise. Help me out please?"

East laid down his pants, undershorts and shirt, and helped Danyluk get out of the *trench*.

"Where are your pants? Jeez, you musta landed head first?"

Although Moose was *caked*, he could see. "Don't worry about me; where the hell are *your* clothes. How come you're only wearin' boots and a beret?"

"I shit myself," came the honest reply. "That fella, Mort, visited me."

The name, Mort, nearly started Danyluk running again.

"He visited me, too. That ghost must be everywhere."

East picked up his bundle of clothes. "Well, there's strength in numbers; let's get to the water-trailer and wash up. You smell horrible."

"Youse is not exactly sweet-smelling yourself. Bergie, ain't gonna believe this." Danyluk then stopped in his tracks and thought for a moment. "Yeah, on second thought, he will."

When morning came, only two cadets were at the company's first-aid station. It appeared Neish and Scott had been eaten alive. Both boys' bodies had lumps galore but dust, dirt, and loose ground material stuck to their skin from head to toe made it difficult for the regular force medical corporal to remedy the situation. He couldn't believe they were human beings.

The NCO tried to understand what had gone on. "Let me get this straight. The two of you live in separate hootchies, yet you both have the same ailments? How the hell is that possible?"

Naked, Neish had difficulty speaking. A honey-loving bug had bitten his lower lip, and that part of his *kisser* had swollen three times its size.

"My buddy here thinks it's just a coincidence ... that it's tree sap. But I ain't near a tree. When I woke up I had honey and insects all over me.

The NCO took a bottle of alcohol and some cotton-wool from a drawer and started working on Neish's face. "What where you wearing when you went to bed?"

"Just my shorts."

"Well, how the hell did you get honey all over you and down your shorts?"

"Dunno, Corporal," Neish replied, his right eyelid swelling by the second. The insides of my blankets were covered in honey this morning.

The Corporal didn't quite know how to tackle the situation. He had no hot water, and the two bodies in front of him had to be cleansed.

"Right! We have to start somewhere. Here are two bars of special soap. I want you both to use the field showers set up behind this tent. Get in there and scrub yourselves as you've never scrubbed before. Use lots of this shampoo on your heads. I don't think your scalps are ever going to be normal again. They appear like you've dunked your heads in molasses."

"But, Corporal, ain't that cold water out back?" Scott asked.

"Yes it's cold water. What do you think this is, the Ritz? Get outta here!"

For the next thirty minutes Scott and Neish scrubbed, scrubbed and scrubbed some more. When they emerged and faced the corporal again they at least resembled something human. Although their hair was still matted in thick gooey knots, the soap and shampoo had started the cleansing job. The rest was up to the corporal with his alcohol. This took one hour per lad, and needless to say, at the end of the process, they faced one unhappy NCO with aching arms. Afterwards, a Medical Corps Sergeant administered a couple of needle shots before sending the boys back to duty.

A furious corporal faced them prior to leaving. "I don't know how you managed to do this to yourselves, but I don't want to see you again. Also, if you didn't do it, and you find out who did ... send him or them to me. Now, get out of here."

Before separating at the junction to their individual lines, Neish scratched his crotch and asked, "Do you think we'll ever find out who the rotten pricks are?"

Scott thought for a second while he scratched his ass.

"Could be MacKay and Sterling? They were the only ones around when we were sleeping."

A discussion followed and by the time they had finished, both boys were red-raw from scratching. Also, Neish's face looked like he'd taken on the world's heavyweight boxing champion and lost. Not only was his right eyelid closed, his upper lip swelled to match the size of his lower lip. They ruled out the implication of their buddies and decided to keep their ears and eyes open, if the bug-bites allowed it.

Scott winced from scratching so much. Although his face wasn't as bad as Neish's, the lumps on his body made up for it.

"My nuts feel like I put 'em in an anthill for an hour to two. They've got so many bites on them, I may never be able to have kids."

Neish tried to smile, but that action his face hurt.

"Mine feel the same way, only worse. It's as though I put them in the anthill, and forgot about 'em. Kids? The way I look, no dame will ever go out with me. If I kissed a broad, my lips would swallow her face. Some rotten ayrab's gonna pay for this. See ya."

"Yeah, see ya. Keep your pecker up," MacKay replied.

Neish turned, saying, "I won't know if it's up or down ... I can't feel it."

While the Scots cried the blues, loud chuckling took place in Wane and Douglas' hootchie. Both boys delighted in the never-ending saga of East and Danyluk. Neither of them had slept much because Douglas kept telling his friend the story. In addition, Wane was ready for phase two. After cutting out the likeness of a large hand and two colossal feet from pieces of a cardboard box, he walked a fair distance and had come back with a long branch of a dead tree. Two full sheets were bundled and wrapped around one extremity of the pole, which now resembled a boxing glove on the end of a large stick. The cardboard hand was then firmly tied on with string.

"I don't care if it's East, Danyluk, Bergie or Jackson. I'll wait at the back of the shitter until one of them arrives, then it's game over. He won't see Mort, but he'll sure feel his hand and see the print. I'm gonna dip this thing in the shitter before I use it. Afterwards when they check the area, they'll find his footprints."

Although Douglas had earphones on, both cadets rolled around on their blankets laughing away. If double-bunks had been present, the person up top would have gone for a *ride*.

At eight o'clock that Wednesday morning, it started to rain lightly, then the Heavens opened up and never quit. The rain was warm, so ponchos didn't have to be taken off hootchies to wear. Cadets walked around in shirts or without them. Although mosquitoes came *indoors* to get out of the rain, at least the dust had cleared and the endless heat from the huge furnace in the daytime sky subsided considerably.

The rain didn't stop the exercise though. Messages continued throughout the day, but slowed down when it was time for pairs to acquire new rations. Additionally, two platoons of (FF) IBT arrived and set up observation posts and listening posts around the area. An additional two platoons of IBT acted as the enemy (EFM) and tried to infiltrate the lines. Both the FF and EFM had .303 rifles and used blank rounds. For night operations, they used Very (flare) pistols.

Special sections were set up to intercept EFM messages and relay the information to platoon and company headquarters.

The rain still pounded when it got dark and training activity increased. All messages were now sent in Morse and because some teams had allowed their Nineteen sets to get wet and short out, line crews laid more line and the relaying of foot messages for those without Tele-L sets became more important. This in itself created a problem because the IBT cadets had set up tripwire and dug small E, L, Y, and inverted-L troop trenches. Although all FF were apprised of tripwire and trench locations, it never failed that certain cadets got *tripped up*.

It was difficult for Wane to get away that night, but he did. He'd studied the locations of both observation and listening posts and made his way around them masterfully considering it was pouring and there was no moonlight whatsoever. Twice he had to hide from grease-painted FF patrols until he found Bergie and Danyluk's *ablution trench*. He then strapped on his cardboard feet, *dipped* Mort's cardboard hand, and waited.

This was a difficult time for Wane. He'd smeared wet mud on his face, arms and hands and he got drenched to the skin while waiting. In the meantime, the night rain turned cold as he lingered for some *activity*, shivering.

That action took two hours to occur, and as fate would have it, the visitors weren't Bergie or Danyluk. Instead, a couple of IBT types had decided they couldn't hold it any longer.

"This is it. Although it stinks like hell, that Moose fella was right. He did build himself a padded throne," said one IBT cadet as he put his rifle down, dropped his pants and shorts, lifted up the back of his shirt and sat down on Danyluk's *special chair* with a hole in it.

The other cadet pushed down his pants and shorts and sat next to his friend, wiggling his rear-end over Bergie's *log*. "Ya got a smoke, Ernie?"

"Biggar, you know I don't smoke, and besides, we've been told not to, even in this weather. What do you think of those two signals types anyway?"

Ernie thought for a moment while relieving himself. "That Bergie character's not bad, but his buddy, Moose, looks and acts like a half-wit. He's always scratchin' his rod. Are all Irish like him?"

"How do you know he's in the Irish?"

"He told me, and ... What the...? Oh, my God, what happened? Christ almighty ... I'm covered in shit! Ernie you rotten prick! What did you grab me for? I'm covered in it!"

Biggar wiped his face with both hands. "Don't blame me you pongo ... You pushed me in! I can't believe this! It's in my ears, up my nose ... You asshole!"

As the two IBT cadets accused each other of who did what to whom, Moose heard the yelling and came running.

"Hey, what's the problem youse guys? Keep your voices down, we've got enemy around here."

"This asshole pushed me in," Biggar yelled before retching.

"It wasn't me, you pongo! Hey, Buffalo, give us a hand out of here will ya! Phew!"

Moose picked up a branch. "The name's Moose, and I ain't grabbin' your shitty hand. Here, take hold of the end of this and I'll ... Heeeellllllppp ... Who pushed? Son-of-a-bitch! Hey Bergie! Bergie, I'm in the shitter again! Did youse pull me in you creep? No, you couldn't have, I felt myself being pushed! Bergie!"

In spite of the fact that Bergie was busier than hell, he came to the rescue. He'd heard the *conversation* from his hootchie and when he arrived and found the trio, he couldn't stop laughing. Bergie knew Moose hadn't created the problem, but somehow he knew Moose would become involved in it. Moreover, for that matter, covered in it.

"That's the first time I've seen three in one shitter. You IBT slobs can't blame us because we were..."

Bergie never had the chance to finish because after a *slight tap*, he landed face down next to Moose. As a matter of fact, Danyluk had to help him back to his feet.

During the commotion, Wane left.

"Son-of-a-bitch Bergie, youse was supposed to help us, not join us!"

A fuming and *coated* Bergie screamed, "I was pushed, damn it! Bloody hell, why am I always in shit ... literally in shit, when you're around?"

It took awhile for Moose to get a footing to crawl out. The banks of the latrine were wet, *muddy* and slippery. When he was clear, he helped the others escape the "pit of shit," as Bergie called it.

"How the hell could I push youse, I was already in there? That's the second shitter I've been in this week. I'm thinkin' about movin' in one permanently."

Cordell Cross

Bergie spotted the handprint on Moose's back. The same large marking appeared on Biggar and Ernie's backs. "Moose, take a look at my back - does it have a big handprint on it?"

"Youse has got one all right, and it's massive."

The unbeliever was now a convert. "Wow ... who or what would have a hand that size?"

Even though he was soaked to the skin, Danyluk took off his shirt to see the impression. "There's no one around so it must have been Mort."

Shortly, the four went and searched the area where Mort must have been when he pushed them. Danyluk couldn't believe his eyes. "Bergie, just look at the size of these foot prints. Mort's a son-of-a-bitchin' giant."

Biggar made a fist with his right hand. "I don't give a damn how big he is. Where's this Mort asshole? ... Give him to me."

"Youse wouldn't want him, he's a ghost, and..."

One-Seven Alpha was called and called to no avail. When a messenger was sent, he reported back that the post had been abandoned. In effect, that's exactly what had happened. Regardless of messages or the lack of One-Seven Alpha's contribution to the exercise, they had to clean themselves up. That objective became complicated, however because enroute to the water trailer, the four were taken prisoner.

An EFM cadet wiped each of his fingers on his wet poncho after frisking a smiling Danyluk.

"What the...? I have shit all over my hands and all I did was try and search him! The others are just as bad!"

Moose grinned. "Youse can try my other pockets if you want?"

The enemy cadet's face became all ill looking. "Get away from me you filthy warped signals abortion! Hey Sarg, these creeps have actually smeared shit on themselves so we can't frisk them! That ain't in the rule-books!"

The cadet sergeant kept his distance. The stench was getting worse and was just too repulsive.

"You four can take off. We didn't see ya, and we don't want to see ya again. Have you got that? If you people go to this extent to win, then we've lost, that's for sure."

After being released, Bergie decided they would have to go to the lake. If they didn't, it would take two fully loaded water-trailers to get their clothes and bodies clean. On the way they passed OPs, LPs, FF patrols, as well as signals stations. The retching and gagging of those they met became part of the picture.

"We're FF," Moose replied when asked to halt.

"We don't give a damn what you are, just keep your distance and keep movin'," was the standard reply. "We can smell ya from here. The new meaning of FF is *effing frightful.*"

The rain picked up as the *frightful* types neared Round Lake and trekked around the back of a two-man signals hootchie with its flaps closed. The busy cadets inside didn't see them, but they sure smelled them.

Cordell Cross

"Roger, One-Four Charlie, out! Phew ... did you take a crap in our hootchie, you creep?"

"No, but by the aroma, you have, ya sneaky little pongo. A tiny bit of rain shouldn't bother you. Get out and head for the shitter, ya lazy asshole."

"Don't call me a lazy asshole, the stench is comin' from you, you creep."

"Hey, it's comin' in from outside. Maybe an enemy patrol came by?"

"Nah, it was probably an officer. One-Four Delta, this is One-Four Charlie, send your message in Morse, over."

"What the hell - you two again? And four more just like you? Is this a joke, or are you people trying to create some sort of record to get on sick parade? Jesus, Tom, come and take a gander at these poor creeps!"

Standing in front of the two medical orderlies were six cadets of the Scottish persuasion. Although all their bodies were covered in molasses and feathers, two of them, MacKay and Sterling, appeared as though they had seen twice the *action*. A layer of honey, bugs and grit lay beneath the insides of pillowcases covering their heads.

The Chaplain Corps cadets had done their thing with the honey, not knowing that shortly afterward six corporals would surprise the Scots from behind, covering the boys' heads with pillow cases. The rest was history as the corporals spread molasses and the wind distributed the wet feathers. Each set of *victims* had got their own back.

One corporal asked Neish, "What's the matter? Has the cat got your tongue? Speak up, man!"

"He can't speak, Corporal," Scott replied. "He has difficulty feeling his lips."

The corporal found it difficult not to smile. Apart from Neish's lips, Scott's nose was as large as Genova's as he said, "A cat didn't get his tongue, Corporal, a spider did with the help of a few ants."

Both NCOs shook their heads and one asked, "Who did this to you?"

"Probably the enemy," offered Sterling. "All of us were taken from the back by surprise otherwise we'd have fought them off. Corporal, what happens when a guy's wang has been bitten by a billion ants?"

The NCO tried to keep a straight face. "We have to amputate. Why?"

Sterling paused, looking quite shaken. "You mean cut it off?"

"Yes, but we'll try and save some of it. It depends on how much of it has been bitten. Do you have that problem?"

Sterling started shaking so much he couldn't answer, so MacKay became the spokesman. "No, he doesn't have that problem, the rest of us do. With him, you're gonna have to cut off his nuts. Not a portion of 'em ... two of them to the hilt."

"Yeah, at least we'll have our balls," said Scot. Then he looked at the others. "Well, I'll have one, anyway. I'm not certain about the other one, it's four times its normal size."

In pain, Neish finally moved his lips and tongue. He sounded like he had a mouth full of marbles. "What good are balls if we ain't got wangs?"

Cordell Cross

MacKay placed an arm around Neish's left shoulder. "Ya can always adopt kids."

"Sure, but who's gonna marry me? The way my lips feel, when I eat food, I won't know if I'm chewin' the fork."

Within minutes, special soap and cold showers became the order of the day again, followed by more strokes with alcohol on cotton swabs. The MIR Sergeant was called in and administered needles before handing out bottles of ointment that would check the itching.

He paused before sticking Scott and Neish's rear-ends.

"Didn't I give shots to you two yesterday?"

With difficulty, Neish spoke again. "Yeah, now after these, I won't be able to feel my ass either. Can't ya give 'em to me on the lips?"

"Yeah, or my nose?" asked Scott.

According to Major Hansford, the Glenemma exercise was a major success. Certainly, there were a few foul-ups, however when he addressed his *troops* on Friday in Camp Vernon after they unloaded from the vehicles and handed in their equipment, his face beamed with admiration.

"You completed your tasks with regular force proficiency and pride.

"The new commanding officer spent a day watching and listening as you performed your skills. His praise is even stronger than mine, if that is possible.

"From what I hear, most of you would rather have stayed in the field for the balance of camp. To me, that is further proof that you have mastered your trade and are prepared to work even harder to earn your professional certificates."

Chuckles filtered through the ranks because the cadets didn't have that in mind at all. They were their own bosses in Glenemma. They didn't miss standing by their beds, polishing, queuing for meals, cleaning, forming up in three ranks on the road, sitting in hot huts, or spending hours on the parade square. Not the number of hours that IBT spent, but near enough.

"It's now 1500 hours. I don't want to see you again until 0830 on Monday morning. There are no tests tomorrow; however, there is a pay parade and a bedding exchange. Also, tonight is not a Mother's Night for you and you will not be required on tomorrow's battalion parade.

"Sort out your equipment, clean yourselves up and relax. Church parade this Sunday is voluntary, but I feel certain most of you will want to attend...!"

Amazed looks and more laughter came from the ranks, placing a smile on Major Hansford's face.

"Have a fine weekend, lads. Thank you all!"

After the normal dismissal formalities, the cadets of Signals Company rushed into their hut, unfurled their mattresses, and flopped down.

The rain had stopped on Thursday morning and the exercise had continued until 0800 hours on Friday morning. That day, it was announced that the FF had won the battle and two-hour platoon critiques covered all strong and weak points.

262 – NEXT STOP, VERNON!

After a swim parade at Round Lake, a wonderful early lunch was brought in from camp and the cadets spent the next two hours cleaning up their equipment and clearing areas, thus leaving Glenemma the way it was when they had arrived.

Although B-25 appeared like a tornado had hit it, it was home, and it felt fabulous to be back. Once again, the showers ran, all toilets were occupied, the sinks were full, the washing machine whined, radios blared and war stories were told. Of course, there were a few problems.

"What the bloody hell are you doing ... that man? Yes, you! I can see you, so can the whole goddamned world! Stand where you are!"

A naked Moose stood by his bed as RSM Gardiner stormed into the barracks.

"Sir, I was placing my radio back on the shelf and I..."

"You again? Christ, young man, when are you going to start wearing clothes? You're not in Glenemma now and there are cars on this highway! Don't you...?"

The RSM paused. "What the hell have you got wrapped around your penis? God's truth, what are you up to now?"

"It's a sock, sir, and there's a bandage underneath it."

"I know it's a frigging sock! What's it doing on your penis? Did you step on the thing?"

"A mosquito crawled up my foreskin and bit me. Bergie thinks it could have been more than one. I'm not sure, but I..."

"You don't have to explain to me what perky thinks. I believe it. You could fit a whole *effing* wasp's nest in there! Corporal Wright!"

A Corporal appeared from the west wing's south-west cubicle. "Yes, sir?"

"Get this bizarre character with his personal mobile roach motel to the camp hospital. Tell them to disinfect that thing and give him the full array of needles! Mister, when you get back, stay away from the windows unless you have some clothes on! Is that clear? Well, is it? Stand still and stop scratching, man!"

The itch drove Danyluk wild. "Yesssss, yes, sir!"

"I can't hear you!"

"Yes, sir! Youse can count on it, sir!"

Cringing after hearing the word "youse," Gardiner marched out, heading towards the next hut where other cadets would receive his *gentle-hearted* wrath.

"A sock on his prick? Someone should put that poor bastard and his partner Perky in a side-show," Gardiner murmured to himself. "No, on second thought, in a *effing* zoo."

The cadets of Signals Company thought it was great to be back. Although they had only been away for a few days, the *shack* seemed like a palace. It was nice to have hot showers, clean clothes, a water fountain, *unpolluted* bedding, comfortable bunks, barrack boxes, movies, a telephone, KiK Kola, the canteen, downtown, pay parade, and girls, girls, even more girls. Now they had been given the weekend off. No Mother's Night, no church parade, and no examinations. It was too good to be true. Rumour also had it that the company was going to Kelowna on Tuesday just for a day trip.

As war stories passed from bunk to bunk, laughter filled the barracks. The stories weren't just limited to the *antics* of cadets from 21 Platoon, because the other

Cordell Cross

three platoons had their mischief-makers as well. A third of 23 Platoon's cadets had been thrown into various *shitters*. Someone stole all the toilet paper in 24 Platoon's area and left leaves strung on pieces of string. A cadet was heard to say, "What, no more leaves? What are we supposed to use, our fingers? Hey Lorne, pass me our map."

"The map's been used," was Lorne's reply. "But some pages of our code books are left."

Considering the weather as well as limited resources, everything antic possible had taken place at Glenemma.

Tripwire outside hootchies appeared to be a popular sport. Not only outside hootchies, but on the edges of latrines as well. Cadets got hung by their feet in snare-traps, had frogs and mice put in their beds, hootchies were moved and set up like they hadn't been touched, sumps and water-drainage canals were diverted under sleeping bodies, hand-crank generator wires were placed under sleeping cadets, and yellow jackets were caught in jars and the uncapped jars tucked into the ends of blankets. Yes, hundreds of *fun-loving* capers concocted on the plains of Glenemma even included putting non-poisonous snakes in kit bags and blankets. Fond tales would make their way around camp this day, and the memories would last a lifetime.

Now, it was spit and polish time once again. Boots had to brought back to shape as well as every other item of clothing soiled in the field.

Cordell Cross

Chapter 20

Upon returning from Glenemma, the cadets worked hard to get back into their routine. While Lyons and McLeod played chess, the balance of the musketeers showered and afterwards got busy sorting out barrack boxes, ironing, soaping and polishing.

Suddenly East looked up from shining his boots and said, "Well what do ya know. Hey guys, vast is here!"

Vast Danyluk didn't really care for the nickname *Vast*, but he'd stopped complaining years ago.

Almost the spitting image of Moose, but a few years older, Vast's grin covered his face as he stood at the doorway and threw Moose the keys to the *chariot*. His wide at the knee and narrow at the ankle light-blue zoot-zoot pants with numerous rows of buttons, fit well in with his pink loose silk shirt, wide-brimmed cream-coloured Panama hat, black banker's shoes and bright-orange socks.

"But I'm not here for long, youse guys. I've five dames expecting me at Polson Park, and another one waitin' for me outside. We're headin' to a weddin' in Calgary. The broad on the road is the bride and she's drivin' her dad's Rolls Royce.

Cadets rushed to the doorway to catch a glimpse of the beautiful blonde in the Rolls Royce parked outside the end door. When she saw them, she smiled, put her compact and lipstick away, waved, and lit up a cigarette. "Tell my big, *big*, baby I'm waiting for him."

While Moose ran up to his brother and smothered him with praise, Rothstein whispered to Cunningham, "If she's the bride, how come she calls *him* her big baby?"

Gordie shrugged. "Who knows? Anything's possible when a member of the Danyluk family is involved."

Rothstein frowned and nodded. "You're probably right, but why do they call him *Vast?*"

"Cause he's got a bigger wang than Moose, that's why. Vast is the oldest in the family - Shaft and Flagpole are younger," the gambler muttered before yelling, "Hey Vee, did ya bring money? Have ya got time for a quick game?"

Rothstein shook his head in disbelief. He didn't think it was possible. "Wow, their father must be something else," he murmured.

"Not with youse, Cunningham!" the hipster replied. "I've got a memory like an elephant!"

And that's not all, thought Rothstein, his astonished facial expression gaining strength.

Over the next fifteen minutes, nearly every cadet in 21 Platoon shook Vast's right hand as he explained his trip with the girls.

"Moose, I'll be back next Saturday to pick it up. What a trip. I had three in the hearse and three in the Rolls."

"Where did youse park it?" an excited Moose asked, jingling the keys.

Cordell Cross

"Just outside the British Columbia Dragoons' armouries. I didn't want to take a chance drivin' it by that mean-lookin' Provost Sergeant. He looks like he chews carpet tacks instead of gum."

"Aw, he's just pissed off because we sung to him today," replied Moose. "Are youse stayin' for dinner?"

Vast wrapped an arm around his *little* brother's shoulders and sang, *"Would youse stay for dinner if youse had six dames waitin' for ya?"*

"Hell no! Youse knows I wouldn't!"

"Well then, that's that. Gotta go, guys. Moose, the old man wants ya to write the old lady. She's written ya three letter and youse ain't replied."

Vast wrung his hands before rubbing his crotch. "After the weddin' I'm gonna have five beauties in the sack with me at the same time."

Moose scratched his head in thought. "I thought youse said ya had six broads?"

Family *amour propre* showed as Moose's brother stuck out his chest. "I ain't sure about the bride. But five dames is a record, ain't it Moose?"'"

Danyluk thought for a moment. "Not quite, *Vee*. I remember a time in Cubs when we raided the Girl Guides camp and..."

"I said, 'beauties' Moose."

"Oh, beauties? Er, yeah, ha, ha, five's a record. Mine weren't *bavishing reauties*, that's for sure."

Seconds later, after more handshakes, Vast drove away with his right arm draped around the *bride's* shoulders.

Moose pocketed the keys. "Who's coming with me to pick up our wheels?"

"Ain'tcha eatin'?" East asked, rolling on his left puttee.

Although Danyluk itched to get behind the wheel, it was decided that the group would have supper before bringing the *auto* closer to camp.

"It's gonna be difficult tomorrow, but with four in the front seat, we'll get sixteen crammed in the back. Jack, youse can lie in the casket with your broad. Then we'll close the lid and five or six can squat on it."

"Stick in your ear, Moose! I ain't lyin' in that coffin. There's been too many stiffs in there."

"Casket, please. Are youse referrin' to my anoty, er...?"

"Do you mean *anatomy*?" asked Rothstein, chuckling.

"Yeah, my anatomy?"

"That too," East replied, catching and returning the contagious grins around him. "Let Lyons have the honour."

Because Lyons was in the showers singing a Seaforth song called *Rubber Duckies are for muffies,* he wasn't around to offer his opinion. After a quick vote, Lyons and his girl became nominated to ride in the *casket.*

After supper that evening, with the funeral *hack* packed to the brim, ten cadets realized the ecstasy of not having to walk back up the hill, but suffered the agony of the alternative. Enthusiastic at first, their eyes soon became moist from the odour emancipating from the *casket*, curtains, seats, carpet, wall padding and everything else the vehicle had amassed over the years from the essence bequeathed by the *dearly departed.*

Cordell Cross

Not wishing to be offensive, rave reviews continued throughout the evening, however, after lights out, some truths were made known. Naturally, it was 'Honest Jack' who offered the first judgement.

"Er, how much did you pay for that thing?"

Cunningham spoke instead of Moose. "I didn't have to pay for it; I won it in a crapshoot. Nice ring, eh? I tried to get his watch as well, but..."

Jeez, Cunner, I ain't talkin' to you - I'm takin' to the Moose. Do you think I give a damn about your winnings?"

The *gambler* shined his ring and smiled. "Well, pardoney meeee."

Danyluk sat up. "My beautiful chariot? Are youse askin' me what it cost?"

"Yeah. How much did you pay for it?"

"I ain't saying. Let's just say I got a good deal. You ripped me off though when I paid you to get rid of the smell."

"Moose, you'll have to blow that thing up to get rid of the smell. How you can get a boner when you lie in that coffin, I'll never know."

"Hey, I can get a boner anywhere, anytime! Smell's got nothin' to do with it, you pongo!"

The corporal's voice joined in. "Danyluk, are you boasting in your sleep again?"

"No, Corporal. I'm wide awake."

"Then keep it down."

"That's a difficult order for Moose, Corporal," Wane said. "With him, it's never down."

"Shove it Banks! Listen, I know it smells, but I'm gonna air it out. Once that's done, every dame will love it!"

Now the sour-faced Corporal came out of his cubicle.

"*Effing* soap and water is all it needs if it smells, ya filthy thing. Air it out? Listen Danyluk, you need to use a whole goddamned bar of soap under that foreskin. Get out of bed and hit the showers now, ya poor excuse for a human being. What have you been doin' to make it smell? You'd let some broad get near that elephant's trunk when it smells? Get in that shower for half-an-hour mister! Move your ass, now!"

"But, Corporal ... I wasn't talkin' about ... I just had a..."

"Move it!

With the Corporal pointing in the direction of the shower room, half an H-hut howled as a naked Moose stomped away grumbling, "You're all mixed up! I was talkin' about..."

"I'm mixed up? Listen mister, I want you on sick parade tomorrow, Danyluk! Do you hear me? It's the blue-ointment treatment for you! *Listen, I know it smells, but I'm gonna air it out. Once that's done, every dame will love it!*' Jeez, you're hazardous as hell!"

Shortly the darkened hut was quiet except for the running of a shower and a conversation in 22 Platoon's end. Two Loyal Edmonton Regiment cadets remained awake. They had heard the conversation and knew that miracles didn't happen.

"How's that Canadian Scottish creep gonna pull back his foreskin to get it clean? What do ya do with three miles of skin?" one asked the other.

Cordell Cross

"Maybe he gets a boner and slides the rest of the skin over his shoulder," his friend replied. "Canadian Scottish? I thought he said he was in the Irish?"

"Same diff ain't it? Canadian Scottish or Irish? They're nearly as bad as the Nineteenth Alberta Dragoons."

At the other end, Wane leaned over to talk to Douglas. "Charlie's visiting us at noon tomorrow ... Great, eh?"

Brice had nearly drifted off, but rolled on his back and looked up at his bunkmate. "Yeah, it's gonna be nice seeing him again. It's my guess he'll sit in the front."

Wane's head disappeared. "Front or back, we'll have to provide him with a clothespin for his nose. Goodnight, Doug."

Douglas chuckled. "Or a gas mask. Goodnight buddy."

"Drivin' in my lim-o, watchin' all the girls go by."
Off key, definitely out on his timing, and dressed only in his *skin*, Danyluk waltzed around his bunk mimicking his radio's song, the Four Lads singing, *Standing on the Corner.*

With the silver strands of his *steady mop partner* draped over his shoulders, and one hand under the towel wrapped around *her* frame, the pleased look on Moose's face indicated Saturday had arrived which meant he would become the tour-master for old Charlie and Fred.

The radio announcer's time-check, "It's nine-thirty on this beautiful Okanagan Saturday morning," got Douglas sitting up and wiping his eyes. The fact that there was no lump or sagging in the mattress up top indicated his bunk buddy was already out of bed.

"Moose, where's Wane?"

Danyluk pranced over singing, *"There's a pawn shop on the corner in Pittsburgh, Pennsylvania.* He's in the showers with Lingus and Bergie. That's where me and my lady are goin' - wanna join us?"

The barracks boiled as Douglas grinned and threw back his upper sheet, saying, "Aren't you afraid of their reaction, when you take that woman into the showers?"

Moose did two pirouettes passing Brice's bunk. "She's seen it all before. As for them, the first one who *cups it* is a pansy. It'll probably be Lyons."

Following Danyluk into the centre washing area of the hut, six cadets from 23 Platoon stood outside the shower room.

"What's the matter; no hot water?" Douglas asked while passing them.

"Nah, that fartin' Canned Scot's in there again, and we don't want him whistlin' Three Blind Mice," came the reply, referring to East's presence in the room. "Even a cold shower's better than being in there when he strains his veins."

As usual, shampoo covered Wane from head to toe. "Doug, you must have been tired. Most of us have been up since eight. I..."

Lyons, smiling and cupping himself with one hand interrupted Banks, by saying, "I'll have you know, Mr. Danyluk, refined gentlemen do not shower with members of the opposite sex. Even if the lady is robed."

As Danyluk slowly pulled away the towel covering the mop pole, a smiling Lyons faced the wall, saying, "Aggghhh, a full-bodied Miss, willingly offering here seductiveness."

"Yeah, and youse knows she heads towards the first boner."

"That'll be you," Bergie said, chuckling and drying his body. "Pay parade's at ten-thirty. After we get our dough, let's drive downtown, grab a burger, and get back in time for Charlie."

After a few moments, the plan to head into town for a snack was approved by the group.

At ten o'clock, a three-ton truck appeared at the doorway to the musketeers' barracks and every cadet from both sides of the hut exchanged one sheet and one pillowcase for laundered items.

At ten twenty-five after all beds were made, a smartly dressed Signals Company marched to B-3 for pay parade. Included with the company were the IBT cadets that assisted the exercise at Glenemma. They had also been given the weekend off.

Without looking up, the pay sergeant asked, "Name?" after Douglas saluted the paymaster and a lieutenant. The armed Provost Sergeant standing behind the officer returned the salute.

"Brice, Douglas, Sergeant."

The sergeant ticked off his name and the lieutenant showed Douglas where to sign before the paymaster counted out five crisp one-dollar bills and laid them on the table.

The lieutenant pointed at a line, "There you are, sign the form … there. Next!"

Douglas signed his name, moved in front of the captain (paymaster), picked up the bills, passed them to his left hand, saluted, turned smartly to his right, and marched away swinging his right arm. The alert Provost Sergeant standing at attention returned his salute.

It wasn't necessary for the company to return to B-25, so after the Musketeers had received their money, they took the back-route to the *limo* parked near the British Columbia Dragoons' armouries.

Shortly, with Bergie and Cunningham sitting next to Danyluk in the front seat, and the rest tucked in the *trailing pagoda*, a happy and whistling Moose drove the hearse to the Silver Grill Cafe on the main drag of Vernon.

Enroute, a few comments were made. Not caustic remarks, just expressions that were necessary at the time. It was East who initiated them.

"For Christ's sake, Moose, open the windows. The hair in my nose is crinkling. God, the smell in this thing would attract a maggot off a pile of shit."

With his hankie covering his nose, Lyons was more kind.

"Yes, old chum, I feel certain we're going to come down with something if air isn't introduced into this malodorous conveyance."

A laughing Danyluk opened his window, as did Bergie.

"Why are you laughing, old comrade?" Lyons asked.

Keeping his eyes on the road, a grinning Moose replied, "I was just thinking. If youse thinks this is a little malodorous now, youse is going to love this afternoon."

Cordell Cross

Obviously, Lyons hadn't yet been told that he and his girl had been elected to ride in the *coffin* that afternoon, so smiles were the order of the day when Lyons asked the others, "What did he mean by that?"

"How much *did* you say you paid for this?" Rothstein asked. "Did I hear you say two-hundred bucks?"

Danyluk glanced in his rear view mirror at his curious friend. "I didn't say."

Harvey chuckled. He knew Moose had told them but he didn't rub it in. "I don't blame you."

At exactly twelve o'clock that afternoon, Miss Millie drove by the Provost shack and parked in the sergeants' mess parking lot. When Charlie and Fred got out, their hands and shoulders were sore from the reception they received from *eight* musketeers. Moments later they were introduced to Lyons and McLeod.

Both men were dressed for the occasion and their neat slacks and open-necked shirts remained pressed even though the sun's rays stayed fierce.

Charlie's face glowed from all the attention he and Fred received. "Thank you, thank you very much, boys. It's wonderful to be here."

"How come you brought Miss Millie?" Jackson asked.

"My car's acting up these days," Charlie replied. "I probably need a new battery."

"Well, whatdoya think?" asked a proudly smiling Danyluk, pointing to the *limo* parked in the same parking lot.

With the boys following, both Charlie and Fred walked towards the *olfactory anomaly*.

Charlie took of his hat and wiped his brow. "Wowee, it sure looks nice."

"Smells nice, too," offered McLeod. "Everyone who has rode in that coffin has added a little *bouquet de body*."

"Casket, please."

"Sorry, Moose. I meant casket."

"How many are ridin' with us?" Fred asked, while East gestured and ushered the group toward the signals kitchen.

"Just twenty," Moose replied, his arm around Charlie's shoulders.

Charlie stopped in the middle of the road. "Twenty? Did you say, twenty? Don't you think that's a little much? Are you sure your suspension can handle it?"

Moose moved him along. "No problem. I only wear them when I've got my battledress on."

"What?"

Rothstein interceded. "He didn't say suspenders, he said suspension."

Moose still didn't understand. "Oh yeah. Haaa, youse is relating my Packard to a suspension bridge, eh, Charlie? Strong like bull, eh? Exactly!"

With odd looks all 'round, the group headed to the front of the line and up the mess hall stairs. No comments, just smiles filled the faces of the cadets waiting in line, but as soon as the old timers passed, middle fingers were offered to the musketeers escorting them.

Inside, Lyons presented the letter from the OC authorizing two extra meals, and the serving ladies piled Charlie and Fred's plates.

Cordell Cross

"I can't eat all this," a wide-eyed Charlie stated.

Moose smacked him on the back. "Youse had better, or you'll end up in the guardroom."

East offered the solution. "What you can't finish ... I'll help you out. How's that, Charlie?"

Dirty looks from the other cadets changed East's mind. "I meant, er, I'll scrub off your plate for you."

As it turned out, both Charlie and Fred thoroughly enjoyed every morsel and even made room for dessert.

Throughout the meal, friends in 21 Platoon came over to say hello and shake Charlie and Fred's hands. For many, it was good to see civilians in the mess hall; it reminded the boys of home. Any change from the colour khaki was a welcome sight indeed, and one very alien to the camp.

After lunch, as planned, ten girls waited in the sergeants' mess parking lot, next to Danyluk's hearse.

"It's wonderful."

"So cool."

"Really mint."

"Real George."

Alma's comment, "Moosie, it's our personal love chariot," got the whole crowd snickering. Alma didn't yet realize that her *love chariot* would literally take her breath away.

Lyons' girl asked, "It's going to be a little tight, isn't it?"

The boys became silent, awaiting *salesman* Bergie's response. "Er, we thought of that and we drew straws for the most cushy place. You and Don will enjoy being comfortable inside the costly, beautifully padded casket, Moose recently had built."

"Oh, how marvellous. Isn't that nice, Don?" she exclaimed, before Lyons could say anything.

The *intelligent one* cringed and glanced around. "Er, yeah ... er, these are really super friends," he said, before turning his back to his girl and facing Bergie. The word, *bastard*, was only mouthed, but Bergie read his lips and understood the meaning very well. He smiled and nodded.

As the couples entered the hearse, a conversation about the cherished vehicle took place in the Sergeants' Mess. The RSM had just arrived and ordered his noon glass of *milk*. "Who died, and where's the undertaker?" Mr. Gardiner asked the bar steward.

The steward sniffed, moving his head in different directions, uncertain to what the RSM was referring. "Sorry, sir. I have a bit of a cold. Everything seems fine to me."

"Who owns the hearse parked in my parking spot? My car's at the headquarters' building, but had I driven it here, that damn funeral auto would be blocking me. Are there any civilians in the mess?"

"Yes, sir ... there's a Mr. Gravely with Padre Ashton. They're sitting in the courtyard. The padre and Mr. Gravely are guests of Sergeant McFee."

Mr. Gardiner had no way of knowing that Mr. Gravely was a liquor salesman who had recently bought a drink for everyone in the mess.

"With a name like Gravely, he should drive a hearse," Gardiner stated. "Why do these padres always hang around with such morbid characters? Is the PMC here?"

"Yes, sir."

"Get him, please."

Shortly, a slightly balding warrant officer second class approached the RSM. "You asked for me, sir?"

"Yes, have Mr. Gravely move his damned professional conveyance out of my parking spot. Also, advise him to obtain a visitor's sticker."

"Yes, sir." the WO2 replied before walking out of the mess and down the stairs to the lawned enclosure below.

The RSM waited and watched out the window as Mr. Gravely stood up, and left the mess. In two minutes, he was back sitting drinking again. At that point, the RSM joined them at their table. Gravely looked about fifty. Although he had a full head of brown hair, his pallor appeared grey. "Padre, Sergeant McFee. Er, Thank you for moving your, er, *business* vehicle, Mr. Gravely."

Actually, Gravely *had* parked his car in the visitor's parking stall, and when Sergeant McFee was about to introduce the RSM, Gravely cut him off.

"Ah, you must be Mr. Visitors? I originally thought the sign meant..."

McFee intervened. "No, this is the Regimental Sergeant Major Gardiner. Sir, Mr. Gravely just bought a drink for the house. He's a..."

"I know what he is. Most kind of you, Mr. Gravely. Business must be good, eh?"

"Not too bad, Mr. Gardiner. We're introducing a few new lines that I thought your boys might like to enjoy. I know you're only here for a couple of months but, well, business is business, isn't it?"

Gardiner just didn't like the man. Mainly because he thought Gravely was an undertaker pushing his wares. "Yes, I would imagine it is. What's different about the new lines? Really, they're all the same aren't they? People get covered, or they get burned. Why do people like you keep wanting to stiff us? A little play on words there, Mr. Gravely."

An expression of surprise and pride came over the liquor salesman. "What? Er, not at all, Mr. Gardiner. Our prices are reasonable. You'll have to try..."

"My God, man, do I look that unhealthy?"

Gravely didn't understand. "I beg your pardon? You're a drinking man, aren't you?"

Mr. Gardiner clarified himself. "Yes, but with limitations. My liver's fine and I would like to think that I won't be needing your services for a long, long time. Even then, I'd clarify that the whole bloody thing would have to done on the cheap. What's the point of pissing good money away on something that hasn't changed in years? Kind of a waste, isn't it?"

Now Gravely got his back up a bit. "Come now, Mr. Gardiner, we've greatly improved our product. There's a difference between rot-gut and..."

"A difference? Rotgut? Ah, you're trying to bury me, are you? You're telling me I'd be able to tell the difference. I'm too tough to be eaten by a shark, Gravely. If you're going to bury or burn someone, you should come to the point, man. Your product should be one price, and it should be cheap."

"Sir, I'll have you know our product prices are very reasonable for the goods. People pay for age, Mr. Gardiner."

"So the older we are, the more we pay, eh? The goods? Christ, man, have you no feelings? The goods?"

Gardiner turned his attention towards Padre Ashton. "Did you hear that? The goods? You're a man of God ... do you use that term? 'Dearly beloved, we are here to get rid of the goods.'"

The padre didn't care for the RSM's attitude. "Why are you carrying on like this, Mr. Gardiner? Mr. Gravely is in the business of selling an excellent product and providing admirable service. To be a good businessman, you must have a better product, and provide better service. I happen to like his commodity and his company's quick delivery."

The RSM stood up. "Quick delivery? Christ, where have I been all my life? Times have plainly changed for the worse. At Normandy, we would have shot any padre saying, 'Get the goods off the beach. We're holding a expeditious business service when the shelling stops.'"

The padre looked confused. "I don't think I understand you, RSM."

"That's quite obvious, padre. How many have you served today, Mr. Gravely?"

"About thirty-four," Gravely replied, referring to *ounces*.

Still standing, Gardiner's eyes widened. "In Vernon? It must be the water that's doing them in. Thirty-four, eh? My God, when I retire, I may just join you in your enterprise. Well, gentlemen, I'm off to dine. Padre, please don't expect me at church service again, and ... er, best of luck with your new *lines*, Mr. Gravely. Look after *the goods*, will you?"

Gravely held out his hand. "That's my job."

Gardiner didn't shake it. "Yes, that worries me somewhat."

After the RSM had left, Mr. Gravely said, "Rather an odd chap, your RSM. He must only like cheap liquor."

McFee replied, "Not normally, I think he's just tired."

"Yes," said Padre Ashton. "I'll speak to the CO about giving him a few days off. I think he really needs it."

Nothing could describe the scene in Danyluk's hearse as it made its rounds throughout Camp Vernon. With Fred and Charlie sitting in the front seat next to Moose, the nineteen teenagers crammed in the back had their faces squished up against windows, curtains and tassels. Backsides met faces, feet met faces, stomachs met faces, legs intertwined, necks discovered boots, boots encountered backs, and when the vehicle went over a bump, all parts of their bodies met - groans of suffering telling the story.

Being a loyal Seaforth, McLeod had worn his kilt, which was now up over his neck. Any effort from him to dislodge his organs from East's left facial cheek proved totally futile. He couldn't even move one of his little fingers. To make matters worse, East couldn't remove his face away from the dangling *dirigibles* complete with *deliverer,* and Jackson couldn't separate his right ear tucked into McLeod's buttocks.

The horrendous heat with the crushing and repugnant smell didn't allow for any conversation, other than up front as well as inside the coffin - on top of which six persons *reclined.* The muffled conversation from within became quite frantic after just three seconds. Poor planning more than anything else had placed Lyons' girlfriend on the bottom.

"I can't breathe, and your breath is horrible," she mumbled.

"It's not my breath ... er, I'm afraid to tell you what it is."

"God, Don, your teeth are up my nose, and your nose is in my left eye."

"I can't help it, my dear, I can't move. Let us out of here!"

"Don, when you talk, you're biting my nose. Oh, that smell. Can you move your right boot, it's digging into my ankle?"

"I'd like to my pet, but my right leg's gone to sleep. Get us out of here, Goddamn it!"

"Don, I've got to pee."

"What do you want me to do, find a bucket? There's no room in here for a thimble. Do you hear me up there? We want out, now!"

Two minutes later the thumping and yelling turned to cries of pure panic and Danyluk had no choice but to pull over. Even Moose was courteous enough to discourage having two unconscious friends on his hands.

It took another two minutes to unload everyone before the coffin could be opened to release two mad, furious, and frantic soaking-wet teenagers gasping for fresh air.

Both Lyons and his girl had to be lifted out because they couldn't walk. But they could talk and Moose got both barrels from each of them.

"Ya don't need the goddamned lid on that thing," yelled Lyons. "It's gonna take twenty years for us to wash away every smell in the universe! East, I thought you washed out that box?"

Rubbing hard at his left cheek, Jack replied, "I tried, but there weren't enough hours in the day. McLeod, if you bare that thing again, I'm gonna hammer you."

Don's girl was a little kinder. "You've got a nerve to put us in there, Moose Danyluk. If I could feel my right hand I'd smack you so hard!"

Throughout, Jackson placed a finger in his right ear trying to pop it.

"What's wrong with you?" asked Cunningham - his nose nearly flattened from being squished up against a window.

"McLeod farted in my ear," came the reply.

Embarrassed, McLeod shot back, "I did not! It was Banks!"

Wane chuckled. "Oh no it wasn't. That was the natural smell of the *trailing pagoda.* Look at it this way, Earl, from now on when someone says to you, 'Stick it in your ear.' You can correct them. It's 'Stick your ear in.' Haaa."

Earl grinned. "Stick it in your ear, Wane."

274 – NEXT STOP, VERNON!

Charlie and Fred laughed with the group as the hearse was *reloaded* and taken back to the sergeants' mess parking lot. Once there, they got out again and the lid was taken off the coffin and left in Mr. Gardiner's parking spot. Douglas now lay in the coffin with Diane on top of him.

On the way, Douglas wrapped his arms around Diane. "Hey, this isn't comfortable, but it sure has its advantages."

Diane blushed. "Wherever we're going, let's get there fast. Then again on second thought..."

Conversation started the whole hearse erupting in muffled laughter as they toured the upper camp, and this time McLeod tucked his kilt between his legs.

At Area 10, they unloaded again to explain the signals practice sessions to Charlie and Fred. Both men were surprised to learn about the great amount of training the boys had undergone during the previous four weeks.

While the pair asked questions, *other matters* were taking place at the sergeants' mess. Although Mr. Gravely had gone, when the RSM left the courtyard, he noticed a coffin lid in his parking spot.

"Damn those undertakers. What a nerve. He's left a sample of his *product* for me to peruse," Gardiner muttered to himself. "Of all the low down dirty ways of conducting business, this takes the cake. The son-of-a-bitch must think I'm nearly ready for his *product*."

The RSM stormed back into the mess. "Sergeant McFee!"

Sergeant McFee stood to attention. "Yes, sir!"

"Where's Gravely?"

"Probably out servicing his clients. I think he said he was heading to the cocktail lounge at the National Hotel. Why, sir?"

"Servicing his clients? Drumming up business, eh? God I hate that terminology! Why? Because he's left a piece of his new *effing* line in my parking spot, that's why! Get him on the phone and get him back here now!"

Sergeant McFee didn't waste any time. "Right away, sir."

As McFee rushed to the phone, the RSM headed to the bar for an *afternoon milk*. Had he stayed outside, he would have seen the coffin lid being tied to the top of Danyluk's hearse. The fully-packed *limo* was now on its way to Glenemma.

Ten minutes later, Gravely rushed into the bar and opened up his briefcase. "Ah, Mr. Gardiner. I knew you'd see the light. That sample is our new line. Have you decided to order the...?"

"I've told you, Gravely, I'm not ready yet. Besides that, you're too pushy. What's the matter with you people? Can't you take no for an answer? When it comes time for me to need your services, my wife will ask any company but yours. Now, get that piece of junk out of my parking lot and don't come back!"

Furious, Gravely asked, "You called me here just to say that?"

Gardiner's intimidating large frame loomed over the liquor salesman. "You bet I did. Don't come around here again. Have you got that?"

Gravely slammed his briefcase shut and headed for the door. "Consider it done! There's no doubt about it, Gardiner, you do need a holiday!"

RSM Gardiner had the last word. "I don't need you to tell me about my health, you charlatan. Move it!"

When Mr. Gravely stormed out of the Sergeants' Mess, the RSM called Sergeant McFee." Is he a friend of yours, or what?"

Although the Sergeant had heard the conversation, he couldn't make heads or tails of it. "Not really, I just like his product."

"My God, man, are you sick too? The man deals with stiffs twenty-four hours a day, and you like the way he does business?"

"Sir, he's the only one who does give us stiffs. He visits us to demonstrate his product. Yesterday, everyone in the house got a free sample and a quality coloured brochure. The others don't do that."

Gardiner stamped down his right foot. "I know others don't do that. Damn it, McFee, it's just not ethical issuing coloured brochures? And you say everyone took one?"

"Everyone but you, sir."

The RSM couldn't believe his ears. "Come now, Sergeant McFee, don't you feel that's a little morose. The son-of-a-bitch takes pictures of caskets loaded with what he calls, 'the goods' and you think that's normal?"

"There was only one picture of a box, sir. The rest were bottles. He's after business and he makes no bones about it."

"What? He uses bottles as well? Bones? Jesus, that's sick!"

"Sir, he's a liquor salesman. What else would he use?"

Gardiner's mouth opened as his face became confused. Whispering and trying to clear his throat, he said, "He's a what?"

"He's a liquor salesman, and a damned fine one at that."

"A liquor salesman? You mean he's not an undertaker?"

A smile came over McFee's lips. "Well, he's got a rum mix called, *Dead in the Morning*, but he's not an undertaker."

The RSM nearly went into shock. "Oh, my God, what have I done? McFee, not a word of this to anyone, do you understand?"

"Yes, sir."

"Why does the man drive a hearse?"

"I've got no idea, sir. Maybe it has more room than his regular vehicle."

"Get him to phone me - will you do that, please?"

"I'll do the best I can sir."

As Sergeant McFee left the courtyard laughing to himself Danyluk had somehow manoeuvred the chariot over the pot-holes of Glenemma where Charlie, Fred and the girls received lessons on what it's like to be pushed into a "shitter."

Another company was training so Moose couldn't drive the expanse of the area. He parked at the centre where the entrance road comes into the clearing. After a few moments with Moose explaining, it didn't take long for the musketeers' guests to understand about the tough training the boys had gone through in the dust and heat.

Ten minutes later Danyluk quickly drove away because two officers fifty yards away started walking towards the hearse.

Cordell Cross

"What the hell was that ... a taxi?" one officer asked.

"No, it looked more like a hearse with a hundred pallbearers," the other replied. "Maybe it was that Mort character all the cadets are talking about," he said before spotting a cadet doing something wrong with a compass. "You, yes you - if you're going to take a bearing with the prismatic compass, you've got to open the top! Get with it, man!"

In spite of the fact that the smell and crushing took its toll, the afternoon was a riot for the musketeers and their guests as they toured the camp and town. Although against the rules, the girls were invited into B-25 with the old-timers. Some recently showered cadets had to cover up in a hurry, but all parties enjoyed the aspect of civilians invading a camp that only displayed one colour ... khaki.

After supper, both Charlie and Fred thanked the boys immensely before getting into Miss Millie and driving away waving. An open invitation was left for the boys and girls to visit Charlie's farm any time they wanted.

Driving south on old highway 97, Charlie lit his pipe, released some smoke, and offered Fred an anthology of wonderful reflections - the final of which was: "Fred, old pal, our lives have been made so much richer by meeting those youngsters. If any guy ever tells me again that this current generation of teens is beyond help, I'm gonna spit in his eye. I've never felt so appreciated, and for that matter, youthful. Kinda makes me want to get mischievous. Wanna go skinny-dipping down by the lake?"

Fred's laughing nearly made him drive off the road. "I think we'd be arrested and placed in an insane asylum. Any other grand ideas?"

"Just joking about skinny-dipping. Let's call Clara and Ruby."

"Clara and Ruby?" I thought you said Clara only wanted to push you towards the altar?"

Charlie grinned. "You said the same about Ruby, didn't you?"

"Er, yeah, I think I did."

"Well, maybe there's a future for a couple of us old farts after all. Whatdoya think?"

Fred thought for a moment and nodded. "Sounds good, but where will we take 'em?"

Charlie nudged him and quietly laughed. "Up in the hayloft of course. On second thought, let's take 'em out for dinner."

Fred agreed. "That sounds better. Then afterwards we'll take them up in the hayloft."

Charlie laughed aloud. "And then we'll go skinny-dipping."

When Fred yelled, "You betcha," Miss Millie weaved.

As Diane and Douglas softly smiled and gazed into each other's eyes, Doris Day's *Secret Love* helped guide the devotion and wonderful affection they felt for each other.

The dance-floor of the arena was packed and dark, but it wouldn't have mattered if they were the only couple there, for no one else dwelled beyond the space where Douglas and Diane shuffled their feet. Time became infinite and background noise just didn't exist as Doris sang, *"So I told a friendly star, just how wonderful you are..."*

Diane ceased staring into Douglas' eyes, nestled her face sideways on his chest and wrapped her arms loosely around his neck. "I've told a friendly star a million times just how wonderful *you* are," she said.

Douglas held her tighter and a lost smile came to his lips. "So have I. I love you, Di - more than you'll ever know. It's funny, when I'm three-hundred miles away, I never see you, and when I'm here I hardly see you. Do ya think I should go AWOL?"

Diane grinned and looked up at him. "What if I said, yes?"

"Then I'd do it," he replied, as *Ebb Tide* started, with Frank Chacksfield and his Orchestra.

"I'd just pack up my things and leave. That's it, gone!"

After taking her head off his chest and kissing him, she said, "Douglas Brice don't you ever consider such a thing."

"If that's an order, I kinda like it."

"Yes it's an order. Don't they kiss when they give orders at camp?"

He laughed. "If they did, there'd be a lot of black-eyes. Just the..."

Their conversation was interrupted by Alma's hand waving between their faces. Her new ring gleamed. "Do you like it? Moose said his mother wants me to have it. She's had it since she was a teenager in love."

A proudly grinning Moose watched Diane take hold of Alma's hand to admire the *present*.

"It really is lovely. Moose, your mother must be a wonderful person."

Alma continued to hold out her hand and move her fingers. "He tells me it won't turn my finger green like the other one he gave me."

"It looks like real gold," offered Diane.

Moose's chest came out. "It is real gold. Nothin's too good for my Alma. Someday, my cupcake I'm gonna smother youse with jewels."

"Er, Moose, I never want to be smothered again. Today's trip in your limo was enough, thank you very much."

Moving on, Moose said, "Alma, from now on it's the front seat for youse. It'll be first-class all the way, baby."

"Oh, Moosie, you say the most romantic things."

Diane watched the *jewellery* disappear into the crowd. "His mother must really be a very considerate lovely lady. Have you met her?"

Brice shook his head. "No, but she sure must have a lot of rings."

Diane's eyes met his. "Why?"

Douglas' amused facial expression said it all, but he added, "Every girl in Vancouver has got one just like it."

Even with Kitty Kallen singing her romantic hit, *Little Things Mean a Lot*, surrounding couples couldn't understand why Douglas and Diane giggled so much.

At eleven-thirty when the doors opened and blasts of cool air entered, the old building shook to the first clap of thunder. Seconds later the sky opened up.

Cordell Cross

278 – NEXT STOP, VERNON!

"Damn, it's pouring," East exclaimed waiting at the hatcheck for his beret. He'd learned his lesson about putting his headdress in his epaulette because even though badges faced their front, sometimes they disappeared. "The smell in the hearse is gonna be worse."

"That rhymes," Rothstein said, collecting his beret. "But at least we won't get soaked."

All the girls had rides home, so after goodbyes were *delicately uttered*, the hearse was only half as cramped as it had been earlier. Even so, the boys were soaked to the skin just running to get into it.

"Jesus, now this thing really stinks," Bergie said, after electing to recline in the coffin. The lid had been taken off the roof earlier and placed alongside the funerary box.

"Hey, youse just watch yer tongue. Ya could be walkin up this hill, ya know?"

Wane took his foot off Cunningham's face. "Must we listen to that goddamned organ music?"

Danyluk turned his head for a fraction of a second. "Yeah, I want Bergie to realize how romantic it is in the casket when the music's playin'. That hymn's called, *Walkin' in the forest with the Lord.*"

Bergie laughed out loud. "In here, it's more like laying in the shitter with the devil."

"Are we parkin' this at the BCD armouries?" Earl asked.

Douglas tried to shift his body because someone's foot dug into his stomach. "If we do, we'll get drenched walking to the camp."

The *driver* offered a solution. "Don't panic youse pansies. I'm gonna park in the sergeants' mess parking lot. It's Sunday tomorrow so half the staff will be away."

Moose was kind enough not to park his vehicle in RSM Gardiner's spot. Instead, he parked it in Sergeant McFee's space. With the doors tightly locked, all ten ran to B-25 as two other *barrrrooooms* erupted after lightening lit up hills to the west.

A corporal walked the darkened aisle while East shut the outer and inner doors. Other cadets were arriving back at the same time. "Hit the sack, fellas."

"Can we have a hot shower?" asked Lyons.

The corporal nodded his approval and asked, "How did the dance go?"

All shivered their endorsement except the *gambler*. Cunningham had been quiet all the way back.

"Some Westie asshole by the name of Stanley took me for twenty bucks. I know him - he's in IBT. Tomorrow he's gonna pay for that. I even lost my watch to the creep."

Heading to the showers, a naked Moose didn't offer solace "Youse should know there's always a faster gun."

Gordie wrapped a towel around his waist and followed Danyluk. "Screw you, Moose. There's no faster gun than me when it comes to the art of gaming. I'm pissed off because the guy was a Westie. Normally Westies hand over their dough with ease. They aren't like the Irish or Seaforths. All those homos do is bitch and complain. When ya win ten-cents from them, it's kinda like the start of the third world war."

"Up your ass, ya black bastard from Beatty Street," an Irish Fusilier yelled from his bunk.

"And the same to you, ya green *effer* from Gilford street," replied Cunningham.

A nearby Seaforth offered his conviction. "The two of you pongoes need to learn a little couth and culture. Join the Seaforths and master the art of becoming gentlemen."

Gordie stopped at the entrance to the centre section. "You mean you fags in rags are starting to see the light? That trying the opposite sex is more apropos than lifting the rear of your nearest buddy's kilt?"

"Stick in your ear, ya BCR degenerate."

"That got him," Cunningham mumbled grinning and heading into the shower. "That's the habit we're trying to rid you of," he shot back.

Fifteen minutes later as the rain lashed Hut B-25's windows, most of its occupants were asleep. Most, that is, except East. Not only had someone frenched his bed, chicken fat had been spread on the floor alongside it. He had a chicken leg under his pillow so the smell didn't really faze him as he took off his shoes and socks, then stood up and slipped, pushing the still parading corporal onto a sleeping Strathcona cadet across the aisle.

The cadet was livid, but still had a sense of humour. "If ya wanna be a cadet. Corp, ya gotta ask the OC."

The corporal didn't waste any time standing up, yelling, East, you reek like a goddamned chicken, and now you're slithering around like a snake! Get that mess cleaned up!"

"But Corporal, it's not me that smells. There's chicken-fat all over the floor."

"I know there is! It's from the bloody food you bring in here. Get that floor scrubbed, now!"

With the corporal now in his cubicle, the wind whipping up the rain, some cadets bitching in their sleep, and Danyluk snoring, a lone East mopped the floor. When he finished, he hit the sack and joined Danyluk in the snoring contest, not knowing that a piece of frozen chicken fat lay placed between Jackson's mattress and springs. The heat from Jackson's body would melt that fat, and all night long it would drip on East's head.

Cordell Cross

Chapter 21

Douglas didn't know what made him wake up at only 0930. After all, he could have slept in until noon had he wanted to.

In seconds, the choice became clear. It was either the cold barracks, the pounding rain, Danyluk's radio offering Hank Williams' *Your Cheatin' Heart*, or the scream East trumpeted heading to the showers. Whatever it was, the hullabaloo was ear splitting. So resounding, all those who remained in bed that Sunday morning sat up wandering what had happened.

Shortly, Brice narrowed the selection down to East because the voice emanating from the centre section didn't stop when it passed Douglas' bed.

"I'm dead, and I've come back as a chicken! If I had feathers, I'd be flying! I can't see, I can't hear, but I can smell, and the whole friggin' world smells like chicken! Guys, what the hell has happened to me?"

A few moments later, Jackson passed Douglas' bunk holding his nose. "East you creep, what have you done? Are you starting a chicken farm around our bunks? Jeez, the smell is making me vomit! Where the hell are you hiding the crap? All night long I've been dreamin' of chickens running around our end of the shack!"

Then silence ensued as Earl noticed Jack's face. "My God man, what the hell have you got all over you?"

"You should know, you're the one who trickled it on me, you pongo," East replied. "You've been slowly dripping it on my face all night long! Have you seen my sheets and blankets? They look like I used them as a bib while I ate a thousand chickens. That's a rotten trick you played, Earl. I'll getcha for this one - you just wait and see if I don't."

Douglas didn't hear Earl's response, but moments later East and Jackson, both naked, hurried back to their bunks with the earnestness of Sherlock Holmes and Dr. Watson. It didn't take them long to figure out the ploy.

East stood in the aisle. "So, some of you assholes are up to your old tricks again, eh? Well I'll find out who you are, and when I do, it's..."

Grinning while returning to the showers, Jack used the forefinger of his right hand to mock-cut his throat from ear to ear.

It took an hour to clean up the mess, including fifteen minutes to *exchange* Jack's mattress, pillow, pillowcase, sheets, and blankets for cleaner items over in the next hut. The inhabitants of the other hut were attending church parade. Earl was more fortunate than Jack; he only had to *replace* his mattress.

Jack East was kind to the occupant he borrowed from in the adjacent hut. He left a bed made better and tighter. As well, the corporal *inheriting* East's *possessions* wouldn't realize it until lights-out. As for the fact that Jack now had to sleep between some IBT corporal's sheets - well anything was better than the chicken *coop's* bedclothes.

Over brunch, howls filled the musketeers' table when they learned that an NCO from IBT was now the new proud owner of the *chicken farm*.

"Haaa, he's gonna give shit to everyone around him after lights-out," said Bergie. "The *fit's* gonna hit the *shan*. You're cruel, Jack."

"Well, someone got me. When I woke up, my tongue was stuck to my pillowcase. What a nightmare."

"Jeez, it's even cold in here," Wane noted, even though he was dressed like the rest of them. The boys wore KD longs, shirts, sweaters, boots, puttees, web-belts, and regimental headdress. Berets, including McLeod's glengarry were tucked in their pockets because if they were left lying around even for a second, the badges would *go south*. In Vernon, badges had a way of vanishing at the blink of an eye.

"That's one hellova cold rain," Douglas said. "It's supposed to stop tomorrow, but it ruins our plans of going to Kalamalka Beach today. What'll we do?"

Gordie counted the bills in his wallet. "Count me out of any plans. I'm meetin' Stanley in our drying room at 1400. He says he's gonna give me the chance to get my watch and twenty bucks back."

"When did you make those arrangements?" asked Lyons.

The *gambler* put his wallet away. "This morning at 0630 when I woke him up."

Don laughed. "You woke him up at six-thirty? What time would you have got him up had you lost fifty bucks?"

When he stood up, a sneaky look of one-upmanship came over Cunningham's face. Taking a coin from Don's ear, he replied, "For fifty bucks, he'd have been up all night."

When Bergie grinned, stared and nodded at Cunningham, the look in his eyes indicating he'd caught on. "You let him win that money, didn't you, Lingus?"

Picking up his plate and utensils, the *gambler* appeared amused. "Who said so?"

"I say so. You've set him up, haven't you? You've never lost to a Westie before. Why would you start now?"

As Gordie walked away, he mouthed, "Bergie, my son, that's for me to know, and for you to find out. I will say this, however; the guy received a solid gold bracelet from home. And as you know, I really like the yellow metal."

While all but Cunningham planned their day, Sergeant McFee grumbled as he parked his car in RSM Gardiner's parking spot. He couldn't park in his own space because of Danyluk's hearse and he didn't want to get soaked parking a great distance from the mess.

"My God, Gravely does own a hearse - and now it's in my spot. Even on Sunday mornings, this guy's out selling. Why the hell doesn't he use the visitors' spaces?" he mumbled, locking his car, turning up his raincoat collar and walking up to the *chariot* to glance inside. Other than the casket with its lid on, nothing else was visible.

"What a weirdo. He must carry his booze in that coffin. Now that doesn't make any sense at all. On second thought it does. Who the hell would steal a hearse?"

Sergeant McFee entered the courtyard and walked up the stairs to the bar area. "Where's Mr. Gravely?" he asked the steward, not realizing that the hearse was now being loaded and would soon be on its way with its occupants singing, *North Atlantic Squadron*.

"The liquor salesman? I haven't seen him," the bartender replied. "Wait a minute, maybe I did. He might be in the dining room with RSM Gardiner."

Although the steward was wrong, the Sergeant now assumed a peace-treaty had been signed. "Ah, so they're making up. That's good - I'll join them," he said leaving and crossing the grass to the other building in the lawned enclosure.

A few sergeants and senior warrant officers were still dining when he entered, but not RSM Gardiner or Mr. Gravely. Shrugging, McFee went to the cloakroom, took off his raincoat and returned to the dining area. Just as he pulled back a chair, the RSM marched in - drenched.

"Sergeant McFee, move that Goddamned car of yours out of my parking spot! No one parks in my parking spot! Have you got that? Bloody hell, yesterday it was a hearse, and now it's your car. It's pissing out there and someone's always in my parking place!"

"Sir, I had to park there because you were talking to Mr. Gravely, and his hearse is in *my* space. I didn't think you were driving today, sir."

Gardiner placed his wet coat, forage cap, and large drill-cane in the place reserved for the RSM's items. "I'm not going to walk in this weather. When was I supposedly talking with Mr. Gravely?"

"Just now, sir."

Gardiner walked up to McFee. "Have you been drinking?"

"No, sir."

"Well, Sergeant McFee, I haven't spoken with Mr. Gravely since yesterday. If I can recall, you were going to have him contact me. Tell me, does this man, Gravely, have a problem with parking in the visitors' spaces? Because he's an alcohol salesman, does he have illusions of grandeur? After all, maybe that's why he drives a hearse?"

"I have no idea, sir. I really don't know the man. It's entirely possible he's with the padre again."

The RSM sat down and glanced at the menu. "Well, if he is with the padre, I wish he'd park his goddamned vehicle in the padre's spot in the officers' mess parking lot. Do you think maybe the padre's got a drinking problem? You know what I mean; he's always with Gravely?"

McFee didn't sit down because he was ordered to move his car. "Are you suggesting that the padre is a closet alcoholic, sir?"

Gardiner fingered the ends of his giant moustache and slyly grinned. "You bet I am, and I'm going to speak with the CO about him. One thing we don't need around here is a padre who fills the communion table chalice with gin, and sips it during the services, eh what?"

McFee agreed, and then left the mess. Shortly, he arrived back and sat down with the RSM. "Gravely must have left - his hearse has gone. I've moved my car, sir."

"Good. You know something, McFee, I'll bet a dollar to doughnuts, that's why Gravely drives a hearse. With his coffin filled with booze, he can fit in anywhere with that vehicle. I'll bet you every damn padre in camp and the Okanagan is sipping away at his products. Did I say sipping? I meant gulping. Anyway, what are *you* going to eat? I think I'll settle for the almond sole with the brandy-flambé."

Cordell Cross

While the two dined, ten musketeers and their girls assisted Alma's dad selling hot-dogs at a Lions Club charity bingo held in the Vernon Arena.

"How in the hell did we get sucked into this?" asked Lyons, dressed in a chef's hat with an apron covering his military summer clothing. All the musketeers and their girls assisted by serving behind long counters, and at least 500 people packed the arena.

"We didn't have anything better to do, did we? East replied with his mouth full. This grub's good"

"You're supposed to serve 'em, not eat 'em," snapped Lyons. "Here we are trying to help the Lions make money and you're eating the profits!"

East pushed the last of a hot-dog into his mouth and wiped his hands on his apron. "They said we could have one, ya know?"

"Yeah, one! You've had ten! And leave those sandwiches alone!"

Jack swallowed, gave Lyons a dirty look, and assisted a customer. "May I help you, sir?"

A pleasant-looking fellow held out two coupons. "Yes, thank you. I'll have two hot-dogs and two KiK Kolas, please."

Talking to his young son, the client held out his hand. East took the coupons, prepared two hot-dogs and uncapped two KiKs. He then moved on to serve someone else, but not for long. East had misjudged the boy's intelligence.

"Daddy, there's a big bite out of an end of my hot-dog."

The boy's father unwrapped the food in question. While the wiener and bun appearing out the end of the napkin looked normal, the rest of it covered by the napkin had indeed been *interfered* with.

"Hey, what the heck are you trying to pull off here? There's tooth marks on my son's hot-dog and it's half gone."

Once again, East swallowed quickly. "Sorry, sir, we've had complaints like that all day. It must be the mice. Bright young little fella, isn't he? Here's another one."

Before accepting the replacement, the boy's father smiled and noted, "Mice? If they have teeth that size, you'd better get yourself a cat. A large one - say tiger size."

Although East grinned, under his breath he mumbled, "There's no doubt about it; that little creep's gonna be a Seaforth or an Irish pongo. The others never said a word. They'll probably join the Rocky Mountain Rangers."

When the fund-raiser finished and goodbyes were said, rain still hammered B-3 during the movie that night. With the building packed to the brim, the old hangar's projector only broke down twice during the showing of *The Snipers*, a British war film about how British snipers *took care* of German snipers during the Second World War.

After mug-up, the cold air in B-25 made the hut's occupants head for the hot showers, or hit the sack just to stay warm. The Musketeers did both, and when the lights went out, the sounds of a platoon on the parade square bellowing, "One two-three one," was just audible over the thumping rain. Other discernible comments were, "Put chicken shit in my bed, will ya? Okay, who did it? We're gonna get soaked until the real rooster crows. God, what a rotten thing to do to me ... your friendly corporal, your mother and father for six weeks! Left, right, left right..."

Cordell Cross

East grinned as he rolled over on his side, muttering, "What kind of a mother and father is he if he doesn't know the difference between chicken grease and chicken shit?"

The scent of fabulous fresh Okanagan morning air didn't enter B-25 until the inner southwest door opened at 0530 and a familiar order rocked the rafters of the barracks.

In great form, Sergeant Bentley rushed down the aisle pulling off blankets and turning mattresses over.

"Stand by your beds! C'mon you lazy people, it's a wonderful day out there and I don't want you to miss it! Egad, it smells like a whorehouse in here!"

"What's a whorehouse smell like, Sergeant? We ain't had that pleasure yet," asked a shivering 15th Field artillery cadet standing at the end of his bunk.

"They smell like this hut," Bentley replied, hastily marching through the centre area to wake the other side.

"You've got exactly thirty seconds to form three ranks on the road! Move it!"

Naked, with his usual morning erection to guide him, Danyluk lined up at the urinal, paying no attention to the dirty looks from the cadet in front who kept his distance even at the expense of bumping the cadet in front of him.

"Is there a Canned Scot in here?" Moose yelled.

A voice from the second *cubicle* confirmed his belief.

"You bet there is, and proud of it," was the reply.

"It smells like it! We in the Irish don't have that problem," Moose offered before returning his attention to the urinal. "Jesus, will you move it up front! I'm gonna piss in someone's ear if this line doesn't start moving!"

"Crass Irish pongo," the second cubicle's voice protested.

Finally making it to the urinal, Danyluk had the last word.

"And I don't care if you are wearing your kilt, use toilet paper!"

Although cold, the air was fresh and the rays of the morning sun had already eliminated any sign of the previous downpour.

"Oh you can't get to Heaven," Bentley sung and his semi-eager charges repeated the words as Signals Company jogged towards the upper camp.

"In IBT kit! 'Cause IBT kit! Is full of shit! Oh ya can't get to heaven in IBT kit, 'cause IBT kit is full of shit! Lord thanks, for the signals course!"

After they returned to B-25 and completed fifty push-ups and fifty sit-ups, the cadets of Signals Company were ready to take on the day. With breakfast only an hour away and the barracks looking like a garbage dump, a lot of work lay ahead.

"One, Two, Three o'clock, four o'clock rock..." sang Bill Haley and the Comets as the musketeers and all members of 21 and 22 Platoons prepared their side of the barracks for the morning inspection. Having the weekend off showed because three full trashcans had to be moved outside.

At 0645 when the line-up for breakfast started, eight musketeers and a Seaforth cadet dressed in coveralls were at the front. East had made sure of that by *reserving* spaces. Bergie decided to stay behind for a few moments.

"Didn't you feel guilty hearing those poor souls on the parade square last night?" Wane asked.

"A little," Jack replied. "But I've been taught to survive in this world. If it wasn't them, it would have been me, or us."

Cunningham went to great pains to display his new gold bracelet. "I wonder what the IBT corporal did with his new bedding?"

Rothstein laughed. "Probably switched it with a cadet. Hey, that's a neat looking bracelet. How come the word, 'Robert' is inscribed?"

The embarrassing question made the gambler put his hand in his pocket. "Well how the hell did I know it was engraved? I'm either gonna melt it down or let him win it back."

"I'd let him win it back," offered Douglas. "Gordie, his parents probably bought him that for his birthday or something. Have a heart."

"Have a heart? Listen Doug, when ya play, ya pay," Cunningham blared. "During the game, he was up and he was down! Do ya think he gave a damn when he won my watch?"

When they were seated, a smiling Bergie entered and rushed up to their table. "Here I am doing the detective work, while you guys just want to eat. Come closer."

Instantly, all heads huddled in the middle.

"What?"

"I don't believe it!"

"That pongo!"

"He waited this long, eh?"

After Bergie got his bacon and eggs, he elaborated further.

"Initially I thought the culprits who'd planted the chicken fat were Scots, but it wasn't them. Johnston's our man. He got the wrong bunk that's all. He came in just before us and asked the corporal which bunk was Moose's bunk. After that, he got mixed up. He had to move fast because he knew we'd be returning soon. Apparently he hasn't yet forgiven you for the Spanish Fly caper, Moose."

Lyons' upper lip twitched. "A Duke did that to Jack? Johnston made more money on that deal than you did, Moose. Okay, Bergie, what do we do?"

Moose put an arm around Bergie's shoulders. "Son-of-a-bitch, you bet he did! What's the plan, old buddy, old pard?"

"I know what I'd like to do," East said, being held back from going up for thirds. "I can still smell the crap. I'd like to kick him in the nuts."

Following breakfast, twelve cadets failed the dress inspection. The fact so many hadn't failed since week two, Major Hansford became thoroughly upset, believing the whole company was becoming slack. "I give you people the weekend off, and I have to witness this type of dress and deportment in week five! I should cancel the trip to Kelowna tomorrow because really, you don't deserve it.

"As of this minute, *you* will straighten out your weak peers! *You* will ensure there are no skuzzballs in this company! If necessary, *you* will shine their boots, wash and press their uniforms, and shine their belts. Do I make myself clear?"

A resounding, "Yes, sir," shook the hut windows.

"Effective immediately, this company will be on the parade square every morning for three hours on the days we have *any*, and I say again, *any*, tramps on my parade! *Moreover,* if your kit and quarters aren't up to par throughout the day, every last one of you will be on the parade square for three hours following supper!

"Platoon sergeants, get these people out of my sight! I also want to see all platoon sergeants and junior NCOs in my office at 1200 hours!"

As far as the cadets were concerned, they had never seen Major Hansford so angry. Marching to the parade square, they knew the platoon sergeants and corporals would get a blast at noon, and that blast would be passed on tenfold, starting now.

"Left, right, left, right, left right! Get your arms up and push down on your thumbs! Get your chins up, chests out and stomachs in! You, you once-horrible excuse for a normal birth, what the hell are you wiggling your ass for? Twenty-One Platoon ... halt! Stand still! Keep your head and eyes to your front!"

Spittle poured out of the sergeant's mouth onto the shirt of the cadet he towered over. "Are you one of those weird ones? Well are you?"

"No, Sergeant!"

"Speak up! Well, are you a woman dressed as a man?"

"No, sergeant!"

"Why not?"

"It's er ... well, it's not my sexual preference, sergeant!"

"What's your sexual preference? Your right hand; someone else's hand, or whatever?"

"No Sergeant!"

"Then you must be left handed! Is that it?"

"No, Sergeant!"

"Well young man, and I use the term loosely, if you wiggle your rear-end on this parade square again, I'll personally volunteer your services for use on an island off the coast of Greece! Is that clear?"

"Yes, Sergeant!"

"By the left, quick ... march! Left, right, left, right! At the halt on the left, form ... squad! Watch your dressing on the halt. Change direction left at the halt, left ... form!"

True to his word, Major Hansford ensured three solid hours of drill on the blazing parade square were carried out with stern military discipline. The pop truck didn't appear, water breaks were not given and during the one-hundred-and-eighty minutes, only once were the cadets allowed a two-minute break. That break wasn't in the shade; it was right smack in the middle of the parade square - the ground that melted feet if they were in the same place for more than sixty seconds.

At noon, the musketeers along with everyone else in the company plopped themselves on their beds, and Wane leaned over, saying, "We haven't been treated like that since last year with Beckford."

"We haven't had that at all," was Douglas' reply. "Beckford gave us more breaks in the shade."

Lyons had taken Driver Mechanics the year before and these last three hours were the most he'd ever spent on the parade square.

"Chaps, every bone in my body is crying to be set. My arms are sore, my legs are sore, my stomach is sore, my neck is sore and my..."

"Balls and wang are sore," offered Moose, yanking a letter out from under his pillow. He'd received the letter on Saturday with another twenty and was just now getting around to finishing them off.

"I've got more blisters than normal skin on my feet," said Rothstein, taking off his boots and wrapping Band-Aids. "Maybe this camp is sponsored by Johnson and Johnson, the bandage people."

"No it's not. It's run by cruel-minded sadists," Jackson replied.

"Actually old chap, that's an interchanging sentence. You see chum, sadists would already be cruel-minded, so you don't have to..."

"Go screw yourself, Lyons." Cunningham interrupted as he put on his new gold bracelet and admired it. Watches, eyeglasses and all jewellery except rings were not allowed to be worn on morning parades. "Here we are dying, and your correcting his use of the Queen's English. Do we know who the twelve are?"

"What twelve?" Bergie asked.

Gordie waved his hand around watching his new bracelet glitter. "The twelve who weren't up to snuff and caused all this shit?"

Although his legs ached, Douglas kicked Wane's springs and said, "Those twelve are in 23 and 24 Platoons."

Banks leaned over. "Don't, Doug. Every muscle and bone in my body aches."

"Sorry, buddy."

East opened his barrack box and took out a partly eaten sandwich he'd stored the night before. "The rotten pongoes. We should run 'em through the gauntlet."

"If they do it again, we will," offered Bergie. "What's on this afternoon?"

Jackson took out his timetable. "We're playing soccer from 1330 to 1430, followed by a swim parade at Kin Beach. Our platoon is playin' a Driver Mechanics platoon. Speakin' of D&M, has anyone heard from Foster?"

Moose stood while removing his clothes. "Whatsamatter with you, Earl? Didn't you see him give us the finger this morning as those jeeps drove by?"

"The creep. He's such a sod," said Lyons.

Douglas laughed. "You did it to us last year. Are you so pure now?"

A grin came over Lyons' face. "Come to think of it, I did, didn't I? Moose, where are you going and what's wrong?"

Naked, Danyluk stood there with a sad look on his face. "I'm goin' for a cold shower."

"But why so sad, old companion?"

Moose put his letter back under his dust cover. "It's this letter from lovely Olga. She's only written six words; she must be really sad."

"What'd she say?" asked McLeod.

Danyluk threw his towel over his shoulder. "She says, *'Moose you scoundrel - the rabbit died.'* What the hell's she blaming me for? I never even knew she had a rabbit.

Cordell Cross

Oh well, I'll get her another one when I get home. Nah, rabbits don't last long, I'll get her a cat."

That afternoon, four Signals Company platoons beat four Driver Mechanics platoons at soccer. Following the games, the trucks arrived and the worn-out company headed for Kin Beach. With the temperature in the high nineties, the cadets in the backs of the trucks didn't concern themselves about 'show' parades. The boys only wanted one thing, and that was the cold clear water of Okanagan Lake.

For an hour-and-a-half, the cadets had the wondrous water and beach to themselves. Only two civilians were at the east end of the shore and although Jack could smell their hot-dogs cooking, he reluctantly kept his distance.

On the way back to camp, the singing in the backs of the trucks indicated that the 0530 awakening had been forgotten, the morning parade square session was out of their minds, and the sweat, blood, and sore throats from yelling on the parade square and at the soccer games had vanished.

Upon arriving back at B-25, Major Hansford stood waiting for them. Obviously, his talk with the NCOs had been a two-way conversation.

"Perhaps I was a little rough on you this morning, I don't know. Your sergeants and corporals tell me you're working hard. I agree with them; the majority of you are putting everything you have into this course. It's unfortunate that a few bad apples can ruin the crate.

"As I mentioned earlier, I want you to sort the bad apples out using *appropriate* methods. *Explain* to them that to survive, we must operate as a team. That there is no room for slovenliness in signals, or this camp for that matter. *Talk* to them and bring up their standards by showing them what is expected of them.

"Damn, we're in week five. All the bad habits bought from home should have been eliminated by now. I feel confident that sloppy cadets can be embarrassed if peers do their laundry, shine their belts and boots, and keep their bed-spaces clean. Only then, will they see the light and get the job done themselves.

"Tomorrow morning we're going to Kelowna for the day. Trucks will arrive here at 0900 hours. The dress has been posted. It is khaki shirts and shorts, boots, puttees and hose tops. Your regimental webbelts and headdress will be worn. In addition, if you wear lanyards at your home corps, you may wear them tomorrow. Any questions?"

An arm shot out. "Sir, can we take our swim suits?"

"No!"

Another arm quickly shot out. "Sir, is this a programmed tour, or are we on our own while we're there?"

"You're basically on your own. Take a look at the town, meet the people, and remember your manners. You represent this camp remember that! The trucks will remain there until 2100 hours and box lunches will be handed out at the vehicles at 1200 and 1700 hours."

Following the dismissal, the cadets shared their joviality by cheering their way into B-25.

Cordell Cross

Unlike the way they felt at noon, the refreshed cadets lay on their bunks joking and looking forward to their upcoming trip.

Shortly the musketeers' side of the barracks was silent, except for Kay Starr singing, *Wheel of Fortune*. Danyluk had forgotten to turn off his radio when East bellowed, "Hey you pongoes, other companies are lining up for supper already!"

As evening fell, it was quiet in B-25. The barracks remained immaculate as cadets wrote letters home, laundered their clothing, ironing it, made trips to the cadet canteen, or sat around each other's bunks telling war-stories.

The musketeers, minus Cunningham gathered around Bergie's bunk, planning their retaliation for Johnston. Cunningham was over with Stanley, *allowing* the boy to win his gold bracelet back if such a thing was possible with a marked deck.

After thirty minutes, a plan was decided upon. The *dirty work* would be done that very night.

"The little bugger won't have a clue," said Moose rubbing his hands together. "Bergie, my boy, I say it again - you are indeed a genius."

"You guys are mean," McLeod stated, standing up to get his chess board out so he and Lyons could start a game.

"How long do you think it will take you?" Rothstein asked. Although he said, "you" he was involved, but his part took place at approximately 2215. "My *job* won't take that much time."

"No more than twenty minutes," Bergie said. "The little creep's been playing baseball and soccer all day, so he'll be tired as hell."

Bergie was right. Johnston snored loudly as seven cadets stood around his upper bunk at 0200 hours. Rothstein had done his job earlier, and Jackson and East were now lookouts. If military police vehicle lights appeared, or sentries walked towards the hut, the seven would learn about it quickly.

As usual, nothing was said. Firmly and efficiently, Johnston's mattress with him on it was transferred by three of them onto a folding table held high by the remaining four.

It was dark in Johnston's hut. Even the centre section's lights had been turned out for some reason, leaving only the lights from the road and the porch lights from each end of the *chicken-fat joker's* wing.

Silently, they moved Johnston into the toilet area where the table was lowered. The mattress was then gently pulled off and pulled evenly along the floor coming to rest under the first two cubicles. Had he opened his eyes, Johnston wouldn't have recognized the location. His face was inches away from the outside bottom of the second cubicle's toilet bowl. His feet rested next to the first one - the partition of the two cubicles separating him at the waist.

Seconds later, after the table was returned to its normal spot, there were only two things left to do ... flush both toilets, and this was swiftly done by Bergie and Moose before they ran. Earlier, Rothstein had visited the hut and clogged both toilets with toilet paper and anything else he could fund.

Cordell Cross

290 – NEXT STOP, VERNON!

The Musketeers didn't stick around to see the results of their caper. Like Johnston did after he planted the chicken fat, they took off back to B-25, calmly shook hands and said goodnight. Johnston now wore the results of their *restitution*.

Chapter 22

"His yells woke everyone up in his barracks and the next barracks," East explained, laughing and pushing a piece of bacon into his mouth.

Prior to breakfast, the morning of the Kelowna trip had started like most other mornings. Up at 0530, Signals Company had completed a jogging trip throughout the upper camp and completed fifty sit-ups and push-ups before cleaning up their hut and heading to the mess hall.

East was so excited, he had trouble telling the story. "Everyone in their barracks is talking about it. They think it's hilarious. Not only was the pongo drenched, but someone had taken a dump earlier and left it after noticin' the shitter was clogged. The little creep got the whole thing. With the room being pitch-black, and not knowing where he was, and being half asleep, he couldn't get up because of the partition, and the shitters kept overflowing. The whole floor flooded. Apparently, his yells could have raised the dead. He's blaming the Irish."

Low chuckles dying to be set free filled the musketeers table, and East still wasn't finished. "Afterwards, he was thrown in the shower with his bedding and mattress and spent the night with a corporal's blanket on the drying room floor. Masterful, Bergie, masterful."

"Well, we've gotten our own back," Bergie said with his chest out. "When are they gonna learn not to mess around with us?"

Moose roared out laughing. "Only after they pay the price."

"There is yeast, yeast, up the asses of the police; in the stores ... in the stores.
There is yeast, yeast, up the asses of the police; in the quartermaster stores.
"My eyes are dim, but I can see, the provost pack, their, butts, with yeast. The provost, pack, their, butts, with yeast!"

It didn't matter which uncovered convoy truck passed the guardroom that morning, each vehicle's chorus sang the same song. Even the appearance of the Provost Sergeant didn't hamper the enthusiasm of the cadets bound for Kelowna.

The ten musketeers were joined in the same truck with another ten cadets from 21 Platoon.

"At least this is one rig we don't have to push to Kelowna," Jackson quipped, taking in the beautiful scenery Highway 97 covered.

Throughout the trip, the lakes' colour and serenity were enough to get all cadets of Signals Company wanting to jump off for *bare and unauthorized* swim parades, but dreaming gave in to common sense.

"We should have told the girls," said East, eating an apple while protecting a brown paper bag.

Jackson held out his hands to the sky. "Now he thinks of it. Where the hell have you been, Jack? The girls are playing softball all day in Lumby. I mentioned that last night."

"I musta been busy when you told me."

"Yeah, you were busy all right. You're back to storing chicken in our barrack box again. What's in the bag?"

Cordell Cross

"Three tasty chicken legs, and their all mine," East replied, placing the bag on his lap and firmly holding onto it with his left hand.

Moose couldn't believe it. "Doesn't the smell make you wanna puke?"

"You won't say that when you want a bite."

Danyluk cringed. "Believe me, I won't want a bite. Youse can eat all the maggots in that decayed dead chicken flesh, you want."

A sour look came over East's face. "Ya don't have to describe it that way. Er, who wants a bite of chicken?"

Bergie held out his hand. "I'll help you, gimmee a leg."

After Jack passed the leg, Bergie handed it to Moose, who finished it in seconds.

East saw the action. "You dirty creep! You wanted one all along, didn't you?" Jeez, that's sly!"

Howls of laughter filled the back of the truck. "If youse ain't gonna share the stuff, we've gotta get it by usin' Lord Strathcona methods!"

There were no Lord Strathcona cadets in the back, but there were a few Westies.

"Or Westie methods," Moose added.

"Stick the bone up your ass," one of the Westies said. "You wanna know somethin'? I'd eat horse manure before I'd lower myself to the standards you Dukes operate by."

"We already know that," came the response. The other musketeers, except McLeod, joined in. Bergie, Rothstein, and Jackson considered themselves honorary Dukes. McLeod took into account that as a proud member of the 72nd Seaforths, under no circumstances would he lower himself to become an honorary Duke. "It just ain't done," he said.

Danyluk took a letter out of his pocket. "Youse guys have gotta hear this. It's from delightful and exquisite Edith, the love of my life in the alley."

"Hey, she's a new one, ain't she? Just how many loves of your life have ya got?" asked Cunningham, displaying his new gold ring. He'd allowed Stanley to win back the bracelet, but it had cost the Westie his ring.

"I didn't say she's a normal love of my life," offered Moose. "She's just a love of my life when we're in the alley. Let me get on with this, will ya?"

"My darling Alley Cat: With the days so short and the nights so long, how long must I wait, for the touch of your prong? That's a little touch of poetry I thought you'll like. I feel so embarrassed writing this way, Moose, my love, but since youse liberated me, I've become a new broad. The other..."

Rothstein interrupted. "She says she's become a new *broad*? Who taught *her* the Queen's English?"

Moose stuck out his chest. "I did. What's wrong with that word?"

East threw a chicken-leg over the side. "Oh, get on with it! Harvey - ya shoulda known that when you heard the word, *'youse.'*"

" ... night I went house to house asking for donations for your Military Police With Sore Buttocks Fund, and I collected twelve dollars and ninety-three cents, which is enclosed. Moose why didn't youse mention the reason the police have got sore asses? One guy who opened the door said he was in the Military Police and he ended up with piles as well. I said piles of what - money? When I

said, let's have some then, he slammed the door in my face. What an asshole, eh? He don't have the dignity you and your friends have. Anyway, just why do the Provost have sore asses? Are they sitting on their butts all day, or what? My friend, Claire says they've got sore asses because they've got the runs twenty-four hours a day. How horrible. When I gets the runs, it only lasts two or three hours. Remember that time I got the runs when we went on the Shoot the Shoot at the Pacific National Exhibition? Why you took off on me I'll never know. Was it because I put my panties in my purse instead of throwing them away?

Anyway, my faithful lover, I've been walkin' our favourite alley just waitin' for youse to return. Here's another little poem I wrote for youse. 'When I walks the alley, with my pally; I stops to piss before we kiss. He hands me a mint, which I stuff in my face; and before I know it, he's lifting my lace. So relaxed, he pushes my body against the fence; Sometimes I wonder if he knows why I'm tense. Then he holds me tight, and hands me a ring, which he says was his mother's, as he fuses my thing.

Great eh, Moose? Remember that it was youse who taught me how to write poetry.

Well, my heartthrob, I'm going to walk that alley right now, just thinking of youse. I'm not going to write again because I knows you're comin' home soon. Give my regards to your best friend, the commanding officer. All of my love is yours ... in the alley of our dreams. Edith.

Danyluk's dreamy face said it all when he sniffed at the letter and put it back in his pocket. From the expression he gave, he indeed really did have the hots for his *love of the alley*, and the stunned sneers he got from everyone else went totally unnoticed.

Douglas whispered to Wane, "Marigold's a princess compared to Edith."

"How about a queen," Wane whispered back. "Jeez, I wouldn't let that girl - if she is one, wash my socks."

Douglas laughed. "She'd like to wash more than your socks."

Banks grimaced. "I doubt it. From the sound of her, I don't think she washes anything. She reminds..."

Lyons' bellowing interrupted Banks.

"What the..." Jack, you wiped your chicken leg all over my crotch when you picked your beret up off the floor. My God, look at the front of my pants! What's the matter with you?"

"It looks like you've peed yourself and said to hell with it," offered Jackson.

East couldn't be more apologetic as he took out his hankie. "I ... I'm sorry, Don. Here, let me try and wipe ..."

The hankie looked worse than Lyons' crotch. "Get your grubby little hands offa me, you pongo! Now what the hell am I going to do? I can't walk around Kelowna looking like this?"

"I'll wash 'em for you when were there."

"You'll what? Oh sure, and I'll just walk around in my gaunch while my pants are drying. Get with it."

Lyons didn't see the few smiles around him, he was too intent on giving East a blast.

The trip to Kelowna turned every signals cadet into a raving tourist. Very little traffic used Highway 97 that morning and the air and scenery captivated the boys' artistic senses, even Danyluk's.

As the trucks rolled, the beauty of Kalamalka Lake and its two neighbouring lakes was beyond imagination.

After they stopped in the parking lot of a red-bricked high-school, the company was formed up, given another pep-talk by Major Hansford and fallen out. Seconds later, groups of cadets headed in all directions.

Douglas, Wane and the rest of the musketeers had visited Kelowna before, but just being in a new town felt exciting. Although Kelowna wasn't a military village like Vernon, the people were just as friendly. Passing adults smiled at cadets, said hello, and questioned the various badges they wore. Short khaki pants were also an oddity. Many residents thought they looked marvellous and cool, not knowing the amount of work it took to make them appear that way.

In many ways, Kelowna's main drag resembled Vernon's. Tall buildings hadn't yet been approved, allowing an atmosphere of open space with blue sky. The many quaint shops lining both sides of the eight blocks of the main street seemed different to big-city boys. Stores offered regional fruit, souvenirs, pastries, and a combination of city, and country consumer goods, leaning more towards country commodities. Times were gradually changing, but the rustic rural hardware stores still marketed saddles, ice-cream and butter churns as well as every other farm necessity.

Had the cadets visited on a Friday night instead of a weekday, the main street of Kelowna would have been packed full of farming families visiting from miles away, making their weekly, monthly, or even their annual trip to the *big* city. Some farmers were fortunate, their farms bordered the town, but ever so slowly, their land was being bought up and developed.

While their parents shopped or sipped beverages in the few local bars, squeaky clean *dressed up* farm kids whose hair hadn't been combed for weeks before they came to town, drank pop and had the time of their lives attending Kelowna's one movie theatre.

"There's the ferry," offered an excited Rothstein, pointing to a little old chug, halfway across Okanagan Lake. "Let's take a ride."

With the wind up a bit, the lake was choppy. Presently, all ten musketeers felt the light spray washing their faces as the aged but cherished vessel made its way to Westbank on the other side.

As usual, Douglas was lost for words as he moved away from the others and found a secluded spot up front. As far as he was concerned, absolutely no one could describe the abounding beauty he saw and the complete feeling of freedom he felt. The burnt barren hills caught by the sky and shared with the lake's mirror, created a miraculous portrait and the *artist* had allowed him in.

It was Wane's voice that ended the rapture. "We should live here."

"Oh, that we could be so lucky," Brice replied. "I'd never want to leave. You know, when I see this I know what God wanted us to see."

Wane's eyes rolled to the sky. "Jeez, Doug, don't start philosophising again."

"Wane, I'm not philosophising, I've just given it a lot of thought, that's all. I figure the chances of being born are about one in a hundred million quadrillion billion trillion. That goes for animals, bugs or any living thing. Just look around you at the changes that are going on. We're starting to pave everything. Some day there'll be no open spaces at all. God doesn't want that."

"Wane's interest grew. " What does he want?"

"He wants us to observe and sense the beauty of the wind blowing the trees and flowers. He wants us to feel the clean rain on our faces; to experience the power of a storm agitate the oceans and the lakes. He wanted us to see ... no, he wants us to feel the beauty of the moon and the sun and the umbrella of stars."

"But Doug, we already do that."

"I don't think so, Wane. Describe a sunset for me, will ya?"

Wane searched for words. He'd seen the striking colours of sunsets hundreds of times, but he couldn't describe the scene. "Er, can you?"

"Not very well. I've tried to, but I can't. They're too beautiful. It's like what Sergeant Beckford did last year when he blindfolded the instructional technique class and then asked Bergie to describe an elephant."

"Wane chuckled. " Or Moose's *parts*."

Both cadets laughed, before Douglas continued. "So you see, we take it all for granted. I guess that's because it's free. It's a matter of values. Most people will shine their car and take hours admiring it, but don't give the moon a second look when it shines in their window at night."

Douglas stopped talking and studied the wash of the lake against his side of the ferry. "I guess I'm rambling again, eh?"

Wane's "No," was almost a whisper. "I knew a girl who had a horse for years. She loved him so much, they were inseparable. She spent every spare minute grooming him and riding. Then one day she lost interest and had him put down. She said she couldn't afford him, or got herself married; one of the two, I can't remember. Others wanted the horse, but she wouldn't share him. The horse was only thirteen and had been a loyal friend. When you talk about the chances of life being a hundred billion trillion to one, I guess she never thought about that. Pretty shitty, eh?"

Douglas looked into his friend's eyes. "She did that? Unfortunately, the wrong animal was put down."

"Hey you pongoes! Moose's steerin' the boat," Bergie shouted sticking his head out of the captain's bridge porthole.

"Is he smoking a pipe and singing a sea shanty?" Jackson asked, appearing with the two.

"No, if anything, he looks a little green around the gills!"

Earl understood. Moose had told him he got seasick easily.

"Then we may never make it! Abandon ship! All passengers to the lifeboats!"

On the trip back, Rothstein and McLeod also got to steer the vessel. Although there were no official papers, the captain appointed them *titular* first mates.

For Lyons, the day was living hell. While walking the streets he kept his right hand dangling in front of his crotch. When he passed two officers, his left hand took over the dangling part and his right hand saluted.

After they had passed the cadets, one officer said to the other, "Did you see that poor bastard? I wonder what happened to him?"

Cordell Cross

Wearing a green hackle, his colleague replied, "Probably a birth defect. Either that or he thinks he's in the showers. Did you see his badge? What regiment is he with?"

The officer glanced back. "I think he's in the British Columbia Regiment. Yes, he's wearing a black beret."

His friend snickered. "It figures."

"Stand by your beds! Come on you lazy lot! You had your fun yesterday. Today everything is back to normal," Sergeant Bentley roared as he pulled down bedding and turned over mattresses.

"You've got twenty seconds to form three ranks on the road!"

"Hey Sergeant, the day before yesterday youse gave us thirty seconds," Moose *advised*, rushing to the jon with his customary massive morning erection.

"I heard IBT gives thirty seconds; this is signals. Get a move on!"

Wednesday's warm sun hadn't been up too long as signals jogged through the upper camp. Although singing started, most boys were too tired to join in due to lack of sleep, or too much fresh air.

Kelowna had been the break they needed. All cadets had walked their feet off exploring the town or following girls. The park by the beach provided shade for them to relax, but few took advantage of it. Instead, they ate their box lunches in the blazing parking lot of the high-school.

The air was cold riding back to camp that night. Some had brought sweaters, but most remained in their shirts. The same shirts that had been removed at the beach, allowing the sun to leave fiery tattoos on its worshippers.

"Just think, Don, you don't have to dangle your hand in front of your crotch anymore," McLeod said.

Despite the fact that Lyons was still upset with East, a smile appeared. "I'm still thinking of that waitress in the restaurant who kept telling me the washrooms were at the rear. She thought I needed the jon."

Bergie slapped Lyons on the back. "Eight people on the street also stopped to direct you to the public washrooms. Didn't you get tired of saying, 'Thank you, but I've recently broken my arm?'"

"You bet I did! That's why I carried an empty box lunch in front of me for five hours! God, that was the most humiliating day of my life! You owe me, East!"

East still apologized. "I'll do your boots for a week."

"Oh, no! Not just my boots. You'll do my whole kit, you creep."

"At least I stuck up for you," East said, searching for a chocolate bar he'd misplaced. "That Canadian Scottish cadet was gonna pound you."

Lyons gave Jack a dirty look. "Yeah, but why was he gonna pound me? Because I told him to go and screw himself when he said, 'There's that BCR who always pisses himself instead of goin' to the jon.'"

After the cadets completed their morning physical exercises, it was back to Morse code, line laying, signal office duties, and every aspect of signals training the company had covered since day three.

Cordell Cross

297 – NEXT STOP, VERNON!

On Thursday, Advanced Instructional Technique was introduced by their platoon officers and the boys found that teaching signals mutual instruction wasn't as tough as they had first thought. When they returned to their home corps' they would teach other cadets and the new-found knowledge would be used on parade nights and monthly field exercises. Most cadet corps held Nineteen sets, Fifty-Eight sets, Morse code keys and buzzers, UCL ten-line switchboards and Tele-L sets.

It was half-an-hour before the start of another Mother's Night process that the cadets of Signals Company learned that their weekend wouldn't be free. The company was formed up three ranks on the road when Major Hansford explained to them that the council members of Vernon had approved the sports trials at Polson Park on Saturday, and the swimming trials at Kalamalka Beach on Sunday.

"You will, however, have Saturday night off and you can apply for a midnight pass. The BCR band will parade on tomorrow morning's parade, so those of you who are a little stale, should bone up on your instruments tonight."

"He must be talking about Danyluk," Cunningham whispered to Rothstein. "Little does he know, Moose *instrumentalizes* his bone every night."

Although Moose was in the front rank, he heard the *gambler*, turned around and offered, "Yeah, and it ain't gettin' stale. Hell, if youse lets your wang get stale, life just ain't worth livin' is it?"

The OC didn't particularly care for being interrupted when he addressed his company. "You! Yes you! If you have something to say, you can pass it along to all of us! Now, what seems to be your concern?"

As he shot to attention, perspiration appeared on Moose's forehead. "Er, I was simply telling my comptrot here that…"

"Compatriot, not comptrot," Bergie murmured, rolling his eyes to the sky.

"…Er, telling my compatriot, that, er, he'd better bone up. Some of us are boned up, and some of us ain't."

The OC appeared pleased that his advice was being considered. "Oh, well that's fine. Have you boned up?"

Moose had stood at ease. Now he quickly assumed the position of attention again. "I never lets my instruments get the better of me, sir! Daily practice keeps me and them in shape!"

Only after a roar of laughter from the company did Major Hansford understand the humour. Slightly red-faced, he let the matter drop. "Thank you, cadet Danyluk!"

"Youse is welcome, sir! I just hopes that those who play the swinechord is boned up!"

"Swinechord? Er, what is it, and who plays them?"

With a smile on his face and his chest out, Moose enlightened his officer commanding. "Mainly Seaforths and Irish. A swinechord is a hair stretched over a pig's ass and is plucked by the teeth, sir!"

No one knew if the OC's mouth gesture was a smile or a gas pain as he ignored the comment and called the CSM to dismiss to dismiss the company.

Inside, many of the Scottish persuasion voiced their *concern* as they passed Danyluk's bunk.

"Bloody BCRs are all the same! Filthy freaks!"

Cordell Cross

"All you black-hats are full of shit!"

"Jealous prick!"

"If anyone plucks hair out of his teeth, it's you, you pongo!"

"Christ, he's got a nerve! He showers with the living-breathing human fart, and he thinks he knows it all!"

"He should put a string on his knob and play it like a fiddle … the abnormal abortion!"

"Better yet, he should play the harp. He could pluck it with his prick!"

Throughout the bombardment, a grinning Moose turned up his radio and hummed along with Les Paul and Mary Ford singing *Vaya con Dios.*

Shortly, bunks were moved as mops and scrub-brushes swung into action. Sweating cadets worked away raking the *garden*, cleaning the windows, floors, toilets, urinal, showers, sinks, taps, mirrors, drying room, barrack boxes, folding tables and benches, garbage cans, fire extinguishers, light fixtures - shades, and the tops of shelves and cubicles.

When that was complete, they rubbed White 'IT' into their running shoes, scrubbed pith helmets and wash-basins, pressed boot-laces, shined boots, pressed puttees, shined their badges and belts, pressed their battledress, and washed, soaped, starched and ironed every article of Saturday's clothing.

At the end of the day, the towels that had been sent to Hop Sing's earlier in the week were individually *sniffed at* and hung at the ends of bunks.

That Friday evening's weather was so hot, many cadets made their beds Saturday morning style and slept under or next to their bunks. Since their mattresses were already rolled, all they needed was a blanket and the cool floor. They really didn't need a blanket, but during the night, it would get a little cold and subconsciously they would cover themselves. Others didn't use a blanket at all; they just stretched out on the slivers of the well worn-out floorboards, or the cold concrete of the shower room. In the morning, their bodies would be a little stiff, but they wouldn't have to waste time making up their beds in the fashion demanded but hated by all cadets.

"Ah, the smell of this towel is pure bliss," East stated, stretching his towel under his nose. "I can actually whiff the aroma of Hop Sing's girls as they slave getting our laundry clean."

"How do you know it was sent to Hop Sing's?" Jackson asked, sniffing his towel. "I can't notice any fragrance."

Moose sniffed at his own towel and butted in. "Yeah, that's Hop Sing's scent. Ya know getting into girls' laundry is quite the job. It's, gotta clean. Earl, youse don't have the nose for it. Neither do you, East. To notice the, er, redo … er, what's the word, Rothie?"

"Redolence," Harvey replied shining his left boot.

"Yeah, redolence – thanks Rothie. Youse has gotta be chaste. Is that the word, Rothie … *chaste*?"

"Yeah."

East hung up his towel again. "Bullshit. I've been chased many times. I was chased stealin' an apple and..."

Cordell Cross

Rothstein put his gleaming boot down and placed a cloth over it. "Not chased like being chased, you pongo. Chaste, like bein' celibate, er, pure with virginity. What Moose is saying is that the two of you ain't got screwed yet, therefore you wouldn't know the difference."

Disgruntled, East came and sat on Harvey's bunk.

"Who says I ain't been screwed. How the hell do you ignoramuses know I ain't done it? Hey, Wane, tell 'em about that night I got lucky in Stanley Park. You saw me in my shorts, didn'tcha?"

Wane put down the Morse book he was studying. "Yeah, but that's because you were goin' swimmin' in Beaver Lake. She had all her clothes off, but you wore your gaunch."

"Well, the moon was shining. I ain't an exhibitionist like Danysuck here."

Moose's eyes lit up. "The dame had her clothes off and youse wore your shorts? Jack, that's an invitation; what's the matter with youse? I wouldda done it in the lake."

"I did do it in the lake, you creep. And don't push the bull that all your dames have clean laundry. Other than Alma, the other ones never wash."

Moose's face showed his frustration. "Jack, I ain't talkin' about peein' in the lake, I'm talkin' about gettin' it on in the lake."

"Yeah, you came out with your shorts still on," Wane said, straightening his book and picking up where he'd left off.

East stood up and went over to Banks' upper bunk. "I didn't piss in the lake! I slipped it to her, didn't I, Doug?"

Douglas peered over the top of a Captain Marvel comic someone had thrown at him. "How the hell do I know? Jack, I wasn't watching you. All I remember is her yelling that something was biting her ass."

Bergie laughed. "Hey maybe Moose was there. Nah, it was probably East. If he had no food, he'd bite the next best thing to it."

"You've got that wrong, old chum," Lyons quipped, moving a chess piece in the game he was playing with McLeod. "If it came to biting an apple, or biting an ass, I'd pick the ass anytime."

Jackson was a still a little miffed. "Yeah, after you cleaned its stall. Moose, what makes you think you're the only person who has screwed a dame? We might not have your calibre of wang, but what we've got ain't exactly useless. We're not all impotent like East. Just because he's sexually inadequate, don't paint all of us with the same brush. Besides, I've read that two inches can turn a dame on just the same as eight inches."

Danyluk grinned and changed radio stations. "Sixteen inches, please. Where'd youse read that? Probably in that goody-two-shoes Sweet Sixteen monthly. Jack can't see his wang, his gut's startin' to get in the way. How the hell could he use it?"

Although Moose was just ribbing East, the *beast* took it personal. "Step outside, you braggart! A man's gotta defend his actions, and I ain't about to let you ruin my reputation!"

Bergie chuckled. "You ruined your reputation when you left your shorts on. C'mon now, did you really get it on?"

Cordell Cross

"I ain't sayin' if I did or I didn't. From now on, you fruits will get nothin' outta me."

Moose had the last word. "Nor will any dame, by the sounds of it."

Jack was going to respond, but his stomach beckoned and he checked his watch. "Time for mug-up ! Who's coming?"

Instantly, the musketeers' end of the hut emptied.

Fifteen minutes later when they re-entered loaded down with sandwiches and cups of cocoa, Vast Danyluk was sitting on his brother's bed. Unlike before, he wasn't smiling or exuberant.

"Moose, where's the keys?" Vast said, looking worn out.

Moose threw him the keys to the hearse. "Vast, what happened? Youse was only gonna be in Calgary for a week?"

Vast shook a few hands moving towards the door. "Don't talk to me about Calgary - I hate that town."

"Why, what happened?" his curious brother asked.

"'Cause last night I got married in a civil ceremony. Shit, I was so drunk I didn't know what had happened until I woke up this morning starin' at a snorin' broad's face. I said, 'Who the hell are you?'"

"Yeah? And what did she say," Moose asked.

"Well, after she put her teeth in, she said, 'I'm your wife, don't you remember?'"

Howls filled B-25, then Vast added, "Oh, so it's funny, eh? Moose, go take a look at your new sister-in-law. Apparently her name's Nora. God, what am I gonna do?"

The rush was on as nearly every cadet in 21 Platoon ran out the other end of the hut to get a gander of Nora sitting in a car. After a glance, they didn't waste any time returning.

"Jeez, she must be ninety years old," Moose stated, adding, "What the hell's the matter with youse? Is she loaded, or somethin'? Vast, the old lady's gonna be pissed off; not to mention the old man. Shit, your new wife is older than them combined."

Vast ran his fingers through his hair. "Please don't mention the word "wife." I'll have ya know she's only sixty-six. At least that's what she says. Hell, I don't think I met her until I woke up next to her. What am I gonna do?"

It was Lyons of all people who came to Vast's rescue. Looking like a minister ready to preach, he said, "How old are *you*, Vast?"

"Nineteen, but I feel sixty-six."

"Then you're not married. Someone's putting you on. You've got to be twenty-one before you can marry without your parents consent. Someone's played one hell of a trick on you old boy."

With every cadet nodding, Vast's facial expression changed from one of hopelessness to jubilation. "Hey, that's right. I've been set up. Stay here, I'll be right back."

In two minutes after his new *wife* drove off, Vast was back with his luggage.

"It was a set up and she admitted the joke to me. She was goin' to Vancouver on a business trip and my buddies put her up to it. Apparently I never touched her, thank God."

Cordell Cross

Grinning sneakily, Moose placed his arm around his brother's shoulders. "Er, Vast ... youse just ain't keepin' up the family image. Ya could have stopped at a hotel tonight and broken it off in the mornin'. What's wrong with youse?"

A typical Danyluk expression came over Vast's face as he said, "Damn, youse is right. I could have nailed her before we arrived. Oh well, there'll be other broads on the way. Where's the hearse?"

Whispering to Wane, Douglas' cringed. "God, it must run in the family."

Wane's extraordinary expression crept from ear to ear. He couldn't believe the action either. "I guess age is no barrier when a Danyluk is involved."

After shaking all the Musketeers hands, Vast picked up his luggage and headed off to the BCD parking lot. "See youse guys next week," were his last words.

Shortly when the lights went out, Moose whispered to Bergie, "My brother must be slippin'. I'll betcha that Nora dame would be great in the sack, eh, Bergie?"

Although Bergie wasn't asleep, he didn't answer. Instead, he felt like throwing up.

Cordell Cross

Chapter 23

During the sixth week at Vernon, an empty phone booth in the cadet canteen indicated homesickness was on the wane. Although the cadets looked forward to the week's activities, they knew mom's cooking, dad's pride, clean civvy clothes, and privacy were not far away.

While these thoughts were pleasant, the cadets didn't know that after homecoming kisses and slaps on their backs were over with, they would soon come to realize how much they missed the disciplined clamour of camp life. The first two days after their return would be too quiet and loneliness would set in. Despite the fact that Vernon restricted them somewhat, the essence of their training allowed each of them to participate as a team, but make their own decisions. Soon, decisions would be made for them at home and at school without the military's method of praising initiative.

Morning runs disappeared during week six, but this didn't mean B-25 turned into a mausoleum. If anything, it appeared that another six weeks of training was crammed into every day.

Signals Company won the pennant on Saturday morning, and the tests were three hours instead of the usual one. Despite the fact that the BCR band was a little stale, the commanding officer had applauded the volunteer efforts of the bandsmen and advised that a 'Bandsman' course was being planned for future summers at the camp.

During the sports practice on Saturday, musketeer couples went their separate ways, however on Saturday night they all appeared at the Vernon Arena for the final dance of the summer. Girl or no girl, every cadet in camp attended and the *maidens* who had held out for six weeks waiting for Mr. Right to come along had to settle for *leftovers*.

Following the event, the couples separated again with the boys eventually meeting at their bunks for the 2359 curfew. There was no merriment as they got into bed. A great summer was coming to a close and earlier, on the girls' porches, the sadness of parting was shared mutually after each couple reminisced about the previous five weeks of fun.

When Monday morning rolled around it was the hut's corporals who walked the aisles getting everyone up.

After he flung back the covers and stood up, Danyluk thought he'd be smart. "What about gaunch, socks, shirts and belts, Corporal? Don't ya want us to wear those items?"

On Sunday, the girls turned up at Kalamalka Beach for the swim practices but unlike the previous year, couples separated themselves from their friends and went their own way. They had many private things to talk about and the only disruptions allowed were the calls from the sports-staff's bullhorns asking the numerous competitors to take their positions.

"Ok, you people - hit the showers! As you know, the dress today and tomorrow is KD longs with boots and puttees! You will wear your regimental head-dress, and don't forget to bring your mess tins, utensils, and canteen bottles!"

Cordell Cross

"Danyluk, how come you're not a hunchback?" asked the corporal, staring at the ninth wonder of the world holding his erection aside with one hand and scratching his testicles with the other. The look of pure bliss on Moose's face was typical when he initiated his morning scratching *ritual*.

Moose dropped his towel on the *pole* and straddled to the showers. "Why do you ask?"

"Because the weight of that thing should bring your upper body forward," was the corporal's reply. "Fully loaded, it must weigh at least a hundred pounds."

Before Moose entered the centre washing area, he put on his proud look. "Twenty-two pounds if youse wanna be exact. At least that's what lovely and gorgeous and ravenous Roberta told me when she weighed it."

Although the animal's reply didn't faze the corporal, Moose's statement became the main source of conversation in the crowded shower room. East couldn't believe what he had heard. "You let some dame weigh that thing?" he asked. "What the hell do you use for a scale?"

Danyluk picked a huge bar of grey sergeants' soap out of a nearby bucket and started rubbing it on his body. "Floor scales. I lay on the floor and put my wang on the scales. Luscious Roberta told me it weighed twenty-two pounds. When I weighed her bazookas, one weighed eight ounces less than the other. All us Westie types weigh our parts. It's in our ROPs."

"Don't you mean SOPs?" asked Rothstein, referring to standard operating procedures.

"No I don't mean SOPs," Moose sang. We Westies use ROPs, er, Reclining Operating Procedures!"

The weird looks Moose received from cadets not in 21 Platoon didn't bother him a bit and smiles filled the faces of those who knew he wasn't a member of the Westminster Regiment. (Now Royal Westminster Regiment.)

"You Westies are really odd-balls," said Wane, his frame covered with shampoo lather. "What other parts do you weigh?"

Danyluk dropped his large bar of sergeants' soap on a cadet's foot. After the boy shrieked and bent down to rub his toe, Moose *borrowed* his shampoo.

"Exquisite Roberta's ass weighs exactly seventy-three pounds. Not bad, eh?"

"A little heavy ain't she?" asked Jackson. "What's her total weight?"

"Likely seventy-four pounds," Douglas quipped, howling his head off.

Moose's left hand reached up and covered the shower nozzle, cutting off the water supply to three other cadets.

"Youse is just jealous. When I get home, I'm gonna buy some new scales and bring my journals up to date."

An Irish cadet asked, "You keep records?"

Danyluk released the nozzle. "Certainly, don't everyone?"

"Er, are all you Westies, er into weighing your parts?" a young Seaforth asked displaying a sour look while twitching his nose. The smell inaugurating next to him emanated from a grinning, whistling East who stopped whistling for a second to say, "You bet we are."

Cordell Cross

The shower room had become too crowded and Jack had reacted quickly to Bergie's unseen motion for a *bomb* release. All other Musketeers had quickly left the room momentarily awaiting the exodus that started immediately, along with the customary bitching.

"My God, what happened? Who would do that?" asked a now *blind* Strathcona cadet that never had time to rinse.

"Who died?" said another. "That Westie creep must belong to the Shit of the Month Club!"

The Seaforth ran out last. "It'll take me all day to get the stench out of my nose - that's if I still have a nose! My one nose-hair is already loose!"

Sixty seconds later, laughing cadets from 21 Platoon had the showers to themselves.

As Wane rinsed off, he said, "Moose, your bullshit had them all sucked in. What a lark."

A broad smile came over Moose's face. "Hey, who said it was bullshit?"

On firing position thirteen, Cunningham took off his beret, put his badge in his pocket, wiped his brow, and then placed his head-dress under his shirt to protect his right shoulder. "This place has to be the hell-hole of the world," he said, referring to the heat, dust, dirt and bugs on the outdoor rifle range, slightly south-west of the camp.

It was nearing noon and since the company arrived, four cadets had been sent back to camp suffering from heat-stroke.

Bergie lay next to him on position fourteen. "Look at it this way - you'll be in the Butts this afternoon and the money you make will keep you happy."

The *gambler* never had a chance to continue complaining because the range officer's voice boomed from a megaphone.

"This relay ... load! Range ... two hundred! Ten rounds application at your target in front - in your own time, fire! I say again, do not fire at the indicators!"

After about five minutes, indicating stopped and each .303 remained at a forty-five degree angle with its bolt open.

"This relay ... unload! Take your magazine off! Remain in your position and prepare for inspection!"

Only after a corporal had declared the weapons clear were the .303s allowed to be placed down on the ground-sheets, bolts open with bolt-heads up.

"Pull, score and patch! Change the flags! Stand up behind your weapons! We're now going to break for lunch. This relay left turn ... quick march! Telephone orderly advise the Butts personnel to come up for lunch after they've finished marking!"

Trucks that had arrived fifteen minutes earlier started to leave. Behind them they left containers of buns, soup, beef stew, sandwiches, coffee, milk and tons of dust churned up by their tires. Not settling, the clouds of dust hung in the burning air eventually joining the beef stew sliding down hungry throats.

Shade wasn't available due to lack of trees, so the company had no choice but to sit out in the open. Not the musketeers though; they'd learned their lesson the year before. The shadow of the range truck became the dining area for all of them except

Cunningham. He found a *sucker* willing to play stuke for ten-dollars he'd just received from home.

East used the last of his two buns to wipe out his mess tins. He'd tried to go back for thirds and was told to get lost. "Just think, this time next week we'll have all the comforts of home," he said, chewing. "We'll be able to sleep in, eat civvy grub, wear jeans, and go to the Pacific National Exhibition. Wow, I can't wait."

"When's our first parade night?" Wane asked Douglas.

Brice stood up to wash out his mess tins. "I think it's the second Wednesday in September. A new year, and a new RSM."

A look of fright came over Danyluk. "Don't tell me. It's already happened, hasn't it? Is it Battlefield?"

Moose could get away with most things with RSMs Brown, Matser, and Laidlaw, but with SSM Battlefield, it was another story.

"Shit, he's got eyes in the back of his head. Before I do anything, he knows about it. Do youse guys remember the time I wore a khaki tie because I'd lost my black one. I had my raincoat buttoned and my collar up headin' to the quartermaster stores. Do ya know what he said? He said, 'Danyluk, get rid of that tie immediately! Do you think you're in the Seaforths? Report for defaulters at the break! You're a Duke, Danyluk, Remember that!'"

Cunningham returned while Moose was reminiscing. He'd heard it all. "Moose, you think that's something? I wait at the same bus stop with the guy and walk four feet behind him to the armouries. Many times I've said, 'Good evening Sergeant Major,' but he chooses to ignore me. He doesn't even talk when I sit next to him on the bus, er, sometimes."

"You suck," said Wane. "You sit next to him on the bus?"

Gordie grinned as he fidgeted. "Well, er, once in a while I do. I keep a deck of cards handy and..."

Banks wasn't finished. "And if you could, you'd let him win."

Wane's statement got the *gambler's* ire up. Banks had overstepped his bounds as far as Cunningham's personal *ethics* were concerned. "Bullshit I would. When it comes to playin' cards and makin' money, everyone's equal!"

"Even Battlefield?" Douglas asked.

A guileful smile appeared on Cunningham's face. "Yes, even JKB. Well, I might let him win a few hands, but I..."

The range officer's voice cut him off. "Right, 21 Platoon you're in the Butts! Let's carry on, *gentlemen*!"

In the minute it took to wash out their mess tins and utensils, East said, "Battlefield's takin' Driver Mechanics ya know?"

Not really interested because he was counting his money, Cunningham casually asked, "How do you know that, Jack?"

"Because Foster told me. Battlefield talks with Foster all the time."

Shoving his wallet back into his right rear pocket, Cunningham said, "He does, eh? He can talk to Foster, but he ignores me! Just wait till I get him into a game!"

After one-and-a-half days of shooting on the outdoor range, the blazing sun had left its usual *marks*. Those who had taken their headdress off to use as padding had burnt foreheads and faces. The others, who kept their head-dress on, had two-tone kissers - their foreheads appeared white. Cadets foolish enough to take off their shirts in the Butts suffered to no end. Even cold showers couldn't ease their agony. As for the rest, when they placed their faces in cupped hands full of cold water, they subconsciously heard the water sizzle.

Despite being confined to camp on Tuesday afternoon, the cadets of Signals Company enjoyed the fact that they got the time off. It gave them the opportunity to wash the dirt, dust, and grime from their bodies and clean up their gear and barracks. Also, the cadet canteen remained open.

As usual, some cadets had returned from the range with live tortoises to keep as pets. These reptiles somehow survived in various mud ponds in the area. After a dressing down from their platoon sergeants and informed that the animals had been on the earth for two hundred million years, the *new owners* quickly returned the *critters*.

Most cadets in 21 Platoon were just lounging around when Cadet Johnston marched into the barracks. He still had no idea that his fellow Dukes had *repaid* him for his kindness of leaving the chicken fat.

"Did you guys hear what I went through?" he asked, sitting on Cunningham's bunk.

"Yeah, we heard," Gordie replied, taking his dice out from underneath his dust-cover. "How much money ya got?"

Johnston gave the *gambler* a contemptible glance. "Forget it, I ain't got any cash. I think it was the Irish who did the dirty to me."

"Why do you think that?" Wane asked, finding it hard not to smile.

"'Cause those creeps do that sort of thing. Jeez, I still have the smell of those shitters in my nose. It took me a day to live it down - no one would come near me."

Danyluk got up to turn on his radio. "That's the norm, ain't it?"

"Screw you, Moose. Er ... didn't you go through the same thing with the, er, chicken fat?"

Moose tuned in the Kelowna radio station and allowed Archie Bleyer's song, *Hernando's Hideaway* to fill the area.

"What chicken fat? Oh, now I know what youse is talkin about. No, I switched bunks with an Irish cadet that night. Boy was he ever pissed off. How'd you find out about that?"

Johnston quickly got to his feet. "What? Irish? So it was them pricks? Oh, er rumours travel fast. Irish, eh? Those green pongoes, I'll fix them. Gotta go guys. See ya on the train."

After the Spanish Fly *spreader* left, Lyons looked over the top of the manual he was reading. "Some *green pongo* is gonna get it tonight, don't you think so, chaps?"

In spite of the laughter, no one missed Cunningham's offer, when he yelled, "KiK Kolas are on me." In seconds, Gordie stood surrounded on the road.

The cadet canteen hummed as Gordie got the pop. This indicated some other companies had been given the afternoon off as well. Since all tables were full, the Musketeers sat on the grass by the west fence.

Cordell Cross

"Earl, is our company picnic tonight, or tomorrow night?" East asked.

Jackson took a small notebook out of his pocket.

"It's tonight at Kin Beach. And don't forget we've got the swim meet at Kalamalka tomorrow and the sports meet at Polson on Thursday. Graduation Parade is on Thursday evening at Polson Park. Tomorrow night, Captain Romer from the regiment is coming up here to take all us Dukes on a night outing. We're going to a place called Adventure Bay."

Banks finished the last of his KiK Kola and held the bottle against his forehead. "Hey Lingus, this will give you a chance to get next to Battlefield. I hear he's always got dough."

Gordie winced. "Jesus, I buy you a pop and you insult me like that? I'm not talking to him again. Like I told you - from now on he talks to me."

Wane laughed. "Oh sure! The new RSM is gonna come up to you and say, 'Hi Cunner, how's it going? Er, Cunner, my friend, the next time we're on the bus, I'll talk to you, is that all right with you?'"

The gambler got up to buy another pop. "You can laugh, but you don't know how stubborn I can be. From now on I'm not even going to acknowledge the guy."

"Unless he's got dough, right?

"Even if he's got all the dough in the world. Jeez, we even go to the same school and he doesn't talk to me." Cunningham paused for a moment. "Did I say that? I must be softening."

That evening at eight o'clock when the cadets of Signals Company arrived at Kin Beach, company staff members were waiting for them and preparing the food. Officers and all NCOs had cooked hamburgers, hot-dogs and a host of other goodies. In addition, watermelon, pop, apples, oranges, potato-chips, and chocolate bars were *on the house.*

After eating, all staff members were tossed into the water. The officer commanding the company, Major Hansford, put up a bit of a fight, but when fifty cadets have their minds set, nothing can change the eventual outcome.

As the sun set, with their faces illuminated by flames, cadets and staff gathered around the beach's fire pit singing *military* songs and telling stories.

It had been a long hard summer and some friendships made during the five-and-a-half weeks would last a lifetime. This break for revelry had been earned at the sun's anvil (camp) and for the first time since they arrived, the cadets had the opportunity to realize that their staff were human beings also. The *monsters* marching into the barracks every morning could smile without their faces cracking. They could tell jokes and they knew the words to most of the songs.

At first, some cadets were leery of the relaxed attitude of their trainers. They couldn't get used to the fact that certain sergeants actually dressed in civvy clothes; that they didn't wear their crisp uniforms and polished boots to bed.

During the singing, a cadet from the Nineteenth Alberta Dragoons summed it up in a sentence. "Jeez, Sergeant, your parents were married after all, eh?"

The sergeant scowled at the lad before grinning, and his reply confirmed that the officers and NCOs of Signals Company were indeed very proud of their charges. "Why do you think that?"

Cordell Cross

"Er, because you're not taking names or speaking quietly."

"This attitude is purely a front, my son. You'll realize that when I turn over your mattress tomorrow. What's your name?"

"Er, Thompson, Sergeant."

"Well, Thompson ... you'll not be getting used to this attitude. Tomorrow you're on KP duty."

The cadet's smile quickly disappeared. "Aw, Jeez, Sarg. How come?"

"Because you've had it too soft. This course has been a swan for you guys."

"Thompson's smile returned when the sergeant's massive arm come around the boy's shoulders before patting him on his back. "Just joking, Thompson me ol' son. Now tell me the words to *O' Provost* so I can sing with ya."

At 2330 when the trucks turned up, cadets having the time of their lives in the moon's shimmering waters, got dried off, changed and boarded.

With each vehicle's chorus wailing away, the cool sweet-smelling air would remain in each cadet's memory for years to come. They were relaxed, clean, full of vigour, and loyal with camaraderie.

As they passed the Provost shack, the NCOs and officers in the backs of the three-tons joined in and sang the song that always made the military police cringe.

Military personnel and civilians packed Kalamalka Beach on the day of the swim meet.

The musketeers' girls had arrived early to find spots to place down their blankets and as Diane lay on her stomach next to Douglas, she thought the fence trees provided ample protection from the sun's rays.

With the swim meet in progress, they had to speak louder than usual and it was difficult to hear each other over the crowd and loudspeaker's noise. Due to the large number of civilians, the musketeers and their girls were scattered all over the beach.

"It would have been nice if we had gone out to the farm this week," Diane said, trailing a finger gently over his lips and nose.

Douglas grinned as he turned his head to stare into her eyes. "I know. I'm still trying to figure out what made this summer go so fast. It seems like we've just arrived. What date are you coming down to the coast to see the PNE?"

Diane nestled closer. "A week this Friday. We're staying at the Austin Hotel in Vancouver. Do you know where that is?"

"Yep, it's not far from where I live. Is Debbie coming with you?"

"Yes, Wane's convinced her to come."

"Great. Wane and I will pick you guys up and we'll have a ball. I hope you don't mind travelling in Moose's hearse?"

Diane took a small gift-wrapped box and a card out of her purse and after handing it to Brice said, "I missed your birthday yesterday, Doug. Happy birthday - I love you."

Douglas sat up with a surprised look on his face. "Damn, I forgot it again," he replied, kissing her as she knelt up. "Thanks, Di."

"Have you received a card from your mom?" she asked.

He chuckled reading Diane's card. "Yeah, a week ago, and I made a promise not to forget. We've been so busy. Uh, you can't afford to buy me a present. Why did you do this? What is it?"

Diane appeared excited as he undid the ribbon. "I'm not telling you. Open it!"

An impish smile appeared. "Not until you tell me."

Tickling each other, Diane finally convinced him to open the small box and adored watching the expression on his face as he took out a chromed British Columbia Regiment (DCO) cap badge.

Douglas was lost for words, but his eyes said it all as he brought her in close to him and kissed her again. "I ... Where did you...? How...?"

"I wrote to your regiment and sent them fifty-cents. Then I sent it back to Vancouver to have it chromed. You won't have to shine your badge anymore."

Chromed badges had just started appearing in the British Columbia Regiment and they were prized.

"Jeez, thanks, Di. This is the nicest present one could have. I think..."

The loudspeaker cut him off. "Cadets entered in the backstroke and butterfly report to the wharf!"

Brice got up quickly. "I'll be right back. Guard yourself and the badge for me, will ya?"

Diane put the item back into its box and placed it in her purse. "You mean if some cadet makes the move on me, I'm to slug him?"

"You bet ... and hard."

"Wilco," she replied, throwing him his towel.

Only a few feet away, he turned back. "Did you say, Wilco? Hey, that's a signals term. Who taught you that?"

Diane's face gleamed. "I took signals in Girl Guides. I'm not just another pretty face, you know?"

"You can say that again."

Laughing, she said, "I'm not just another pretty face, you know."

Douglas got the last word in before he ran off. "Not just another shapely leg, either."

Even though cadets fiercely competed against each other during the swim meet, the rivalry ended after they walked away from the wharf. Company pride didn't interfere with friendships that had built up over the summer. Following an event, signals cadets left with their arms around the shoulders of D&M cadets or IBT cadets and vice-versa. The meet was a great opportunity for each of them to get together before leaving for home.

When Douglas returned, he noticed Debbie and Alma had moved their blankets next to Diane's. Some civilians had left, leaving a little room on the crowded beach.

Alma wore a gold chain around her left ankle. The inscription read, *Alma - youse is my love. Moose*. It wasn't professionally inscribed; instead, it appeared Moose had taken many hours scratching out the lettering.

Alma asked the boys, "It's gold, do you like it?"

Banks put his glasses on. "Yeah, neat - but your ankle's turning green."

"Moose says that's just the reaction of the fresh lake water. That it'll wear off."

Cordell Cross

"What, your ankle or the mildew?" asked Wane, fully knowing he'd be chased all over the beach, which he was.

At 1600 hours, the cadets formed up for presentations. A company of IBT had won the swim meet. Signals Company was second, followed by Driver Mechanics.

As the cadets boarded the trucks and blew kisses to their girls, Lyons noticed Cunningham's forlorn face.

"Whatsamatter old chappie? Couldn't you find enough suckers?"

Gordie shook his head. "No, I made a good amount of money, but Battlefield really got to me."

"Don't tell me you followed him again?" asked Rothstein.

"I didn't follow him! I ended up next to him on the wharf, so I congratulated him. Do you know what he said?"

"What?" asked Lyons.

"He said, 'Thank you - are you new to the cadet corps? I don't believe I've seen you before …er, what squadron are you in?' Seen me before? Shit, I've been sayin' hello for the past year!"

As the trucks rolled past the Vernon golf course, the rest of the musketeers laughed just looking at the expression on Cunningham's face.

"I guess some people can make an impression and some can't," offered Lyons. "It's quite obvious old chum - you can't."

The *gambler* didn't say anything else. He just took out his wallet and counted his winnings. While doing so, the laughter stopped and twenty other sets of wide eyes counted with him.

Two hours after supper, the cadets of the 2290 BCR (DCO) thought it was great getting together as a group in the Okanagan. Adventure Bay sits at the center end of the snake's tongue peninsula separating the north arms of Okanagan Lake. An arrangement with the owners of the property allowed the BCR officer, Lieutenant Romer to set up a barbecue and the head of the VACC swim staff *volunteered* four lifeguards. In addition to watermelon and cold KiK Kola, Romer purchased hot-dogs and hamburgers from the camp. The commanding officer of the British Columbia Regiment (DCO) had sent Romer up from Vancouver to conduct a Duke's picnic for all BCR cadets and that's exactly what the officer did. That evening throughout the region, other regiments did the same. McLeod was at Kin Beach attending a Seaforth party, conducted by a Seaforth regimental officer.

From eight o'clock until eleven-thirty, a hundred-and-nine BCR cadets and some guests from camp filled their stomachs, swam, sang songs, and told stories. Throughout, Cunningham followed Battlefield everywhere, even offering to be his horse in the water games. Unfortunately, the gambler's presence remained unnoticed by the new RSM so Gordie took out his cards and won money off Romer and a few other BCR NCOs.

"Do youse know who is not here?" asked Danyluk, chomping on a large piece of watermelon. "Genova hasn't shown his face in weeks."

"He's still around," Banks replied, leaning against a tree and sipping a KiK. "He arranged the boxing matches last week. The creep still manages to pull out the boxer's shorts so the boxers can breathe easier. I thought some of the elastic waist bands would snap. Jesus, I can't stand that man. Did I say man?"

"You did," replied Bergie.

"I meant..." Wane shook his head. "I can't think of a name for someone like him. He should be banished to an uncharted island."

Later that night, half-an-hour after midnight and lights out, naked cadets from D&M company raided B-25. Dressed only in running shoes, the Driver Mechanics *bare-buttocks crew* ran down the aisles lightly sitting on the faces of snoring signals cadets. The operation had been well planned and it was over in sixty seconds.

"What the...? What the hell happened?" East asked, sitting up and wiping his face. "Was I dreaming? I dreamt a fat broad sat on my kisser! I thought dames' asses were supposed to be smooth? In my dream, whoever sat on my face had skin like sandpaper."

Bergie had been missed because he was sleeping on his side. "No, you weren't dreaming. A fat ass *was* on your face."

East rubbed his cheeks. "I knew I was irresistible! What was she like? Was she one of the broads from the kitchen?"

Now the whole barracks was up and the lights were on.

"From the glimpse I got, she wasn't bad if you like a set of balls in your face," Bergie added. "We were raided, you pongo. Got any ass-hairs in your teeth?"

Jack didn't answer. Like most others who had had their faces "ass-cupped," he rushed for the sinks to wash and rinse out his mouth. When he arrived, all cadets in the centre area cursed the unknown intruders. They didn't know who the culprits were, but they vowed to get their own back.

"What happened to you?" a Loyal Edmonton Regiment cadet asked, checking his tongue in a mirror.

"Some fat slob sat on my face," replied East, gargling.

"At birth?" asked a nearby Irish cadet. "Yeah, the mould did a good job."

"Up yours, ya potato chewer," yelled East

"You're lucky," the LER cadet said. "Someone farted in my face."

East spat out the water. "I'll get the lard-ass, you just wait and see."

"Same here." Suddenly the cadet recognized the shower-room *emptier* and backed off quickly."Jeez, he'll die if *you* fart in his face."

The talk at breakfast the next morning was all about the raid, and the company that had the guts to pull it off. Shortly, some weak-lipped Driver Mechanics cadets spilled the beans and the news spread like wildfire. The marauding expedition had been planned for a week, which explained why it was pulled off flawlessly.

After breakfast, a signals planning committee was set up to repay the *evildoers*. The committee would meet at Polson Park during the sports meet to plan the counter-strike.

Dressed in blue PT shorts, white T-shirts, pith helmets, heavy wool socks and running shoes, the large parade in column-of-route filled both traffic lanes of the highway heading towards the park. Cadet companies still passed the Provost shack as the band of the 2290 BCR (DCO) cadet corps turned into Polson at the bottom of the hill. Half an hour later, the meet started.

As the cadets performed their mini field Olympics, cheers from the bleachers grew louder and louder. Like the swim meet the day before, company pride was on the line and as far as signals and driver-mech were concerned, cadets from the instructors' basic training course were not going to sweep this encounter.

Throughout the morning, dutiful young *sportsmen* performed to the best of their ability during the 440, the 100-yard dash, the tug-of-war, javelin throw, shot-putt, relays, jumps and other competitions.

At noon after the kitchen staff handed out box lunches, the retribution-committee only took a few minutes to decide the fate of Driver-Mech. The bare-assed cadets that carried out the *dastardly deed* would be left alone. Instead, the Driver Mechanics hut corporals would be *fixed*. They would naturally blame their cadets and the vengeance would be ten-fold to what signals could otherwise do.

"Bergie, that's a super plan," said a *committee* member from 23 Platoon.

Bergie waived away the praise. "Just make sure we keep our lips shut. If this is going to be successful we can't go bragging about it like driver mechanics did."

Handshakes sealed the deal after five cadets from each signals platoon were picked to make their move at 0100 hours in the coming morning.

Other than competing in the open playing-field of the sun's oven, the cadets took advantage of the cool paradise provided by Polson Park's magnificent green cover of trees. When the bullhorns called, however, the exposed *hearth* became hotter. Every iota of each individual's energy paid homage to company esteem.

During lunch, Douglas, Diane, Wane and Debbie sat by their favourite tree next to the small stream.

"Will you send me a platoon picture?" Diane asked, resting her head on Douglas' chest. She knew platoon and company photographs had been taken the week before.

"Yep. I ordered two and we pay for them tomorrow."

Debbie ran her hand through Wane's hair. "It seems like you just arrived yesterday. Where have you been all summer, soldier?"

Wane chuckled. "Learning about Morse code, the Nineteen set, the UCL ten-line switchboard, line-laying, the Tele-L sets, other radio sets, and splicing. When I get back, I just may quit school and work for the telephone company."

"You forgot signal office duties," uttered Brice. "How can you forget the exciting action of signal office duties?"

Wane nodded. "Yeah, and those goddamned signal office duties. Jesus, I hate that subject. I kept falling asleep."

"You and me both," said Douglas. "I hope we don't have to teach it back at the corps."

Moose and Alma came running by. "Hey youse guys, guess who's talking with Battlefield?"

Douglas and Wane quickly sat up and Douglas asked, "Who? Foster?"

Cordell Cross

Moose winced. "No, you dummy. Cunnilingus. He's been trailing him like a bee all mornin'. A minute ago I saw him take his wallet out of Maggie's purse and show it to Battlefield."

Wane got to his feet. "The braggart. He must be talking about all the money he's won. Doesn't that guy ever give...?"

Wane didn't get the chance to finish because Cunningham and Maggie appeared out of nowhere. Once again, the *cardsharp's* face was downcast.

"What's the matter with you now?" asked Wane.

"Battlefield, that's what's the matter," the *gambler* replied. "I went up to him and asked him how he was today and..."

"You suck," bellowed Danyluk.

"Stick it in your ear, Moose! He asked me how the Irish were. He thought I was in the bloody Irish. Can you believe that? When I took out my wallet and showed him my BCR card, he said, 'Where'd you get that?'"

"What did you say?" Douglas asked.

"When I told him I'd been in the Dukes for over a year and I ride the bus with him every parade night. Do you know what he said?"

Banks thought the situation was hilarious. "What?"

"He said, 'Those cards are for cadets in the 2290 British Columbia Regiment Cadet Corps. Who'd you steal it from?' Then he walked away. I tell ya, I ain't gonna talk to him no more. RSM or no RSM, that's it!"

Moose placed an arm around Gordie's shoulders. "That'll teach youse to suck-hole. I'm surprised youse didn't try to get him into a game?"

"Who says I didn't? I've got my reputation to consider," Cunningham shot back. "Naturally I did, but the guy said, 'I don't gamble with people I don't know; particularly if they're in the Irish.' Shit, why does he think I'm in the Irish?"

"Because you're pushy," said Wane "All Irish are pushy."

Joviality filled Polson Park that afternoon and eventually Cunningham joined in. He had done his damnedest to get on the good side of the new RSM of the 2290 BCR Cadet Corps, but obviously, Mr. Battlefield didn't want any part of him.

"Screw promotions. I'll be happy being a career cadet," Gordie said, starting up a stuke game with Maggie and a few of her girlfriends. He knew without a doubt, he'd win their money and keep it.

Driver-Mechanics won the sports meet that afternoon, and their cheers were loud. Signals came in second and an IBT company took third.

"The bastards. We'll get them tonight," Moose whispered, watching the exhilarated faces of the driver-mech cadets as their spokesman collected the trophy. "They won't be cheerin' tomorrow, that's for sure."

Lyons wasn't too certain. "They just might because it's pay-day tomorrow after we hand in our summer gear. Do you chaps realize tomorrow's our last day? On Saturday morning, we're actually heading back to civilization."

No one answered Lyons. Instead, solitary looks captured the faces of the Musketeers and their girls. Each of them had the same feeling last year and now it was happening again. Although they wanted to go home, the boys would miss their girls, the City of Vernon, and the madhouse atmosphere of the old camp on the hill.

Cordell Cross

Chapter 24

When brown wrapping paper is soaked and rolled, it remarkably resembles a cylindrical form, lump or a ball of excrement. Rolled in warm tea without leaves, the similarity is uncanny. As well, strained chicken noodle broth when placed on white sheets would convince the most ardent scholar that it wasn't broth at all - that it was urine.

Following supper on Thursday evening, these items were quite easy to obtain and the mixing and straining process took place in the drying and shower rooms of B-25 just before the final parade of the year. Bergie, Brice, Danyluk, East and Banks would participate in the *distribution* of the compounds at 0100 hours. They were the five cadets chosen to *represent* 21 Platoon.

With the temperature still hovering around ninety degrees, boots shone like mirrors below short pants with creases that could cut hard butter as the graduation parade progressed.

It appeared as though half the citizens of Vernon turned out at Polson Park to witness the graduation ceremony as Lieutenant-Colonel J.C. Cave and his entourage weaved in and out of the ranks of the cadet battalion.

Because they formed part of the band, Brice, Banks, Danyluk, Lyons, Cunningham, and East, did not get the opportunity to occupy supernumerary positions. Bergie, however, was appointed Signals Company commander, Rothstein the platoon commander of 21 Platoon, Jackson the company sergeant major, and McLeod the battalion adjutant. Many other battalion supernumerary positions were filled with IBT and D&M cadets.

Following the initial review and march-past, designated cadets from each company participated in displays demonstrating what they had learned during the summer. Only a few cadets passed out, and medical personnel quickly took them to the sidelines.

Throughout the evening, the audience's rousing applause never stopped. Spectators even enjoyed the speeches given by Lieutenant Colonel Cave, Vernon's Mayor, and RSM Gardiner.

When it came time to say goodbye and the guard fired the feu du joie (fire of joy) followed by the band playing *O' Canada*, appreciation in the stands was resounding.

When the band led the parade out of the park, the citizens of Vernon, along with the camp's staff gave the parade a send-off that could be heard at Silver Star Mountain.

During a playing break heading back up the hill, Danyluk chuckled and Lyons asked him what was so funny.

"I always love Gardiner's speeches. Did youse hear him referring to my hearse? I'll betcha he'll never forget that chariot. Also, if he knew I owned it, I'd be dead."

"None of us will forget it," replied Lyons. "I'm going to be claustrophobic for the rest of my natural life."

Moose belted out a giant laugh and received a dirty look from Barry Kelly who was still Acting Drum Sergeant Major.

Cordell Cross

"I can't help it," Moose whispered. "If Gardiner knew I owned the hearse, he'd have shit himself then sentenced me to death. Youse all knows how he feels towards *me*? I didn't know it was his parking space. Oh brother..."

Apparently Moose's voice wasn't that low. The whole band started laughing, even Kelly. They all knew too well.

After handing in their instruments, the Musketeers took in the movie *Normandy* at B-3. As usual, the projector broke down three times and non-smokers (the large majority) went outside for a breath of fresh but still hot night air.

"I'm totally beat," said East, chewing a chocolate bar. "What a day. If we had to get up at 0530 tomorrow, I think I'd pull a mutiny. I can hardly wait to get on that train and sleep in something other than a bunk."

Harvey Rothstein gave East a disconcerted glance. "Oh, no you wouldn't. You'd be at the kitchen door at 0500 waiting for one of the ladies to sneak you a sandwich and a glass of milk. No wonder they cut the bread supply at mug-up, you eat it all in the morning."

East grinned, saying, "Who told you I did that?"

Harvey put his arm around East's shoulders. "Jack, we've been living with you for six weeks. When you burp, we know you've just finished a jam sandwich. When you belch aloud, we know you've had a chicken leg, and..."

Jackson interrupted. "And when you fart in the showers, we know you've had fourths of something ... anything."

"Well, you guys always demand the extreme bomb! I need the nutrients to produce the explosive. Do you think I can do it on an empty..."

Danyluk came out of B-3. "Hey youse guys, the movie's starting again. East, get rid of your wind now before youse comes in. Okay?"

Jack gave Moose the finger. "You don't say that when you need my *services*, you pongo!"

Following the film, a maniacal atmosphere engulfed B-25. Paper of sorts filled the hut from top to bottom as boys jumped on beds, jumped in and out of windows, squirted the fire extinguishers, climbed over the tops of cubicles, mooned the cars on Highway 97 and did the normal things that typical cadets do on their second last night in camp. They also knew it all had to be cleaned up in the morning, but that didn't matter. On the following night, the same thing would happen but the British Columbia cadets knew the Prairie cadets would be sticking around to clean up the mess. Prairie cadets left on Sunday, not Saturday.

At 0100 hours when snores filled each bed space, twenty signals cadets (five from each platoon) met in the drying room. After a short meeting, they headed off in four different directions towards the same hut, each group carrying their own combination of artificial *turds* and *urine*.

Half an hour later, the same twenty returned to the drying room, shook hands, washed out the buckets, and hit the sack.

Although Cunningham hadn't participated, he joined the rest of those awake in 21 Platoon in welcoming back the 'midnight marauders.'

"Any bets on what time they hit the parade square?" he asked with a grin, writing out the wagers in his *little black book*.

Cordell Cross

Most bets were from 0500 on, so Gordie made money.

With each D&M cadet calling out the time, the whole city was probably awake as the clamour from the parade square erupted at 0430. The recipient-corporals were not at all happy directing their subjects who were dressed only in undershorts, socks and boots. Those who slept *au naturel*, marched *au naturel*.

"Left, right, left, right! Get your arms up, up, up! Never in my life have I experienced such childish and filthy inconceivable acts! If you're going to shit, you'll shit in your own beds from now on. And if you're going to piss, you'll piss in your own beds! My God, what is this world coming to? You! Yes you without the gaunch, get your arms up!"

The *special* parade ended at 0630 and only then did the corporals realize the mess in their beds wasn't the real thing. Still, they were thoroughly upset and the cadets of Driver Mechanics had a full day of regular force *displeasure* ahead of them.

At 0700 after cleaning up the barracks, breakfast never tasted better as the cadets of Signals Company dressed in half-battledress whispered among themselves. Those who had slept through Driver Mechanics' *torture* chuckled and pounded their tables trying to hold back their laughs.

At 0900 they were formed up and Major Hansford's speech got their chests sticking out. The officer informed them that he'd been around the world and worked with many troops, but he had enjoyed this summer more than any other posting. As far as he was concerned, the cadets of Signals Company had excelled in learning their trade and he and his staff would work with them anytime, anywhere.

"When Sergeant-Major Wong falls you out, you will get your gear and board the trucks that will take you to the upper camp. When you return, each individual in your specific platoons will form up alphabetically to read and sign your course reports. Afterwards, although you have the morning off, you are confined to camp until lunch. There will be a pay parade at 1100 hours and a mail call at 1130. Are there any questions?"

There were none, so the OC continued.

"My staff and I will be around at various times to see you before you leave. It has been a great pleasure working with you. Good luck and have a safe journey home!"

"Well, here we are again," noted Rothstein as he tried to wave away the dust filling the back of the three-ton truck. "These uniforms will look like washed-out rags before we return home. Wow, it's hot."

All musketeers and other members of 21 Platoon were loaded down with gear heading towards the clothing hangar in the upper camp.

"Are we going to meet you at the PNE, Rothie?" Moose asked. "And how about youse, Earl?"

Rothstein, Jackson, and Bergie all agreed that they'd be in Vancouver for the PNE. Arrangements were made so that Harvey would stay at Cunningham's house, Bergie at Danyluk's, Jackson at East's and McLeod decided he would stay at Lyons' house. Actually, Lyons could have stayed at McLeod's house, since, as they discovered earlier, they didn't live that far from each other. The only person who hesitated and really wanted to stay at a hotel was Bergie. For some reason he was leery of Danyluk's house, but he bowed under pressure.

"Bergie, I'll introduce youse to loveable and dainty Aphelia. I calls her *I'llfeelya*. You'll love her breasts."

Bergie knew from Danyluk's grin that he was being set up.

"Why? I suppose she's got three?"

"No, she's only got two, and they're normal. I couldn't arrange one with three. Five maybe, but not three. You'll also like her teeth."

With Danyluk and Bergie getting weird looks from others sitting with them, silence filled the truck. Everyone waited for Bergie's next question.

"How many teeth has she got?"

"A beautiful set of 'em," replied Moose, proudly. "This dame is what youse would call, indubitably appealing."

Bergie clapped his hands at the fact that Moose had pronounced "indubitably" correctly.

"Listen, Moose, if you're going out with her, something's wrong. What is it?"

When a grinning Moose turned his head away and mumbled something towards the cab, the whole truck broke out in laughter. The only person who didn't hear him was Bergie.

"What did you say?"

Clearing his throat, Danyluk replied, "She might have three legs, but just look at the advantages."

"Forget it! I'm staying at a hotel!"

Only after the trucks were unloaded did Moose admit Aphelia was normal. "She has two arms, two legs, a great set of teeth, two eyes, and two breasts. In fact a set of everything *and* she's smart at school."

When Bergie heard that, he forgot about the hotel.

In the outside line-up, East whispered to Banks. "I've met her and while Moose wasn't exactly lyin', she's not quite as normal he says she is. He also calls her *Blowie*."

"*Blowie*? What's wrong with her?" Wane whispered back.

Jack put his mouth to Wane's ear. "Bergie won't care for her two noses."

As Bergie entered the hangar to hand in his gear, he didn't hear the howls of hilarious laughter going on outside.

When the company returned to the lower camp, each platoon sorted itself out alphabetically outside its own end door of the two wings. Individual platoon officers and NCOs sat at tables in their respective areas, and one by one cadets were invited in to read and sign their course reports prior to receiving a few handshakes.

It was announced during the signing that an individual company standings list would be posted on the two bulletin boards after pay parade.

Following the course reports procedure, signals marched to B-3 and each cadet received fifteen dollars. The total bonus for attending camp was one hundred dollars. Since the cadets had already received three payments of five dollars each, (they weren't paid during the first two weeks) a cheque for seventy dollars would be mailed to each of them within a month of them returning home.

Cordell Cross

When the standings list was posted, Jackson took his notebook and fought his way in. To no one's surprise, Harvey Rothstein attained the highest marks in the company. He had studied relentlessly throughout the six weeks. Bergie followed Harvey by tying for second with an Irish cadet. Brice was third, Banks tied for fourth place with a Seaforth cadet, and Lyons and Cunningham tied for fifth. Cadets McLeod, Jackson, East and Danyluk tied with others in the top twelve. Only three cadets failed the course, and one of them should have passed because he received forty-nine percent. The boy wasn't in 21 Platoon, but the pass/fail mechanism bothered Wane. He suggested to Douglas, "They could and should have stretched it to fifty. Sergeant Beckford would have."

Following mail call, the girls joined the Musketeers for lunch. Although the mess hall became crowded, plenty of food was available and East took the opportunity to return three times. He would have gone back for fourths, but time didn't allow for it.

After lunch, the hill became alive with cadets heading into town to buy souvenirs and have some fun. The bowling alley, movie theatre, and restaurants soon got packed and Polson Park became the sobbing sanctuary for departing couples.

After bowling, two banana splits, and a movie, each musketeer and his girl entered Polson and respectively found their own little place under the trees. It was a sad time for the girls because their *soldiers* were leaving, but the boys looked forward to a rest at home. Although they had slowly got used to the sun, the sergeants, the corporals, the early mornings, cleaning, cleaning, cleaning and training, military life in general had created a few lines under the boys' eyes. Even if they really didn't want to leave, sleeping in at home was a dream each of them longed for.

After an hour of saying their first goodbye, each musketeer walked his girl home and then took on the hill alone. The second goodbye would be *fulfilled* at the train station the following morning.

Douglas Brice felt a little dispirited heading up the hill. Though the hill was chock full of cadets, his friends weren't with him. To make matters worse, he thought the world of Diane and now the summer was over.

For the past year before coming to camp he had decided to spend every spare minute with her, but it wasn't to be - there was just too much to do and so little time. At camp, spare time was treasured and an inviting bunk always beckoned cadets out of the heat. What with studying, drill, lectures, cleaning, cleaning, and more cleaning, excess time hardly existed.

When a passing Provost told him to get his arms up, Douglas was laughing at the thought of the timetable using the term 'spare period.' It should have said, washing and cleaning period, he thought. In addition, when training ended each day, more washing, cleaning, and studying followed.

Even so, Douglas Brice loved Camp Vernon. The onus was on him to survive. Whether he did it alone or with friends, the total essence of just *being* was to take what they passed out and make something of it without complaining. He realized of course that he couldn't have made it alone. It took teamwork.

Cordell Cross

Douglas knew the cadets who arrived six weeks ago were not the same going home. Perhaps they didn't notice the change, but in a big way, they had partially opened life's steel door to maturity.

Upon entering B-25, Brice took off his itchy battledress pants and the rest of his clothes and headed for the showers. Although it was 1700 hours, the temperature hovered around a hundred and all he wanted was to stand under the cold water and sort out his mind. With most people over at the mess hall, he had the shower-room to himself until Lyons entered looking a little melancholy. Obviously, he had mixed feelings about leaving as well.

"Hi, Dougie, old chum. Any cold water left?"

Although Brice grinned, his sigh indicated he wasn't in the mood for small-talk. Just after he replied, "Lots," a smiling and naked Moose came in and picked a bar of sergeants' soap out of a bucket.

Danyluk appeared chipper. "Hello, men ... How the hell are youse two doin' this fine afternoon?"

Both cadets ignored the *animal* and Lyons asked, "Doug, can you believe what movie they're showing tonight? It's called, *Young Love*. Damn, don't they realize what we're going through?"

Moose agreed. "Yeah, Alma's just filled two handkerchiefs with her tears."

Lyons finally acknowledged Moose's presence. "What? Two hankies? My good fellow, she must really be going to miss you."

"Yeah, that too," replied Moose. "The first one-and-a-half hankies were used because I stomped on her foot by accident. Poor gal probably won't be able to walk for a week. Lord knows about her neck."

Brice winced. "What the hell happened to her neck?"

"We were in the bushes at Polson Park and I head-butted her Adam's apple by accident. Her arm won't be in a cast for very long."

A quizzed look hit Lyons' face. "I thought you said it was her foot?'

Danyluk covered his head with Sergeants' soap *lather*. "I did say it was her foot, but I also rolled over on her arm. Damn ... for a tough girl, she's also tender. She says she has to see a doctor about her back."

"What's wrong with her back?" asked Douglas - his grin getting wider, as was Moose's.

"I had to kneel on her back to relieve the pain of her left knee cartilage. She caught her knee under a stump. That's how she bruised her tailbone, and lost the hearing in her right ear. She doesn't know if her sight of her left eye will take a week or a month to return. I think..."

Loud laughter filled the shower-room, and as the three of them dried off, Moose explained Alma was fine. They'd taken in a movie and he had walked her home, that's all.

Moose had the knack of sensing when goings on bothered people. As far as he was concerned, his job was to get everyone on track again. "Well, at least I got youse guys outta the dumps, didn't I? What do ya think I am, some sort of a wrecking machine?"

"Yeah" Brice and Lyons replied in unison.

Cordell Cross

The word "humidity" appeared to be on all sets of lips the night in camp. Even with all the windows and doors wide open the temperature in each hut had to be over a hundred. Visiting officers and NCOs didn't waste too much time shaking hands and offering their goodbyes because the air boiled.

During the movie, B-3 was almost empty. Not just because of the heat, but because of the film. A good roaring war picture would have filled the bill, but someone goofed and ordered a film loaded with tears.

After pandemonium and lights out, it was just too hot to form tunnels out of bunks as cadets had done the year before. Instead, throughout the camp, platoon bunks were moved together so the boys could *shoot the breeze*.

During the summer, cadets had made fun of each other's regiment. Now Irish sat with Dukes, Seaforths lay with Canadian Scottish, Calgary Highlanders, Cameron Highlanders and Lake Superior Scottish cadets. US Marine Corps Cadets sat with Canadian Guards cadets and they all chewed the fat with Royal Canadian Engineers and Royal Canadian Signals cadets. Fourteenth Canadian Hussars joked with King's Own Calgary Regiment cadets as well as the Queen's Own and British Columbia Dragoons cadets. Royal Canadian Electrical and Mechanical cadets and Provost Corps cadets got together with LdSH (RC), British cadets and Fort Garry Horse cadets. Royal Winnipeg Rifles types chatted with Princess Patricia's lads as well as the boys from the North Saskatchewan Regiment and the Regina Rifles. Royal Saskatchewan Regiment types talked with Manitoba Dragoons, the South Alberta Light Horse, and the 20th Saskatchewan Dragoons. Nineteenth Alberta Dragoons rapped with Rocky Mountain Rangers, Westminster Regiment, the Loyal Edmonton Regiment, Yukon Regiment types and Artillery cadets. Those who weren't affiliated with various regiments who wore RCAC badges (Royal Canadian Army Cadets) or CSofC badges (Cadet Services of Canada) got their two bits in as well. (Author's note: Whew. I'm sure I've missed some. It's been a long time. Sorry.)

As faint party music emanated from the officers' and sergeants' messes, a lone bugler's lament followed a cadet piper's air echoing in the nearby hills. Camp streets, sports, and training areas stood silent, the hill was alone, Polson Park provided its quiet for locals, and Glenemma's prairie lay isolated. During this tranquil time, however, a sporran parade marched the parade square and some cadets painted the canon *again*.

Amidst the low chitchat, Moose asked Bergie, "Are youse coming back next year?"

Because it was his last night, the *animal's* friend had been trying to stop an Irish cadet from gambling with Cunningham. He figured that on this night all regiments should be one.

"Yeah, I'm gonna take Driver Mechanics. How about youse? Damn, did I say youse? I meant, you."

Danyluk chuckled. "I'm getting to ya, aren't I?"

"Moose, old buddy, *youse* got to me last year when *youse* read your first letter from home. I wondered who the hell I was bunking with, and as a matter of fact, I still wonder."

Cordell Cross

"We should all take D&M," Rothstein said, dressed only in shorts and reclining on a lower bunk.

Except for Lyons, nods all around indicated most agreed.

Wane, who had been quiet, stood up and stretched. "God, I'm beat. Sitting around like this is unnatural. I'm so programmed I feel like I'm cheatin' the government. All I did today was press my battledress pants, and my shirt."

East took a sandwich out from under his bunk. His favourite kitchen girl had packed a few in a brown paper bag.

"Nice, ain't it? No sergeants yelling, no corporals nagging, no ass *cupping* my face. I could get used to this life. And tomorrow were headin' home to ecstasy."

Jackson snickered. "I met that driver-mech type that sat on your face. He says his ass hasn't been the same since. Something to do with wanting to fart all the time."

Between the chuckles, East yawned and replied. "I'd like to meet that SOB. I've got a few chicken bones I'd like to shove where the sun don't shine."

An hour later as the barracks cooled, most cadets were asleep. Not necessarily on their own bunks. Snoring bodies lay side by side with other snoozing bodies reclining on mattresses placed widthways, lengthways, or anywhere there was room. Some cadets slept on the floor, under bunks, or even on the cold concrete of the shower-room.

At two o'clock in the morning, clouds came rolling in and the Heavens opened up. Even the rain joined by eruptions of thunder didn't raise an eyebrow.

With breakfast over with, their bed spaces brushed and kit-bags on their shoulders, British Columbia cadets boarded trucks in the pouring rain.

Platoon Sergeants had awakened everyone early, and that allowed time for the BC cadets to say goodbye to officers, NCOs and their Prairie counterparts who would leave the next day.

Poor planning more than anything else left the tarpaulins off the vehicles, but the rain didn't stop some of the boys from mooning the Provost or throwing pennies at the Provost shack.

After forming up at the train station, the cadets were dismissed and allowed to say farewell to new friends they'd met in Vernon - mainly girls.

The musketeers and their girls met with Charlie, Fred, and Mr. Brewer, the Native gentleman they'd met the previous year. Mr. Brewer got along great with Charlie and Fred and after shaking hands and saying goodbye to the boys' the three went to a local hotel for a few beers.

As Cunningham boarded, a Sergeant said, "You, yes you, you horrible little man! What the hell have you got in your right hand?"

Reminiscent of his first day's arrival at the station, Gordie swallowed heavily. The voice was none other than the sergeant he'd *encountered* six weeks earlier.

"A deck of cards, Sergeant! I know, I know! I'll put them away!"

Sergeants remember faces. To Cunningham, the Sergeant's smile could have been a gas pain, but this time it looked like the real thing.

Cordell Cross

"Like hell you will! I'm travelling on this train and I want to see just how good you are! I remember you when you arrived!"

A hut-corporal very familiar with Cunningham's *expertise* whispered to a friend, "That's the first mistake the sergeant's made this summer."

"Yeah, and it'll be his last," his buddy replied. "He'll be broke by the time he reaches Vancouver."

Engine noise, hissing steam, a few thousand people, and pounding rain didn't stop couples from quietly saying farewell under crowded umbrellas. Not just cadets, but staff members as well.

After saying goodbye, Debbie and Diane watched their *men* walk through the aisle of a railcar trying to find their seats. Moments later, Wane and Douglas opened a window and stuck their bodies out.

While Wane and Debbie and hundreds more yelled to each other, Diane bellowed, "Doug, will you write to me when you get home?"

Douglas took hold of Diane's offered hand. "There's no sense. If I write, you'll be in Vancouver before my letter arrives. I'll phone instead ... all right?"

Diane's lost look amplified as she nodded, wiped the *rain* and tears from her face, and anxiously reached up to stroke a face she couldn't reach.

"Look after yourself, Doug. I miss you already!"

Douglas found it hard to smile. "Same here. I feel like getting off the train. Say goodbye to your mom and dad for me."

Their hands were parted by the train's first initial jolt as it slowly moved out of Vernon's station. With all windows open, hundreds of sets of wet arms waved goodbye to visions viewed through welled up eyes. Douglas and Diane kept their eyes *locked* on each other until the train rounded a bend.

Bedlam set in ten minutes later as cadets' unpacked radios, guitars, mouth organs, playing cards, and took off their boots and damp clothes.

Those who had felt lonely and insecure on the train six weeks earlier weren't noticeable - those tendencies had vanished. Also, Camp Vernon had taken *care* of the cadets with brazen and a host of other uncontrollable personalities, forever.

Cordell Cross

EPILOGUE

To teenagers, train rides are fabulous. The trip back to the coast was no exception for the Lower Mainland cadets of British Columbia. Prairie cadets leaving for home the following day would feel exactly the same way.

Even though train berths aren't the most comfortable places to sleep, more logs were sawed through on those trains than in the sawmills they passed. As well, military bunks were now redundant until the following year.

A week after camp, the musketeers" girls visited Vancouver and the group drove to the Pacific National Exhibition in Danyluk's *sweet-smelling* hearse. Yes, it really did smell wonderful because Moose paid East to scrub and disinfect the casket from top to bottom. East slaved for two days, only to end up losing his hard-earned five-dollars to Cunningham. The *beast* forfeited another twenty as well.

As for Cunningham - well, on Sunday morning as the train coiled its way through misty clouds filling the Fraser Canyon, Gordie sat alone counting his money when RSM Battlefield entered the railcar and joined him." Are you Cunningham?"

Sitting to attention, the gambler's face looked like Jesus Christ himself had paid him a personal visit. "Er, yes ... yes sir, I am, that's me, I mean..."

"Have we met before, Cunningham? You're in the Irish aren't you?"

Gordie started fidgeting with his hands. He didn't know whether to say yes or no. As it turned out, the widening grin on Battlefield's face indicated an answer wasn't necessary. The recently appointed RSM had been putting the *gambler* on from the beginning.

"Just joking, Gordie. Congratulations on your excellent marks. Lance Corporal Cunningham, you're as persistent as a bulldog. See you at the Drill Hall."

East appeared after Battlefield had shook Cunningham's right hand and departed for his own railcar.

"Shit, ya made Lance-Corporal, eh? Now you'll never wash that paw – right, Lingus?"

The new lance corporal couldn't say anything. He just sat there with his mouth wide open. After *cleaning out* the sergeant and most others on the train, the world's best *risk taker* had been caught at his own game.

In September, when training started at the Drill Hall on Beatty Street in Vancouver, knowledge learned at Vernon was thoroughly passed along. The 2290 British Columbia Regiment (DCO) Cadet Corps remained very strong, as did the 72nd Seaforth Highlanders of Canada, the Irish Fusiliers (Vancouver Regiment) and all other army cadet corps in Western Canada. The same thing took place in Central and Eastern Canada as cadets passed along what they had learned at their camps.

On the third parade night of the new training year Cadet Gordie Cunningham was promoted to lance corporal and Lance Corporals' Brice, Banks, East, Danyluk, and Lyons were promoted corporals.

As the boys marched up to the commanding officer to receive their stripes, another meeting took place in the grand old building. The Regiment's Regimental

Sergeant Major (Pat Patterson) gave Warrant Officer Second Class Genova his walking papers.

In the 50s, Canadian teenagers who joined cadets were treated fair, firm, and friendly by their peers who trained at Canada's many cadet camps each summer. All the techniques passed along by regular force troops were passed along again. What a fabulous period in time.

Cordell Cross

OTHER BOOKS BY CORDELL CROSS

THE HIMMLER STRATAGEM
At your bookstore, or (order on net) https://www.createspace.com/3555767
Revised ISBN 978-0-9696248-8-2
A must read if you enjoy fast moving suspense, intrigue, and mystery in a world of intense hatred and sleaze.

MANIAC
At your bookstore, or (order on net) https://www.createspace.com/3604911
ISBN 978-0-9869503-0-8
When a sixteen-year-old girl disappears in the neighbourhood of Greg Britton, a Seattle police lieutenant on compassionate leave, the police officer holds nothing back and decides to find her dead or alive.

STAND BY YOUR BEDS!
At your bookstore, or (order on net) https://www.createspace.com/3613071
Revised ISBN 978-0-9696248-5-1
Is the hilarious story of seven 14-year-old cadets sent to a summer military camp for six weeks training. Regular force troops returning from WW2 and Korea were also sent to the camp thinking they would be training officer cadets. When these hard-nosed battle-scarred veterans found that the boys were only 14 and 15 years old, they trained them the way they would train regular troops. The boys in turn form a very close group to survive. Both groups learn a lot about each other. Extremely funny. Get ready to roll on the floor laughing. You'll love this book.

FORM THREE RANKS ON THE ROAD!
At your bookstore or (order on net) https://www.createspace.com/3617672
Revised ISBN 978-0-9696248-6-8
It is three years later, and the cadets continue their capers. This time they are in charge, or so they think. A refreshingly funny book.

MAP FACTS (instructional) Order from: vanbrugh@telus.net
Revised ISBN 0-9696248-3-2
The ultimate map and compass guide, is required reading for all those involved with topographical maps and magnetic compasses.

COMING SOON FROM CORDELL CROSS
WHERE THE WIND HIDES - ISBN 978-0-9869503-1-5
RUBBER GEARS NEXT YEAR! The last novel in the Vernon Army Cadet Camp series. The hilariousness continues.
RAIN ON MY TONGUE
THE STOPOVER

Cordell Cross

www.ingramcontent.com/pod-product-compliance
Lightning Source LLC
Chambersburg PA
CBHW060247100426

42742CB00011B/1663